As seen in the **PBS** documentary *The Challenge of Grief*

Finding Daylight after Loss Shatters Your World

seven
choices

Elizabeth Harper Neeld, Ph.D.

"A joyful book of hope...written with touching candor and a deep wisdom."
—Harry Lipscomb, Texas A&M University College of Medicine

ACCLAIM FOR *SEVEN CHOICES*

"Compelling substance . . . a gifted writer. . . . Elizabeth Neeld clearly meets Samuel Johnson's first criterion for genius."
—Washington Post

"Sound advice on how to adjust to change and form new life patterns and human bonds. **—Publishers Weekly**

"A useful, wide-ranging work . . . trenchant . . . pertinent."
—Kirkus Reviews

"A highly original and meaningful approach to the grieving process." **—Psychology Today**

"An affirmation of the power of the grieving process, a source of hope and validation. Dr. Neeld clearly goes well beyond a focus on coping (which is necessary) and acceptance to the importance of integration and self-empowerment."
—Dr. John Schneider, author of *Stress, Loss and Grief*

"A profound book . . . deeply compassionate and very wise."
—Coast Book Review Service

"Elizabeth Harper Neeld gives lessons written from experience and from the heart on rehabilitating your life when you are alone. This book is about becoming a person of joy.
—Liz Carpenter, author of *Getting Better All the Time*

"Unfortunately, there is no one-minute way to grieve. But Elizabeth Harper Neeld gives us the steps we must take to lead full lives again." **—Ken Blanchard, author of *The One Minute Manager***

Also by Elizabeth Harper Neeld, Ph.D.

Writing, 1, 2, 3 Editions
Writing Brief, 1, 2, 3 Editions
Readings for Writing
The Way a Writer Reads
Writing: A Short Course
Options for the Teaching of English: The Undergraduate Curriculum
Either Way Will Hurt & Other Essays on English (ed.)
Harper & Row Studies in Language and Literature (ed.)
Fairy Tales of the Sea (ed.)
From the Plow to the Pulpit (ed.)
Yes! You Can Write (audio)
Sister Bernadette: Cowboy Nun from Texas (co-author)
A Sacred Primer: The Essential Guide to Quiet Time and Prayer

seven choices

FINDING
DAYLIGHT
AFTER LOSS
SHATTERS
YOUR WORLD

ELIZABETH HARPER NEELD, PH.D.

GRAND CENTRAL
PUBLISHING

NEW YORK   BOSTON

AUTHOR'S NOTE: The stories told in *Seven Choices* are true. In order to honor the privacy of the more than sixty generous individuals who were willing to tell me the stories of their grieving process, I have altered names and other distinguishing features of the accounts. In addition, in telling my own story I have looked backward with eyes that can now see pattern, order, significance, and progression in what at the time was often only random, unconnected events. I have told the *truth* of my story at the same time that I have, on occasion, telescoped events, consolidated meanings, and altered strict chronological sequence in order to provide lucidity and precision in the discussion of the grieving process.

Grateful acknowledgment is given to the *New York Times* for the following: From "About Men—The Death of a Son" by Albert F. Knight. Copyright © 1986 by the New York Times Company. From "Sea Sculpture" by Ronald Pease. Copyright © 1981 by the New York Times Company. From "Middle-Age Dating" by Noel Perrin. Copyright © 1986 by the New York Times Company. Reprinted with permission.

This Grand Central Publishing edition is published by arrangement with Centerpoint Press, a division of MBI Publishing, 6706 Beauford Drive, Austin, TX 78750.

Grand Central Publishing
Hachette Book Group
1290 Avenue of the Americas
New York, NY 10104

www.HachetteBookGroup.com

Printed in the United States of America

First Hachette Book Group Edition: August 2003
20 19 18 17 16 15 14

Grand Central Publishing is a division of Hachette Book Group, Inc.
The Grand Central Publishing name and logo is a trademark of Hachette Book Group, Inc.

The publisher is not responsible for websites (or their content) that are not owned by the publisher.

Library of Congress Cataloging-in-Publication Data
Neeld, Elizabeth Harper.
    Seven choices : finding daylight after loss shatters your world / Elizabeth Harper Neeld.
        p. cm.
    Originally published: 3rd ed., rev. Houston, Tex. : Centerpoint Press, 1997.
    Includes bibliographical references and index.
    ISBN 978-0-446-69050-8
        1. Bereavement—Psychological aspects. 2. Death—Psychological aspects. 3. Grief. I. Title

BF575.G7N44 2003
155.9'37—dc21   2003041076

Cover design by Brigid Pearson
Book design by Charles A. Sutherland
Text Illustrations by HRoberts Design

For
Rachel and Tommie

ACKNOWLEDGMENTS

Just as it takes a village to raise a child, it takes a team to bring a book from a thought in the author's imagination to a bound copy in a reader's hand. Without Chris Tomasino, my agent, who has represented and supported my work for more than a decade, this edition of *Seven Choices* would still be an idea instead of a reality. Chris's creativity, indefatigable energy, and commitment both to this book and to its author make her a friend and colleague I never want to be without. Caryn Karmatz-Rudy, my editor at Warner, is one of the most compassionate human beings I have ever met. Her commitment to making this book available to as broad a readership as possible has never wavered from the day she first read *Seven Choices*, while riding on the train from Pennsylvania to New York City, to the day we could all say the long publishing process had been completed. I count myself blessed to have both Chris and Caryn as partners.

Carol Anderson put a professional touch to the copyediting of the book, and Charles Sutherland created the new design. Howard Roberts drew the map of the Terrain of the Active Grieving Process. Brigid Pearson is responsible for a cover that speaks quiet hope. Keri Friedman saw that readers, the media, and professionals knew that the book was available. I am grateful for their specialized, creative skills. Adina Neufeld made sure all the research and references were accurate and up-to-date. Joey Bieber shot the author's photograph at the same time that she delighted me with her exuberance for living.

In the Directory can be found the wisdom of three friends who contributed generously to *Seven Choices*. Ann Rachlin, M.B.E., of London, provides suggestions for selections of music that are appropriate for each of the seven sets of experiences—from Impact to Integration. It was Ann's support and ingenuity that made *Seven Choices* available to many of her associates and friends in Great Britain. Ione Jenson, educator, author, lecturer, and psychospiritual therapist with degrees in education, counseling, and psychology, writes about how to help children who are grieving. A new section on helping teenagers deal with grief and loss is provided by Colleen O'Grady, supervisor, consultant, and trainer of family therapy in child and adolescent psychiatry at the University of Texas Mental Science Institute in Houston. Professor John Bradley suggested a list of movies about grief. Charles Anderson, professor at the University of Arkansas in Little Rock, contributed a story that appears in the "Working Through: Finding Solid Ground" chapter about the definition and power of memory that readers say is one of the most helpful insights in the book.

Susan Echrich, in her leadership in the Grief and Loss Program of AARP, together with her colleagues Susan Duhamel, Kathy Wood, Judy Fink, Tim Wollerman, Selima Nelson, Nancy Griffin, Bill Moore, Tom Young, Eunice Hofmeyer, Dorothy McConnell, Ida Nezey, Florence Williams, Mary Yarber, Ann Black, and all the AARP Grief and Loss Program volunteers around the United States, inspire me to continue to do whatever I can to be of help to people who are grieving.

Kathi Appelt, Cynthia Whitcomb, Christine Head, Lee Herrick, Yvonne Donaldson, Eva Archer-Smith, Joe Mercer, Beth Mercer, Ernestine Hambrick, Sheri Harper, Gail Daniels, Dee Poole, Cathy and Russ Setzekorn, Ken Appelt, Robert Unterberger, Faye Walker,

John Bradley, and Paula Hunter are family members and friends whose presence I count on and am grateful for every day of my life. The late William Stafford not only enriched my life with his poetry but gifted me with his friendship as well.

Dr. Betty Unterberger, who holds the endowed chair in history at Texas A&M University, has been a mentor, an inspiration, a friend, and a companion on my spiritual journey for more than twenty years. She is the person who taught me about silent prayer. Her support and love are with me every day.

My sister, Barbara, my brother, Frank, and my aunt Frances are daily connections to the very riverbed of my origins; they let no time go by when they do not remind me of their love and support. In so doing, they resonate for me the care and encouragement that my late parents, Tommie and Rachel, provided for all of us.

My husband, Jerele, once told me that he thought the reason I had come into this world was to write *Seven Choices*, and that the one person I had written it for had already read it . . . therefore everything else in my life after that could be pure pleasure. It's that kind of jollying up—and that kind of faith—that makes my life with Jerele fun and fruitful. And our shared commitment to the Holy Other empowers each of us every day. For all of this, I am always thankful.

CONTENTS

Contents

INTRODUCTION: A PROLOGUE

Let me tell you a story . . .

How many times has such an offering been a boon to our lives: a break from doing sums in arithmetic class, a just-frightening-enough last activity around a campfire, a moment to laugh, a clarifying example that helps us understand.

And sometimes even a gift. A life-saving, life-giving gift.

A few months after my young husband, in perfect health, dropped dead one summer by the side of the road at our cabin in Tennessee, I went to a distant city on business. A friend, thinking to help, arranged a dinner in that city for me and another widow. When the woman was seated at the table where I waited, she immediately began to cry. And she cried during the entire meal. When the waiter brought the dessert menu, my dinner companion came close to becoming hysterical; she kept talking about how much her late husband loved chocolate.

It wasn't that I didn't empathize. How many meals had I cried through, just as she was doing now? But I must admit that I was a bit puzzled, for the whole idea of this dinner was that I would have an opportunity to talk with someone whose insights and experiences would benefit and help me.

As we walked out of the restaurant, I ventured to say, "I'm so sorry for your pain. How long has your husband been dead?"

When she answered, "Eighteen years," something snapped for me. I said to myself, in that very moment, "Elizabeth, whatever it takes, eighteen years from now you are not going to be walking out of a restaurant carrying in front of you a life-size cardboard cutout of a widow." I already knew enough about grieving from books I had been reading to realize that people have sad experiences and cry years and years after a loss. But I also knew enough to realize that this was not the case here. This person, instead of being caught in a momentary experience of "shadow grief," was living—it seemed to me—the lifestyle of someone whose very identity was the loss she had experienced.

What could I do to avoid this?

Perhaps because I was a researcher by training and a teacher of poems and stories, I decided to watch for people who had experienced loss and tragedy and ask them to tell me the narratives of their lives. But I wanted to hear the stories of a particular kind of person. I wanted to talk to people who, in spite of the awful things that had happened to them, had found some way to love life again. People who, through some means (though what these means might be, at this point, I didn't have a clue), had managed not to get stuck in the pain and emptiness of their loss. I wanted to learn from people who could say, like Mr. Manette in Dickens's A Tale of Two Cities, "I've been recalled to life."

I ended up, over time, talking to more than sixty people. When I began, I had no thought in mind except my own need. I had to know what people did or what they thought or what they learned that made the positive difference in their lives after loss had shattered their world. I would talk to them, and then I would go home and write what I remembered in my journal.

Later—in fact, years later—as I reflected on the stories and on my own experiences, I thought I saw a pattern of movement from the time when we feel the first blast of loss to the time when we can say, "I have found equilibrium again. I have freedom from the domination of grief. Life now has a 'new normal.' I am not stuck. I am again a participant in the wonderful mystery called life." This was the genesis of the book you are now holding.

From the testimonies of so many individuals who read the first editions of *Seven Choices*, I now know that the mapping of the terrain of active grieving that I made for myself—based on the experiences and examples of the generous community of people who shared their stories with me—offers something for all of us when loss blows our lives to smithereens. It is this mapping—flexible, personal, individual, and private—that forms the structure of this book, from "Impact: Experiencing the Unthinkable" to Daylight, when we can finally say that Integration is now a mark of our daily lives.

Buttressing the personal stories people told me are the works of scientists, medical professionals, philosophers, spiritual thinkers, and poets who provide evidence or offer powerful observation that such an "active grieving process" does exist and that it is within the power of each individual to make the choices that allow movement through that process. The process is unique to every individual; each of us moves at a pace and in ways that are right for us; nothing is automatic, and everything derives from our active participation in the ebb and flow of our own lives. Yet we all share the same humanity. We recognize the common elements of our grief, at the same time that we recognize that no two of us experience a loss in quite the same way. Each of us is a member of a community that is known the world over, a community of "those who mourn, those who have lost."

I begin each of the seven chapters of this book with a narrative of the loss of my husband. You will find, however, that my story merely serves as a mirror to reflect the disasters and the triumphs we all experience during the process of grieving many kinds of loss:

divorce, death (parents, children, partners, brothers and sisters, friends), estrangement from a friend, loss of the shape of life as we knew it, financial and career setbacks, reversal of expectations, disappearance of a dream.

But enough framing of the tale.

Let me tell you a story . . .

1

IMPACT:

EXPERIENCING THE UNTHINKABLE

Well, everyone can master grief
'cept he that has it.
William Shakespeare

I looked at my watch: 8:17 P.M.

"He really should be back," I thought. "I know it's harder to jog here than it is back home. But, even so, he's had enough time to finish his run by now."

Every summer, as soon as the spring term ended at Texas A&M, Greg and I came to our cabin in the Tennessee hills. We had bought the place four years earlier, just after we got married. We could barely believe our good fortune: The cabin cost us almost nothing, because it was so old and run-down (a condition Greg found most appealing—he loved to wield a saw and a hammer), and the location reminded us so much of the beautiful spot where we were married.

In fact, the mountains around our cabin were part of the same range that sheltered Cade's Cove, the site of our wedding. While we were dating, we came upon the tiny cove that appears so unexpectedly and incongruously among the rugged and steep mountain peaks. Here a few families of pioneers, trekking in the early nineteenth century toward a new life, had found a haven among the cove's meadows. The barrier of mountains that surrounded them required the settlers to rely on their own ingenuity. Their cabins, water mill, barns, churches, and pasture fences are still standing, now preserved as a national treasure, a testimony to the pioneer's self-sufficiency. When we decided to get married, it was the oldest cabin in the cove, the John Oliver place, that Greg and I chose as the wedding site. That cabin, with its hand-hewn timbers, its doors fastened with carved wooden hinges, its floor worn smooth by generations of living, was a symbol for us of the way we wanted to live our new life together: simple, strong, in harmony with the environment.

Our own cabin had been built only forty years ago, not over 150, but it and the surroundings had the same sense of timelessness and peace as Cade's Cove and John Oliver's cabin. Whether it was down at the feed store listening to the farmers guess about rain or on my parents' front porch with our chairs tilted back against the wall, listening to night talk, we felt our spirits renewed whenever we came here.

My seventy-two-year-old daddy, a Holiness preacher who had retired from pastoring but not from preaching, as he was quick to tell you, had settled himself and Mother a few years earlier in a little wood-frame house on Possum Creek in Soddy-Daisy, which was right nearby. Greg and I loved to walk up the road at the end of the day and visit with my parents on their front porch.

"Got two bushels of butter beans out of the garden today," Daddy would report. "And if we get rain there'll be more the day after tomorrow. . . . Here, Elizabeth, take this dishpan and see if your thumbs still know how to open a bean."

And then there'd be discussion about the progress of Mother's fourteen-day cucumber pickles and whether or not there were enough tomatoes to begin to can. Most nights there'd be homemade peach ice cream around bedtime; and then Daddy would say, "Time to turn in." Greg and I would start for our cabin.

We always seemed to be able to see the moon and at least one bright star in front of us as we walked down the country road. I would look up at the sky and chant a rhyme from my childhood:

I see the moon;
The moon sees me;
God bless the moon
And God bless . . .

Instead of "God bless me," I always said, "And God bless us."
Greg would answer:

Star light, star bright,
First star I see tonight;
I wish I may, I wish I might,
Have the wish I wish tonight.

"But," he'd say, pulling me close, "I've already got my wish. I've got you!" No matter how predictable this ritual, we still laughed every time he said those words.

Greg and I were both professors, and we used the summer months to do our writing. We had come to the cabin this summer to finish a book we were writing together, and our work was going well. In the five days since we arrived we had opened up the cabin, unpacked our books and supplies, and decided where each of us would work.

Greg's spot was at a small table on the tiny screened-in front porch. "Lets me see who's going up and down the road," he joked, as if any more than one or two neighbors were likely to pass in a whole day's time. I worked inside, at a table we had placed beside a long wall of windows. I could watch the chameleons that scampered along the old stone foundation, where, in some earlier time, another part of the cabin had stood. And if I looked up I could see the tops of the pine trees that grew all around the cabin. "Virgin pines. Hundreds of years old," Greg explained. "They've never been cut—that's why they're so tall."

*　　*　　*

Work had gone well today, and after supper Greg had said, "Want to join me for a six-mile run?"

"No, sir, offer declined," I said. "I'll do the two-mile route and see you back here when you're finished."

So I had run to the Possum Creek bridge and back, and it was now time—past time—for Greg to be home. Minutes passed. "I bet these hills *did* get to him," I said to myself. "He's probably walking the last miles. I'll take the car and go pick him up; he'll appreciate a ride back home."

I started the car and guided it carefully over the big roots of the trees that grew all the way up to the edge of the cabin. I turned onto the paved road from the cabin lane. It was that time between daylight and dark that makes one feel lonesome and melancholy. Reaching the bridge at Possum Creek, I noticed how still and deep the water looked. Everything was covered with that kind of gray-green light that's left in the mountains when the sun has almost gone down. I crossed the bridge and rounded a curve.

There I came upon a scene of confusion. Large groups of people were standing on both sides of the road and spilling out into it. Carefully, I threaded my way through the crowd. I drove past the black-and-white car that belonged to the sheriff's patrol. I drove past the orange-and-white ambulance parked in the gravel on the left-hand side of the road. What held my attention was getting back onto the open road.

The trees and bushes were thick and grew close to the pavement. "It'll be easy to miss him if you're not careful," I reminded myself as I left the crowd behind. So I drove slowly, looking carefully to the right and to the left.

There he is! I see him! It was a glimpse of Greg's orange running shorts. I had known I would find him taking it slow and easy up and down these hills! I accelerated the car and exhaled a sigh of relief. How long, I wondered, had I been holding my breath?

But when I got to the spot where Greg was, the orange turned out to be a cylinder that had been mounted on a post, meant to hold a newspaper. By now I had reached the country store that I knew was Greg's three-mile turnaround point. "I've just missed him somewhere on the road," I said, speaking aloud to no one but myself. "I'll turn around here. I know I'll see him on the way back. I've just managed to miss him."

When I got to the curve above Possum Creek, the crowd was still there. So was the black-and-white car that belonged to the sheriff's patrol. And so was the orange-and-white ambulance.

I noticed a man standing in the middle of the road. He seemed to be directing traffic.

"What happened?" I asked, rolling down the window when I got abreast of him.

"Lady, move on. You're blocking traffic," was the man's reply.

I eased the car down toward another man who was also standing in the middle of the road. This man appeared to be in charge.

"Sir, what happened?" I asked again.

"We found a man in the ditch," he answered.

"Well, I'm looking for my husband," I said. "My husband went for a six-mile run, and he hasn't come home yet."

For a few seconds the man said nothing. Then he spoke in a voice so low that I could hardly hear him. "Ma'am, I think you should pull your car over to the side of the road." I felt no emotion. I asked no additional questions. If there was any connection between what was happening beside that road and my life, it still was not apparent to me. But I did what I was told. I pulled over to the side of the road.

There was a place on the gravel where I could park. I pulled in beyond the ambulance and turned off the motor. By the time I put my feet on the ground outside the car, that man and another were there by my open door. They were waiting for me to get out of the car.

From my seat, I looked up at the two strange men. It was only then that I realized that the man they had found in the ditch and the man I was looking for were probably one and the same.

"Is he dead?" I asked.

There was a long silence. One of the men finally answered.

"Yes, ma'am. He is."

I got out of the car. One man stood on my right side and one on my left. We began to walk, not touching, toward the ambulance. Greg, my husband, was dead.

We reached the back door of the orange-and-white ambulance. The crowd standing there quickly moved aside. No one was talking. I stepped up to get into the ambulance. The wire-mesh grate under my feet did not seem stable. I held on to the railing to keep from falling.

A shiny chrome bench ran the length of the ambulance; it was cold when I sat down on it. In front of me a body lay on a stretcher, covered by a white sheet. A pair of jogging shoes rested on top of the body's stomach. Blue Adidas. I knew they were Greg's.

When the man pulled down the sheet, I felt no emotion. How can you cry when you know it is not possible that your husband is dead? "Look at him," I thought. "There's nothing wrong with him. He looks exactly the way he did taking a nap on the front-porch swing this afternoon. He couldn't have died from those gravel burns on his cheek. There's just some mistake; I know he's not dead." Nevertheless, when the man standing at the door of the ambulance said he needed to ask me some questions, I covered the body up again.

"Is this your husband? . . . What was his address? . . . What is his date of birth? . . . What is your name? . . . Does he have any children? . . . Are his parents living? . . . What was his occupation? . . ." I felt so competent, knowing all the answers. There was not a single one I stumbled over.

My mother and father arrived. I heard my father crying and calling out before I ever saw him. "I don't believe it's Greg," he was saying as he pushed his way through the crowd. "Let me through. I've got to see if it's him."

When he got to the door, I said, "Yes, Daddy, it's Greg." I got out of the ambulance so he could see. Then I saw my mother running through the crowd. She was crying, but there was no sound. Mother did not go to the ambulance; she came straight to me. We got into my car, and I drove back to the cabin.

I spent the next hours being efficient. People must be called: Make a list. Find the telephone numbers. Sit down and dial. Greg's two sons, his ex-wife, his mother. My family. Our friends. People we worked with. When one is emotionally frozen, one can deliver even devastating news without cracking.

My sister, Barbara, arrived from Chattanooga. She, my brother-in-law, and I went to the hospital to release the body. I went back to the cabin and chose the burial clothes. Neighbor women brought chocolate cupcakes and hot, strong coffee to my parents' home, where we had gathered. Neighbor men sat in silence on the front porch with my father. My friend Felicia arrived from Knoxville. My brother, Frank, came from Atlanta. Others were flying and would arrive tomorrow from more distant places.

Everyone sat in the living room all night. Frank, Barbara, and I planned the memorial service—I sat on the couch, Barbara on the floor, and Frank on the fireplace hearth. Frank wrote on memo paper that Mother brought him from beside the telephone.

Details were decided. We would hold the service down on the grassy slope by Possum Creek. Frank would be in charge, and we would ask several of Greg's friends just to stand and talk. We'd put flowers in big tin buckets and place the casket down by the water. Mother and Daddy's minister would give a final prayer. Greg's body would be buried in the family plot in the country cemetery nearby.

Only once all night—when Barbara first arrived and came running through the door calling, "Oh, Sister! Oh, Sister!"—did I almost feel tears. Only once, as I walked through the empty dining room and just happened to glance up and see the moon and one star framed by the windowpane, did a deep groan sound from somewhere far, far away, from somewhere outside me.

As I stood in the lumberyard the next day buying plywood to put down by the creek for the memorial service, I realized how strange this all was. But all I could think to say was "Daddy, we never thought we'd be buying plywood for this purpose, did we?"

I went to the memorial service wearing the only dressy thing I had brought to the cabin, the white suit and bright red silk blouse I had bought for Frank's graduation from law school the month before. Two small ceramic stars that Greg had bought for me—one red and one black—were still pinned on the lapel.

When it was time for Frank to begin the service, he stepped up to the rock wall that edged the water and began to talk:

We are here to celebrate the life of Gregory M. Cowan. We are having this service here by the water because it was one of Greg's favorite places, and one he would want us to remember him in. A few of Greg's friends are going to speak of what Greg meant to them and what he contributed to their lives. . . .

I felt pride when I heard the eulogy given by David, Greg's friend and our department head at the university:

We come bringing our garlands of flowers and of words in honor of a man who loved loveliness in all things. . . . In his presence we all thought better of the world and spoke better about each other. This is why the sad occasion that has brought us here has its affirmative, its joyous side. Where Greg led, we shall follow. The memory of his smile, of the twinkle in his eyes, of his patient voice, will disperse and blend into the mystery of each of our lives and of life itself. The spirit of affirmation that was the light of Greg's life has rejoined the spirit of affirmation that lights the lives of good men in all times and places and that enables us to find our way.

As David spoke the funeral eulogy, I heard his words; but I was also participating in another ceremony . . .

The wind is blowing the pages of the marriage book, and the dairy farmer-turned-justice of the peace is having trouble keeping his place. Greg and I stand in front of him, our backs to John Oliver's cabin, Greg with a big white daisy in his lapel, me carrying a bouquet of daisies tied with yellow streamers. The vows . . . Will you have this man to be your wedded husband? . . . Will you have this woman to be your wedded wife . . . to live together according to God's holy ordinance . . . till death do you part? . . . I do, I do. *The prayers . . .* I will lift up my eyes unto these hills from whence cometh my help. . . . *This was my promise. And Greg, turning his head to take in the numinous beauty around us, quoted a prayer he had written in a letter to me several months before:* May we be blessed by the birds, the bark, and the slanted rock.

I returned to Possum Creek. The service was coming to an end. Frank was speaking:

After hearing what Greg meant to all these people, if you can imagine that a hundredfold, you will begin to understand what he meant to his family. One talent he had that we can all try to emulate was his ability, and willingness, to express his feelings toward others. An example of this was just three weeks ago, when everyone came to Atlanta for my graduation from law school. That night, after Greg and Sister had gone back to Texas, Greg called to let me know how much the day had meant to him and how much he enjoyed being with me. Here today, before each of you, I pledge for myself that I will try to let each of you know what you mean to my life, and I urge you to make that same commitment.

It was time for the closing hymns. The congregation, gathered on the hillside, began to sing an old spiritual, "I'll Fly Away." I heard the words: "Some glad morning, when this life is o'er, I'll fly away, to that home on God's celestial shore, I'll fly away. I'll fly away, oh, glory, I'll fly away. When I die, hallelujah, by and by, I'll fly away."

Again, I suddenly found myself somewhere else . . .

It's a Sunday morning in Mexico. I'm on a path cut out of the edge of the jungle. The bougainvillea grows so close to the path that we brush the flowers as we jog past. A yellow-and-green parrot is sitting high up in a plantain tree.

"Let's sing," I say.

Reaching for my hand, Greg replies, "It's Sunday, so let's sing a hymn."

"How about 'I'll Fly Away'?" I answered.

We sing, jogging along together.

The congregation is now beginning the final hymn. "Amazing grace, how sweet the sound." I listen, but I am not present at a memorial service on July 4 at noon by the side of Possum Creek, in Soddy-Daisy, Tennessee. I am far away . . .

In a big white room in a house in Texas. The sun shining through the east windows gives the softest light you have ever seen. It's Sunday, and the New York Times *covers the floor. The coffee cups are almost empty. Greg says, "Hey, I haven't heard our concert this morning. Isn't it about time?" And I go over to the piano I've had since I was a little girl and begin to play "Amazing grace, how sweet the sound . . ."*

I come to myself as the audience sings the last refrain. Some friends, carrying big buckets, are moving among the people on the hillside. The buckets are filled with flowers. Everyone is being given a white daisy to take away.

I looked and saw the light sparkling on the water in front of me. As the sounds of the hymn echoed from the mountains across the creek, I noticed that a flock of ducks had swum up to the edge of the water. The ducks were all lined up in a row, as still as they could be.

Then there was the drive to the cemetery and the walk up the hill to the spot where Greg's body would be laid. The minister reads: *The fruit of the Spirit is love, joy, peace, long-suffering, gentleness, goodness, faith . . .* My sister, brother, their spouses, and I sing a little song that we made up one summer night when we three couples were vacationing together: *You are my lovely daffodil, that grows upon the yonder hill . . .* Somebody prays. Then the kind funeral director asks if we want to stay or leave as the casket is lowered into the ground. I suggest that we leave. The sun feels excruciatingly hot on my head as I step away from the graveside, and my feet slip several times on small pebbles as we walk back down the hill.

In the days and weeks that followed, I must have told the story a thousand times: *It was Monday afternoon, we were at our cabin, he went for a jog. . . . He died in stride as he ran along the road . . . a congenital heart defect so small the coroner said it would never have been detected. . . . The doctor said he would have died that night no matter what he was doing. . . . He had a heart that was going to last forty-three years, and that was it.*

I wrote long letters to all our friends, giving them every detail of the weeks before Greg's death—what he had done, what I noticed and remembered now, the amazing things I could see in hindsight. I answered note after note, acknowledging the kind words people had written: *Hans, I know exactly what you mean when you say you feel as if you've lost your biggest fan. . . . Dear Amilde, Yes, he was so relaxed; and I, too, always felt he was listening, that he always had time, that I had his full attention when he was with me.* I relived our last day over and over and over again. The way he made a flower out of the butter lettuce for our salad at lunch. The way we worked on the manuscript all day together. The book, *Gift from the Sea*, that he left turned down at his worktable. How I called out, "Grego, those legs look terrific," as he jogged away from the cabin.

I took little notice of the strange things that were happening to my body—or to my mind. My appetite disappeared. For days I felt no hunger. It was more than two weeks before I remembered that there were good things in the world to eat. One morning I smelled Mother's biscuits baking in the oven and realized that I wanted breakfast. It was the first food I had tasted in days—a plate of gravy and biscuits. The meal made me feel good because it brought back cozy childhood memories.

I lay awake for hours when I went to bed. Every night, when I finally did get to sleep, I would wake up at exactly the same hour, 3:00 A.M. I had dreamed that someone had stolen my wedding bracelet. The same dream night after night. The first thing I would do when I woke up was reach frantically for my arm. Was the bracelet still there?

After this, I could never go back to sleep. I would lie there imagining that the insurance company would find something wrong with the policies and I wouldn't have the money to buy a monument for Greg's grave. I would think of my two stepsons and fear that I wouldn't be able to save anything for them. I would think of all the bills piling up and try to figure out how I was going to pay them with only one salary.

My menstrual period started fifteen days early and flooded like a hemorrhage. And when it finally ended, it began again after only seven days. I couldn't think clearly. I did strange things. I carried gravel around in my coin purse, gravel that was speckled with blood from the scratches on Greg's face when he fell. Every time I got change out, I picked up the pieces of gravel and squeezed them in my hand. Once, when I was washing my hair, I saw a crack in the sink. For a moment, I was certain that the crack was blood from one of Greg's scratches.

On the fourth day after Greg died, I finally cried. Two friends who had not been able to come to the funeral flew from New York to Tennessee. I wanted to drive to the airport to get them. When I sat down behind the wheel of the car, every detail of Monday afternoon came back to me. Leaving the cabin. Looking for Greg. Asking the man what had happened. Stretching high to reach the wire-mesh step at the back of the ambulance. As I remembered, the tears came in a torrent.

And now I could not stop crying. I cried as I typed letters. I cried when I went to bed at night, and I cried when I woke up in the morning. At times during the day I would feel rushes of grief, like waves, and I would sob convulsively. Often, I felt that I was choking.

I took a trip to see one of Greg's sons. We talked for hours about his father. I ordered what I knew Greg liked when we went to a restaurant. I was angry that he wasn't there to see how neatly Fred had cleaned his apartment in preparation for my visit. I was loath to leave because being with Fred and his brother, David, was the closest I could now get to Greg.

My sister, my brother, and I went to the Pacific Northwest to attend a memorial service in Greg's hometown. While on board a small boat, crossing a bay, I thought of how many times Greg and I had made this trip together. I had always loved the exhilaration of the spray on my face and the wind whipping around me. On this day, however, I only felt dull. My eyes wouldn't focus. Instead of seeing the water, I saw only other years and other days. Suddenly, I thought, "I could jump! I could jump right into the water! I could go where Greg is." But would I find him? That was the question.

Everywhere I went, I looked for Greg. I had to go to New York to discuss the future of the book we had been writing; and when I wasn't working, I roamed. I went to the apartment house where Greg and I had lived before we moved to Texas, to the restaurant where he surprised me with an engagement ring set with jade. I retraced the route we took the day we carried a sheet of plywood on our heads from the lumber store on West Broadway to our apartment on Bleecker Street. I ate cannoli at Ferrarro's and ordered a full plate of antipasto at the Greek restaurant, even though I knew it was too much for one person.

I stood in the entry of the Little Church Around the Corner and imagined the candles being lit on Christmas Eve. I rode the A train to the end of the line and walked up the hill to see the unicorn tapestries hanging in the Cloisters. I ran my hands over the coolness of the stone walls and sat in the opening of the arched walls, watching the shadows move across the courtyard. Everywhere, I tried to find my past. But all I found was incontrovertible evidence, assaulting evidence, that Greg was not present. And that everything—the past, the present, and the future—was irrevocably altered by the fact that he was dead.

I went to see a therapist. "I feel so abandoned," I said to him again and again. "Do you think Greg misses me the way I am missing him? Do you think he cares about me anymore? Does he see me? Does he know I'm still here?"

The wise therapist reassured me that my questions—and my feelings—were normal. "Don't hold anything back," he counseled. "Cry as much as you want to. Don't try to be strong and brave. You have not just lost a husband; you have lost a part of yourself. You are mourning not only for Greg," he reminded me. "You're also mourning yourself. You're mourning your own death."

In the absence of any purpose for life, my mind was constantly swirling with emotions and thoughts that repeated the same message.

Guilt. Was I responsible for Greg's death? If I hadn't been so keen on jogging, would Greg be alive today? Had there been some sign of his problem that I ignored or just missed? Why wasn't I kinder to him the last time he had a cold? Did I kill him by thinking ugly thoughts when I was angry? And why did *he* die and not me? He was a much better person than I was, much kinder and more loving. And those times I had enjoyed being by myself, happy that he was gone on a trip, even fantasizing about being an independent woman completely on my own again, back in my apartment in New

York . . . did God know about those thoughts and punish me by killing Greg?

Regret. Why didn't I run with him that day? At least I would have been with him when he died. Why did I agree to such a tight time line on the book? If we hadn't been rushed, maybe he wouldn't have worked so hard and then he might not have died. Why hadn't we spent more time with his children?

Resentment. What good did it do that we took care of ourselves? What did it matter that we ate well and always exercised? Who cared now that we took all those vitamins? Why did he have to die before we completed the book? Why did he go off and leave me with all the remaining work?

Anger. In New York the bell captain at the hotel where Greg and I had stayed many times in the past asks when I get out of the cab, "You alone this time, Mrs. Cowan? Where's the boss?" At that moment, I hated Greg. I hated him for deserting me. I hated him because I was the one who had to tell this man that he was dead. I hated the empty hotel room. I hated the double bed. It seemed preposterous to me at that moment that a human being could just disappear from the earth. I sat down at the desk in my room and wrote furiously: "I absolutely cannot believe at 10:50 P.M. on Tuesday, July 31, that Greg Cowan is dead. No Greg Cowan. An empty space. No one to fill the Greg Cowan space. There is no Greg Cowan anymore on this planet. I hate the world! I hate the world! He was a presence felt. He occupied space. He was. Where are you, Greg? Where, where are you? Can you really have gone away?"

Mystery. There were mysterious happenings. One day while sitting in a fifth-floor office at my publisher's, editing a chapter of the book, I saw for the first time a note in the margin in Greg's hand: "Get butterfly haiku." Only the day before, I had called my graduate assistant in Texas and asked her to find a short poem for the text, and she had given me this Japanese haiku:

> Spring Scene
> On the temple bell
> Has settled, and is fast asleep
> A butterfly.
>
> Anonymous

Reading Greg's note, "Get butterfly haiku," I think, "I've already done that. I did that yesterday!" I was so stunned by this coincidence that I turned in the swivel chair to look outside. There I saw, hovering against the glass, five floors above Third Avenue in New York City, a bright orange butterfly.

Then another kind of mysterious happening. Returning to Tennessee from New York, as the plane touched down on the runway, I felt as if I were suddenly engulfed in darkness. I could not breathe. I could not stand without holding on to the seat in front of me. When I tried to walk down the aisle, I stumbled from side to side; everything was black in front of me. The same words kept circling: "What am I coming back to? Nothing but more of the same. Nothing but an empty cabin."

And then the unexplainable happened. As if a voice had spoken, although I heard no sound, the words came: "Look outside. The sun is shining. Life is good." In that moment, I felt a release from the heaviness that had been pressing in on me since we landed. Somehow, in that split second, I knew that I was going to be all right. It was a genuine moment of grace. And even though the feeling did not last, I never forget the miracle of its occurring.

Visions. As I was flipping through a magazine back at Possum Creek with my parents, a photograph caught my eye. It was a sepia-tinted photograph of an old town in the West, a town very similar to one Greg and I had stayed in once when we were traveling through South Dakota. As I stared at the picture, I could feel Greg and me pulling into that town in the late afternoon. It was as if we were driving right into the picture. I knew exactly what we would have said. I felt how we would have felt.

Hearing an insect buzz, I looked up from the magazine and out toward the yard. Suddenly, as if slides were being flashed on a screen, I saw three scenes suspended like a mirage in the glare of the hot August sun.

An Irish fisherman's wife was sitting by a fire on a cold, stormy night. The oil lamp on the table beside her cast a warm yellow light. The woman was knitting rapidly and nervously; the rain was beating on the windowpane. As I watched this scene, I knew the woman's husband would never come back. I knew he would be drowned at sea that night during a storm.

A Native American woman was preparing her brave for battle, telling him goodbye as he left to fight. His face was painted with diagonal stripes of blue. His short loincloth struck against his thighs. There was one brief moment when the woman reached up and straightened the band around the warrior's head. As she made that gesture, I knew the brave would die in this battle and never come home again.

The third scene was a lonesome prairie. There was nothing but emptiness as far as the eye could see. The grass was tall and spiky, the kind that hurts your legs when you walk through it. Standing among this wiry grass was a family, their covered wagon behind them. The mother stood motionless, looking down at the ground. Two children huddled beside her,

their faces buried in her skirts. The father stood a short distance away.
He, too, was staring toward the baby's tiny grave.

In the few seconds that these three scenes flashed before my eyes, I gained wisdom. I realized that death was impersonal, that women—and men, too—in all times and the world over had felt the pain of losing a loved one. And millions more would experience it also. I saw that death and grief were a condition of living. Death was not something that had happened only to me. I was not special.

I cried from the depths of my being. I cried for the Irish fisherman's wife, for the Native American woman whose brave did not return from battle, for the pioneer family who had to leave their baby on the lone prairie. I cried for the human condition. I knew that what had happened to me was not a personal thing, that in my grief I was participating in a way that the world was. The way life was set up to be. And even though this wisdom could not shield me from what lay ahead, it nevertheless did allow me to get in contact with and express my deepest pain.

As each day passed, I realized more fully that I had not only lost a husband but that I had lost the very purpose and shape of my life. The bulwark I had built against randomness, the chaos of existence, that bulwark had been destroyed. My life no longer had any contours; there was nothing into which I could fit. I had no expectations. I had no plans. At night I dreamed of thin crystal vases, broken while being washed. I dreamed of sheets hanging on a clothesline above an ocean, being whipped, whipped, whipped by a very strong wind.

Day after day it was the same. In the twilight period between sleep and waking, I would hear the words "Oh, Greg, oh, Greg," except that they sounded like "Oh, sad, oh, sad." When my mother asked one morning, "How are you today?" all I could say was "I feel so weary. So stretched out and caught. I'm the loser for being alive."

I wrote to a friend: "The nothingness of life. Nothing is important. There's no reason to be here. Greg's dying has done more than just leave me alone. It has rocked me to the foundation and shaken all my optimism about life. I feel like running head-on into a tree."

That is what it means to grieve. You allow yourself to see the truth—the devastating truth. The continuity of your life is gone. The connections are broken. The web of human relations that you had with courage reached out to build turns out to be so fragile. So quickly destroyed. And you are impotent. Powerless. The force—the robber—has struck. About this you have no say.

Grief is excruciating pain. You understand why for centuries, in cultures around the world, the wail of grief has sounded. That wordless cry into the night. The lament of life and death. You now know the meaning of those long, mournful wails.

〜⌒⌒⌐

This is Impact. This is Experiencing the Unthinkable. Shattering. Surprising. Gut-wrenching. Debilitating. Overwhelming.

Our lives have changed, but without our permission. We are disoriented, frightened, confused. We reel, stagger, stumble, unable to regain our balance. This response to the unwanted change that has intruded into our lives is natural. For what we have lost is the very shape of our lives, the structure that tells us who we are and what we are about. How could we, then, *not* react with such intensity?

But there is also a paradox in our behavior. We may respond to the news of the loss in such a way that people say things like "It hasn't hit her yet" or "He still hasn't let himself realize what has happened." But regardless of appearances, these people are wrong.

It is true that for a period of time—minutes, hours, days, even weeks—we may pay little attention to a reality in which people concern themselves with long-range planning, or with making their way in the world, or with friendly, sociable discourse. But never think for one minute that we are not in touch with reality. We are in touch with the most profound reality there is. The kind of reality that is grounded in our deep interconnectedness to everything around us. The kind of reality that centers on the personal world each of us has constructed—the people we love, the work we do, the place we live in, the family we belong to, the things we enjoy. The kind of reality that we sometimes get in touch with when we stand over our children as they are sleeping or when we gaze out at sea or when we finish planting a garden or painting a picture.

Yes, the grieving person is in touch with reality. It is the most elemental of realities, the ground of realities. To this, attention is being paid.

It may be, as researchers at the Institute of Medicine suggest in their study of bereavement, that during this time of stress our brains secrete special neurohormones that allow us to register or recognize things that are happening around us in a detached, slow-motion way. It may be, as Dr. Beverley Raphael points out, that our ego "virtually closes its boundaries and defenses against the trauma that is perceived as overwhelming and a threat to its survival."

Yet for the neurohormones and the defenses even to go into action, we have to first know that something terrible has happened. So while we are perhaps protected for a time from realizing the *external* implications of the loss, nothing protects us from the immediate *internal* knowledge that something has threatened our lives. That some alien force has intruded. That we are in danger; our survival is at stake. We know *this* immediately—before we even know the facts or the details. We register the loss through some frequency that bypasses words and conscious thoughts and at some velocity that is quicker than sound.

We are never more aroused than when we have experienced a loss. Our body is in a state of emergency. As with all emergencies, even emergencies of far less significance (think of our response when pipes burst during a winter's freeze), we devote our entire and immediate attention to reacting. We may react by becoming numb and detached. We may react by becoming efficient and able. We may react by crying or falling to pieces. But we *do* react. We are not dumb to what has happened. We know it to the very core of our being.

This response is so elemental that we even share it with animals. Konrad Lorenz took note of how greylag geese responded when they lost their mates. The goose's first reaction was to begin looking frantically for its partner, moving about "restlessly by day and night, flying great distances and visiting places where the partner might be found, uttering all the time the penetrating . . . long-distance call."

Many of us read the story, which appeared in newspapers worldwide, about elephants mourning at a rail track in India's Assam state. Seven elephants had been killed by a train that derailed. Khagen Sangmai, a top official of the Digboi police station in Assam, reported that, within minutes of the train's hitting the elephants, a herd of about one hundred other elephants "came from nowhere." The elephants, "with tears rolling down their eyes," circled the pachyderms that lay dead by the railroad track.

The scientist Cynthia Moss also described the response of a family of elephants to the death of one of their members from a gunshot wound: stopping at the scene, becoming quiet and tense, and then slowly and cautiously beginning to touch the body. When the family finally moved on to find food, the mother elephant kept looking back, as if to get one last glimpse of the body they were leaving behind.

The reactions we have when we experience a loss, then, have a long evolutionary history. We find ourselves in a state of alarm. We behave as if we are searching for the one who is lost, even though we do not consciously expect to find this person. The restlessness we experience—going from place to place, from room to room—is one way we search. So is the alteration in our perception that causes us to think we see or hear the person who is absent, and the slip in attention that results in our setting the lost person's place at the table or looking for the absent one in a crowd. We are aroused at a deep, evolutionary level, and our actions—shock, crying, anger, pining, searching, ignoring, detaching—are automatic and testify to the connectedness and bonding that have existed among human beings as well as animals for millions of years.

What is "normal" behavior during the first days, weeks, and months following a loss? That is a question that we ask often, for we find ourselves behaving in erratic ways and sometimes even fear that we are going crazy. We are occupied almost every minute with thoughts of what has happened and experience everything—including ourselves—as unfamiliar, unreal, and unpredictable. Stories I have heard from men and women who talked about their early grieving reveal that in the first hours, days, weeks, and even months, any of the following reactions can take place.

Spontaneous Emotion

A young father remembers:

When they called me at work, they said, "Daniel has stopped breathing—he's been taken to the hospital." All the way to the emergency room, I figured it was something bad, but I didn't think he was dead. Maybe it was just because I didn't want to think my three-month-old son was dead. I mean, it happened so fast.

When I got to the hospital, I saw my cousin standing outside. He didn't say anything as I ran past, only shook his head. So I ran inside to the desk and asked the nurse, "Where's my son? His name is Daniel. Where's my son?" She pointed toward a door. I ran inside, and Jill said, "Our boy is dead." I fell to the floor, and I cried.

A TEMPORARY SHUTTING OUT OF THE LONG-TERM IMPLICATIONS OF THE LOSS

A widow recalls:

When my husband died, I was so calm and so efficient that my sister-in-law, who had come from Ohio to Pennsylvania to be with me, called her family to say she was coming home early. "Joan is doing so well," I heard her say on the telephone. "You should see her determination! She's got fire in her eyes! She's taking care of everything. She doesn't need anyone here to help her."

If my sister-in-law had only known. A week later the reality hit me, and for months I couldn't function.

SEEING THE LOST ONE

A young widow speaks:

I walked past the stairs, and out of the corner of my eye I saw him sitting on the top step. He was putting his tennis shoes on. The image was so vivid. He was bent over tying his shoe just the way he always did, with his racket up against his knee. The scene startled me so much that I jerked to a stop. But when I looked again the step was bare.

CONFUSION AND DISORIENTATION

A grieving partner told this story:

I cannot remember my own phone number. I took the wrong turn coming home from work today, and we've lived in the same place for four years. My mind just will not work. I start from one place to another in the office and forget where I was headed or why. I cannot make sense of reports, the same kind of reports I've been receiving from my colleagues since I came to work at this company. Our boss asked us in a staff meeting one day this week to consider a particular business situation from a completely different point of view than we would ordinarily have done. In the past, I've always enjoyed this kind of challenge, to think "outside the box." But for the life of me, I could see only the obvious. I was unable to imagine a single alternative.

RESTLESSNESS

A mother whose son was killed in an automobile accident recounts:

When I'm home, I roam from room to room. I can't sit still. I hunt for something to occupy my time and can't find anything. When I'm at work it's no better, because Dan worked with us in the family business.

Today was my first day back at work, and all I did was walk from laboratory to laboratory. I suppose, in one sense, I was looking for Dan, although I knew, of course, that I wasn't going to find him. Finally, I started talking to him quietly as I went through the building. "I love you," was the thing I said the most. "Dan, I love you." I also told him how much I miss him. Sometimes, if no one else was around, I'd call out his name.

When the crew sat down for lunch together, as we do every day, Dan's absence was so obvious. I found myself several times looking to the place at the table where he always sat, and I was surprised every time when he wasn't there. You would think I'd realize, after looking for him the first time, that he was gone; but I guess it was such a habit to expect him to be there. During the entire lunch hour I never stopped expecting to see him at his place at the table, no matter how often I was disappointed when I looked.

IRRATIONAL FEAR

A man reports:

The day I rented the apartment, I didn't notice that there were no lights in the ceiling. The house Marie and I had lived in for twenty-eight years had lights in the ceiling, so I just didn't think about an apartment being wired only for lamps. So here I was, staying my first night in the apartment, with no light except a photographer's light that I used when I developed pictures. The bed I had bought hadn't come yet, so I slept on the floor. I can tell you, I was as scared as a ten-year-old. The dark scared me. The sounds scared me. When the icemaker came on in the refrigerator, the noise almost made me jump out of my skin. Off and on all night, I got up and walked around the empty apartment. I hardly slept at all.

FORGETTING THE LOST ONE IS GONE

A widow recalls:

Our son-in-law called from Germany. Beth had had the baby, a girl. I was so happy! As soon as we hung up, I called Frank at the office. It wasn't until the receptionist said "Hello" that I remembered that Frank was dead. I put down the phone and just stood, looking around the house. Nothing belonged to me. Nothing was familiar. This could just as easily have been a strange hotel as the home in which I had lived for thirty-five years. There was nowhere now that meant anything to me, nowhere that I cared about or felt that I belonged. Even the air in the room felt dead.

DISBELIEF

A sister recalls:

My older brother and I went to Joel's apartment. It was just as he had left it. Half a bagel on a paper towel lay on the countertop. A grape jelly jar stood open—the brand we had all eaten since we were little kids—with the case knife inside. The navy sweatshirt I had bought him at the Gap was spread out on the back of one of the kitchen chairs. In the bedroom, the covers were hanging half off the floor. "As usual," we said to each other. In the living room, CD cases spilled all over the coffee table. We wanted to know which CD was in the player, but we also didn't want to know. What were the last songs he had listened to before going to work? It wasn't possible that our brother wasn't coming back. It just wasn't possible. There had to be some mistake. If we waited long enough, Joel would burst through the door. When I said this to my brother, he said, "Oh, Lisa, if he only would." But we knew the truth, even in the middle of our disbelief.

ANGER AND RESENTMENT

Hear this story:

I was walking along the streets in New Orleans. Everywhere I looked there was a couple. All I could see was couples. Couples laughing. Couples with their arms around each other. Couples shopping. Couples eating oyster sandwiches at the Desiree Bar. At that moment I hated Joe more than anything else in the world. I hated him; I hated being one-half of a couple. I thought, "If I had a knife in my pocket, I would stab every couple I see."

FEELINGS OF GUILT AND BLAME

Listen to this widow:

I knew my husband was sick, but I didn't know how sick. I had to go to a business meeting at four-thirty that afternoon with some disgruntled clients. "I'll be back by seven," I told him as I left. He must have had the convulsion almost as soon as I was out the door. I don't think I'll ever be able to forgive myself for going to that meeting. If I had been there, I believe the convulsion wouldn't have been so bad or gone on so long. I could have gotten him to the doctor sooner. I called him from the meeting but the line was busy, and, of course, I thought he was on the phone with someone. He must have tried to call me, because when I found him moaning on the floor—his face as gray as death—the phone was there beside him. If only I hadn't gone. I could have saved him so much suffering.

PHYSICAL DISTURBANCES

A daughter reports:

A few days after my mother died, I was at work and suddenly felt a heaviness in my chest and my upper arms. I couldn't get my breath. I just sat at my desk gasping, feeling as if I were going to die. The attack lasted for two or three minutes, but the heaviness stayed. For several days, I could hardly lift my arms high enough to get them on the steering wheel to drive the car. Finally, when the breathing attacks began to occur more frequently, I went to the doctor. "Stress angina," he said, and prescribed some nitroglycerin patches, which I now wear every day. "If the situation gets worse," the doctor said, "we'll have to consider other alternatives."

TOO BUSY TO MOURN

A young woman talks about the months after her husband's sudden death:

It is clear to me that I haven't started mourning. How can I? Hardly a day goes by that there isn't something else to do that's related to Martin's death. Find his retirement-fund papers. Get five new copies of the death certificate. Change my will so that the children will have guardians if something happens to me. Talk to the insurance agent, again. Fill out forms and more forms. Decide whether to sue the driver of the other car. Look for a smaller house. Think about finding a job. Spend as much time with the kids as possible. My sister asked me the other day if I thought my being constantly busy and not taking time to let the situation really sink in might be why I've had something close to pneumonia for weeks and never get enough sleep to feel rested. She's probably right. The truth is that I know I'm putting off something that it's necessary to do—dealing with the feelings and pain and thoughts about Martin's death—but so far I just don't feel I have the time or the energy to do this.

OBSESSION WITH MEMORIES

A widow recounts being haunted by a recurring image:

Every time I close my eyes, I see the room in the hospital where the attendant met me. "Here is the form you need to sign to release your husband's body." That was all she said. I suppose I expected her to say something else—maybe "I'm sorry" or "How are you?" or "Would you like to sit down?" But she didn't. All she did was hand me the paper and say, "Sign on the line at the bottom of the page."

"But I'd like to talk to someone," I said.

"I'm the person to talk to," she responded.

"Will there be an autopsy?" I asked.

"No need for an autopsy," she replied. "Your husband was a hit-and-run."

"But I'd like to have an autopsy," I said.

"The coroner did not request an autopsy," she answered. "We already have your husband ready for the morgue."

As the attendant took the paper and started to leave the room, she handed me a small yellow envelope. I had no idea what it was. When I turned the envelope upside down, my husband's watch and wedding ring fell into my hand.

Nothing has ever hit me harder than sitting in that hospital cubicle by myself, staring down at my husband's watch and ring. Not even the first news of his death. I cannot forget the scene. It flashes before my eyes, I guess, a hundred times a day. Over and over I see myself turning the envelope upside down. Over and over I see his wedding ring and his watch falling out into my hand.

EXPECTANT BUT STILL SURPRISED

A daughter recalls:

Our mother had been ill for more than two years, so my siblings and I expected her death at any time. In fact, given how much she suffered, we would say among ourselves that it would be a blessing when Mama died. We hated to see her in such terrible pain.

But, you know, even though I had done a lot of what I've heard is called "anticipatory grieving"—after all, we had already lost our mother as we knew her—I was surprised by my response after she died. I hadn't realized the difference, I guess, between her continuing to be present in our lives, even if she was sick, and her being completely absent, as she was after her death.

As long as she was alive, she still figured daily in my life—whether I was calling or going to the nursing home, talking to the doctors, asking about new medicine, talking to her when she was lucid, or volunteering to be on the family council. A big chunk of the structure of my time altered when she died. I had to find new things to do. And I was surprised to discover that I had to grieve having no mother, even though I thought I had faced this loss a long time ago.

Unexplainable Experiences

A widow reports:

I was riding in a taxi. Elliot had just died. I was going home from the hospital to get burial clothes to take to the mortuary. Suddenly, the taxi was filled with the smell of violets. I looked out the window to see who might be carrying flowers, or where the flower stall was located. But there was no sign of flowers anywhere on the street. "The violets must be in the front seat with the driver," I thought.

"What a beautiful smell," I said. "Where are the flowers?"

The driver looked startled. "I was about to ask you what perfume you're wearing," he said.

Neither of us could come up with an explanation for the sudden smell of violets that we were both experiencing. It was one of those weird, unexplainable occurrences. In some strange way, though, that mystery was comforting to me. I was uplifted by the smell of those violets. I felt as though I'd been touched by Elliott, or by the hand of God.

CRITICAL CONSIDERATIONS WHEN EXPERIENCING THE UNTHINKABLE

Upheaval, topsy-turvy, lost, strange, painful, vacant, engulfing: words that we think of when we hear these stories. The cluster of feelings, thoughts, and actions when we are hit by the impact of loss make us feel that we are "not of this world." Little matters except what is going on in our interior being. We know that nothing can make our situation better except a reversal of the terrible thing that has happened. Yet even in these dire straits there are things we can do and ways we can think that are useful and valuable responses.

TAKING CARE OF OURSELVES

When we experience a loss, a very ancient reaction is triggered in our brain: the flight-or-fight response. More than one researcher has remarked on the deep evolutionary roots of this response to loss. The reason we have such terrible pain, they say, is that far back in the timeless past we learned, as a species, that we had to bond with others in order to find food and to protect ourselves from enemies. To break those bonds was to die ourselves. Even now, when the bonds we have with others are disturbed, at some deep level we fear for our very survival.

Because we sense that we are in danger, the body mobilizes to protect itself from the intruder or, if that's not possible, to escape to safety. But loss is no hostile tribe that we can guard the camp against; nor is it an enemy that we can run from. Therefore we are caught in a state of tension. Our brain has stimulated us to take action; but, since we cannot undo the loss there is at this moment no action we can take. We are, therefore, held taut. This means that our bodies are under enormous stress.

The results of this stress show up immediately. Medical studies report that the chemical regulation of our breathing may become defective. Our vital processes are altered; the biological rhythms of sleeping and eating are disturbed. Our immune system becomes impaired. In fact, as the Institute of Medicine reports, our bodies have multiple reactions to grief: The autonomic, physiological, biochemical, and endocrine systems are all affected. Hormones go haywire; T cells stop protecting us from infections and viruses, as they previously did; our blood flow and cardiac rate increase; our digestion, metabolism, circulation, and respiration change. We experience irregular heartbeats. Our adrenal system is activated. Our ability to concentrate and pay attention decreases; our anxiety increases. In response to loss, then, our bodies are out of balance; homeostasis is disrupted.

What can we do about this?

The most important thing is to understand that we are in a state of emergency. Our very self has been assaulted. Our bodies and minds are reacting intensely to the loss. We need to take as good care of ourselves as we can. This means taking sufficient time off from work. It means eating as well as we can, when we can, drinking water, and resting in ways that support our well-being. It means going on walks or bike rides, running, swimming—whatever allows us to feel our bodies moving. It means taking special measures, such as getting massages or other kinds of bodywork, putting a cold cloth over our eyes, and listening to music.

The most important thing to say about the subject of our well-being during this initial response to our loss is that, while these intense experiences are occurring, we need to do everything we can to stay healthy. Unfortunately, it is precisely at this time that we feel little inclination to care for ourselves. Often, it is only by an act of sheer *intention* that we do what we need to do in order to stay in good health.

RELYING ON OTHERS

Over and over people remark, "Without my friends, without my family, I wouldn't have made it." The nurturing given by those who care for us provides a kind of cocoon of comfort, peace, and safety that we desperately need at this time. I remember hearing Buckminster Fuller say once that love is metaphysical gravity. We never realize the truth of this statement more keenly than during a time of loss, when it seems that the presence of our family and friends is all that allows us to hold anything together.

This is the time to rely on those around us in practical matters, to let them do for us. Accept their offers of help. Welcome their gestures of care and support. Let others take care of the children, run errands, prepare food, assist with arrangements, help with immediate business or legal affairs.

It is also the time to rely on our family and friends for emotional support. Spend as much time with them as possible. Talk about the lost one, even if you find yourself doing so incessantly. Cry unashamedly—wail and scream. Sit mute if you wish, or speak quietly. Just being in the presence of people who love us sends a message somewhere deep inside us, even if we don't realize it consciously, that we are still connected in this fragile web we call life and that, in spite of the rupture caused by the loss, there is still some continuity.

RESERVING JUDGMENT ABOUT GUILT AND ANGER

Since no human being is perfect, we're bound to feel guilty about something that's related to the lost person. We wish we hadn't done something that we did do, or that we had done something we didn't do. We remember thoughts we are now ashamed of. We recall mixed feelings about our relationship with the lost person. We remember hurting the person unnecessarily. We wonder why we are still alive and the other person isn't. And the list goes on.

The important thing at this point in the grieving process is to withhold final judgment about these matters until we are under less stress and can think more clearly. We should hold out the possibility, at least, that our judgment of ourselves may be more harsh than is warranted. And if we are at fault in some way this period of Experiencing the Unthinkable is not a good time to try to work out appropriate action to take in response to the situation. It would be better to put the matter of guilt aside for a while and say, "I'll think about that later. I'm not in a frame of mind now to do justice to the matter."

We are also likely to feel anger toward others. We may be angry at the person who is gone: he could have stopped smoking, but he didn't; she abandoned us; he left me with this responsibility. Perhaps we feel that someone else is to blame for what happened: the hospital staff could have done more, and they didn't; his mother made too many demands on him; there was never appropriate attention paid to the children; she drove after drinking and caused the accident. Or we may just be angry in general, over trivial things: how long the clerk takes to pack the groceries; what clothes the children put on in the morning; whether the grass is cut first thing on Saturday.

It is true that we are not much in control during this time. But if we can be aware that anger is a common response to grief, and that we may not be angry about exactly what we think we're angry about, we may be able to express our feelings in ways that do not tear at our relationships and have us gouging at others.

ASKING QUESTIONS

It is important to learn as many facts as possible about the circumstances of the loss. If we do not, it is likely that for months or even years ahead we will be obsessed with questions. What kind of heart attack did he have? What really happened? Where exactly on the road did the collision occur? When such questions can be answered, we should ask for the most minute details about what happened. Accurate information will take the place of fantasies, fears, and haunting mysteries.

I saw the positive effect of getting all the facts a few months ago, when friends whose son had died in an automobile accident spent time learning everything they could about the accident. They examined the car; drove out to the site to look at the skid marks on the pavement; asked the officer all kinds of questions. The end result was that they felt as fully informed as they could be. This didn't, of course, answer all those painful existential questions— Why did it happen? Why a young man? Why couldn't it have been different?—but the family did get an accurate picture of what had happened. They knew the facts as far as they could be known. It was clear to all of us that, for them, this made an enormous difference.

But what about those questions that cannot be answered? *Why wasn't I home when she called? Why does God let these bad things happen? Why did we fight the last time we were together? Why did I gossip? Why didn't I work harder on our relationship? What have I done to deserve this? How can life be worth living when such awful things as this happen?*

A friend of mind calls these "messy dot questions." My friend loves art, especially pointillism—the style of painting in which an artist uses thousands of tiny dots to create a scene. If you stand back from one of these pictures, you can see clearly the sailboat in the harbor; the women sitting at the café, the streamers of their hats floating in the breeze; the waiter bringing the wine. But, my friend reminded me, if you go right up to the canvas you cannot see the picture at all. All you can see is "messy dots."

To ask questions about the way life happens, about the place of human beings in the scheme of things, about our own complex makeup and behavior, is, at this point of Impact, to put our noses up against the canvas. It isn't as if there won't be a time later when we can engage with such essential questions in a meaningful way. But now—when our bodies are under siege, when our thoughts are scattered, when our ability to focus productively is impaired—is not the time to try to find definitive answers.

GIVING ATTENTION TO RITUAL

One of the things people often tell me they regret when they look back on their grieving process is that when the event happened they rushed through the goodbye services or ceremonies. Or they bowed to convention and didn't have the kind of service or event they really wanted.

It is important to honor your inclinations. To return to the community of origin, if that is important, no matter the extra trouble or the distance. To hold the service in an environment that is right even if it is unconventional. To have the songs that you desire sung even if they are not funereal. To take some symbolic action in private or with close friends, if being public is not what you want.

Even if the loss occurred in the now distant past, there are still other opportunities. Many of the individuals who have spoken to me of their regrets told me, also, of services or ceremonies they held in memorial, often at a later date: a musical evening in which a string quartet played Mozart concertos; a picnic on a hill; a memorial service held on the anniversary of the event. These were a kind of second acknowledgment that allowed the individuals who were grieving to plan and to do things that were not done initially.

TELLING THE TRUTH ABOUT OUR LOSS

Again and again during this cluster of behaviors, thoughts, and feelings related to being stunned by what has happened, we discover how much our lives have been changed by our loss. It is important that we deny none of these changes.

But many people want to make things better for us. Loss is an awkward subject. It is hard for many people to be around someone who is grieving—not only because a friend or an acquaintance is in distress but also because another's loss reminds all individuals of their own vulnerabilities and their own mortality. And perhaps it reminds these individuals, too, of losses they have already experienced that are painful to remember.

Whatever the reason—whether out of concern for the grieving person or out of concern for themselves—many people have a natural tendency to try to say or do something that will make us feel better: *There's a purpose for what has happened; I know you'll see it later. You have (or will have) other children. He's released from his suffering. You'll be so much stronger as a result of this experience. She had a good life. He would not want you to be upset like this. She would want you to be happy.* And so on and so on.

Such statements are, for those of us who are grieving, totally irrelevant. It doesn't matter that some of the sentiments might turn out later to be accurate or even useful. Now they truly do not matter. Now everything is destroyed, and life is in shambles. Nothing anyone says can make *that* any different.

We can remember that these attempts at consolation, which we find so banal, are the way many people attempt to stave off the harsh realities of loss—both for us and for themselves. We are not hardened or evil or self-indulgent because we are unmoved or even angered by these "words of comfort." Unfortunately, we often think we *should* believe or act on the "truths" others remind us of; and, when we cannot, we feel small and perhaps even guilty.

However, this is not the time to try to be philosophical or trusting or reasonable or logical. It may be that in a few months (or years) we *will* see things differently. But none of this matters now, as we deal with the affront of our loss. So we must keep telling ourselves the truth. We must acknowledge all the ways in which this loss has changed our life and mourn each one of these changes.

TREATING WITH RESPECT UNEXPLAINABLE AND MYSTERIOUS OCCURRENCES

Almost everyone experiences some kind of strange phenomenon following a loss. But most people are embarrassed to talk about these unusual events for fear that others will think they are crazy.

There are many theories to explain strange events that occur. Physicists talk about "implicate order" and "morphogenic fields." Scientists talk about "laws of seriality" and "object-impact interactions." Theologians talk about "grace" and "a higher Being." The most useful way to hold these mysterious events early in the experience of grieving is not to try to understand them but merely to acknowledge and reflect on them. And to realize that a grieving person who sees or hears something unexplainable has not suddenly become addled or weak-minded. We don't have to be able to explain a phenomenon in order to take comfort from it or to marvel at it. Perhaps the most important thing about experiencing such occurrences is the truth they put before us: that we do not know everything. That there are sources of comfort and of Presence that we cannot explain. That life contains mysteries, and that it is possible to be greatly enriched and even strengthened by these mysteries. That we can be blessed by moments of grace.

THE CHOICE

Since our initial responses following a loss are automatic—rooted far back in time and designed to protect us and to keep us connected to others—the idea that we can make a choice seems improbable, if not ludicrous. The loss has occurred. About that it is clear we can do nothing. We are helpless and hopeless. Sick, frightened, hurt, disoriented, left behind. How could we possibly have any choice in the matter?

But there is a choice that we have the opportunity to make and remake, a choice that enables us to move appropriately and at our own pace through the active grieving process and achieve a life-affirming outcome:

We can choose to experience and express our grief fully.

You might wonder: If the responses during this time are automatic, how could an individual *not* make the choice to experience and express grief fully?

That's the paradox. The automatic, natural responses occur, but *we* decide whether to experience fully these responses or to try to stifle and suppress them. And there are many reasons that we might choose to suppress our grief rather than express it. The pain might seem unbearable. It may seem more reasonable, since nothing can be done about the loss, to try to forget it—to put it behind us—as quickly as possible. People around us may encourage us "to be brave," "to be strong," "to pull ourselves together." Or we may feel that if we don't rise above the loss we are denying tenets of faith we have affirmed and lived by. People around us may indicate—and we ourselves may believe—that sufficient time has passed for us to be finished with this particular cluster of responses to our loss. We may be embarrassed to express our grief in front of others. We may fear that we are going crazy because we think strange thoughts and do weird things. We may decide to curtail the expression of our grief because it is interfering with our daily activities.

All of these reasons not to choose to experience and express our grief fully can be rooted both in our own reluctance to feel the pain of grief and in the general attitude toward grieving that is present in our culture. The first, of course, is understandable. We don't want to stare into the emptiness of this black abyss. We don't want to be overcome by waves of sorrow and lose control. We don't want to open ourselves to hurt. But there is a natural, normal—albeit individual, unpredictable, back-and-forth—process of grieving that leads to balance and new perspective. These initial responses are an authentic expression of the beginning of that process.

Society, however, gives us little permission to grieve. The better we appear to be coping, the easier it is for people to be around us. We know that the reports people want to hear are: "He is holding up well"; "She went back to work on Monday." The anthropologist Geoffrey Gorer says it bluntly: "Mourning is treated as if it were a weakness, a self-indulgence, a reprehensible habit instead of a psychological necessity." And Lily Pincus, the noted family therapist, commented that she had recently attended a funeral rite "that lasted altogether seven minutes." She describes society's attitude toward mourning as a general conspiracy that death has not occurred.

So the cards seem stacked against us, both within ourselves and in the outside environment. We can understand, then, why the choice to experience and express our grief fully may not be easy. But despite the difficulty, when we do make the choice we will have begun the process that, at some point in our own life story, helps us find a new equilibrium.

Dr. Anthony Storr, researcher and author, points out how dangerous it is not to choose to express grief fully. Objective studies, he notes, show that widows who suppress their emotions have more physical and psychological ailments during the first month, remain disturbed much longer, and, even as long as thirteen months after their husband's death, still display more marked disturbances than widows who were willing to "break down" during the first weeks.

Dr. John Bowlby, too, talks about the positive side of giving way to grief. According to him, people who will achieve a healthy outcome to their grieving are people who let themselves "be swept by pangs of grief." He adds, "[The] tearful expression of yearning and distress will come naturally."

Of course, the manner in which each of us expresses our grief varies. I remember that my seventy-two-year-old father showed little outward emotion while he was with the family in the weeks following Greg's death. But he spent an inordinate amount of time by himself on the creek, in his old wooden boat. He later told us that during these periods of solitude he talked out loud to Greg, prayed, or just let the boat drift where it wanted to go on the water. He honored his need to experience and to express his grief fully.

Colin Murray Parkes, M.D., reminds us that there is an "optimal level of grieving" that differs from one person to another. Some people will cry and sob; others will exhibit their feelings in other ways. The important thing is for feelings to be expressed. How they are expressed is of secondary importance.

If we do choose to experience and express our grief fully, there will come a time of release. This will not mean, of course, that the grieving process is over; but it will mean that we are free of the constant, suffocating crush of Experiencing the Unthinkable.

The following story illustrates the release that can come from expressing grief fully.

A mother told me:

When our son John died at the age of twenty-seven, for weeks I was crushed by the pain of his death. One night my husband, Gray, and I were sitting at supper. I was suddenly overwhelmed by the realization that I would never see our son again in this life—that this was the end, physically, of my relationship with this little baby that I had carried. I began to cry, and I cried and cried and cried, uncontrollably. I went into the bedroom, took off my clothes, and put on my bathing suit. I went out into the pool, jumped into the water, and swam and cried and cried. I did maybe fifty laps. When I got out of the pool, I felt better. The dam had burst. Gray drew me a hot bath. As I took the bath, I realized that the welled-up emotional grief was gone. From that night on, whenever I thought of John I saw him the way he always came into the house, his long blond hair flying, saying, "Hi, Mom." The grieving wasn't all over, of course, but I found that when I was doing something that reminded me of John I would just talk to him. Not with any philosophical or ethical meaning . . . it was always "Are you there, John?" And that's the sort of relationship we've had ever since.

WHAT WE NEED FROM FAMILY AND FRIENDS

One bereaved person after another has told me that hearing family and friends say three simple words brought them the deepest comfort. Three simple words: *"I am sorry."* Spoken with no elaboration. Followed by no awkward attempts at consolation. Just *"I am sorry."* Words that reveal the speaker's understanding that a terrible rupture has ripped our life and that we are in torturing pain.

In the days, weeks, and months that follow our loss, what we need most is the love, support, and presence of those who care for us. We should not hesitate to show how much we want to be with our family and friends; to admit how scared, how alone we feel; to let others take care of us and do everything they can do look after us.

One of the most frustrating things for our friends and family is not knowing how they can help us. As time goes on, it will become even more important that we let them know what we need. For once the immediacy of the event has passed, with customary rituals and initial activities completed, loved ones are often at a loss as to what they can do to help us. We should, therefore, ask for what we need: *I know I've talked constantly about Clifford for weeks, but it's so important to me to be able to keep him in my memory. . . . I'm waiting on the insurance payment—can you lend me some money? . . . May I drop the children off while I go sign the Social Security forms? . . . Will you go with us the first time we return to worship? . . . I'm feeling lonely—can I come over and watch television?* This is a difficult time for everyone. Our family and friends will deeply appreciate our letting them know specifically what they can do to help us.

Sometimes, of course, we don't know what we want or need. Dr. Bowlby points out how important spending time with an accepting person can be to the outcome of our grieving. He talks first about the damage done when the bereaved are told to pull themselves together and control themselves, when they are reminded that they are "not the only one to suffer, that weeping does no good and that [they] would be wise to face the problems of the future rather than dwell unproductively on the past." Individuals who are given such advice, Dr. Bowlby asserts, often suffer the debilitating effects of unresolved grief even years later. He adds, "By contrast, a widow with a good outcome would report how at least one person with whom she had been in contact had made it easy for her to cry and to express the intensity of her feelings; and would describe what a relief it had been to be able to talk freely and at length about past days with her husband and the circumstances of his death."

So even if we don't know specifically what we want or need during this period of intense grieving, we can spend as much time as possible with someone who is comfortable with however we are and whatever we need to say or do. Someone who gives us total permission to grieve, who encourages us to talk if we wish, to be quiet if we are, to show our anger when it is present. Someone who does not try to make us feel better or urge us to make the best of what has occurred or attempt to show us all the good that is still in our lives. Someone who, instead, says, "I'd love to look at all the pictures," or "Tell me about him when he was younger," or "Do you want to talk about what you are feeling today?" Such a person knows that although it may seem as if we are crying or talking about the same thing over and over, in actuality each experience is different, following a logic that is consistent only with a bereaved person's heart.

We should also indicate to others that we are not upset by their expressions of grief. Many of our family members and friends are hesitant to let us see them grieving, for fear that their sadness and tears will make us feel worse. But the truth is that we are comforted by the knowledge that the person we have lost is important to and loved by others. I remember how much I appreciated people telling me about experiences they had had with Greg that meant a lot to them. When they cried or showed their feelings in other ways, I felt that my husband was being honored. If we will let those around us know that we want them to share their memories and experiences with us, the situation will be good for everyone. (Likewise, if we don't want to hear more about the person who has died—as is sometimes the case—we should be straightforward in making those wishes known also.)

Of course, as Colin Murray Parkes, M.D., so succinctly puts it, we don't need someone around us who tries to "pluck at the heart-strings" until we have a breakdown. But neither do we need people around us who "connive" with us in endless attempts to avoid the grief work that we absolutely must do. "Both probing and 'jollying along' are unhelpful," Dr. Parkes tells us. We have a painful and difficult task to perform that cannot be avoided and cannot be rushed. Our family and friends who understand the behaviors, thoughts, and feelings that make up this time of Experiencing the Unthinkable will recognize that fact and will help us find the time and the circumstances in which to do this grieving.

Just being near those who love and care for us is life-giving. Even if there is nothing they can say or do, their presence is a solace and a comfort. At a time when we feel lost and dismayed, we also feel loved.

There is no easy way through this time when we are Experiencing the Unthinkable. To paraphrase the old prophet Isaiah, "The bed is too short and the covers too narrow." Nothing fits. While we are living this emotional raw experience, we often don't know what we are doing or why we are doing it. We move forward by trial and error (mostly error), by default, by the grace of God, by the help of family and friends. It is only in hindsight that we can see what we have lived through.

THE TERRAIN OF OUR ACTIVE GRIEVING

Life As It Was *Life and Loss Integrated*
The Event of Loss *Freedom from Domination of Grief*

IMPACT: Experiencing the unthinkable
CHOICE: To experience and express grief fully

SECOND CRISIS: Stumbling in the dark
CHOICE: To endure with patience

OBSERVATION: Linking past to present
CHOICE: To look honestly

THE TURN: Turning into the wind
CHOICE: To replan and change our lives to include but not be dominated by the loss

RECONSTRUCTION: Picking up the pieces
CHOICE: To take specific actions

WORKING THROUGH: Finding solid ground
CHOICE: To engage in the conflicts

INTEGRATION: Daylight
CHOICE: To make and remake choices

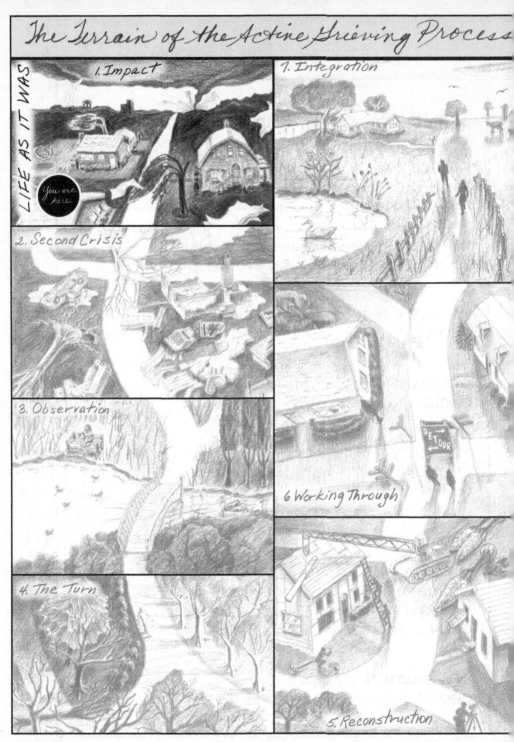

To remember: A map never tells us how to travel. A map does not determine that everyone travels the same route, moves at the same speed, shares a set itinerary. A map does not dictate, prescrib*or even describe an individual's movement. A map does, however, name. A map can help us find where we are when we think we are lost. A map shows possibilities and provides ideas for where else there is for us to go. At all times, however, every individual is the person holding the map.

IMPACT: Experiencing the unthinkable

What Is Normal?

Presence of strong emotion
Absence of emotion and feeling
Need to roam; inability to sit still
Inability to concentrate or focus
Yearning and longing
Dominated by memories
Body biorhythms disturbed
Feeling numb
Plagued by anger, guilt, blame
Experiencing fear, confusion, disorientation
Having no hope

What Can I Do?

Stay close to people who love you.
Talk to the person you have lost as if she or he were actually present.
Ask for anything you need.
Spend as much time as you can with someone who encourages you to grieve in *any* way you wish.
Take care of yourself.
Talk to a professional. There are counselors, pastoral care professionals, social workers, and therapists who can be a guide in this painful grieving process.

IMPACT: Experiencing the unthinkable

My active choice?

To experience and express my grief fully (again and again)

2

SECOND CRISIS:

STUMBLING IN THE DARK

I want to go home, to ride to my village gate.
I want to go back, but there's no road back.
                         Mei Shêng and Fu I
                         First Century B.C.

It had been almost eight weeks since Greg's death, and I was now making plans to return to Texas. The fall semester at the university would begin soon, and I had students to teach. In many ways I was looking forward to being home—in my house, among my things, getting on with life. But I also dreaded what was next.

As the time to leave drew nearer, I lost ground. All I could think of was how much I missed Greg. Everything seemed edged in black—the lake, the mountains, the meadows. I would stand in the yard and look down toward the water of Possum Creek, and my heart would sink. I felt so desolate, so alone.

The terrible dreams began again: young women, with only one arm and no legs, sitting in wheelchairs; rooms with strange walls, every inch covered with dresses, gowns, robes, scraps of fabric—all black. I began to wake again every morning at 3:00 A.M. in terror. Again, I thought my wedding bracelet had been stolen.

Life felt stagnant. "I must begin to think, do, be in some way not connected to Greg's death," I told myself. "I must get on with it." Then I'd ask myself, "But what is *it*? How do I fill the space of Greg?"

A day or two before it was time to leave, my mother showed me an interview in the newspaper. A reporter had asked a widow whose husband had also died suddenly, "Looking back now from a vantage point of four years, what was the wisest thing you did after your husband's death?" The widow had responded, "Going to his grave a few weeks after he died and telling him everything I wanted to tell him." As I read the interview, I thought, "This is something that I should do, too. If it helped her, maybe it will help me." So the following afternoon, my last day in Tennessee, I drove myself to the cemetery.

I walked up the hill to the place where Greg was buried under the dogwood tree and sat down. I could look across the valley and see the foothills of the Smoky Mountains in the distance.

What had the young widow done that was so valuable?

"I first told his body goodbye," she had said. "I recognized that however I was going to relate to him in the future, it would not be to his body. That was now gone."

So I began.

I imagined Greg's body in the coffin. I started with his head. "Goodbye, curly hair. Goodbye, forehead. Goodbye, eyes. Goodbye, beard. Goodbye, tiny scar on cheek." I continued until I had said goodbye to every part of his body.

"Then I told him the things I was sorry for," the young widow had told the reporter.

So I apologized to Greg and asked him to forgive me for all the times that I got angry and wouldn't speak; for last winter when he had a cold and I didn't do anything special to take care of him; for being so angry at him at times that I wished we weren't married. The list was long—I tried to remember everything.

"The last thing I did," the young widow in the interview had said, "was to thank him for all the things he did that made me happy."

So I began my list: Bringing coffee to the bathroom every morning when I was getting ready. Leaving love notes on the entryway floor. Surprising me by putting sausage and biscuit and orange juice in my office while I was teaching an eight o'clock class. Hiding presents all over the house on our last anniversary. Cooking veal stew on the days I had to work late. Carving the letters J-O-Y for my office wall. That list was long, too; there were so many things to thank him for.

It was late afternoon when I left the cemetery. When I got back to the house, I walked down to Possum Creek. The sun was about to go down, but there was still enough light to see by. I dragged an old green wooden armchair from the picnic area down to the edge of the water, unfolded the notepaper I had brought with me, and wrote Greg a letter:

Dear Greg,

I just walked down to the water for the final time before leaving for Texas. I wanted to come to the place where your service was held. I walked over to the spot where your casket stood and looked out at the water which you would have seen if you had been able to see that day. I can hardly believe I'm leaving here without you.

Do you remember the T-shirt you wore on the drive from Texas to the cabin—the one that said "Adios to Summer Races"? Well, it's now Adios to Everything. I think about the days we came down here and played in the water on our floats. I think about all the afternoons we walked down here after work. I've come to say goodbye to everything.

I'm saying goodbye to your spirit in the sunset, the rocks, the grass. What does it all mean? I don't know. Where are you? I don't know.

Do you remember that story "The Old People," by William Faulkner? The one where Sam Fathers, one of the ancient ones, speaks to the deer. "Hail, Grandfather," he says, his arm raised in homage to the buck who is bounding across the mountainside.

Well, sweetheart, today I say to the water, the grass, the rocks, the East Tennessee hills, the mist, the view, the cabin, "Hail, Greg." They are all you.

I love you, Greg.

Your wife,
Elizabeth

The next morning it was time to leave. My family would accompany me to Texas in their cars. I was going to pick up my sister in Chattanooga to ride with me, but when I left my parents' house I was alone in my car. I thought, "How different this is from the way I arrived." I realized that I was closing one chapter in my life and starting another one. And I didn't like it. In fact, I hated it. But there was nothing else I could do.

"What is that ritual when a cavalry officer has been killed in battle?" I asked myself as I drove past the cabin. "Doesn't his horse walk in the parade without a rider?" As I approached the end of the lane and prepared to turn the car onto the highway, I reached over and patted the empty seat.

For weeks after I returned to Texas I lived a vagabond existence. I was afraid to stay in my house alone. This made no sense. Wasn't I the same professional woman who had lived by herself for three years in New York City, relishing every minute of the experience? Why was I now so frightened? An ominous dread and a chilling fear permeated the rooms of the house, and I could not stand to be there. I slept at one friend's house one night, at another friend's house the next.

But roaming from place to place became unacceptable. I was embarrassed that I now felt so needy when I had always been proud of my reputation as a strong, independent woman. I also hated not belonging anywhere. "This is *my* house," I finally said to myself angrily, "and I am going to live in it!" So I mustered up the courage to spend a night alone.

I timed my return from school in order to arrive as late as possible but still before darkness fell. I turned on the television as soon as I entered; that way, at least, I could hear voices. Then I went through the house, looking under every bed, in the bathtub, in every closet. When it started to get dark, I put a towel over the kitchen window.

I spent the evening sitting down and getting up. I made lists of things to do and then decided not to do them. I skipped supper and instead ate a quart of vanilla ice cream. At bedtime, I moved from the upstairs to the downstairs bedroom in case I needed to get out of the house quickly to escape some intruder. I was afraid to undress, so I slept in my clothes. I put a pistol from Greg's college ROTC days by the bed, even though I didn't know how to use it. I was still awake when the alarm went off in the morning.

So much of every day was taken up with unfamiliar and painful business. The legal and business affairs related to Greg's death seemed unending. Entering the lawyer's office, I would reassure myself, "No need to be concerned; this will be no problem. It's just a piece of legal business." I felt strong and capable. But when I started to tell the man why I was there, I discovered that I was crying.

Every day brought new instructions. The accountant informed me, "The IRS requires that you make an inventory of the items in the house and put a valuation on them. The information will be used in determining the tax you owe the government." A valuation on everything in the house? An antique Lionel train set? An old guitar? Pots and pans? The contents of all the closets? Even though I realized that the accountant didn't expect me to take his words so literally, I still found trying to estimate the value of our possessions an onerous task.

I was frightened by the surprise visits from investigators employed by the insurance company. They had written: "Since Mr. Cowan had not held this insurance for the mandatory two-year period, we must investigate this claim. Might there be a chance he had a heart condition prior to his death, a condition about which we were not informed?" I was furious. Didn't they know that if there had been any symptom of a heart condition our doctor would have found it and Greg would still be alive today? The question was an insult. Yet I lived in fear that they would find some reason not to pay.

I worried constantly about not having enough money. At night I dreamed of dying a shriveled-up old woman in the poorhouse—a scene that always looked like something from a Dickens novel. When I got my first paycheck for the new school year, I realized that the monthly bills amounted to more than my salary. Greg and I had made several long-term financial commitments that I now had to pay alone, commitments that meant little to me now but that, at least for a few years, were irreversible. The only way I could make ends meet was to dip into the small pot of insurance money each month; I had already figured out how long it would be before security was gone.

Such were the concerns of my daily life. Nothing was the same. Everything was unfamiliar.

My place in the world was also drastically altered. People who had been friendly in the past were now awkward around me. The first time I went into the mailroom at the university, some of my colleagues were gathered around, passing the time and chatting. I walked in, and everything changed. The easy conversation turned to silence. The joviality turned to haste to get out of the room. Within seconds, everyone was gone. Several people said hello to me as they passed; but no one mentioned Greg, even though some of them had written me notes when he died. One day an acquaintance came to the house to visit and stayed for two hours. Not once was anything said that indicated that my husband had died, even though the woman had earlier sent me a lovely note of condolence. I understood this reluctance to talk about death, this awkwardness and avoidance, but I also hated it.

Greg and I had belonged to a gourmet cooking club for three years. I decided to attend the first meeting in September. Everyone was happy to see me, and I felt genuinely welcomed back into the group. When the list of members was passed around, however, I realized that I was the only single person there. It dawned on me how naïve I had been to imagine that I could continue to enjoy being in the club. What I would have enjoyed taking on as a challenge in earlier times—*why couldn't a single woman belong to any group she was drawn to . . . what was wrong with doing things alone . . . didn't I have plenty of friends who also loved to cook and eat good food?*—was now only a defeat. Something had happened to my confidence; something had sapped my ability to come up with creative solutions; something had taken away my spunk. All I could think about now was how I would have no one to help me prepare the elaborate and complicated dishes. But, worse than that, I would be the odd person at the table.

At a professional conference I attended that fall, a colleague from another university said to me, "You must be devastated to be here by yourself. You and Greg were such a golden couple, and you must already be realizing that you will never shine that way alone." Did he mean to be cruel? Did he realize what he was saying? I cannot say. I do know that I lost interest in attending the conference and left.

The routine and structure of daily living were gone. I had lost the identity I had come to know as myself in the years since meeting Greg. As the weeks passed, it also became clear to me that an equally devastating loss was the loss of the future I had assumed I would have. I had expected to have Greg's children. Katie Rachel Pearl . . . Jeremiah Cade. Now there would be no babies. I mourned these never-now-to-be children.

I had expected always to be a part of Greg's family—a daughter-in-law to his mother, a stepmother to his sons. Now I worried if the four and a half years that we had been married had been long enough for me to establish a place in their lives. When they called, I listened to catch every nuance in their voices. Was I still included in the family?

I had also expected to grow old with Greg, retire with him. We were going to polish agates on the Oregon coast and climb mountains in Tennessee. I now had to reinvent my entire future.

These new stresses brought repercussions. I began to revive old resentments toward certain people. I took umbrage at the slightest affront, whether real or imagined. I nursed these grudges privately and became bitter.

It was in reliving my life with Greg that I took refuge. I found myself fixated on the smallest details of our life together: What he ordered on a hot pastrami sandwich at the Grapevine Restaurant. What camera we used when we took the movies in the Grand Tetons. How cold it was the night we went out in the ice storm to see the frozen crystals that halloed our neighbor's tree. How I always smiled when I saw him coming home from the university on his Yamaha, dressed in a suit and tie and wearing that silly motorcycle helmet.

I became afraid that I would forget things about him, so I made a list—"Things I Never Want to Forget": the time we went to church in Chimayo; the poems we read in Room 222; how he sat in his chair grading papers while I weaved at the loom; how he cooked steaks that time in a fireplace and opened champagne with a nail; his request for a bud vase for his birthday one August. I had already begun to feel that I was forgetting his voice, his image, his words. "Oh, come back, sweet one," I wrote. "Come back and call me Bessa."

Things came to a climax one rainy Sunday in early November. My sister and brother-in-law had been visiting for the weekend, and they had just left to catch the plane for Tennessee. Even a few minutes with nothing to do were intolerable, so as soon as they left I drove to the shopping center to see a movie. Four films were playing, none of them familiar. One title, however, caught my eye: *Starting Over*, with Burt Reynolds and Jill Clayburgh. I bought my ticket and found a seat.

For two hours, I saw my life on the screen. Oh, to be sure, the movie was about a man whose wife had left him, not a woman whose husband had died. But this man's life had the same vacancy, the same lack of direction, the same empty, shapeless future that mine did. The man on that screen was me—resenting, hesitating, fighting, pulling back, crying, wandering. The only difference was that by the end of the movie he had found the courage to start his life over.

I hated the movie. Hurrying across the parking lot toward my car, I castigated myself: "Why in the world did you go to *that* movie? Just to hurt yourself? Isn't it enough to live it—do you also have to go watch your empty life on a stupid screen?" I understood that there is terrible pain and suffering when people lose someone important in their life. There is no way to avoid it. And, in the face of that loss, every person has an inescapable option: to choose to be courageous and make the changes necessary to start life over or not to. Yes, I hated the movie because I had gotten the message.

It was almost dark when I got home, and a light rain was falling. I could see the kitchen from the carport. I had left a light on, and through the mist the room looked warm and cheerful: tall, bright, red chairs clustered around an old circular oak farm table; red-and-white napkins on the table; green plants on the shelf. But I knew the scene was a lie. That kitchen was not warm and cheery; it was empty. There was nothing to do in that house, no one to be with. There was nothing in that house but coldness and a deathlike stillness.

Something snapped inside me. I was overcome with fury. I found myself running into the house. I headed straight for Greg's study, where everything was the way he had left it. On the wall was a large paper butterfly kite I had bought him. I jerked the kite off the wall and began to break it into a hundred pieces. I made balls of the crushed paper, scattering them all over the room. I cracked the sticks until they were hardly larger than match stems. I knew Greg had loved that kite, and I could hardly believe I was destroying it. But I hated Greg for what he had done to my life by dying. I had loved my life the way it was; it had been just the way I dreamed life could be. I had worked hard to achieve the kind of life we had together. And now everything had to change. Everything *was* changed. Whether I wanted it or not, a new life lay ahead of me. And I didn't want it. I didn't want to change my life. And now I knew I had to, regardless of whether it was a change I had asked for or not.

When the kite had been destroyed, I tore through the house like a madwoman. I ran from room to room, bumping into the corners of hallways, hitting doorjambs as I passed. Then I saw the firewood. I grabbed the largest piece I could manage and began to beat the sofa in the living room. I beat the sofa, and I screamed: *"But I don't want to start my life over. I want my life the way it was. I want my husband. I want things to be the same. I want what I had worked so hard for. I want what I had. I hate you, Greg, for dying. I hate you, life, for doing this to me. I hate being without the partner I love. I hate not knowing what to do. I hate having no direction to go in. I hate having to make up a new future."*

Finally, my fury was spent. I dropped the log and collapsed on the floor by the sofa. With my head in my hands, I first cried quietly, and then I sat on the floor for a long time in silence.

For a day or two after this outburst, I felt clearheaded. I talked sensibly to myself: "There is loss in the world, and this is what it feels like. The way you acted on Sunday is one of the normal ways that people act when they experience loss. And everybody experiences it. Loss, like grief, is impersonal. It is just a given in life—you cannot avoid it."

Something else also became clear to me. I realized that in all my reveries, Greg and I never got any older. We never had any new problems, nobody ever got sick, we never changed from how we were. "That," I said to myself, "is totally unrealistic. Maybe things would always have been good, but you don't know. One thing for certain is that life would have been different, and you have no way of knowing how it would have turned out." I could see that in my memories and my fantasies I had frozen my life with Greg in time.

But the clearheadedness didn't last. I could not keep these insights in focus when every day was such a vacuum. I didn't care about anything. Nothing mattered. One morning, as I was dressing, it came to me that nothing from the past now gave me any pleasure. Not only was my husband gone—so was everything that I had valued in the past.

Just the evening before, I had gone with friends to hear the Houston Symphony play some of my favorite music. It had meant nothing to me. I never sat down at my loom to weave anymore, because that now meant nothing to me. I had no enthusiasm for teaching; work was just a place I had to go to in order to make the money I needed to make. I hated Sunday mornings, because reading the newspaper and drinking coffee were the last things I wanted to do. My house could have fallen down, and I would hardly have noticed. My family was important to me, but it was clear now that they alone couldn't give meaning to my future.

Whether I wanted to or not, I was beginning to see more and more clearly what I was facing. I began to realize that I had to establish entirely new habit patterns—how I came into the house, what I did in my spare moments, what I did when I got up. "New paths must be made," I realized, "like new veins for blood to run in." I had seen what I had to do, and I didn't want to do it.

It was Thanksgiving—a joke of a holiday. "Would you come to Chicago for the weekend?" my cousin Ernestine had asked me. "Yes," I had said, thinking that perhaps being with a family member in a new environment would help. I was disturbed by my behavior. Just the day before, in filling out a form for the department secretary, I found myself wanting to write "the Land of the Dead" under Foreign Travel.

"Let's go into the lounge and get you a doctor's jacket," Ernestine said on the first afternoon of my visit. "Then you can do rounds with me." Three months my junior, Ernestine was a highly respected and well-established surgeon. She was poised, confident, and professional.

As we went through the hospital, I realized that dying young could be a virtue. At least Greg, by dying at forty-three and in perfect health, had never faced what I was seeing as we walked through the hospital: illnesses, operations, tubes, oxygen tents, vital-sign machines, pain, suffering. This was what the rest of us had to look forward to. What an ending! I was disgusted.

Driving home, I asked Ernestine, "How do you do it every day? How do you stand the responsibility of all those people's lives resting in your hands? How do you live with the fickleness of life—some people living and some dying?"

She took my questions seriously. "I think of each patient as a hand of cards that has been dealt me," she replied. "A hand over which I have no say-so. My patients are in whatever condition they are when I meet them. I treat them the best way I know how, doing my best not to hurt them or make them worse. In other words, I attempt to make the most of the hand that's been dealt me." What my cousin said made sense. But it only showed me how useless it is to pretend that we human beings have much to do with anything. I thought, "We're only living some kind of busy charade."

That night, I could not sleep. I finally got up and stood looking out the window. Crusts of dirty snow and ice lay everywhere. Grotesque shapes hid in the shadows—shapes I would recognize in the daylight as doorways, garbage cans, concrete embankments. But tonight they looked like specters of the dead. I stared into the darkness.

"Life is meaningless," I said. "You can pretend that things matter, but they don't. Finally, you have to admit that there is no meaning in anything we human beings do. We just fool ourselves. We need to think our actions matter. We think the little worlds we make, the purposes we organize our lives around, the things we commit to, matter. But life is nothing. And death is the end of it all. So what is the use of pretending? Why put effort and care and commitment into anything when it finally makes absolutely no difference? When nothing matters? Everything is vanity. Emptiness. Nothingness."

At the airport on the way home, I deliberately tried to hit people with my suitcases. "Get out of my way," I yelled at strangers. When I got to my dark, cold house, I didn't even notice. Because nothing now mattered. I cared about nothing.

For months, I faced this disillusion daily. Questions plagued me: *If trying to be a good person . . . if working in outside jobs since you were fourteen . . . if putting yourself through school, the first person in your family ever to go to college . . . if getting yourself from the hills of Tennessee to a wonderful job in New York City . . . if taking the risks and making the changes required for two adults who have fallen in love to create a life together . . . if giving one's best and earning the rewards of tenure and full-professor rank at a major university . . . if feeling a deep desire to make a contribution to others . . . if none of these things finally matter because you come face-to-face with the truth: Things happen in life that destroy everything you've worked for, and you can do nothing about this—so what is the use of anything?*

I began to live in ways that denied my values. I courted danger. I tried to learn to smoke and drove my car fast and furiously. I dated men who also were running from life. I spent money foolishly, depleting my already limited resources. I planned ridiculous career changes. Perhaps I'd stop being a professor and become a financial planner in Florida or a free spirit in California. Or maybe I'd just stay where I was and be neat and cool, defiant of all conventions. I enjoyed the adrenaline rush that came with taking high-wire risks. These were the only times that I felt alive in what otherwise were days and nights of numbness.

But the truth is, I was desperate for some answers to what life is really all about. Clearly, it wasn't enough to be self-sufficient, to believe that hard work will get you what you want, to plan to shape your own destiny. It was the first time in my life that I felt completely stopped in my tracks. Greg's death had blown to smithereens the belief system and life practices that I had assumed could always be counted on. I didn't know how to be or what to think. All I could do, it seemed, was try to avoid being swallowed up by the emptiness. But I was failing on all accounts. Everything I did was self-destructive.

Why would someone who drops by all the time—someone who is your best friend—call suddenly to say she's coming over? When Emma arrived, she didn't want to sit down. She said she'd just stand in front of the fireplace.

"Elizabeth," she said, "I've kept quiet as long as I'm going to. I know the loss of Greg has been devastating. That's why over the past months, when I saw you becoming more and more self-destructive, I never criticized. I knew you had lost your footing. And I knew it would take time, maybe a long time, for you to regain your equilibrium."

She paused. I had no idea what she was going to say next.

"But I have lost my patience," she continued. "I want you to know that I am really angry at you; in fact, I am furious. You are acting as if you want to lose *everything* in your life, not just your husband. You seem to think that, alone, you are nothing. But there's something very important I think you've forgotten. You were a whole person before you met Greg, and you can be a whole person after him. It's time for you to remember that. That's all I came to say."

Emma paused.

"Except this. We have been best friends for a long time, but I won't continue to support you in how you are living your life. If you want to start being the terrific person you really are, then I'm your friend forever. But if you don't, then don't count on me."

Her mission completed, Emma gave me a hug and said goodbye. "I'll call you," I said quietly as she was leaving.

I sat on the couch for several minutes, thinking. I wasn't angry at anything Emma had said. In fact, I was relieved. It was as if I had just been waiting for someone to tell me to stop running. To face the emptiness in front of me. To deal with the words from that awful night in Chicago: *Everything is vanity. Life is empty. Nothing matters.* I knew Emma was right. I had to do something. I had to set a new direction.

The next day, in a most mundane situation, I surprised myself by taking action. A young man servicing my car told me I needed some air in my tires and asked how many pounds the tires were supposed to carry. My first thought was to respond as I had in other situations like this: *This is my husband's car, and he died a few months ago . . . I don't know how many pounds of pressure for the tires . . . I don't know what to tell you.*

But this time I did not tell my usual story.

"Just a minute," I said to the attendant. "I have to look it up." I opened the glove box, took out the owner's manual, and located the information the young man needed. I sat back in the seat as if I had just climbed Mt. Everest. I felt such satisfaction! I felt so capable, so strong! Why, I even felt like someone who might have a future!

As I drove away from the service station, however, the cost of what I had just done hit me. By being competent and taking care of the situation, I had lost something very important: I had lost the opportunity to talk about my husband. Now this service station attendant would never know what a wonderful man I had been married to and how much I missed him. Talking about Greg was the only way I now had to keep him present. If I didn't get to talk about him, I would lose him completely. And if I lost him completely I would have to do something else with my life. My dilemma was crystal-clear, and I hated it.

This is the experience of Stumbling in the Dark. A time of Second Crisis. Bleak. Hopeless. Empty. The structure, shape, focus, and direction of the past are gone, and there is absolutely nothing to take their place in the present. Every assumption one has ever had about how life works and what an individual's role is or can be is assaulted. You have been completely knocked off course. You don't know what to believe, what to think, what to hold on to. The underpinnings of your life have been destroyed. The world as you knew it has been shattered. And you have neither the desire nor the resources to rebuild it.

If anything, this cluster of experiences is worse than the initial experience of loss. You cannot now avoid knowing how permanent this change is, how forever the loss. You cannot avoid the knowledge that all there is to do is to make a new and different shape for your life. At the beginning, you have no idea how extensive and deep are the patterns: how much milk you buy at the store; what you schedule to do after work; how many holiday cards you order; how the income tax is handled; what you do on birthdays and anniversaries. There's no one to call out "I'll get it" when the telephone rings and nobody to help bring in the groceries. When I was a child our house burned down, and I can remember that for years my mother kept remembering things she missed or needed that had been lost in the fire. This is how it is when you lose someone or something that's important to your existence. As each week and month passes, you see new ways in which your life has been affected. You come to understand that this loss cannot be compensated for. It is irreversible. You realize that you are ultimately helpless in how things go in the universe. Nothing you do, in the final analysis, matters. You lose all hope. All of this becomes *inescapably* known.

Peter Marris, the British social scientist, talks about it this way: The lost person has been a "keystone" in our lives and "the whole structure of meaning in . . . life collapses when the keystone falls." A relationship is gone that identified who we were and what we did each day. Our purposes, our satisfactions—even our "important anxieties" and "resentments"—involved this person. So whether we were happy, ambivalent, or unhappy in the relationship (an irony those experiencing the loss of someone with whom they had a "bad relationship" know all too well), the familiar world we live in has been shattered.

The collected wisdom perhaps would say, "Since that's the way it is and there is nothing you can do about it, you just have to quit looking to the past and build a new structure." Not so easy, says Professor Marris. We can't "escape from this distress by adopting new purposes," he reminds us, because "purposes are learned and consolidated through a lifetime's experiences." The task we find staring us in the face, then, is nothing short of a "painful retrieval of purpose from the wreck of dead hopes," but while we are Stumbling in the Dark it is clear that we do not have the wherewithal to accomplish this retrieval.

Dr. John Bowlby suggests another reason this period is so painful. "In the course of our evolution," he says, "our instinctual equipment has come to be so fashioned that all losses are assumed to be retrievable and are responded to accordingly." But this time we know undeniably that the loss we have sustained is not retrievable—we will not be able to "restore the bond that has been severed." The loss is permanent. It is undoable. It is forever. And we are deeply affected by this realization.

As I have listened to people tell me about their experiences of Stumbling in the Dark, I have heard both pain and strength in their voices. It was clear that the trauma of these experiences of the grieving process is devastating. But it was also clear that these individuals—even as they told their stories—were recognizing what it meant that they had lived through this terrible time in their lives. Their conversations were, for me, a kind of celebration of the resilience that is part of the gift of being human.

These women and men from whom I learned say that such experiences as these were characteristic of those weeks and months in which they were Stumbling in the Dark.

THE LOSS OF IDENTITY

A man recalls:

It was a time of chaos. My life was liquid—it had no form. I didn't know who I was; I didn't know where I was; I didn't know where I was going. You see, I had been defined before. I was Sandra's husband. I lived on the corner of Greenwich and Dawson. I had an identity as a married man with a family. And now I couldn't even tell you my new address. Most of the time I gave people the wrong phone number. "I live out by Kmart," I'd say, and that was about the best I could do on directions.

I was just an unknown quantity. I didn't exist. I wasn't attached to anything. I quit doing anything extra at work. I avoided people whenever possible. And I just . . . sometimes I think I felt like I was, as some people say, drifting. Just floating along, like these wisps that come off cottonwood trees or dandelions; they just float off into space and they drift down and they float up and drift down and they float up; and you don't know where they're going to end up.

THE ALTERATION OF LIFE'S BASIC STRUCTURE

A woman with young children describes the change:

Everything about you changes. You have to do even the normal things differently. You have to get up thirty minutes earlier in the morning because you're the only one to check to be sure the kids get dressed and their teeth are brushed, since your husband isn't there now to help you.

Just on a day-to-day basis your life is going to have to change, because you're now everything to the children. I mean, you can't cook dinner and clean the dishes and let Daddy bathe them. You have to cook dinner, clean the dishes, bathe them, and listen to them read. You have to be different because you have to fit all that in, and there's still just twenty-four hours in the day.

THE DISAPPEARANCE OF THE FUTURE

A widow talks:

It's one thing to remember the past, the good and the bad, and you remember both. But it's another thing to grieve over what's not happening now that would have happened if the person were still here. I'm always thinking, "If Cam were here now, we'd be doing this or doing that, things would be this way, and the future would look like this."

Cam was the major moneymaker. And because his business was construction we were always looking for a big payoff in the future. He'd say, "It's not good now, but we're going to stick it out; and next year it'll be better, and the next year it'll be even better." But now that he's dead it's irrelevant to me and the kids whether the construction business gets better in the future.

I had to let the rental houses go, for instance, because now I don't have the luxury of waiting for things to turn around. But it was so hard for me to accept that the future has been wiped out. That now I have to get in a position to earn enough money to meet the responsibilities. That's a weight that just adds to the shock and sadness of Cam's death.

It has taken me many months to get to the point where I can say, "All right, the future is not going to be what you thought it was. It's gone, and you're not going to get it back. You just will not have it. Now you've got to build a new one." That is traumatic. I don't feel sorry for myself anymore for the past; I just miss all the things that are now never going to happen.

FEELINGS OF DESPAIR

A man remembers:

I decided that I would finally unpack and settle into this new place. The first thing I took out of the box was a Mr. Coffee. Well, as I unloaded the coffeemaker the glass decanter fell out and broke on the tile floor. I was so heartbroken that I just sat down, broken glass and all, and cried. Like a little baby. I lost control.

I'd cut my finger on the glass, and some combination of things— the broken glass, me sitting there on the floor, completely worn out from dealing with all this, completely spent, the blood on my hands, the boxes around me, nothing, no good smells, no food cooking, no anything—made me feel total despair. "This is the beginning of death-in-life," I said to myself.

For at least a month I shook a lot; my voice trembled. I cried easily, I was angry and short with people without notice. I began behaving erratically. I'm not a drinker, but I'd buy a bottle of wine and drink the whole thing in one night. I started cooking enormous meals, which I then couldn't eat because I didn't want them. In fact, I'd go for days without eating, just living on orange juice, coffee, candy. I lived a life of nobody-ness. It was a time of being help-less and hopeless.

AN AVOIDANCE OF OTHERS ON THE SUBJECT OF DEATH OR LOSS

A widow remembers:

Four months after Claude died, I gave my first dinner party. I worked for days preparing a wonderful menu for eight people with whom he and I had spent many evenings, weekends, and vacations. When the dinner began, I expected that at least one of our friends would suggest a toast to Claude or at least acknowledge in some way his absence.

But I was wrong. Not once during the entire evening did any of the eight mention him. It was as if he had never existed. They probably thought, "She's having her first dinner, so we won't say anything to bring the evening down." But I was so hurt. I felt like standing up and yelling, "How can you just sit there? Claude is dead." I should have. But I didn't. During the course of the evening, one man made reference to death in some other context; and I felt a bond with him because at least he had risked mentioning the word.

FRANTIC ATTEMPTS TO FILL THE EMPTINESS

A man talks about the reaction to the loss of his partner:

About a month after Ben died, I started doing everything I could to avoid thinking about it. I went out and bought a Dodge con-vertible, which I couldn't afford, and all I did was drive that car from party to party. At one of these parties, I met up with some rich but questionable characters; and I ended up serving as their confi-dant, companion, and even their lawyer. This meant that my days were almost entirely filled with conflict, as I tried to help these new friends extricate themselves from their legal situations. This, of course, only added to the upset I already had over Ben's dying. So at night I'd try to forget by going to more and more parties.

At these parties I began to drink heavily and started using cocaine. To try to get away from myself, I even took three trips abroad in six months—to places like Egypt, the Philippines, London—and ran up huge bills on my credit cards. That, plus the amount of money I was spending on drugs, pushed me to the edge of bankruptcy. I was caught in a vicious cycle.

A Loss of Faith

A mother speaks:

You know, when a child dies, in addition to the sense of loss there is a sense of outrage because it's unnatural. It's not in the scheme of things. A parent should go first. There's also the sense of a wasted life. So many years to live. So much to live for. Now, as a parent, you can never know what the child might have become.

We have not been able to make the loss of our daughter compatible with any scheme of fairness or with any belief in a plan in the universe. We have lost our faith. We were fairly regular temple-goers before Charlotte died, but Carson hasn't set foot in the temple since her death. He says he can't reconcile a loving God with the loss of his young daughter. I've been back once or twice when they have a special service that our family always participated in.

Strain in Relationships

A daughter discusses events after her father's death:

When my father died, that was it on my being part of the family. Three years before, my sister and my mother died within twelve months of each other. With no immediate family left, I tried to cling to my father's brothers. I had never been close to them, so I don't know why I thought all of a sudden I would be close; but I made advances in that direction. It turned out to be a horrible disaster, because what they wanted was my dad's money.

Everything revolved around some property that had been in the family for a long time. Many years before, the family had been getting ready to sell the property; but my father decided he just couldn't let it go out of the family, so he paid the other members of the family for their shares and bought the land himself. Several years later, Dad got a phone call: "We think there's oil on your land—will you let us drill?" My father said okay. Well, the minute the oil well hit, all of a sudden my uncles are saying, "If we had had any idea there was oil on the property, we wouldn't have sold it." It really got ugly.

Then, after Dad died, they started pressuring me. "If your father were still alive, he'd give it back," they said. It was terrible for me. A shock. When I didn't return the property, which they had sold so many years before, my uncles and their families stopped speaking to me. This taught me that just because you're related all the feelings aren't necessarily going to be good.

SYMPATHETIC ILLNESS

A daughter recalls:

My father died on January 19, and on March 12 I came down with an affliction just like his. He was in his eighties when he went into the hospital for excruciating lower-back pain. They operated on him, but he never got well. I felt that my illness was somehow related to my father's death. I even had a dream the day I woke up with the pain. In the dream, my father said that I didn't have to do what he did. Finally, though it took many weeks, somewhere in my head I got the message, and the pain went away.

A SUDDEN ACCIDENT

A teenage son tells this story:

A few months after my dad's death, I injured my leg. It was on a Saturday, and I was getting ready to go to the locker room to suit up for the game. I ran out of my dorm room in my stocking feet, and when I turned the corner my feet slipped and I fell. One leg bent back under me. I went on to the game, but I didn't get to play.

I developed what the orthopedic surgeon called cavalryman's disease. Soldiers would ride their horses so long and hard that their muscles would tear and bleed, resulting in atrophy. That is what happened to my leg. Even today, I have a calcium deposit in that leg that affects my mobility.

In the months after my dad's death and before the accident, I would sit in my dorm room, in the dark, and look out at the trees and the sky. I had never felt so blue and lonely in my life. I wouldn't be thinking of my father directly, but I'd just be so empty. When the accident happened, it was as if it were a continuation of something that began back in those terrible afternoons.

ANGER

A friend talks:

One of my closest friends just died of AIDS, and I'm so angry at the reaction of some members of his family. Near the end, Cal spent all his resources on treatment. He had no insurance, and he was still desperately fighting for his life.

But the attitude of several members of his family was so callous. When Cal asked them to help him financially, they responded by saying, "Are you really sick, or have you just overcharged on your credit cards?" They reminded him of all the times he had gotten into trouble with his money and how they had often helped bail him out. They argued that he wasn't ill. This hurt Cal so much that he severed all relationship with his family. When he finally died, not one member of his family was with him. I'm so angry about this that I can't even grieve for Cal. So very, very angry.

TAKING CARE OF ONESELF

A man dealing with multiple losses says:

Last year my wife of sixteen years left to go live in a spiritual community. We love each other, but since I didn't want to join the community we divorced. This continues to be a deeply painful loss. Last year my stepfather died. He had been married to my mother for thirty-five years and we had a close attachment. Then last month my mother died. I find myself dealing now with at least these three losses simultaneously, and perhaps more. (My father died when I was a child, and I don't think I've ever fully mourned his death.)

The other day, a friend asked me what I was doing in this stressful time to take care of myself. I replied, "I'm taking care of myself by not working too hard at my law practice, going to synagogue every Friday night, joining a choir, and doing my best to nurture myself and not put myself down. I'm seeing people, although not in a serious relationship, and I'm going out and not being alone. I would like to have a serious relationship with a woman, but I'm not ready. I would love to have the closeness again, but it's not the right time for me. I am deliberately not seeing my wife, because to see her would be hurtful to me in view of the fact that I still love her. So, despite her wishes to see me, I am refusing to do so. I have a regular massage, and also I'm seeing a counselor on a weekly basis. Last week I attended the scattering of my mother's ashes at the cemetery, which threw me. I ended up in bed for two days, and on the way to work I nearly fainted twice. I allowed myself not to go to work, although I find it difficult looking after myself alone and not having someone to care for me as previously. I regularly go to synagogue and obtain spiritual nourishment, and I'm reading a good book on grief."

GUILT

A daughter recounts these circumstances:

I blame myself. I am a registered first-aid person. If I had only been home that weekend I could personally have saved my mother, because I would have recognized her symptoms. My father didn't recognize that she had had heart failure because her symptoms were different from his when he had a heart attack. But he had digitalis right there in his pocket, and if I had been there . . .

I think a lot, too, of how I could have helped my mother be happier. I'll see a talk show about people who are chronically depressed, and I think of my mother. I remember things from my childhood—like my mother coming home and saying she stood for twenty minutes in front of the green beans trying to decide which brand to buy. I would just look at her sort of quizzically and say, "Mother, that's weird." I really feel guilty about that now. I wish I had known more then and could have helped her.

I watch the movie *'Night, Mother*, with Anne Bancroft, over and over. You know, the movie where Anne tries to save her daughter, who is going to commit suicide. I identify with the Bancroft character; I wish I could have saved my mother. Or I'll watch *The Big Chill*. There's this line where—I think it's JoBeth Williams who says it—something like "If only I'd known, maybe I could've helped." And one of the other characters snaps back, "Oh, do you think you have that kind of power?" I guess I do think I have that kind of power. I think that surely I could have helped if only I'd said the right thing or been there at the right time.

CRITICAL CONSIDERATIONS WHEN WE ARE STUMBLING IN THE DARK

As we can see from these stories, there is little to relieve the bleakness, the despair of this cluster of experiences, thoughts, and feelings, this time of Second Crisis. It is a period when things seem the blackest. When we are living in a no-person's life, caught in a place we can only call limbo.

Why are we having such a hard time? What else about life is this loss now uncovering and revealing? And what will be our response after we see this? These are the difficult questions that lie at the heart of this time of Stumbling in the Dark. Never more than now will the way we think and the actions we take be more critical in determining the quality of our future: whether and how we move through our grieving and whether or not we ever reach a place of new equilibrium.

UNDERSTANDING THAT WE ARE ALSO GRIEVING THE LOSS OF OUR "ASSUMPTIVE WORLD"

While we are Stumbling in the Dark, we are dealing with much more than the loss of someone who was an essential part of our lives, as central as that loss may be. We are also dealing with a loss of meaning and a loss of those purposes that determined not only how our life had been but also how we thought it would be in the future. We've lost the structure that informed our life, the mental map that served as the source of our choices and plans. We've lost our "assumptive world," the life we expected to have.

I read a father's poignant account of what it is like not to be able to count any longer on one's assumptions. Writing in the *New York Times Magazine* about his son's death from a fall in Yellowstone, the man said:

A year ago, I learned of the death of our only child, our 22-year-old son, Paul. One of my early thoughts was that my wife and I would have no grandchildren. There would be no passing on of either our tangibles or intangibles. There would be no children or grandchildren to inherit our antique organ, the glassware blown by Betsy's grandfather, our silverware, our china or our modest financial estate. Nor would there be children or grandchildren to listen to the family stories about my father and his colorful relatives, the stories of my youth, of Paul's youth, of my wife's family, or of our solid, if uncolorful, married life. . . .

On our way to Yellowstone, I felt many emotions, including anger and the irrational hope that this was all a mistake. But above all else, as we traveled that long day, I felt lonely. I thought how strange it was that, with my wife of 25 years beside me, in a plane full of passengers and crew, and in airports like Newark, Minneapolis and Denver that swarmed with people, I felt alone.

As the months have gone by, the sense of loneliness has diminished somewhat, but it has never completely gone away. I have been surprised by how the assumptions that a man's child will marry and have children—and that they will outlive him—are his constant companions, molding thought and action in innumerable subtle ways. Suddenly, my thoughts and actions were inappropriate, because the assumptions on which they were based were no longer valid. Until some new assumptions replace those shattered by Paul's fall, I feel like a ship without engine, sail or rudder, floating helplessly without direction.

This father speaks for all of us. When life has no center that holds, when we can no longer live and plan according to our assumptions, we are left without direction. Now, not only must we mourn the absent one but we must mourn the loss of the future we naturally assumed we were going to have.

EXPECTING THAT WE MAY NOT BE TREATED THE SAME BY SOME PEOPLE

We begin to notice a change in some people around us. We don't get invited to places we used to be invited to. Some acquaintances are awkward when we run into them in public places. Even certain old friends start to avoid us.

How do we account for this behavior that is so hurtful and confusing? Is loss so threatening to others—something they will go to such extremes not to acknowledge—that they choose to confuse the griever with the grief and try to ignore us completely? (Dr. Colin Murray Parkes puts his finger on this issue when he says that in our society we don't burn our widows; we just pity and avoid them.) When these reactions do occur, they come at a time when we are least able to understand them. This behavior of others therefore exacerbates what we are already experiencing as an almost unbearable situation.

In *The Guardian*, one of the daily newspapers in the United Kingdom, in a column called "Private Lives," someone wrote about feeling deserted by friends after the death of his wife. Readers were invited to send in their responses to the man's experience. One reader wrote:

> *Death is the modern taboo. Most people are scared and embarrassed by it. Many do not know how to deal with another's bereavement, are scared of saying the wrong thing and of releasing a strong emotional reaction— so they ignore it in the hope that it will go away. This is probably what your friends are doing. . . . You must go out, do things, and be with peo-*

ple. *Do something, anything, that you are interested in where you will be with people—whether it's bell ringing, brass rubbing, morris dancing, train spotting, or, probably most useful of all, voluntary work. You can and will make new friends.*

Life goes on whether we like it or not, so get out there. If you don't, two people will have died, but only one will be lying down.

REALIZING THAT OUR LOSS IS SOMETIMES NOT RECOGNIZED BY OTHERS

It may be that our loss is one for which society makes little or no allowance for grieving: a miscarriage, the birth of a stillborn baby, an abortion, the death of a pet, the death of a companion whom the general public is reluctant to acknowledge as a primary relation.

I remember standing at a counter in a shop and overhearing a young mother-to-be talk exuberantly about the sonar pictures that had just been made of her baby. "Can you believe," she said, "that even at twenty weeks we could see the baby's esophagus! And watch the baby reach down with tiny hands and grab its feet! The doctor even made a video of the pictures so my husband could see it at home. My dad keeps asking when we're going to make eight by tens for the rest of the family!"

As I listened, I realized how much this mother—and millions like her—knew and loved her baby long before it breathed the oxygen of the outside world, and thought with sorrow of how often that love is not acknowledged and honored by others when a miscarriage occurs or a baby's life is lost. How unkind it is when someone tries to comfort by saying something like "But you are still young—you can have other children."

Similarly, the pain of the loss of a partner only intensifies when others are uncomfortable about acknowledging the relationship. I remember when the relationship of a friend of mine ended. The two women had been partners not only in life but also in their medical practice. Many people closest to my friend commiserated much more about the business losses involved in the breakup, often never even alluding to the personal pain she was experiencing.

BEING ON THE ALERT FOR THE WAYS WE ATTEMPT TO DEFEND AGAINST LOSS

Dr. Bowlby tells us that it is almost inevitable: We *will* attempt to defend ourselves against the pain of our loss and all the awareness that comes with it. What are some of the ways in which people attempt to protect themselves against feeling or dealing with the pain of loss?

- Becoming ill
- Having accidents
- Losing ourselves in work or other frenetic activities
- Giving excessive care to others
- Copying the mannerisms, behavior, or even the physical condition of the lost person
- Engaging in destructive behavior
- Engulfing ourselves in anger, guilt, and blame
- Falling into depression and making little effort to get help
- Flying high with euphoria
- Making rash, often costly, decisions

While we are Stumbling in the Dark, we may exhibit some of these or other defensive behaviors. Such behaviors seem, for many of us, to come with the territory. If we become aware of them as defenses, we stand a much better chance of stopping them before they become irreversible. Dr. Bowlby reminds us that while "defensive processes are a regular constituent of mourning at every age, what characterizes pathology is not their occurrence but the forms they take and especially the degree to which they are reversible." In other words, if the defenses we put up to ward off the reality of our loss are something we can "come back from" when we move forward in the grieving process, then we will not experience what Dr. Bowlby calls "pathological grieving." If, however, we do not become aware of the defensive behaviors and stop them before they take an irreversible toll, we run the risk of getting stuck in an identity as a griever or of having the defensive behaviors become a destructive way of life for our future.

WATCHING OUR HEALTH

Dr. Beverley Raphael warns us that "bereavement may also be fatal." There are many statistics to support this assertion. One study showed an increase of almost 40 percent in the death rate of widowers over the age of fifty-four during the first six months of bereavement. Another study looked at the death rate of close relatives of people who died over a six-year period. Of these close relatives, 4.8 percent died within the first year of bereavement, as compared "with only 0.7 percent of a comparable group of nonbereaved people of the same age, living in the same area."

A study reported by the Institute of Medicine says: "The mortality rate was at least seven times greater among the young widowed group (under age 45) than for the matched young married control group. The mortality rate for death from cardiovascular disease was 10 times higher for young widowers than for married men of the same age." Another study showed a death rate of 34.3 percent over five years for bereaved individuals, as contrasted with a death rate of 6.9 percent among those not bereaved.

Suicide is also a hazard. Studies show that the suicide rate among a group of 320 widows and widowers was 2.5 times higher in the first six months after bereavement and 1.5 times higher in the first, second, and third years after bereavement than in the fourth and subsequent years. When this group was compared with a control group, the "age-standardized suicide rate for widowed men was 3.5 times higher than among married men and for women the rate was twice as high."

We can see from these statistics that it isn't only during the first year of bereavement that we need to be concerned about the increased likelihood of death. The editors of the study done by the Institute of Medicine tell us: "There is some evidence suggesting that mortality rates remain high for certain categories of bereft individuals beyond the first year—perhaps into the sixth year after their loss."

What are some of the illnesses that contribute to these high death rates? Numerous diseases have been linked to grief and mourning, especially among individuals who are predisposed to such medical problems. Here is a partial list: cardiovascular disorders, heart disease, cancer, pernicious anemia, ulcerative colitis, leukemia, lymphoma, lupus, hyperthyroidism, pneumonia, rheumatoid arthritis, diabetes, tuberculosis, influenza, cirrhosis of the liver, glaucoma.

As early as 1944, Erich Lindemann, M.D., found that mourners were at high risk for these seven illnesses: "myocardial infarct (the so-called heart attack), cancers of the gastrointestinal tract, hypertension (high blood pressure), neurodermatitis (chronic itching and eruptions of the skin), rheumatoid arthritis, diabetes, and thyrotoxicosis (thyroid malfunction, most frequently seen in women)."

And to these seven Dr. Glen Davidson adds "chronic depression, alcoholism and other drug dependencies, malnutrition (both under- and overnutrition), and electrolyte disorders in which the blood chemistry, particularly salts, are out of balance." Dr. Davidson says that other disorders that mourners often cope with include "headaches (particularly the migraine variety), lower-back pain, frequent bouts with colds and flu, excessive fatigue, impotence, and significant sleep disturbances."

We must be on the alert for an onset of illness even beyond the first year of mourning. There is some indication that the number of incidents of illness actually increases in the second and third year following bereavement.

On the other hand, we must also monitor the temptation to use the "sick role" to get the attention we want and need, to avoid responsibilities, and to be passive rather than active in the face of our grief. It is natural during this bleak time to need desperately the sustenance and nurturing that friends and family can provide for us. But it is easy to see from the statistics above that the "sick role" is not a good way to ask for this help.

ACKNOWLEDGING SELF-DESTRUCTIVE BEHAVIOR

Being self-destructive is another defense that can destroy us. In the face of the harsh realities of mourning, some individuals choose to take on "the derelict role." The Institute of Medicine reports: "All studies document increases in alcohol consumption and smoking and greater use of tranquilizers or hypnotic medication (or both) among the bereaved." And Dr. Raphael points out other types of destructive behavior that mourners often engage in: "antisocial, delinquent, and criminal activity (for example, stealing or shoplifting); sexual behaviors including promiscuity leading sometimes to pregnancy; dependency disorders such as alcohol or drug dependence; and eating behavior disorders."

Often, we engage in such behaviors not only to block out painful experiences but also to have some sense of aliveness at a time when, otherwise, we feel dead. And it is true that destructive behavior can provide its own kind of high. When we engage in dangerous activities, we have a feeling that we're on a roll, making things happen, living it up. The danger, the risk taking, gives life an edge. But only for so long. There is always the emptiness, the loneliness, the nothingness of grief to come home to. Defending behaviors like these, therefore, can only compound our mourning. Until they finally destroy us.

IDENTIFYING DYSFUNCTIONAL RELATIONSHIPS

The misuse of personal relationships is another defense we may carry to such an extreme that our grieving does not proceed normally. There are several ways that we may relate in an attempt to avoid the pain of grieving. We can become overprotective of others or become an excessive caregiver who is always compelled to look for someone weaker to help. We can establish a relationship that is little more than a replacement, hoping that being with this person will allow us to skip the necessity of mourning. We may choose to engage only in relationships that require no intimacy, hoping thereby to protect ourselves from future losses; or we may engage in relationships that provide a battleground for the display of our hostility and anger. Whatever form our defensive use of relationships takes, we create for ourselves double heartache. For we are stuck in our mourning, and we are also denied the satisfaction that can come when we relate to others authentically.

AVOIDING BECOMING A PATHOLOGICAL MOURNER

One of the outcomes of excessive behaviors is that we can become pathological mourners. Pathological mourning can take many forms: (1) *chronic or prolonged mourning*, a state in which the initial intense grief of the early phases of loss continues unremittingly and the bereaved seems to take on "a new and special role, that of the grief-stricken one"; (2) *absent grief*, a situation in which the bereaved carries on "as though nothing has happened" in order to fend off threatening emotions that are too painful to bear; (3) *delayed grief*, which entails a long period of absent grief, perhaps months or years, after which grieflike symptoms emerge; (4) *inhibited grief*, a condition in which the expressions of grief are "toned down or shut off"; (5) *distorted bereavement*, which takes several forms: "intense pervasive anger in the absence of sadness and mourning and overwhelming guilt linked to intense ambivalence about the relationship between the mourner and the lost person; absorption in caring for others who have been bereaved; and denial that the person is permanently lost."

How likely are we to continue our defensive behaviors until we become pathological mourners? Opinions vary. Dr. Davidson says, "The best that can be determined is that between 5 and 15 percent of the population have unhealthy grief reactions." But Dr. Raphael suggests a much higher percentage: "The levels of morbid outcome or pathological patterns of grief are known in only a few instances, but they may represent at least one in three bereavements." Whatever the number, it is high enough to alert us: Our defending behaviors can become dangerous. Not only can these behaviors destroy all chances that we will be able to move through our grief normally but, as we have seen, they can also become fatal. The thrush's remark in Aesop's Fables may be useful for us to remember: "I am not half so much troubled at the thought of dying as at the fatality of contributing to my own ruin."

RESPONDING TO DISORGANIZATION

For those of us who have a lot of blue days while we are grieving, it comes as a relief to read Dr. John Bowlby's words: "I suggested that depression as a mood that most people experience on occasion is an inevitable accompaniment of any state in which behavior becomes disorganized, as it is likely to do after a loss. . . . For until the patterns of behavior that are organized for interactions that are no longer possible have been dismantled, it is not possible for new patterns, organized for new interactions, to be built up." Dr. Bowlby then makes this encouraging statement: "It is characteristic of the mentally healthy person that he [or she] can bear with this phase of depression and disorganization and emerge from it after not too long a time with behavior, thought, and feeling beginning to be recognized for interactions of a new sort."

Is there anything we can do to avoid this disorganization and depression? Perhaps the better question is: "Should we try to avoid depression when it comes?" Dr. Raphael reminds us how important it is to "know, and name, and express the pain that a [loss] causes." Many people, however, attempt to block their experience of depression (and sadness, too, which is a different experience, though it is often mislabeled as depression) through medication, drugs, alcohol, and other means that "do little to improve outcome in such bereavements." It is important to remember "that part of the work of adaptation requires a period of depression and personal reassessment."

Dr. John Schneider, who has been a mental-health professional for more than thirty-five years, has studied the difference between sadness and depression where those who are in the process of grieving are concerned. He points out that most of what people think of as depression after a loss is not depression: "Most of what is happening isn't depression or even an illness. Most of what is happening is a healthy response to a shared defining moment." It is important, Dr. Schneider says, to know the difference between depression, discouragement, and grief. Dr. Schneider suggests to people who are responding to loss that they first say, "I am depressed," and then try saying, "I am grieving" or "I feel discouraged." To a de-

pressed person, each statement feels the same. To those who are experiencing appropriate feelings of sadness and discouragement but
not depression, there will be a difference.

What can we do when we feel so disorganized? "Noble deeds and
hot baths are the best cures for depression," Dodie Smith, the English playwright, quipped back in the late 1800s. Individuals have
told me about other things that supported them as they Stumbled
in the Dark: getting regular exercise; keeping a journal; painting
and drawing; sewing; cooking; spending time with friends; seeing a
professional; listening to music; talking with a priest, a rabbi, or a
minister; going camping or walking in the country; doing hard
physical labor; fishing; gardening; praying.

On the basis of my own experience, I would recommend these
two things in particular: slowing down and speaking with a professional. Let me talk first about slowing down.

Grieving is hard work. It requires much attention and enormous
energy. Therefore it helps if we place some kind of moratorium on
as many other activities as possible, and that we have as few responsibilities as possible. And when we can't relieve ourselves of
certain duties and obligations we should do everything we can to
take care of ourselves: eating food we like, taking as much time off
as is feasible, getting massages, resting and relaxing when we can,
continuing to ask friends and family for help.

Part of slowing down should be getting a physical examination.
Doctors recommend a checkup perhaps between the fourth and
fifth months of bereavement. "If a mourner is developing an illness," Glen Davidson says, "the symptoms will usually appear during this time and yet be in an early enough phase of development
to allow effective medical intervention."

Another form of slowing down is to delay making major life decisions. Research shows that we do think differently when we are
under stress. For instance, even with a common illness like a severe

case of the flu, people are likely to experience mental dysfunction. This dysfunction may take the form of losing perspective and being unable to visualize objects or form thoughts from more than a single viewpoint. Or there may be some loss of the ability to reason. Perception, too, may be altered. Drs. Sidney Zisook and Stephen Shuchter warn that "acute grief frequently creates degrees of mental disorganization, confusion, anxiety, memory disturbances, and distractibility." If we must make major life decisions, it is good to ask others whose opinions are respected to help us check our own thinking.

Slowing down can also include the kinds of activities people told me helped them: gardening, walking, writing, playing music, making scrapbooks, organizing pictures, piecing a quilt, building a birdhouse or a fence, praying, listening in quietness, sitting by a pond watching the ducks.

My second personal recommendation: Speak to a professional. Peter Marris gets at the heart of the matter when he says: "I think a stranger, who understands grief in general, and stands in an acknowledged therapeutic role, can probably give more support to the working out of grief itself. Because this support is, in a sense, impersonal, it does not threaten to preempt the personal resolution of the crisis. For the most part, it simply offers reassurance that the crisis is natural, that it will find a resolution."

I liken talking to a professional to having a guide when you are rafting down a river. Once friends and I took a white-water-rafting trip down the Snake River in Idaho. What would we have done without a guide who knew that river? I remember so well words like "We are about to come to a No. 7 rapids. Lean in. Hold on. Don't turn loose the ropes, no matter what." I also remember words—oh, such welcome words—like these: "We're going to have smooth floating for a while now. You can sit back and enjoy the ride. I'll warn you when the situation changes."

What a professional who understands grieving can do is help us recognize where we are in the grieving process; encourage us as we make the choices that are appropriate for movement, in our own time and in our way, through that process; and point out pitfalls and highlight opportunities. It may be, though, that we have to be courageous to seek professional help. There may be people around us, in their biased ignorance, who suggest that only "sick or weak people" ask for help or go for counseling. However, when we are grieving we are going through perhaps one of the most severe physical, mental, emotional, and spiritual crisis of our lives. And to have as part of our support team someone who understands grief and loss is to show the opposite of weakness. It is to show a courageous commitment to our future.

There is one circumstance where we *must* seek the help of a professional: if we continue to experience chronic depression and cannot seem to get free of it, no matter what we do. The Institute of Medicine warns: "Grief may . . . give way to depression; approximately 10 to 20 percent of the widowed are still sufficiently symptomatic a year or more after their loss to suggest real clinical depression. Although this proportion is relatively small, out of the approximately 800,000 people who are widowed each year, this means that 80,000 to 160,000 people suffer serious depression in any given year. The number of depressed individuals following other types of bereavement—death of a child, sibling, or parent— is not known." Talking with a professional will allow us to understand whether our feelings are appropriate or whether they are symptoms that call for intervention and help.

What about taking medicine, especially drugs such as tranquilizers or antidepressants?

This is a controversial and difficult question.

Of course, we have to be responsible for our physical and mental condition. But where do we draw the line between being duly responsible and using medicine or drugs to blunt our experience, when such blunting is to our detriment? Unfortunately, many physicians interpret the prescribing of barbiturates and tranquilizers for grieving individuals as an automatic "standard of care." And the majority of the general public, not understanding the grieving process, see mourning as something that "must be suppressed."

Other physicians are adamantly opposed to the prescribing of tranquilizers, barbiturates, and antidepressants for those who are grieving. My own doctor, when he read an early manuscript of this book, wrote me:

> One of the reprehensible practices in medicine in the past fifty or so years has been the pushing of drugs on the bereaved—probably to make sure that they didn't embarrass themselves or the family with their true feelings: screaming rage, gnashing of teeth, pulling of hair, falling on the ground, and so on. Maybe if doctors could encourage patients to "let it all hang out," we wouldn't be faced with hidden, prolonged grief (guilt and the like), which is the fodder of contemporary psychiatry.

Dr. Colin Murray Parkes, who spent many years working in the area of grief and loss at the Tavistock Clinic and Tavistock Institute of Human Relations in London, as well as at Harvard Medical School, also questions the use of tranquilizers and antidepressants by people who are grieving. While Dr. Parkes acknowledges that he does not doubt the efficacy of these drugs "in reducing the intensity of the unpleasant features of grief," he also notes that anything that keeps us from going through the "unlearning" process central to grief "can be expected to prolong the course of mourning."

One would hope that we and our doctors will make decisions that take the necessity to grieve into account. If there is a legitimate need for drugs, scientists like Dr. Parkes urge that these medications be used with caution. And, as Dr. Glen Davidson points out, there are alternatives. For instance, changing one's diet to include carbohydrates eaten about ninety minutes before bedtime can often induce sleep most effectively because, as the carbohydrates are digested, the brain releases a natural opiate or barbiturate. This is only one of many possible alternatives to taking drugs. A good doctor who practices preventive medicine or a professional health practitioner can offer many other suggestions.

Let me say one final word about speaking to someone about our situation during the Second Crisis. For many people, one of the most disturbing experiences following a loss is a crisis of faith. What we believed before, we now question. What we thought could be counted on turns out not to have helped. What we asked for, we did not receive. Our ideas of good, fairness, right, God—all may now be uncertain. We may feel anger toward a Power that would let this terrible thing happen. Our deeply held belief system has been assaulted and, so far, nothing has put it right.

This is a good time to talk to someone who has given thought to the "eternal questions" that now plague us. People have said to me, "But I'm ashamed of the thoughts I have; I feel like a rotten person for no longer believing what I used to believe. How can I tell someone what I think or feel?" I make the recommendation to talk to someone who thinks about such questions deeply and profoundly not because such a conversation will provide certain answers but because often it is only in dialogue that we find out what is really true for us. Talking with someone we regard as wise and honest and qualified lets air blow through the stultifying repetition of questions in our minds. It allows us to hear our own voice, to pay attention, and to honor our inquiries.

Healing, insights, epiphanies, clarity—we never know when these may occur. One place they often show up, however, is in conversations between caring people who are striving to be as authentic as they can be.

THE CHOICE

We can choose to endure with patience.

What does it mean to endure? Maya Angelou says in her wonderful poem-book *Phenomenal Woman*: "All of my work is meant to say, 'You may encounter many defeats but you must not be defeated.' In fact, the encountering may be the very experience which creates the vitality and the power to endure."

When we experience a loss, we have definitely had, to use Maya Angelou's words, an encounter with defeat—the defeat of our hopes, expectations, dreams, and attempts to make a shape of love and care with our lives. How can this "very experience" of loss and pain create the energy, "the vitality and the power to endure"? Alexander Shand, in his classic work *The Foundations of Character*, asserts that despair tends to elicit courage. He then goes on to explain, "Despair tends to evoke . . . a resolution capable of attempting the most dangerous and uncertain actions."

I think the key word here is "resolution," which *Webster's New Collegiate Dictionary* defines as "the act of answering." When we are Stumbling in the Dark, we come to know awful truths: No, we won't ever have the relationship back again as it was. Yes, everything around us has changed and nowhere can we find a fit. These truths bring despair. The despair means that at some level we have given up any illusion that things are not as they are. But while this despair feels empty, like a vacuum, the very fact that we allow ourselves to experience it means that the vacuum becomes also a place of possibility. Talk about something that is both an irony and a paradox!

Letting ourselves know these terrible truths and still choosing to endure in spite of the emptiness and the despair means that at an appropriate time new patterns, new ideas, new thoughts have a chance
to emerge. Perhaps this is an illustration of the familiar biblical saying "You shall know the truth, and the truth shall set you free."

WHAT WE NEED FROM FAMILY AND FRIENDS WHEN WE ARE STUMBLING IN THE DARK

For many people around us, grieving is what we do during the first
days or weeks after our loss. After months go by, these individuals
often think we are now okay. Those closest to us may continue to
try to be helpful—perhaps by suggesting someone we can date or
something we can do with our time, not recognizing that it is much
too early for us to be receptive to this kind of assistance.

The kind of assistance we do need as we struggle with the long-
term implications of our loss and experience the incontrovertible
truths of what we are now facing may strike some as no assistance
at all: We need to be allowed to do whatever we do. To feel as bad
as we feel. To behave however we behave. To think in whatever
ways we think. To make whatever mistakes we make. For we have
to find our way through this quagmire, even if it means that we hurt
ourselves or flounder or act in ways that our friends and family
think are unlike us. We are at this time engaged in "a struggle of
conflicting emotions which advice can do little to resolve." We
cannot hear the wisdom of others at this time or see the pitfalls that
they are seeing. We are trying to find firm ground on which to
stand, to identify the boundaries of a world that we do not know.

At the same time, we do need the companionship of those who
love us and understand that what we are now going through is central to our grief and very private. As much as possible, we need to

allow ourselves to be sustained by the continuity of our relationships with others, for often this seems to be our only link to life. Perhaps it's a friend we jog with every morning; a family tradition we participate in even though we don't feel like celebrating; a niece or a nephew we take shopping or a son or daughter we take to the movie; a wise aunt we feel we can talk to. To know that the presence of these people is abiding—that is what we need and must ask of our family and friends during this lonely time in our grieving.

But there is a paradox. While it is true that we must be left alone to make our own way, at some point we need to listen to—and actually *hear*—either our own wisdom or the wisdom of someone around us, wisdom that urges us to do something about the quality of our lives. (One of the greatest challenges for those around us is to know when and for how long to be quiet and when and for how long to speak.)

Perhaps it will be an inner voice saying, "Enough is enough—you must stop this destructive behavior, this apathetic way of being." Perhaps it will be the shock that comes when one day we are hit with the reality of what our actions have cost us. Perhaps it will be the words a friend speaks or some passage we read. Perhaps it will be an experience we have outdoors or the message of a minister. It might be the impact of a traditional ritual or the love of an animal. But something, somehow, will bring us to a new threshold of seeing.

The choice of this experience of Stumbling in the Dark—to choose to endure—is captured for me in the haunting words of a folk song that was part of my preschool years spent in the pine woods of South Georgia. I learned this song from Annie, who was my special friend. As Annie helped my mother, who was expecting my little sister, Barbara, with the work of the house, she sang, her voice low and moaning: "You gotta walk that lonesome road; gotta take that trip through the long, long vale . . ." Even a four-year-old could hear the accumulated pain, hardship, sadness—and courage—captured in that song. I loved Annie.

It was someone as special as Annie who taught me that I, too, could make the choice to endure, only this time her name was Thornell. The granddaughter of slaves and the mother of a daughter who was a computer specialist and a son who had a Ph.D., Thornell exemplified what it meant to choose to endure. I would sit with her for hours, listening to her stories. In those stories I saw my own way forward, even if it would be a long time before I could take the necessary steps. I saw that it is possible to live through terrible times, to refuse to give up, to refuse to become bitter but, instead, to find the courage to do what you have to do.

Thornell held the center of gravity while I whirled and flailed during the months of my Second Crisis. "You're a good person," she would counsel me. "A woman's gotta do whatever she's gotta do. When you get through, you come on home."

When her husband, Charlie, died and she herself was learning to live alone for the first time in her long and fruitful life, Thornell told me one day, "No matter that we are having a hard time ourselves, we still can do whatever we can to be useful to others. There's a woman in my community who has a disabled son. I'm going to offer to sit with him one day every week." And that is what she did.

For me, Thornell was evidence of the truth of the old quotation "There is a strength of quiet endurance as significant of courage as the most daring feats of prowess." Her generosity was a point of light in my dark night. Her actions said to me, "Yes, I have been hit hard. I am hurt. I don't know how everything is going to work out. But I do know this: *I will endure.*"

THE TERRAIN OF OUR ACTIVE GRIEVING

Life As It Was   *Life and Loss Integrated*
The Event of Loss   *Freedom from Domination of Grief*

IMPACT: Experiencing the unthinkable
CHOICE: To experience and express grief fully

SECOND CRISIS: Stumbling in the dark
CHOICE: To endure with patience

OBSERVATION: Linking past to present
CHOICE: To look honestly

THE TURN: Turning into the wind
CHOICE: To replan and change our lives to include but not be dominated by the loss

RECONSTRUCTION: Picking up the pieces
CHOICE: To take specific actions

WORKING THROUGH: Finding solid ground
CHOICE: To engage in the conflicts

INTEGRATION: Daylight
CHOICE: To make and remake choices

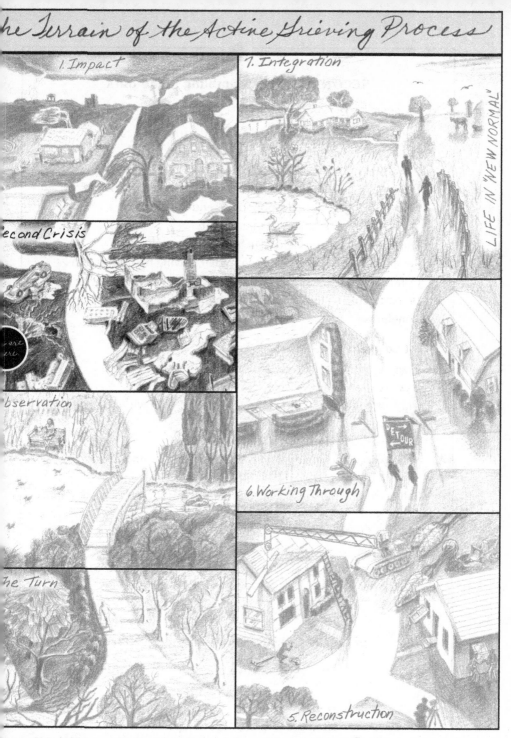

1. Impact

Second Crisis

Observation

The Turn

7. Integration

LIFE IN "NEW NORMAL"

DETOUR

6. Working Through

5. Reconstruction

Remember: A map never tells us how to travel. A map does not determine that everyone travels the same route, moves at the same speed, shares a set itinerary. A map does not dictate, prescribe, or even describe an individual's movement. A map does, however, name. A map can help us find where we are when we think we are lost. A map shows possibilities and provides ideas for where there is for us to go. At all times, however, every individual is the person holding the map.

SECOND CRISIS: Stumbling in the dark

What Is Normal?

Daily life feeling disorganized and in disarray

Loss of our "assumptive world"; recognition that the future we assumed we would have will never happen now

Feelings of emptiness, helplessness, and hopelessness

Sadness, depression, despondency, and despair

Decline in health; increase in accidents

Questioning of long-held beliefs and philosophies

Feelings of being suspended in midair, having no foundation

Continued obsession with anger, guilt, blame

Being unable to find structure or shape for our lives

Loneliness

What Can I Do?

Keep a journal, paint, garden, build a birdhouse.

Exercise, take nature walks, get a medical checkup.

Pray. (If you want to pray but can't, spend time with someone who can.)

Continue to ask others for what you need.

Work with a professional who can be a partner and a guide in this dark time.

Talk to a wise person about the "eternal questions" that are haunting you.

Eat good food.

Slow down.

Spend time with others who express love and concern for you.

SECOND CRISIS: Stumbling in the dark

My active choice?
To endure with patience

3

OBSERVATION:

LINKING PAST TO PRESENT

*Danger and deliverance make their advances together, and it is only in
the last push that one or the other takes the lead.*

Thomas Paine

I'm going to be in the city to meet with my publisher," I told his secretary on the phone. "I'd like to make an appointment to see Mr. DiMele."

Armand DiMele was the therapist I had visited when I was in New York just a few weeks after Greg's death. After a friend in the city recommended him to me—"Have you thought about seeing someone who can help you through this? . . . I know a man who is excellent and who has worked a lot with people who are grieving"—I went to see Armand several times during those early critical weeks.

It was Armand who told me about the phonograph album that I played night after night when I could not go to sleep. "Jean-Michel Jarre's 'Oxygene,'" he said. "Buy it. Perhaps the sound of that music can give you some sense of life in another dimension."

It was Armand who gave me a special present. The last time I saw him before returning to Tennessee, he held out a small object. "See, Elizabeth," he said as he showed me a tiny glass figurine. "We have to be whatever we are at any given time in our lives, even when we are wounded. We have to live that moment on the way to other moments." He handed me a beautiful crystal bird. One wing had been broken.

I suppose I expected something similar from Armand when I saw him this time—wisdom offered with gentleness and indirection. But today he did not speak the way he had in the past. His words were sharp and straight.

I began by speaking of feeling lost and without direction, of loss and tragedy; Armand responded by speaking of the limits of human perception.

"How do you know death is a tragedy?" he asked me. "For people who die, it may not be a tragedy at all. They may be far happier than they were here on earth—who can say? Those of us left here certainly don't know. It may well be," he concluded, "that tragedy is something only the living imagine."

When I spoke of my desperate desire to find something or someone that would make me happy, Armand spoke of the futility of my efforts.

"You will never be so happy again," he warned me. "You will never be so innocent and trusting. You will never know anyone else who will love you the way Greg did. You may," he said, "meet someone to love and be loved by, but you will then be a different person. You will never be able to repeat what you had with Greg. You might as well stop looking. The only place you are going to find happiness is within yourself."

When I spoke of the impossibility of living without Greg, Armand spoke of actions to be taken:

"Invite a friend to go to dinner tonight. And have this as a rule: Don't mention Greg once during the evening."

I spoke of the emptiness and loneliness of every day, and Armand challenged:

"Well, Elizabeth, what are you going to do about that?"

When I said I wanted my life the way it used to be, he asked:

"Are you going to be like the person I met the other day whose husband has been dead twenty-eight years and she has never taken one item of his clothing from the closet or changed one item in their bedroom? It would be amusing if it weren't so tragic. Because she keeps wondering why she can't get over her sadness. She's such a lonely and unhappy person.

"Oh, I could tell you stories, Elizabeth, of grieving people who attempted to lose themselves in causes—or in excessive care of others," Armand went on to say. "Of those who have retreated to a safe environment and settled for so much less than they had dreamed of for their lives. People who have given up their zest for living and exist in resignation. Many avoid new relationships; if they don't care for anyone, perhaps they will never be hurt again. Some give up all their ideals and beliefs, some withdraw from life, some—"

"But I can't see that I have done any of those things," I said defensively. "What am I hiding behind in order not to have to get on with living?"

"What do you think?" he asked me.

We sat in silence for several seconds. I knew it was time for an honest appraisal.

"Well," I began tentatively, "I have tried to run away from the loss—to try to find something or someone to substitute for Greg so that my life would have meaning again. I have also tried to become a different person, perhaps so I wouldn't have to solve the problems that plagued the person I used to be."

"But were these activities also beneficial?" Armand asked.

"Well, yes, at the beginning. I suppose they were a way to stay alive. But I think now they are walls I hide behind. I wanted to show that I could overcome any loss."

"But you haven't, have you?"

"No," I answered quietly.

"What is the next step?" I asked after we had sat for a few moments in silence.

Armand did not answer right away. Then he began to read from a paper that he held in his hand. It was something another griev-

ing woman had written, and it began: "There is a time to stop traveling . . . A time to refuel yourself . . . A time where the only number you dial is your own." He gave me the paper to take back with
me to Texas, and I read the words every day for many weeks.

It was one of those nights made for outdoor parties. As I drove
onto the grounds, I could see the lanterns in the distance bobbing
in the breeze; and as soon as I stepped out of the car I heard music
coming from somewhere across the small lake. I followed the
sounds, walking down a winding rock path that had been lined
with *farolitos*.

"The party of the year," the gossips billed it. A local real-estate
agency's open house for the business community, held annually on
the country estate of one of the agency's owners. As a professor I
had, of course, never come to this big event; but my friend Emma
came every year with her businessman husband, and this time she
had seen to it that I was invited. So here I was, feeling out of my el-
ement, but excited.

As I circled the lake and came closer to the central location of
the party, I felt more and more as if I were entering a world of
magic. Women in gauzy cocktail dresses looked ethereal as they
moved among the willow trees that grew along the edge of the
water. I could now see the musicians playing from the raised plat-
form in the gazebo, their clarinets and saxophones gleaming. The
buffet tables, covered in white linen and lit with tall silver cande-
labra, were constantly being replenished by waiters in tuxedos. I
wandered, looking for my friend Emma.

When I did not see Emma or her husband, I began to chitchat
with the strangers who were near me. A lawyer from Dallas and her
husband. A horse trainer and his small son from the Rio Grande

Valley. Several local people whose faces I recognized from pictures in the newspaper or from having seen them in their places of business. I was having fun. Not once since arriving had I thought of my misery.

It was at the buffet table that I met him. He walked up behind me as I was attempting to extricate a shish kebab stick from the pineapple it was stuck in. "Let me help you with that," he said, deftly pulling the shish kebab out and placing it on the plate he had taken from me. He was a handsome man, with hair that reminded me of Greg's. "You a regular at this shindig?" he asked, smiling the kind of smile that suggests you and he may soon discover you are both imposters or maybe co-conspirators.

"No, it's my first time," I answered. "What about you?"

"Yes, my first time, too. Just came in from Tulsa to visit my mother." We walked away from the buffet table together.

Finding a bench down by the water, we sat down. As I ate, he talked about his job—he was an anchorman at a local television station in a small town in Oklahoma—his last vacation in the Bahamas, how he came to town as often as he could to see his mother. Then he turned his attention to me. What did I do? Where was I from? And what was an attractive woman like me doing alone at a party? When I told him I was a widow, he patted my arm sympathetically and said he understood, that he had just broken up with his girlfriend. "Let's go somewhere and talk," he said. "I know we've got a lot in common."

I suppose it took me about fifteen minutes into the conversation to come to my senses. I had followed this man into town in my car, and we were now seated in a dingy roadside café. He was talking about his misfortunes. The women in his life hadn't understood him . . . they seemed never to be able to realize that it was to their own good that he gave priority to his work . . . always became bitter when he had so little time to give to them . . . oh, it was all such a sad history . . . yes, he knew how awful it was to be alone. "We wounded ones," he said, reaching over to pat my hand. "We wounded ones just have to stick together."

That was when it hit me. I had left an elegant party for this! To sit in a plastic booth in a run-down restaurant, listening to this self-centered, garrulous man tell his boring stories. And I knew where the scenario was headed. "Why don't we leave here and go somewhere a little more private?" Loneliness trying to lose itself in loneliness.

I realized now that this was what my decision not to let Greg go would always bring me: weak, whiny men, pandering to my own weakness and whining. "It must work something like radar," I thought. "Those signals one sends out that say, 'I'm living a sad story. Tell me about yours.'"

But tonight was going to be different. For something had suddenly shifted. I was no longer willing to play the role of a destitute widow, even to keep Greg close. And I was no longer willing to listen sympathetically to a man's pitiful tale just to get to be with him. So, without saying a word, and even as the man continued to talk, I picked up my purse, walked out of the restaurant, and drove back to the party.

I suppose that waking up in one area tends to make one more observant in others. I found myself, after that party, paying more attention to all of my behavior. It was as if through that event I had come to realize that I was an actor in my own story, that I myself played a significant part in what happened to me and around me.

It became a challenge to question my reactions. To try to understand things about which in the past I would have said, "That's just the way it is," or "This is natural and unavoidable." More and more often, I was able to put two and two together to make meaning of something that I had just done or something that had just happened.

⁊

The graduate faculty meeting had gone badly, the work of a whole year down the drain. The committee and I had been sure that our curriculum proposals would be accepted, but they were all returned, marked "Further study needed." I was so hurt and angry that it was all I could do not to cry as I walked down the hall to my office.

As I sat down at my desk, I looked outside and noticed that the grackles were back. Hundreds of them, flying all over the campus. Suddenly, in memory, I saw Greg that first year that we were living in Texas, running into the house, excited. "You won't believe the number of birds that are flying over at the university. Come on. You've got to see it."

That was the same day he'd written a verse and left it on the kitchen table.

Partners
You make the salmon loaf.
I make the sandwiches.

As I sat in my office now, looking out at the birds, I longed for Greg as if he had died yesterday. I missed him so. I put my head on the desk and sobbed uncontrollably.

It wasn't until I was on the way home that the question flashed into my mind: Could there be any connection between that faculty meeting and this relapse in my grieving? Had a new hurt opened up the wound of an earlier hurt? Was I transferring the upset at school to my loss of Greg?

We were five for dinner: an elderly couple, a child, and two young women. As the hostess crossed the floor, it was clear that she did not know whom to address. Who in this group was in charge? The one male among us wasn't stepping forward.

Seeing the hostess's awkwardness, I said, "May we have a table for five, please?" She was clearly relieved and, smiling her best hostess smile, led us to a table.

As we sat down, I exploded. "Have you ever seen anybody so rude?"

"Who?" My companions had no idea why I was so angry.

"That hostess," I sputtered. "She let us stand there looking foolish. If I hadn't spoken to her first, I guess we would still be standing."

"I didn't notice anything," the older woman said tentatively.

"I didn't either," said my friend. "But then I also wasn't paying any attention," she added placatingly. It was clear that no one except me had noticed anything unusual.

Later that night, while I was brushing my teeth, truth broke through the illusion. "You weren't mad at that hostess at the restaurant," I admitted. "You were mad at Greg for deserting you. You hate having to change roles and construct a new identity."

I went over to the physical education department to take a special fitness test they were providing for the faculty. My results were excellent, and I should have been happy. However, as I walked back across the campus, I felt sad. "What's wrong?" I asked myself. "No one there knew your husband had died" came the answer. "And you didn't tell them. They didn't know, then, that you live

such a contrast: Though you are healthy in body, your spirit is broken."

When I got back to the office, I sat at my desk and wrote:

> Upon Taking a Physical After Her Husband Has Died
> It's amazing that the electrocardiogram doesn't show irregular beats
> And the stress test printouts don't show blocked and partially blocked
>   valves
> The water test doesn't reflect the extra weight of the heart
> The pulmonary tests didn't catch the inability on occasion to breathe
> Imagine that.
> What's wrong with those machines?

I was now beginning to understand the source of moods to which,
previously, I had felt only a victim.

I was clearing out Greg's desk at home. A file marked "Divorce"
caught my attention. The folder contained copies of the divorce
decree from his first wife, the property settlement, records of child-
support payments, and other assorted documents. As I thumbed
through, I saw a copy of a letter he had written to a friend during
the divorce proceedings. I sat down on the couch and read the letter. One paragraph touched me deeply. Greg had written:

> Sometimes I worry about the boys. What kind of lesson was I giving them?
> I could define myself as a pillar of the community, an example to my chil-
> dren, a mainstay of my spouse. But the point of life isn't pretense; it's once
> around, baby, not a single tick more; and damn serious people damn well
> better see that nice things are nicer than nasty ones and good appetites,
> good digestion, good spirits, sound sleep all grow out of living life good—
> not ends in themselves but benefits accruing to the pilgrims who dare.
> Now, if you were somebody's son, wouldn't you like that for a lesson?

When I read the letter, I felt so guilty. Why had I not realized how painful it must have been for a good man to leave his children? Why had I never appreciated fully what he had lost? All I could think about was the numerous times I had criticized him for a divorce settlement that I thought was too generous. And the way I had not been big enough to try to include the boys in our lives more centrally. I was ashamed, so ashamed. I knew I had been a petty person, and that there was no way I could undo my selfish behavior.

One day, however, when it seemed that this guilt would just about suffocate me, a thought came out of nowhere, it seemed: *Human beings are mistake-makers*. It wasn't an excuse. It wasn't a rationalization. It wasn't a justification. It was just the truth. *Human beings are mistake-makers*.

Yes, I had made mistakes. And I deeply regretted them. There was no making up for those mistakes. Nothing could undo them. But I realized that I had become more conscious as a result of recognizing those mistakes. I could not now be so blind about my pettiness in any area, including that of Greg's children. That, it seemed to me, was something valuable to realize and something that could lead to new and different actions in the future.

It was interesting to watch what happened as I became more reflective and introspective. I had days when my life seemed to lighten up. Times when I was able to find enjoyment in simple activities. Occasions when I could imagine regaining a sense of humor.

One afternoon I decided to wash the car. I polished the headlamps. I scrubbed the tires. I oiled the leather. When I finished, I realized why, when Greg called me out to admire his wash job, he was always so happy. I felt a deep satisfaction.

As I was getting ready for bed one night, I went into the bathroom to take a shower. Just at the moment that I took off the final piece of my clothing, the lightbulb overhead blinked. I laughed and said, "Greg, you rascal. Is that you?" The next morning, as I was walking out to get something from the utility room, I hummed a song in my head: "All I Need Is You." For a second I thought the song was about Greg, but then I knew I was singing it to myself!

I found myself spending more time alone, being much quieter. Betty, a senior professor in the history department at the university and now a new friend, had given me a book to read. My thinking had been stimulated by the book, especially by a chapter titled "A Philosophy to Live By."

"I want a personal, workable way of life," someone quoted in that chapter had said. This simple statement resonated deeply within me, for I desperately wanted to make meaning of the loss in my life, which until now seemed only senseless and useless. The author had put forth a simple philosophy: *Realize first your relationship to the Creative Forces of the Universe, or God; formulate your ideals and purposes in life; strive to achieve those ideals; be active; be patient; be joyous; leave the results to God; do not seek to evade any problem; be a channel of good to other persons.* I wrote this list in my journal and thought about it often.

It was Betty, too, who introduced me to a new form of prayer: just sitting quietly in the presence of God. Formal prayer had been infrequent in my life since I had given up the strict doctrine of my youth, but I found this sitting quietly—"in communion with God, Who is also within us" was how Betty put it—calming.

I found that there were times now when I could think about Greg with peace and not pain. For instance, one day I was watching the Joffrey Ballet troupe dance on television and thinking about how much Greg loved to go to the ballet. I felt sad. Then I really looked at the dancers, their grace, the simple beauty of their movements. It seemed as if I were seeing not only the dancers but

Greg's spirit. I felt his beautiful self in the dance, his gentleness. It was amazing, but in that moment I felt closer to him than I had at any time since he had died.

On another day I saw a guest on *Donahue* talking about ethics and morality, and I remembered the decision Greg made a few months before he died always to tell the truth, to himself and to others. I had been inspired by that commitment then but, listening to the man on television, I recognized that the commitment continued to inspire me now. I realized that Greg's ideals had lived past him, and in this very important way, he was still part of my life in the present.

It's amazing how like calls to like. When I was still telling my sad story, I seemed to draw people who also had sad stories. But in the past few weeks things had been different. It seemed the quieter I got, the more people I met who were deep and reflective. Like my new friend Betty, who had given me the book and told me about a kind of prayer that was new to me. And my new friend Tommy.

I met him first at a chili cook-off where Emma and I were two of the judges. I had sensed that there was something different about him, even in passing. He was . . . well, it wasn't impersonal . . . I suppose you would say detached. Observing. Standing back, almost as if he and life had a solitary pact. I liked this man and wanted to get to know him.

"Don't get your heart broken," Emma warned. "Tommy is a very private man. Many women have been attracted to him, only to discover that when they pushed he disappeared." So from the beginning I determined to do something I had not done since Greg's death: Let a friendship develop with a man instead of acting as if I expected him to be my beau.

It was Tommy's relationship to the land that most attracted me to him. We spent many a Saturday or Sunday on his family ranch, checking to see if the washes between the bunkhouse and the river were or were not passable, hunting for twisted grapevine sticks to add to his collection, scaring up jackrabbits, deer, and armadillos. We combed the landscape looking for mesquite branches and broken limbs to make a brush pile in front of the bunkhouse.

At night we'd sit on the porch waiting for the moon to rise and the wind to die down. When it was time, he would light a piece of kindling and put it to the mounds of dried grass and leaves at the bottom of the brush pile. The fire caught fast. Flames licked twenty, thirty feet up toward the sky.

We sat on the ground near the fire. Tommy talked about the Native Americans who used to live on this land. About the wild boar we had seen that morning. About the stand of trees in the bottom. The scene was almost eerie—nothing but sky and earth enveloping us; familiar constellations of stars distinct and clear above us; dark shadows all around us, except where the brush was burning. "Like a primitive tribal rite," I thought to myself. "Or a fire made by nomads to ward off danger." I felt out of time, like one of the ancients.

Then Tommy began to call the coyotes, making sounds long and plaintive. We waited in silence. At first there was no echo, only stillness. Then, after a few more calls, the coyotes began to return the sound. Over and over. Again and again. We sat there until long after midnight, watching the fire burn and listening as the coyotes answered. Experiences such as these gave me a sense of connectedness with the earth deeper than any I had ever known. They brought me great solace.

It must be that the law of compensation works in everything. When I was feeling more peaceful than I had felt since Greg's death, news came that threw me off center. My girlfriend Felicia called from Tennessee; she and Al were separating after fifteen years of marriage. I had been friends with Felicia and Al since graduate-school days. Now she was alone with a young daughter. "Could you come for a day or two?" she asked. "Just until I can pull some of the pieces together?" Naturally, I went.

We talked long into the night. I lashed out in such hatred. "I despise him," I said. "How could he do this? How could he leave someone like you?"

The morning I left Felicia's house to drive to the airport, I was feeling sad for her pain and loss; but the countryside through which I was driving also made me feel happy. These mountains of East Tennessee were my home, and I had never seen them look more beautiful. It was early, and the mist that gives the mountains their smoky look—and their name—was lifting. A blue haze lined the far horizon. The road turned back and forth through cuts of granite, and now and again I could see tiny lines of sparkle where the sun hit the thin streams of water running down the rocks.

I was thinking about my conversations with Felicia and how angry I was at Al, how hurt. "Does love always have to cost so much?" I asked myself. "Does caring always have to bring loss and pain?" Of course, the questions were moot, for I already knew the answers. "Nothing—no one—can be counted on," I said in bitterness.

Then, suddenly, from somewhere far back in the past, I began to hear the notes of a children's song. *Three blind mice. Three blind mice. See how they run. See how they run . . .* Where in the world was that song coming from? Then I remembered. How many years had it been since our teacher played that phonograph record in elementary school? "Pick one of these songs," she had said, "and when you get scared, begin to sing it. Whatever you pick will always be your song of courage."

Now the notes of that nursery rhyme were sounding of their own accord. *Three blind mice. Three blind mice.* And I knew the question they were asking: Would I have the courage to love—to love people, to love life—in spite of the fact that things often turned out rotten? Would I run the risk of caring anyway, even if nothing and no one could be counted on?

It was a critical moment. Was I willing to forgive life for what had happened to me? Did I have the courage to love life, even with the pain?

I heard the sound coming from deep inside me. It was with a wavering and a teary voice, but I was singing: *Three blind mice. Three blind mice. See how they run. See how they run.* Something—some deep part of me—was saying "Yes." Suddenly, waves of love flooded over me. Love for the world. Love for every person in the world. Even love for Felicia's husband. I looked out at the sky, which by now was a midmorning blue, and I shouted aloud, "I yield. I yield. I surrender. I will expand my love for Greg to all my life and to everyone. Yes, I will love."

This is Observation, the experience of Linking Past with Present. A time of review, of reminiscing. Of noticing and paying attention. Of sifting through the past—the good and the bad—in order to bring truth into the present. A time of attempting to make sense of our actions and responses. A time of coming to terms with guilt and anger; a time of forgiving. A time of being still and quiet. A time for gaining wisdom.

"Mourning requires that a person review the relationship, mull it over in memories, dreams, fantasies," says Mardi Horowitz of the University of California at San Francisco Medical School. This review is "at the nub of mourning," for it "allows an update of a person's mental map of himself [or herself] and his [or her] world, to adjust it to the reality of the loss. You scan your memory banks to see what is still relevant to your life, what is not. You want to know, 'What do I have to let go of? What will I have to find in someone else? What can I contain within myself?'"

Much of this review involves "a very intense reexperiencing of much of the past development of the relationship, back to its earliest times." The review, of course, has been part of the mourning process from the very beginning, but when we get to this point in our movement through grief the review is a more defined activity. In a way, the past is now more contained. The images are now "not growing and active," so we can review "piece by piece, memories, thoughts, and feelings associated with the image" of the lost person or the lost shape of our lives.

Dr. Beverley Raphael offers this description:

> Many powerful feelings well up as memories of the relationship are sifted through: regret that more was not valued when the partner was alive; resentment over those things that were not made right or over being cheated by death of what was hoped for the future; ineffable sadness over what was and can no longer be; sorrow for the lost past and the younger years that are gone with it; anger at life, the dead person, the self for what one did not have and now may never have—perhaps children, perhaps love; guilt for the love that was not perfect, for the hate that was nurtured, the care that failed; release from the suffering of illness, from the suffering of relationship; triumph that one did not die oneself, guilt that such a feeling could appear; depression at the emptiness of self and world; and envy of those who have not lost, but live unscathed by death.

Memories of the relationship are *sifted through*. Those key words from Dr. Raphael's description encapsulate the activity of this phase of our grief work. We are *sifting through* our feelings and experiences—"studying and investigating thoroughly," as the dictionary defines *sift:* "separating out as if by putting through a sieve," as the root word for *sift* tells us.

It is during these experiences that we realize, if we have not already done so, that "the work of mourning is, by its nature, something which takes place in the watches of the night and in the solitary recesses of the individual mind." Friends and family can help us, as Dr. Bowlby points out, "to confirm or disconfirm [our] initial evaluations," but it is we who make these first evaluations. Therefore much of the work of Linking Past to Present must be done in solitude and quietness.

What can we expect during this time of observation? Men and women who have paid attention to their own process of mourning report such experiences as these. . . .

AN AWKWARDNESS IN LEARNING TO BE ALONE

A young woman recalls:

At first I could not be alone. I stayed busy constantly, even though I didn't know I was doing it when I was doing it. I just stayed real busy, thinking about what my next thing was going to be, that next thing I was going to do right then. If some friends came over and said they wanted to take Jeffrey to the Dairy Queen to get an ice cream, I said okay. Then, after they left, I left, too. The empty house was just too scary.

But one day I thought, "Okay, you have to wean yourself. You have to sit here and just sit . . . you can't just be doing something, you have to make yourself literally be by yourself." I made myself get in the recliner—it was a Sunday afternoon, which has got to be the worst time in the week to be by yourself. "Just look outside," I told myself. And I just did it, and I didn't run from it.

Now I enjoy my time alone. My mom took Jeffrey home with her the other night, and I put music on and was just sitting here singing. I would never do that before. I mean, the amazing things that change inside you as a result of your actions . . . it's unbelievable.

AN INCREASED CLARITY ABOUT WHAT YOU HAVE LOST

A son who was fourteen when his father died says:

When my father died, I couldn't figure out why I continued to be so upset so long after the event. My parents had been divorced for so many years, and I had adjusted to that fairly well and was reconciled to it. Therefore I couldn't understand the devastating effect the loss had on me.

It's taken a lot of reflecting for me to get a handle on this. But I see now that, even though I didn't live with my father and wasn't even especially close to him, as long as he was alive there was still the possibility of relating with him and going to see him when I did. On Father's Day I could send him a card and things like that. I see now that what I'm mourning is the loss of the opportunity to relate to him and develop and nurture my relationship with him as an adult. When my father died, I felt I was in the most positive place I had ever been with him—it felt like the start of something new. I was growing up, maturing. I could imagine us doing all kinds of father-son things in the future. So the loss of never getting to develop our relationship as two adults is what has continued to gnaw at me. It has been freeing just to realize this.

A GAIN IN UNDERSTANDING WHAT IS RIGHT TO DO

A widow with two small sons recalls:

I began to observe the boys and how they were about the death of their daddy. One day, several months after Lee's accidental death, the boys and I were pulling into the driveway and the four-year-old suddenly asked, "Mama, what does *accident* mean? What's an *accident?*"

Before I could answer, Jeremy, who is seven, said, "I don't want anybody else to ever talk about Daddy in front of me again. You just don't have to talk about him in front of me."

I stopped right there and said to myself, "It's time for the three of us to stop trying to avoid what has happened and to face up to it." So I said, "Jeremy, that is not the way it's going to be. Anybody that wants to talk about Daddy is going to be able to talk about him any-time he feels like it. It's a lot better for us to talk about it than it is to just sit and think about it." Then I told him, "I'm going to be talking about him, and if your brother has any questions or wants to talk about his daddy he is free to do it. That is going to be a new rule of this house. Each person can talk, and nobody will keep the others from talking."

That probably wasn't very sensitive, but I was being truthful. I went on, "You're old enough to know we can't ignore this. We're not going to pretend Daddy never lived, because we had happy times and we ought to talk about them and remember them. It will be especially nice if we talk about the good times, but we'll talk about the bad times, too, when we remember them. And sometimes when we talk it will make us sad and we'll want to cry. You're going to see Mama cry. And it won't be your fault that Mama is crying, and it won't be Daddy's fault. But if I feel sad, or if you and Danny feel sad about Daddy or anything else, it is perfectly all right to cry.

And we're not going to hide any of these things in our house. We're not hiding anything that we feel about Daddy, good or bad."

I guess that really sank in, because a few days later we were putting up the Christmas lights—this had always been a job for Lee and the boys—and they wanted me to hurry and turn them on. So we turned off all the lights in the house and just had the tree lights on. The three of us were sitting there in the living room looking at them, and Jeremy spoke up and said, "Oh, Mama, this is so nice. If Daddy was here, he'd love it 'cause he always liked the lights. This would be even happier if Daddy was here."

And I held him and said, "You're right, Jeremy. We wish he was here, but he's not. And it's all right for us to remember how happy it used to be."

It's been several months now, and both of the boys talk about their dad. About six weeks ago Danny, the little one, came running into his grandmother's kitchen and said, "You know, Grandma, what I really miss about Daddy is his wrestling with us." He said this right out of the blue. So I know, though the boys don't seem to dwell on it, that they do think about him and miss him.

A DECISION TO STOP AVOIDANCE BEHAVIOR

A mother whose son died told this story:

I hadn't catered a party in more than two years, and, suddenly, a few weeks after Jack's death, all these people started calling me. Within a week I had five jobs, ranging from a company picnic for five hundred to an intimate dinner for six. I grabbed at all the work. It was much more than a one-person operation could handle, but all I could think was that the jobs would fill my time and keep me from dwelling so much on Jack. And that's the way it was for months and months afterward. People kept calling, and I kept taking work.

But now, a year later, I'm burned out. I'm tired. And I also think that the purpose of the frenzied work is over. Now, instead of wanting to keep Jack out of my mind, I want to think about him. I want some time now to think about what it means that he is gone. I see now that my antidote to the pain of losing Jack—working in a frenzy night and day—just delayed what I'm going to have to do: get used to life without my son.

AN HONEST ASSESSMENT OF BEHAVIOR THAT IS DAMAGING

A widow tells her story:

Ever since Carter died, I have blamed his business partners, who couldn't see what Carter was trying to show them about the company's future. Carter's upset over this ate him up. All of his physical problems started then.

I realized something the other day when I was watching one of the talk shows and a doctor on there said that depression was anger turned inward and that you couldn't hold a grudge, else it would really hurt you. That's when it snapped for me that it was really Carter's grudge against those company officers that killed him. That's when I decided that I would stop holding a grudge against them—which means, I guess, that I forgive them—because I can see now the damage that kind of thinking can do. It destroyed a man's health, ruined him. Now I try to see where the other person is coming from. But if I'm not able to do this, I let go of the grudge, if only for a selfish reason—so my life won't be damaged by it. I watch myself and my children and try to teach them about grudges. I've done a lot of that since I saw that program.

AN OPPORTUNITY TO UNHOOK FROM ANGER

A man describes an important realization:

When everything was over and I was living alone, I was so angry. Finally, I realized that the anger was destroying me. So I began a conscious effort; it wasn't something you do like slice a piece of cake, or at least for me it wasn't. I'd have to repeat: "Don't let that anger ruin your life." I'd say, "Look, anger is anger; it's an emotion, and it's just stored in a closet in your mind; and you let it out, and it does all kinds of cruel and mean things to you."

When worse comes to worst, and I can't get rid of the anger any other way, I go out to the flower beds and start digging up weeds. The ground is really dry, and there are lots of clods. I have this brick wall around my backyard. So if I'm so angry that I can't talk myself out of it, I pick up those clods and swing them as hard as I can. They just explode when they hit the wall. I confess, sometimes I even get to talking to those weeds and those clods: "Okay, you so-and-so," I'll say. "You're going next—just hold on, you're going next!" I tell you, I'm killing weeds! I'm breaking clods! And what worked out so well when I threw the clods against the brick wall is that they fell back into the flower beds as soil!

A RECOGNITION THAT IT IS TIME TO START RELYING ON YOURSELF

A woman whose companion died advises:

You're surprised when you find out that you're going to make it. That there is some kind of ability we all have that just shows up on your front porch, so to speak. You have to have some kind of rationality present, however; and for so long, of course, you don't have it. But there comes a time when you do.

I would say there is far too much advice out there on what to do about these matters. One thing I've discovered is that there are a thousand advisers; and I'm sure it's all good advice, but it's also confusing. So, somehow or other, I think you need to take time to sort it out alone. I think all the major decisions after loss finally have to be made alone. They are made when you're driving the car or standing in the kitchen or mowing the lawn.

I know people say, "Don't try to do it alone; turn to your friends for help." And that's good advice for a certain time period. Goodness knows, we need love from others; but I think there's a tendency to turn to other people so much that you forget about your own abilities and forget about the fact that it is only your decisions that are going to carry you through in the long run.

A REALIZATION THAT GRIEF OVER ONE THING MAY MASK GRIEF OVER ANOTHER

A woman recalls:

I loved classical music, and when I played it after being alone I would cry so hard that I had to turn the music off. And then one day I realized that my crying over *Moonlight Sonata* had nothing to do with losing my husband.

I thought back to when I had first heard that piece of music. It was in a movie when I was a young girl—I think about fourteen. It was during the Depression, and I would go with the other girls in my little country town to the movies. I would sit there watching John Payne and Betty Grable or Kathryn Grayson and long for the world out there. I can even remember where I was sitting in the theater the night I heard *Moonlight Sonata* for the first time. I don't remember the name of the movie, but I remember the song so distinctly. I sat there and dreamed of singing and dancing the way the stars on the screen did. I dreamed of being in their world, which looked so wonderful. I longed to have that.

So when I thought I was crying over my current loss as I listened to *Moonlight Sonata*, I was actually crying over my lost youth, over the fantasy world I had thought existed out there. I was crying for the little girl back during the Depression.

COMING TO TERMS WITH GUILT

A young man reports:

I did wrong, and my best friend paid for it with his life. I drank too much at a party and drove home recklessly. I lost control going around a curve and turned the car over. I wasn't injured, but my buddy was killed.

This is something I will always live with. Right now, I'm doing retribution. The judge said, "In addition to giving you a probated prison sentence, I am going to require you to pay retribution." I work construction, so each week when I get paid I send my friend's parents a certain amount of money that the judge said I must pay them. I know this can do nothing about the loss of my buddy, but it's a way of saying I'm sorry. The thing that matters most to me—and something I will never forget in my whole life—happened at the trial when Jim's mother came up, put her arms around me, and said, "Jacky, I forgive you."

AN ABILITY TO SEE WHERE ONE IS STUCK

A widow recalls:

It was almost a year after Donald died. A man came to the back door—he worked for the telephone company—and asked if he could check some wires at the back of the property. When he returned, he rang the doorbell to tell me he was through, and he said, "This is a beautiful home." I said, "Thank you. My husband built most of it himself." But I didn't stop there. I went on to tell him that the house was Donald's dream, and that I couldn't move from it because Donald was now dead.

The lineman said, "Oh, I'm sorry he's dead." I said yes, and then told him the whole story. I told him Donald committed suicide. I showed him where he did it. I told him how awful it was to find him. I just told this stranger every tiny detail. It was awful. I'd cry and talk to him and talk to him and cry. Just wallowing in my loss and stirring up his.

After he left, I thought, "This is the pits. This is the worst. Stop a stranger to tell him about your problems, and your husband has been dead over a year. I'm down to the last person, I guess. I've told everyone else until they're tired of hearing it. So now I grab at somebody new I can tell my story to."

I haven't done that since. I realize that I've told many people how Donald died when it was completely unnecessary. I know it's healthy to be truthful when someone has committed suicide, but you don't have to use the method of death to get more sympathy. That's what I saw I was doing. I know now that it's very important to question why you're continuing to do what you do. Whether you can quit right away or not, there's value in asking yourself the question.

AN ACKNOWLEDGMENT OF AMBIVALENT FEELINGS

A young widow discloses:

I don't know if we would have made it or not. He died in December, and since October we had talked about getting a divorce. I told him I couldn't stand the way he tried to dominate me. He had to be the macho husband, and he wanted me to be the sweet little wife. I wanted to finish high school, and he didn't want me to. I wanted to have a career, and he said, by damn, he was the breadwinner. We were headed for some change—either through counseling or divorce—and I doubt that it would have been counseling.

So now that he's dead I feel two ways. I'm sad and lonely; I miss him more than I ever thought I would. But sometimes I'm relieved and, I guess you would say, even grateful. In some ways I'm lucky that he died, because now I'm my own person. I can live my life to the fullest. But, you know, even saying that makes me think something bad will happen to me. You aren't supposed to feel that way about the death of your husband, but that is the way I do feel.

AN EXPERIENCE OF EXISTENTIAL LONELINESS

Listen to this story:

Now that I'm spending more time in solitude I have recurring feelings of being alone in the universe. You may laugh when I tell you, but as early as age six or seven I would be lying on the bed before I went to sleep at night, looking out the window to see if I could see the stars. I would find one star and think about going up into the sky. I would get such a peculiar feeling. The star was so way out there . . . and where was I? I would keep thinking about this, getting a little afraid. Out there would seem like such a void. And, even though I was that young, I would wonder: "How do I fit into life?" I would feel so lonely then. And that's the kind of loneliness I feel now in my grieving. I feel alone in the universe. I wonder often how I fit into everything. It's the kind of loneliness that sometimes also feels like fear.

A RECOGNITION THAT GRIEVING IS NOT BEING DONE

A mother talks about her adult sons' response to their father's death:

Don has been dead for two years now; and my three sons, all in their forties, are still awkward when their dad is mentioned. The other day Don's brother, who looks a lot like Don, came to visit. Afterward, the boys kept asking didn't it bother me to see Uncle Gene sitting in Daddy's chair. The truth is, it hadn't bothered me at all. I didn't even think about it until they mentioned it.

One of my sons in particular is trying to live his life as if he doesn't have grieving to do for his father; and, of course, he does. So he's upset most of the time about other things—his work, his relationships, his health—and I think a lot of this is because he's avoiding grieving.

I've noticed something else. Every time I step out and do something on my own—like drive myself to the dentist or say I'm going to take a ceramics class—my sons get upset. It's as if they want me to stay the way I was when their father was alive. Any changes I make seem to be threatening. I haven't figured this out yet, but I certainly notice it.

And I notice things about myself, too. I bought a new stereo a few weeks ago, and when Don's brother came I found that I was embarrassed to mention the stereo or show it to him. It was as if I was embarrassed that I had stepped out in this way. I think I was afraid he would think I had spent too much money.

So there's "east" to go, as I've heard people put it. There's grieving yet to be worked out, and there's a whole set of family dynamics enmeshed in and around that grieving (or the absence of it). But one thing I'm clear about is that I'm going to keep observing myself and keep myself moving on through this process. Even in the worse of these situations, I notice that I'm walking two and a half miles every day with my neighbor and having my prayer times. Something strong is there, even in the middle of all these complications.

A Recognition of Ways the Lost Person Continues
to Be Present

A granddaughter recounts a realization:

The morning after my grandmother died, my husband wrote a little dedication for her and put it by my coffee cup at breakfast. It read: "For Grandmother, I'd wear jogging shorts and a New York Met's cap." I knew why he'd said this. My grandmother at seventy-nine was active beyond most people's imagination. She had just recently finished painting the outside of her house herself, and had even managed to fall—with no repercussions—into the kitchen through the back window when the concrete blocks slipped out from under her. She was also an avid Mets fan who would take her portable radio to bed with her when they were playing on the West Coast so she could follow the game, even though it was two o'clock in the morning.

I missed Grandmother after she died; she had been such a spirited presence in our family. Then one day I noticed something: I had started buying stationery and cards that had beautiful flowers on them. "Ah," I said to myself. "That's Grandmother!" Grandmother always had flowers in her yard, and these flowers were always a topic of conversation when you were with her. I would say that she and flowers were so connected in our family that you couldn't say one without thinking of the other. I had also begun to write to my family, who live in different parts of the country, every week instead of my usual once or twice a month. Grandmother wrote all the children in the family every week, no matter what, and chided the rest of us when we were with her for not "keeping up the family tradition," as she put it. "Family is important," she would say. "You must write to your family."

So, without realizing it, I had started doing what Grandmother said—"keeping up the family tradition." This was comforting to me, because I knew this was a way that Grandmother was still present in my life. She will never go away as long as there is flowered stationery and family letters!

CRITICAL CONSIDERATIONS WHEN WE ARE LINKING PAST TO PRESENT

What ways of thinking and behaving are most useful as we sift through the past to bring what is relevant into the present? What are the issues that predominate? In some ways, during these experiences, we face confrontation: Facts and situations that are painful now call to be paid attention to. Yet in other ways the experiences result in a sense of calm: We begin to focus on something over which we *do* have control—our own thoughts and reactions. Here are some of the opportunities:

DISTINGUISHING BETWEEN LONELINESS AND SOLITUDE

There is no question that after the loss of those who are important to the structure of our lives we are lonely. Their absence is part of our constant awareness. In our loneliness, we feel an incompletion, a lack, something is missing. Our need to bond, to connect, to love, has been tampered with; our desire for communication and companionship is very present.

Solitude, however, is very different from loneliness. While we are still alone when we allow ourselves time in solitude, we are not lonely. The companionship we have is with ourselves, our own thoughts and dreams, our relation to life around us. We explore our internal world, making discoveries that enlarge us, having insights that feel like openings. We find that we are more creative. Perhaps we experience unexplainable feelings of union and connectedness or oneness with all living things. Solitude brings growth and stillness, nurturing those parts of us that have been so deeply wounded by our loss.

In her spirited and inspirational book *Getting Better All the Time*, Liz Carpenter, that vivacious person who became so beloved by the public when she worked with Lyndon and Lady Bird Johnson in the White House, tells the story of making the critical distinction between loneliness and solitude after her husband died suddenly of a heart attack and she moved from Washington back to Texas:

No gradual transitions for me—I wanted it all to happen immediately. I confessed this to my doctor, John Tyler, confessed it with tears I couldn't stop.

"Stop racing and look around. Let your environment enrich your life," he said. "You have a place you love, so stay put long enough to love it."

One morning as I sipped a cup of coffee while I was on the phone talking with an editor in New York, I looked out the picture window and saw a baby deer walk gingerly by, sniffing at the pink geraniums. It paused, framed against the pink granite dome of the capitol of Texas in the distance. Here it was, God's world and my new world laid out before my eyes.

"I'll have to call you back," I hastily told the editor. "I've got to take this in."

And I sat there for a full five minutes gazing at the wonder of it all, reflecting that I had just learned how to move from loneliness to solitude. There is a vast difference.

That's what I had prayed for. That's what I had made the move for, and I had found it at last. God had really given me a chance at a second life, and gradually, in a different way, it became as full as the old life, the Washington life.

Authorities tell us that even babies need solitude in order to "discover [their] personal life." If infants are capable of being alone, says Dr. Donald Winnicott, first "in the presence of someone" and then without the "*actual* presence of a mother or a mother-figure," children will learn how to "have an experience which feels real." And, Dr. Winnicott points out, "a large number of such experiences form the basis for a life that has reality in it instead of futility." Dr. Anthony Storr, commenting on Winnicott's study, says that "the capacity to be alone thus becomes linked with self-discovery and self-realization; with becoming aware of one's deepest needs, feelings, and impulses."

There are practical benefits, too, that accrue from our time of solitude. Paul Horton suggests that "the ability to give solace to oneself is the basis of such major positive feelings as joy, awe, forgiveness, and generosity." Work he has done shows that spending time alone talking to oneself, reading, listening to music, praying, going for a walk, and recalling pleasant memories bring solace. He emphasizes the importance of this "private behavior" in our being able to comfort ourselves and "lift the weight of a depression."

REMINISCING

Sadly, I have heard people advise others who are grieving, "Quit thinking about the past. The future is what you can do something about, so that's where you now need to be looking." But this advice is wrong. First, we must reminisce. For reminiscing—recalling events, conversations, occurrences from the past—is one of the important ways that we mourn. (In fact, the word *mourning* in Sanskrit means "to remember.") And, paradoxically, reminiscing is a way of thinking that can result in our getting free from our sadness and even our depression if we are caught in that place of blackness.

"How so?" someone might ask. "How can thinking about the past help break the darkness of the present?" Pietro Castelnuovo-Tedesco, who has studied reminiscence at Vanderbilt University, points out that this form of thinking is "one of the principal means by which a person continues to have a relationship with old parts of the self." Through reminiscing, he says, we are able to maintain an "inventory" of the key images of ourselves from the past and are therefore able to keep "a thread of continuity among them."

Reminiscence also allows us to discover that the past "has not vanished but is still available and serviceable." "Serviceable?" someone might ask. "How can a past we can never return to be serviceable?" Because reminiscence "comes close in substance to thinking as a form of trial action." Through reviewing both our past accomplishments and our failures, we can better set goals for the future. Reminiscing, too, "offers guidance and direction" because we are reminded of those ideals and precepts that we have believed in.

Reminiscence is a type of thinking that may occur with others but mainly "occurs silently, when the individual is alone, and is a most private form of mental activity." It allows us to be "simultaneously observer and participant," which is why reminiscing is such an important part of this time in our grieving process. For now, during this time of solitude, observation, and reflection, it is necessary for us to begin to reflect on how we are reacting to the loss and to make judgments, decisions, and changes in relation to those reactions.

Castelnuovo-Tedesco reports that reminiscence "may even be positively related to freedom from depression and to personal survival." When we reminisce about the past, this way of thinking can actually provide consolation because it can serve "as buffer against loss and depression." Reminiscences confirm "that *something* actually took place," and that what remains "has enough substance to comfort and reassure." Through this way of thinking we find that our minds are " 'peopled.' The figures of the past are not just 'memories' or mere abstractions" but are still present and available to us in certain ways: as sources of awareness, learning, and wisdom; as reminders of goals and ideals; as part of the context we have for making decisions in the present.

ACKNOWLEDGING BOTH THE GOOD AND THE BAD

In the beginning, we are prone to go to extremes. We either idealize the person who is gone by turning her or him into a saint or we find fault—by painting this person as the blackest of villains. Perhaps we lived in a love-hate relationship with the person, not only experiencing alternating happiness and unhappiness but also having "contradictory and interdependent feelings of love and hate for the same person." Perhaps there was unresolved anger. Perhaps we even harbored fantasy death wishes about the person. Perhaps even now we have mixed feelings about the person's absence—in some ways we are glad, and in other ways we are sorry. We may also remember our own role in the relationship from a skewed standpoint, or we may attempt to gloss over unresolved issues.

Not to admit these ambivalent feelings—which are common to all of us—is to determine that we will never complete our mourning. Lily Pincus says, "The greatest obstacles in the way of making new relationships after bereavement and being able to live meaningfully again are ambivalent feelings about the deceased and the denial of one's own hating self. By denying [the] hate," the family therapist goes on to say, "the mourner impairs love, and with it the capacity to be in loving contact with other people."

I remember talking to a mother whose daughter had died in an automobile accident. The two of them had fought constantly because the daughter had dropped out of college just six credits shy of graduation, an act that infuriated her mother. After the young woman died, her mother would not admit that there had ever been an argument between them. And everyone else in the family skirted the issue also, being careful never to allude to the animosity and anger between the mother and daughter. The cost of this unwillingness to see the bad as well as the good in a past relationship? The mother—and the rest of the family—was caught in her mourning, unable to reach any kind of integration.

When we experience Observation, however, we have an opportunity to begin to find a balance. This is no small point, for Dr. Beverley Raphael warns: "Critical to the issue of resolving the loss is the way in which the average of the good and bad of human relationships is accepted and balanced." In fact, one of the benchmarks we have for measuring our progress in mourning is that we begin to remember our relationship with this person as a combination of the plus and the minus. "When the bereaved person remembers the dead person as the 'real' person he was to her," Dr. Raphael says, "then mourning is progressing successfully."

TAKING RESPONSIBILITY FOR OUR GUILT

One of the outcomes of looking at the past from a balanced point of view is, for many of us, a feeling of guilt. Human relationships are complex. We cannot live and relate to others without doing something that, in retrospect, we feel or know was wrong or harmful or insufficient or thoughtless. Therefore few of us—if we tell the truth—are free of at least some degree of guilt after a person is gone. The question to ask, then, is not "Did I do something that I should feel guilty about?" but, rather, "What responsibility am I taking for dealing with my guilt?"

Alfred Camus, the French essayist and novelist, suggests a reason that we may fixate on our guilt instead of working through it. He says, "A world that can be explained, even with bad reasons, is a familiar world." We keep worrying our guilt, perhaps, as an attempt to keep the world sensible and understandable—a world that our actions do directly impact and cause things to go this way or that.

Dr. Colin Murray Parkes also helps us to understand this:

A major bereavement shakes confidence in [our] sense of security. The tendency to go over the events leading up to the loss and to find someone to blame even if it means accepting blame oneself is a less disturbing alternative than accepting that life is uncertain. If we can find someone to blame or some explanation that will enable death to be evaded, then we have a chance of controlling things. It is easier to believe that fate is indifferent, or rather positively malevolent, than to acknowledge our helplessness in the face of events.

We don't want to feel impotent, of course. Therefore we continue to search for causes and to assign blame and guilt. When my husband died, for instance, I felt responsible for his death because I was the one who wanted us to take up jogging—even though the coroner told me that Greg's death had nothing to do with the fact that he was running. I had to give up that guilt when I realized how much I belittled Greg by acting as if he didn't have full choice in the matter of whether he jogged or not. I also had to stop looking for something that "caused" his death—something he could have done something about, like jogging.

I also had another kind of paranoid guilt. Hadn't I caused Greg's death by wishing at times, after we had had a fight, that I wasn't married to him, even that he would go away? The turnaround in this situation came to me one day when I was telling a friend how guilty I felt, and he said, "Well, if you had the power to cause his death by something you thought or said, why don't you bring him back by thinking or saying something now?" That question ended my preoccupation with grandiose imaginings that my thoughts had controlled my husband's life and, therefore, that I was somehow guilty of causing his death.

On the other hand, perhaps we have actually played a part in the event(s) that brought about the loss. We were driving the car too fast; we didn't give sufficient attention to clear symptoms of decline. "Wrong doings," Dr. Glen Davidson says, "cannot be addressed unless it is possible to identify what they are. . . . Rather than trying to suppress the feelings, mourners should express them in order to be able to discern what the limits of their responsibility are. . . . Only in clarifying what they should feel guilty about—either through omission or commission—can they know what they need to feel no guilt over."

It is our potential development that is at stake when we engage in authentic questions about our responsibility for what has happened. What we stand to discover are those things that will allow us to know ourselves, to rectify our behavior, and to make appropriate commitments for restitution that can bring feelings of completion.

Finally, the bottom line of any engagement with the subject of guilt is this: We must forgive ourselves and others. There is no alternative if we are to live fully and freely, if we are ever going to find a "new normal" through our grieving. So it isn't just a moral issue—it's a personal issue of our own well-being as well.

REALIZING THAT EARLIER LOSSES HAVE BEEN REACTIVATED

As if the loss we are currently mourning weren't enough, often we must deal simultaneously with the upset and pain of earlier losses that were never fully grieved. It's as if one loss calls up all losses. We think we are grieving for one thing, and we are actually grieving for another. It's hard to distinguish.

To sort out these losses is one of the tasks of the ways of thinking and acting that make up the experiences of Linking Past to Present. To the mourning we are doing now, we may have to add mourning for something that happened in the past. I remember talking to a young woman who was angry over the loss of her husband. Suddenly she began to cry. "It's the same way it was when I was fifteen, and my daddy died," she said. "I've got to make changes that I don't want now, just the way I did then."

"What kind of changes?"

"Since I was a little girl," she answered, "it had been set in our family that when I went to college I would go to my mother's alma mater. That was where I wanted to go more than any other place in the world. Then, when my father died, all that changed. There wasn't enough money for me to go away when I graduated from high school, so I had to attend the local public junior college. So much about my future life was determined by that necessary decision."

The young woman realized that although she had mourned her father's death, she had never mourned the "inconsequential" loss related to her choice of college. Yet the anger and sadness had been there for fifteen years. The similarity between her situation now— things she would have to give up, changes she would have to make as a result of the loss of her husband—stirred a deep memory. She was grieving for a seventeen-year-old who had been forced to attend a junior college as well as for a thirty-year-old woman who now had to make a new life without her husband.

RELEASING RESENTMENT AND ANGER

Almost everyone experiences anger when there is a significant loss of any kind—anger at the person who is gone, anger at ourselves, anger at "the system." But during this time of sifting through and reflecting, many people begin to see the importance of expressing their resentment and anger and becoming free of it. They see the damage they are doing to themselves, as well as to others, by continuing to harbor these negative feelings and they try to find a way to release them.

But this resolution does not happen for some—particularly those who feel they have been done wrong, treated unfairly, taken advantage of and used, abandoned. The other day, a social worker told me that the people she works with who seem never to find a new equilibrium after their losses are the ones who will not give up their anger and their bitterness. These individuals, she told me, determine everything about their lives in relation to its value as retaliation. And even if they choose to express their anger passively, the anger hampers their self-expression and sets the parameters of their lives. The cost, of course, is enormous: constant conflict, fear of living, withered existence, early aging, disease, and ill health.

Another kind of resentment and anger that is extremely difficult to overcome is that which results from acts of prejudice, ignorance, and callousness. Many people who have lost someone to AIDS know too well the damage such unconscionable behavior can inflict. But somehow, as hard as it may be, the anger and resentment need to be transformed. Not only do we have an opportunity to reflect on the cost to ourselves of harboring these self-devouring emotions but we have the chance to think about ways of using the energy present in our anger for good. Some people become involved in educational programs designed to alter society's attitudes toward a disease. Others help raise the money needed in the search for a cure. A friend who was an FBI agent decided that the best way for her to respond authentically to life was to resign her job and become a full-time artist. Recently, when I was privileged to attend one of my friend's gallery openings, I saw in all her pieces anger transformed into strong, powerful colors and images. I saw, to quote that lovely poem in the Old Testament book of Isaiah, beauty that had been made from ashes.

SHIFTING OUR FOCUS

Victor Frankl, a Viennese psychotherapist and a survivor of the Holocaust, once said, "Each man is questioned by life; and he can only answer life by *answering* for his life." As we observe and reflect as part of our grieving process, we have the opportunity to begin to answer for our own life. We begin, during this time, to direct our gaze to ourselves, to our reactions, to our role in determining how our mourning is progressing.

This is a time of hard appraisal. How am I behaving in the face of this loss? Am I in any way taking advantage of the situation to get sympathy or to avoid responsibility? Are there things I could do to make the situation better? Why am I not doing them? Do I really want things to be different? Or do I want to grieve forever, so that I can avoid living my life? Excuses are detected, fear pinpointed, strengths called forth and acknowledged.

"It often helps to write down one's thoughts," Dr. Richard Sackett says. This writing can take the form of a list, "with a column listing one's thoughts and feelings about the matter, and another column enumerating a rational response to each thought." Such writing makes it "easier to see when you are distorting things."

I think of a friend, Lucia, who made a commitment to answer for her own life after a painful loss. She reported:

For a long time I would just escape. With the radio in the car, with TV, with friends. But one day a customer gave me the key to her cabin on Camp Creek and said, "Go—stay as long as you like." I had no distractions there, so I began to sit, and I asked myself: What do I want to do?

How am I going to react to what has happened in my life? Wallow in self-pity? Have the courage to take new risk? How will I live my life?

Lucia said that she wrote down every thought that came into her mind. She also read *A Woman of Independent Means*, a novel that reminded her of the possibility of creating your own life, rather than just living as others want you to live. "It became clear to me," Lucia said, "that I wanted to go to my native country in Central America to see what I could see and then return to America to set up some kind of project that could help."

I must admit that when Lucia told me her story I recognized the authenticity of her decision, but I also thought that, as time went on, the realities of life as a single mother and a businesswoman would alter the form and scope of her dream. But imagine my surprise—and pleasure—when I saw this lead to an article in our local newspaper: "Lucia Adams is on a mission to provide Central American refugee children with the necessities of life." The article went on to state that Adams had formed Friends of Central American Children, a nonprofit organization established to collect clothing, food, and toys for refugee children. And accompanying the article was a photograph. There, among eight small Nicaraguan children in a refugee camp, stood my friend Lucia. A woman who had answered life, as Victor Frankl said, by answering for her own life.

THE CHOICE

There is a choice of real value when we are Linking Past to Present:

We can choose to look honestly.

This is a choice that requires enormous courage. It requires us to be alone with our thoughts; to focus on our responses rather than on the event of the loss itself; to remember in a balanced way rather than to remember only the good or only the bad; to admit the cost of guilt and anger and to be willing to forgive.

The choice to look honestly requires us to call a moratorium on what we may have been doing to "cope" with the loss—things like losing ourselves in our work, involving ourselves excessively in the care of others (usually others we perceive as being weaker than we are), running constantly, dwelling obsessively on the past, depending on sleep, drugs, alcohol, television, spending money, or partying to ease our pain. Instead of these, we choose now to grapple with the only questions that can lead to wisdom: What meaning does this loss have in my life? How am I choosing to respond to what has happened? How do I intend to act in the future? These are questions of import, questions of power.

WHAT WE NEED FROM FAMILY AND FRIENDS WHEN WE ARE LINKING PAST TO PRESENT

A young widow told me about her dilemma. A neighbor rushed to the back door one afternoon in a panic. "I've been calling and calling," she said to the young widow. "Are you all right? I saw your car in the driveway, but when you didn't answer the phone I just knew you were sick or depressed or something."

The young woman had to speak to her neighbor firmly: "You know, Alicia, that I told you I wanted time alone. And that I was not going to answer the telephone every time it rang. I've realized I need to be by myself more now. I'm finding time alone to be valuable."

"You just don't need me anymore," the neighbor said with a catch in her voice. "And it's terrible not to be needed."

Unfortunately, this neighbor was well intentioned but uninformed. She didn't know that the need to withdraw, to be alone, was a sign that her friend was progressing through her grieving in a healthy way. In similar situations, we must do as this widow did and take the initiative to ask for time alone if others do not understand, explaining that this is an important and necessary part of the process of our grieving.

But often we are ambivalent about the matter ourselves. What if people forget us while we are engaged in matters solitary? What if those with whom we like to do things get accustomed to our absence and stop thinking of including us?

Again, it is a matter of balance. For although we need time by ourselves to begin to make sense of our reaction to what has happened, to think toward the future, we also continue to need our family and friends. We do still get lonely, and we are often sad. We do not, then, mean to cut ourselves off from our family and friends; we seek to engage with them in ways that are appropriate to our needs now. Perhaps they can be a sounding board for the ideas or realizations that come to us when we are alone. Or they can offer suggestions that help us implement changes we are thinking about making. Or perhaps they can share our happiness at new possibilities we have seen. Family and friends may also be able to provide guidance and advice in areas about which, in our silence, we have discovered there is particular pain.

The solitude of these experiences is, I think, as much an attitude as it is an action. We can be alone in a crowd if we choose to be introspective and contemplative. This doesn't take the place of the time we need alone, of course, but an attitude of solitude can serve us anywhere and at any time. Because this is so, I think another role our family and friends play while we are Linking Past to Present is to be a source of things to read, do, and think about. What we couldn't hear months ago because we were experiencing the pain of separation or were engulfed in bleakness, we can now respond to: a book someone recommends, a place to go for inspiration, an activity that others have found beneficial. Often, a casual comment by another person will open up a whole new vista for us. A conversation can lead to entirely new areas of inquiry. A movie or a television program will spark ideas for the future. A discussion, a sermon, or an event will lead to a powerful reevaluation of our beliefs, our values, and our faith. So with the attitude of solitude—in addition to the actions—we can be both with our family and friends and separate from them.

I saw Armand DiMele, the grief therapist in New York, a few months after he had given me the "only number you dial is your own" piece of writing. This time I told him, "I have something for you." It was Richard Brautigan's short poem called "Karma Repair Kit: Items 1–4." After listing silence, sleep, and food, the poet gives his final instruction:

4.

Seeing Armand smile at this wordless instruction for how to repair one's life, I said, "This is to let you know that I got the message."

When we are Linking Past to Present, such is the wisdom of our experiences.

THE TERRAIN OF OUR ACTIVE GRIEVING

Life As It Was   *Life and Loss Integrated*
The Event of Loss   *Freedom from Domination of Grief*

IMPACT: Experiencing the unthinkable
CHOICE: To experience and express our grief fully

SECOND CRISIS: Stumbling in the dark
CHOICE: To endure with patience

OBSERVATION: Linking past to present
CHOICE: To look honestly

THE TURN: Turning into the wind
CHOICE: To replan and change our lives to include but not be dominated by the loss

RECONSTRUCTION: Picking up the pieces
CHOICE: To take specific actions

WORKING THROUGH: Finding solid ground
CHOICE: To engage in the conflicts

INTEGRATION: Daylight
CHOICE: To make and remake choices

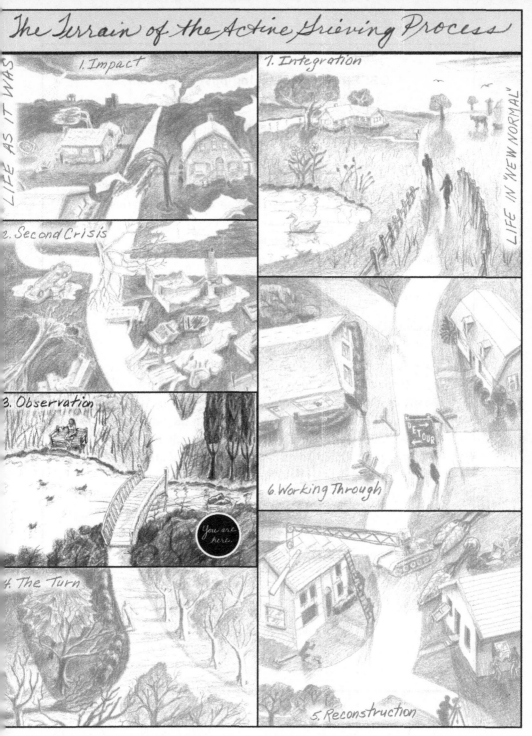

To remember: A map never tells us how to travel. A map does not determine that everyone travels the same route, moves at the same speed, shares a set itinerary. A map does not dictate, prescribe, or even describe an individual's movement. A map does, however, name. A map can help us find where we are when we think we are lost. A map shows possibilities and provides ideas for where else there is for us to go. At all times, however, every individual is the person holding the map.

OBSERVATION: Linking past to present

What Is Normal?

Reviewing both the positive and the negative in relation to the past
Gaining some distance
Dealing with anger, guilt, and blame; forgiving
Having insights that give meaning to what has been experienced
Taking stock, especially of reactions and responses to this loss
Considering priorities
Coming to rely more on oneself
Choosing quietness and solitude
Recognizing truths about your experience of grieving
Reminiscing, sifting through memories

What Can I Do?

Spend time alone, reflecting and reminiscing.
Look at photograph albums; relive events of the past.
Work through debilitating emotions like guilt, blame, and danger.
Go to places that were important to you and the person you've lost.
Think about things you might want to do in the future.
Consider what values, dreams, things that made meaning from the past you would like to bring forward into the present.
Make scrapbooks.
Write stories about the past that you can share with family and friends.
Recognize the value of solitude.

OBSERVATION: Linking past to present

My active choice?
To look honestly

4

THE TURN:

TURNING INTO THE WIND

Life can only be understood backwards.
It must be lived forwards.

Søren Kierkegaard

At Easter I went to Greece. Chrysoula, a friend I worked with, invited me to go home with her to visit her family. The flight was "cheaper than flying from Houston to Los Angeles," she promised, and we would be staying with her mother and father. After having been so financially irresponsible, I was worried about making ends meet. This, however, looked like something that I could do without wrecking my budget.

Chrysoula's parents live on the island of Crete, on the outskirts of the town of Kania, where her father, Mr. Bouyotopoulos, runs a small woodworking business. The rest of the family—uncles, aunts, cousins, grandfather—live in Vlatos, the ancestral village, high in the mountains at the end of the island. "A very simple life raising goats and tending olive trees," Chrysoula told me. "Nobody has much, but when I go there I find it hard to leave."

Being in Greece at Easter was a mixture of pleasure and pain. The pleasure was everywhere. . . . Walking in the strong sunlight on the baked dirt outside the Bouyotopoulos house. Picking bright orange kumquats off the trees and pressing their warm flesh through my teeth. Bicycling with Chrysoula and her mother to visit a monastery in the hills, where brown-robed monks served us schnapps in a stone-floored room as cool as a cellar. Hiking to the ruins of a temple—built by the Venetians centuries ago, many of its arches and bridges still standing—scrambling down steep rocky slopes to find caves with secret altars. Eating tiny fish fried whole, chicory salad, and homemade "flower cheese" that tasted like cake. Drinking Greek coffee and pouring the dregs on the plants growing in pots outside the door. Playing with new kittens. Watching the way the light came through the lace curtains that had been part of Mrs. Bouyotopoulos's dowry. So much pleasure.

Yet equal amounts of pain. I was full, almost to bursting. Only someone who knew me the way Greg did, who cared about what touched me, who loved to know what I thought and to tell me, in turn, what he thought—only Greg could make these experiences complete. Without someone to share them with, the place was almost too beautiful, the experiences too poignant.

There was Good Friday, when we went to the neighboring village of Gavalachori . . .

In the village everyone gathers in the churchyard for the ritual of ringing the bell commemorating the start of Easter weekend. One after another, women, men, and children walk solemnly up to the bell rope and pull it. When the last person is finished, Mr. Bouyotopoulos turns to me and says, "I will teach you to ring the bell. You must learn to ring the bell sorrowfully." There was something in the incongruity of ringing a bell sorrowfully that made some statement about life, but I couldn't quite put my finger on it. I needed to talk to Greg.

There was the religious procession through the streets of Kania the night before Easter . . .

Everyone rushes to get from one good vantage point to the next in order to catch a glimpse of the holy statues. Chrysoula's family and I run through the streets trying to catch up with the procession, a human chain, each of us holding the hand of the next person. As we turned corners and were pulled along by the momentum, I thought of the whip games I played when I was a child. When we finally caught up with the procession, we fell against each other in breathless pleasure. It was like the day Greg and I jogged up a ski lift and finally made it, leaning on each other when we got to the top because we were so tired, but laughing because we were so happy. But who here would understand, even if I told them how much this event reminded me of that earlier one?

There was a midnight mass . . .

We sat in a small village church built in the 1200s—dark, quiet, solemn. Sitting in the shadows, we watched the service as if it were a tableau being performed in the center of an illuminated circle. At home, following the mass, we ate the traditional Easter supper, which we did not finish until almost daybreak.

In bed later, I could not sleep. The service had been so simple and so beautiful; when I closed my eyes the images swam in front of me. And at the supper table I had felt that I was living the meaning of *family* and *tradition*. Without Greg, there was no one to talk to who would understand that every cell in my body was alive from the impact of these experiences.

Chrysoula's family spent every Easter with Mr. Bouyotopoulos's father in the ancestral village. Papa Bouyotopoulos, seventy-seven and a widower for many years, prided himself on his self-sufficiency. It was he who always prepared dinner every Easter, a family tradition.

During the three-hour ride to Vlatos, on treacherous roads that seemed to hang between the mountains and the sea, I sank into moroseness. Perhaps it was because my stay was almost over. Perhaps it was because the previous day had been so exuberant. Perhaps it was because this was the morning of the Resurrection, and in my life I felt no resurrection. Who can say what was the source of my feeling so low? All I knew was that I felt so alone and empty, as if I were being slowly but inexorably sucked into an immense black hole of nothingness.

Mr. Bouyotopoulos parked the car in the sandy square of the small village. "Papa lives farther up the mountain," Chrysoula told me. "We have to walk from here."

We twisted back and forth on the trail for almost an hour, walking silently, single file. Then, suddenly, the path ended. We were there. In front of us was a small yard surrounded by orange and lemon trees. A kitchen table, set with bowls ready for soup, occupied the center of the open area. "We can never all get into Papa's kitchen," Chrysoula said, laughing. "So we always eat out under the trees."

Papa must have heard us coming, for when we stepped into the yard he was standing at the table breaking eggs. "When you make lamb and rice soup," Mrs. Bouyotopoulos explained, "the egg yolks always have to be whipped at the very last minute."

"Oh, and when you taste it . . ." Chrysoula added, turning her eyes toward the heavens.

Two widowed aunts, who also must have heard our footsteps on the rocky path, came into the yard simultaneously. They were dressed all in black, even to the babushkas that covered their heads. The aunts rushed to the orange trees and picked a piece of fruit for each of us. "Sit . . . sit down and eat . . . this will refresh you. Jacob's soup will soon be ready."

We ate the soup, while the aunts worried about us. Papa was busy removing the young goat from the spit, where it had been roasting at the edge of the yard. He brought it to the table and began the carving. When we finished the soup, we ate the succulent meat with its crisp, almost burned edges pressed between pieces of thick, coarse bread and washed it down with pungent homemade retsina.

As I sat there—simple, satisfying food in front of me, hospitable, generous people around me—I felt the blackness lifting. I looked across at Papa and his two sisters, each bereft of a partner but clearly relishing being alive. I looked down at the sunbaked earth beneath my feet and then up toward the blue patches of sky that showed through the orange and lemon trees. Suddenly, I felt a shift occur in my body; there was an actual physical alteration. Something released inside me. This shift was immediately followed by an inexplicable sense of well-being, of calmness and serenity. The vague foreboding—the sense that "something is not right; something bad is about to happen," which had been a constant presence in my life since Greg's death—had left me. Instead, sitting there as if in a round of sky and trees and light and earth, I felt in touch with something elemental, strong, ineffable. In touch with what at that moment seemed to be all one would ever need to know, with something deeply healing.

After dinner, it became clear that Papa had plans. "He wants us to go with him up the mountain—he has something he wants to show us," Chrysoula told me. We followed the spry old man, who was carrying two wooden buckets filled with water, as he led us to a path that seemed to go straight up the mountain. We climbed for many minutes.

Then we turned a final curve in the path. Ahead was what Papa had brought us to see. Planted in the large clearing were hundreds of tiny oak seedlings. Row after row of little trees lined the steep hillside, narrow furrows plowed between them. It was Papa's forest. He proceeded carefully to water every tiny tree.

I stood there in amazement, looking first at Papa and then at the hillside of seedlings. I could imagine the amount of work this project required: how the old man's back must hurt from all the bending and how his arms must ache from hauling water up the mountain.

"Why would he do this?" I asked myself. "This man is seventy-seven years old. He cannot possibly live long enough to see these seedlings become a forest." Chrysoula's mother seemed to read my mind, for she turned and said, "Papa has planted these trees as part of a reclamation program sponsored by an environmentalist organization active here on the island. 'For the land,' he says. 'So the family will always have trees on the land.' "

As we walked back to our car at the end of the visit, I thought about this all the way down the path. Seeing Papa Bouyotopoulos's forest had deeply stirred me. I didn't quite know what it was that had touched me so, but it had something to do with making a contribution that will live on after you, something about looking out at life instead of always obsessively peering inward. I knew the experience had made an opening in my thinking, because for the first time since Greg's death I found myself considering the idea that there might be projects worth doing in life, commitments worth making.

I now looked forward to going home. I was enthusiastic. It was going to be the start of a new era.

But that wasn't how it happened.

When I returned, instead of energy I experienced a new depth of darkness. It was just like the weeks right after Greg's death. I was afraid to be in the house by myself again. I lost my appetite and couldn't sleep. I cried easily, and I had no desire to go to work. The worst part of it was that I had no way of understanding this setback. I knew that I had made progress in grieving. Why, then, was this happening?

Confused and distraught, I called Armand DiMele in New York. "Now, just exactly when was it that Greg died?" Armand asked. "I know it was last summer, but what was the date?"

"July 2," I replied, just a little aggravated. I couldn't see what the date of Greg's death had to do with how I was feeling now.

"I'm looking at the calendar," Armand went on. "It's been nine months . . ." He paused as if I would find that useful information. Then he continued, "For some uncanny reason, people often have a severe relapse nine months after a loss. It happens often enough that researchers even write about it. So if you consider that you may be experiencing the nine-months-since-death syndrome, and if you add to that the fact that you spent Easter in Greece, where you participated over and over in activities associated with death and resurrection . . ."

"And with a family who has lived in the same place as a unit for hundreds of generations," I added, beginning to see the picture.

"Then you come back," he went on, "with the idea that you would start life newly—"

"But what I found," I interrupted, "was the same old empty house and a pattern of life that was no different."

"Enough to make one feel down, isn't it?" he asked.

"It feels just like that day," I said—and as I spoke I began to experience an almost suffocating fear—"when I realized that I'd have to make new patterns for my life, like new veins for blood to flow in. But when I did then was to fall to pieces and spend months living in desperation. I don't want to do that again."

"You won't have to," Armand said. "You're much stronger. Now you'll be able to look at what you need to do more quickly and more directly, and do it."

Still feeling in low spirits, I returned to work. The nights were especially difficult. I kept dreaming that I was driving on what I thought were open highways, only to find, at the end of every road I took, the wall of a heavy concrete underground bunker. When I was with people, I felt separate from them, as if I were encased in a shield of plastic. I was present, but I was not present.

One evening Ann, a neighbor, asked me over for dinner. While she was making the picante sauce and her husband was putting the fajitas on the grill, I went into the dining room to set the table. "Add a couple of extra plates," Ann called from the kitchen. "Beth and Joe are joining us. In fact, they should be here any minute." I went to the hutch to get the silverware and the dishes.

I put five brown ceramic plates down on the white linen table-cloth. Suddenly, the place where the sixth plate should have been laid stood out so prominently that it actually startled me. As I stood there, looking at the blank spot on the table, anger welled up in waves from my stomach to my throat. I felt hot tears in my eyes, and my nose was stinging. "I must get out of here," I said to myself, "before somebody comes in and sees me." I could hear Beth and Joe arriving as I ran from the dining room to the empty den to take refuge.

I grabbed a pencil off the desk and began writing furiously. The words seemed just to appear on the page in front of me. In rapid-fire progression, I wrote:

Tonight
The 6th place at the table.
Empty,
Like a socket with no eye.
I hate it.

Wipe It in Your Face
The 6th place at the table.
Shouting, "You're by yourself.
Ha, ha, ha, ha, ha, ha
Ha, ha, ha, ha, ha, ha
You can't come and get me."

Golgotha
The 6th place at the table.
White mark of the cross.
No way to ignore it.
Even a bowl of salad doesn't help, really.

Say What?
The 6th place at the table.
What kind of plate can a ghost eat from?

In Your Honor
There really should have
Also been
Flowers
                    And butterflies
                              And stars
                                        And rainbows
At that 6th place at the table.

Delphi
A praise offering.
That's what should have been
At that 6th place at the table.

Celebration
To commemorate your release
To the cosmic playground
Airy Ferris wheels
Ethereal merry-go-rounds
And plenty of room for washing your car.
Who needs that limiting, earthly, binding 6th place at the table?

When the last word had been written on the page, I felt light, unburdened. I sat for several seconds wondering what had happened to me, and then I thought I understood. As I wrote those lines, I had stopped thinking only about myself and my loss and had begun to think about Greg. What was good for him? What did he deserve? What would honor him? I had changed from being Greg's angry critic and enemy to being his champion and friend. And I had located him somewhere in a place where he had some other form and was happy. I went down the hall and joined my friends in the kitchen. No one had even had time to miss me.

During the following weeks, I turned my attention to several things that, up until that time, I had been avoiding. I wrote the remarks to be delivered at a regional conference, where the first Gregory Cowan Memorial Teaching Award would be given: "Tonight, with Karen Davis presenting this award, there is evidence of the best kind of immortality. Greg's dedication to students and to teaching is re-created in Karen, one of his students. He would not want a better legacy." I decided how to spend the money that colleagues and friends had contributed to a memorial fund at the university. I would invite the poet William Stafford, who had been Greg's friend, to come from Oregon to present a special evening of poetry and to honor ten of Greg's graduate students by giving them gold Cartier writing pens. As I worked on these activities, I could see that there were many ways in which Greg would continue to be a part of the lives of the people who knew him even though he was not present. It was a different way of thinking.

The first anniversary of Greg's death was approaching. I had read many books warning that birthdays, anniversaries, holidays, and the anniversary of the event itself were dangerous times: You could almost count on having a relapse in your grieving. I thought at first that I'd do whatever I could to avoid paying attention to the anniversary. Perhaps my sister and I would go on a trip. Or I would go and stay with my parents.

But finally I decided not to do any of these things. "I know I'm capable of facing whatever I need to face," I said to myself. "I will go to work as usual and perhaps have some friends over for dinner. But I'm not going to run from Texas to Tennessee to try to escape this anniversary."

I continued to talk to myself. "Yes, you'll be able to do it," I said confidently. "You know by now that you don't die from pain, even if you don't like it. As bad as it is, you do live through it."

So I went to work as usual on the day Greg died one year earlier. With a group of other professors, I spent most of the morning discussing a possible exchange program with a dignitary from the Middle East.

It must have been 2:00 P.M. when I arrived home. The light was flashing on the answering machine. I pushed the button.

"Hey, Sis, are you ready to be an aunt?"

I could hear the excitement in my brother's voice.

"Your niece, Sarah, was born a couple of hours ago. She weighs four pounds seven ounces and is seventeen inches long. She'll have to stay in the hospital for a little while, but basically she's okay. She has all her essential parts."

I sat down on the couch, dumbfounded. My brother's first baby was here! And she had arrived six weeks early. Born on the very day Greg had died twelve months earlier. A birth and a death—both unexpected—had occurred in our family on the same afternoon. This was amazing! On a day that our family had expected to be sad and lonely, we would now also be cheerful and happy. Every year this particular afternoon would always be a reminder: There is exit from life, and there is *also* entrance.

I suppose I needed something to deflect me from the intensity of the moment. So I picked up the magazine the gentleman from the Middle East had given me a few hours earlier and began to flip through it while my mind tried to accommodate what had happened.

As I turned the pages, a page of poems caught my eye, and I began to read. When I came to the second poem, I could hardly believe what was before me. It was as if the poem had been written for today, for my family. It was as if the gentleman had given me the magazine just for this occasion.

A Song

I sing a sad song—
sadder than the sunset's walk
in the city streets;
I feel grief in my blood
flowering from some hidden spring;
my friends, we die—
we sail into the end
without pausing to say goodbye;
our dreams, hopes, loves
come to an end
like footprints in the sand
chewed by the desert.

I sing a happy song—
happier than the sunrise
on another shore;
happier than the smile
a birthday-child smiles;
happier than a new kiss;
I feel a stubborn joy
conquering my blood;
my friends, we live—
we live each instant
to its deepest cores, collect

its treasures, trifle with its secrets,
lave ourselves within its ecstasy.

Of death and life I shall
a happy/sad sad/happy song
    sing . . .
        Shaikh Ghazi Al-Qusabi

When I finished reading, I thought, "*The cycle of life*. You hear that phrase; you understand with your mind the truth of it. But then comes the day when you *know* what the words mean. You *know* with your whole being."

There are some things that you never understand, however—things that defy all logical explanation. The note from my mother, written on the morning of the anniversary of Greg's death, arrived a few days later. I stood at the kitchen counter, reading:

Dear Sister,

    We're thinking of you this morning and pray that everything works out well . . . An almost unbelievable instance happened yesterday! As we were going to church last night, about 6:30—way before dark—when we got to the exact spot where Greg fell, there came a young man jogging, facing us on the exact side of the road. As we passed him, you could see that he had a dark beard, close-cut like Greg's. Was such a feeling, seeing him right at that spot, resembling Greg so much. Neither of us said a word and haven't mentioned it since. Seems almost sacred-like. Don't mean to make you sad, just wanted to mention what a coincidence it was! Especially right at this time.

    Daddy is in the garden seeing if it is too wet to pick beans. We had a little rain yesterday.

                Lots of love,
                Mother

I was packing a box to put into storage. As I reached for a piece of the newspaper I was crushing to protect the breakables, an article caught my eye. THE WORDS OF JEAN-PAUL SARTRE, the headline read. Melvin Maddocks of the *Christian Science Monitor* had written a perspective on the philosophy of Sartre, who had died a few days before the article was written.

I started reading. It is hard to anticipate that sitting in your den packing boxes can be the occasion for a life-changing epiphany, but it happened. As I read, one sentence jumped out at me. A character in one of Sartre's plays had said:

"Freedom crashed down on me and swept me off my feet."

When I read this, I finally understood the aftermath of Greg's death: Freedom *had* crashed down on me.

Until Greg died, my life had a particular purpose and direction. After he died, I was free—within the bounds of my abilities and my resources—to do anything, live anywhere, act in any way. But this was a freedom that I despised, a freedom that I didn't want, a freedom that frightened me. For this freedom was also a form of emptiness, of nothingness. The freedom provided only openness; it offered no structure. And without structure, without some specific shape, I was dangling out in nowhere. I experienced, as Sartre's character said, a freedom that had "swept me off my feet."

I don't know why, but just understanding what I had experienced, just understanding what I had been running from, why I had been so tentative, so uncertain, made me feel stronger. I think I realized, perhaps for the first time, that I had reacted in a normal way to a frightening condition of human existence. Greg's death had altered everything that mattered to me; and the freedom that resulted—"the absence of necessity or constraint in choice or action"—had confronted me.

The article also summarized the philosopher's credo:

"Let us say that one can improve one's biography. . . . There is always a possibility for the coward to stop being cowardly. . . . [There is always the] possibility of being a hero. . . . The self is a choice; we are what we do."

I was responsible for my life, and it would be choices I made—not the circumstances in which I found myself—that would determine the kind of life I had in the future. There are hardly words to describe that moment. I felt an enormous energy. There was something I could do! I did not have to be a victim of what had happened. I did not have to resign myself to a sublevel existence. I did not have to have as my highest goal "accepting and living with" what had happened to me. It was true that I could do nothing about what had happened, but I could do everything about how I continued to react to what had happened. I could act on the realization that I had the power to make choices about my future, and then I could make the choices that best served.

From that point on, I held my grief in a larger context. I now felt a sense of *possibility*. I didn't know the context for this philosopher's credo; perhaps the way I interpreted those few quotations in the newspaper was completely in error. But it didn't matter. In reading them, I had seen a new future for myself, and that was the interpretation that mattered.

I don't know what possessed me. I was walking across the university campus when I got the idea. I would go over to the president's office and ask if I could work for him! No matter that I didn't know him and had seen him only once in the three and a half years I'd been on the faculty. We could get to know each other! No matter that no professors worked in the office of the president. I could be the first! No matter that I wasn't exactly sure what I would offer to do for him. I'd make a list! The more I thought about it, the more excited I became. The job would be perfect. It would give me something new and challenging to do at the same time that I remained a part of the university.

That afternoon, I called and made an appointment. As soon as I got off the phone, I began to make my list and to decide what to wear that would look "administrative."

"President Tyler," I said when we had completed the introductory amenities, "I'd like to come to work for you. Here's a list of ten things I can do." Balancing a cup of coffee in one hand, I reached awkwardly across the president's desk with the other.

In the short time it took the president to read the list, I lived a dozen scenarios. He would laugh and find the whole thing ridiculous. He would feel sorry for me and be as nice as possible while he summoned his assistant to see me out the door. He would be embarrassed at having to find a way to refuse me. I wouldn't like to work here anyway. How did I ever come up with such a harebrained idea in the first place?

Then he looked up. "Professor," he began, "there are four or five things on this list that I have been losing sleep over. I can see how you might be a help in these areas. Give me a couple of weeks to see what I can do; I believe we'll be able to work something out."

And that's how I started taking action and being responsible for the direction my life would take. That's how I launched a new future.

These are the kinds of thoughts and experiences we have when we are Turning Into the Wind. They can be described as a series of realizations, understandings, actions, and commitments that allow us to establish a longer-term and larger framework for the grieving process. We shift our focus. We experience a change in perspective. It becomes clear that a new plan—one that includes the loss we have experienced but is not dominated by it—is required for our life.

Up to now it was important, life-and-death important, to acknowledge and experience all the ways in which the loss hurt us. We, appropriately, spent much of our time looking inward. By this point in our movement through our grieving, we have expressed—and continue to express—our grief fully; we have suffered and endured the dark times of sadness and even despair; we have sifted through and reminisced about the past; and we have now arrived at a new place. We can now examine our new situation and consider how to meet it. We, in effect, begin to redefine ourselves and to make the necessary plans for a new future.

Dr. John Bowlby puts it this way:

> Because it is necessary to discard old patterns of thinking, feeling and acting before new ones can be fashioned, it is almost inevitable that a bereaved person should at times despair that anything can be salvaged and, as a result, fall into depression and apathy. Nevertheless, if all goes well this phase may soon begin to alternate with a phase during which he starts to examine the new situation in which he finds himself and to consider ways of meeting it. This entails a redefinition of himself as well as of his situation. . . . Until redefinition is achieved no plans for the future can be made. . . . Once this corner is turned a bereaved person recognizes that an attempt must be made to fill unaccustomed roles and to acquire new skills.

We don't experience Turning Into the Wind automatically. We don't do this because time passes and "heals all wounds." Turning Into the Wind does not "naturally follow." Dr. Bowlby reminds us that it is not with our emotions and feelings that we make this commitment to redefine ourselves and our place in the world around us. This is a *cognitive act*, he says, something that happens in our thinking and speaking. We commit to making the longer-term adjustments that are so essential to a satisfactory outcome for our mourning because we *decide* to do so.

I remember an ad sponsored by Shearson Lehman/American Express that ran in the *New York Times* and the *Wall Street Journal.* "COMMITMENT," the bold headline read. Then these words followed: "Commitment is what transforms a promise into reality. It is the words that speak boldly of your intentions. And the actions which speak louder than words. . . . Commitment is the stuff character is made of; the power to change the face of things. It is the daily triumph of integrity over skepticism."

This message, it seems to me, reflects the kind of thinking and behavior we are called on to do at this point in the mourning process. It is the "words that speak boldly of [our] intentions." It is with "the daily triumph of integrity over skepticism" that we find ourselves making the Turn, a momentous act that in its very nature is an act of creation.

During these experiences we come to understand Dr. Anthony Storr's assertion that "mourning is . . . a long drawn out mental process leading to an eventual change in attitude." We make the choice to begin to dismantle old ways of thinking and behaving that are no longer appropriate—that could only keep us caught in some kind of permanent "grieving limbo"—so that we can create new ways of thinking and behaving that are useful, that will allow us to create a satisfying life in the future.

As I have talked with people whose choices moved them through the challenging process of grieving, I have been awed by their heroism. They have been willing to feel the shock, pain, and tearing asunder of their early grief. They have been willing to endure the dark times when life seemed hopeless, full of sadness and despair. They have stepped aside to look at their own responses to their loss and to think about what could and could not be brought from the past into the present. And, in being willing at the time that was right for each of them to begin Turning Into the Wind, they have had conversations with themselves and have had the willingness to begin to make the hard changes that their situation in life requires of them. When I asked these men and women to describe the insights and actions that characterized the Turn, they related the following experiences.

RECOGNIZING THAT YOU HAVE SURVIVED

A young widow speaks:

You know, there's really no making sense of the loss itself. To keep on attempting to figure out why him on that particular day or why the valves weren't capped on the machine or why he didn't have his hard hat on . . . that's useless. There's just no sense to be made of it.

But I see that there is sense to be made out of my experience of the loss. I am beginning to make sense out of who I am and how I feel about that. I'm beginning to sort out what's worth keeping out of the experience, what's worth recognizing about myself and about life, and what's not.

For instance, one thing that has come to me in the last few days is the realization that I survived. I survived, and I really actually am turning out well in the face of such a traumatic event. I didn't die from it. I didn't go permanently crazy. I didn't kill myself. I did things, yes, that hurt me. But that's relatively minor compared to the part of me that was strong enough to endure a process like that.

Now what I have to do is make a stronger identification with that important part of myself. I don't think you get that kind of training when you grow up. You have to decide on your own to cultivate the part of yourself that is strong.

Redefining Oneself

A man relates:

I'm not sure that this loss is anywhere near complete, but I do feel that I have definition. I am Mark Allen, a stockbroker, a friend to a lot of people, and I'm the father of a couple of children. I'm a person who can now maintain a nice household, who fixes some very good meals, who is beginning to write again, who is getting some national recognition in my field. My life has started forming again, from a liquid to a solid, so to speak. And, incidentally, the solid turns to liquid every once in a while. So I'm not without my troubles and everything is not settled. But I am beginning to see where I am and where I have come from.

Making Distinctions

A widow states:

It is very educational to be left behind. You realize that there are some things you can do something about and some things you cannot. You can decide what kind of clothes you want to wear; you can pick a house to live in; you can decide what kind of career you're going to have. You are in charge of your everyday life.

But there's a higher level of existence, and I think when you've experienced loss you come to realize that you don't have control of that higher level. You realize that at that level you have to be prepared to roll with the punches. If something happens and you didn't plan it, it's still a part of life. You have to decide if you are going to be a survivor or not. You have to choose to continue making choices on the everyday level, no matter how enticing it might be to throw your hands up and quit because you don't control the higher level.

I recognized this so clearly some time after Ash's death. I told my son, "Look, we weren't killed; we didn't die. We're alive, and we've got to stay alive. We can't just go into a cocoon and shut ourselves up, because we won't be able to exist like that. We have to decide to be a part of life. We have to make decisions in all the parts of life that we have any control over."

RECOGNIZING CONTINUITY

A widow recalls:

We took Akio's ashes back to Japan the year after he died. That was when I got a sense that life itself has continuity—in spite of the death of individuals. We went to central Japan, to the place where Akio's parents are buried. Actually, it's the family graveyard, and there's a temple that has been the family temple for centuries.

We had a burial service at this family temple, and then we walked to the graveyard and the Buddhist priest put the ashes in the stone. I felt a deep calm after the ceremony. For me, Akio was now part of that temple that had been there for centuries and, as far as I know, will be there for centuries long after I am gone. I got a real sense that life started before we were born and will go on afterward. For me, this was very peaceful.

When I got home, I found myself building on that sense of continuity. It became very clear to me that I wanted to keep up the Japanese side of my life. I am an American, but Akio and I were married for over twenty-five years, and I have been greatly enriched by the Japanese people and culture.

So I said to myself when I got back from Japan. "I'm not going to lose all that." I read about Japanese things. I keep myself abreast of the culture. This is providing me with continuity.

Making a Decision to Turn from Loss to Living

A senior citizen whose sister died asserts:

It has taken me a while, but I've decided that life is worth doing anyway. Because you have to live until you die, so you might as well perk up. Attitude is everything. The hardest thing to do after a loss is to know when to say, "I've grieved enough." It's hard to time. But you do get to the place where you know you have a choice. I mean, if you're a living, breathing, semiconscious person, you realize finally that you have to make the choice to have enough nerve to do something.

Deciding Not to Be a Victim

A woman told this story:

One day I said to myself, "Sally, you've pined long enough. Get up from this couch and make yourself some clothes. You've got to go out and get a job." So I began to sew. As soon as I had a couple of outfits made, I decided it was time to start looking for work. I had contacted my friends and said, "If you hear of anything, let me know." So now it was "Sally, get ready. It's time to take yourself out into the world because no one else is going to do it for you."

Acknowledging Responsibility for Being Happy

A mother says:

You can't drag a ghost and be happy. That's a choice we all finally make. At some point after our daughter died, I realized I was operating on a dead-end street. I had been dragging the past around and feeling sorry for myself and waiting for someone else to do something that would make me feel happy again. But I've come to see that nobody else is responsible for your happiness. Nobody! Not your husband, not your parents, not your children, not your best friend—only you. Every tub must sit on its own bottom.

And that goes double for anybody who wants to be happy after losing someone. Your state of mind finally comes down to your choice, no matter what has happened to you. And I'm not saying that tomorrow I won't revert to "Here I am, little Janinne, saying, 'Poor me.'" But I can assure you that I may go ahead and feel sorry for myself for a little while, but then I'll do something to get myself out of it. I choose not to stay miserable, and I know I'm the only one who can do anything about it.

Recently, I was lonesome and blue, missing Meredith terribly. So I got out my knitting needles and started knitting a sweater for her boyfriend. I knitted and cried into my knitting. I put all my love for Meredith into that sweater for a few hours, and I got myself out of feeling sorry for myself.

My husband said to me when he saw me crying, "Go ahead and cry. That's okay. Because I know you well enough to know that you're going to get tired of feeling this way before twenty-four hours are up. And that you're going to do something about it." Isn't that a wonderful attitude for a husband to have?

UNDERSTANDING THERE IS A NEW FORM FOR THE RELATIONSHIP

A woman recalls:

One day I realized that it had been almost three years since Martin died, and I still had so much of his stuff everywhere. I had gathered up a lot of his things and put them in one place upstairs, and there they were, staring at me every time I went in that direction.

Suddenly, I had the urge to get rid of all this stuff. The urge shocked me, but that was what I really felt like doing. I asked myself, "What are you trying to do—forget Martin? Pretend he never existed?" But that wasn't it. All those things belonged to a Martin I had loved and who had lived in this house. And the Martin I loved now was different: he was not present; he did not need old college notes and service-station records. I knew I would always be close to Martin but that closeness was not related to holding on to his things.

So I went into the living room and made a fire in the fireplace. Then I started burning everything that would burn. It was a chilly day, but can you imagine how hot a fire gets when you're burning years of accumulation? I finally had to turn on the air conditioner.

I think if you're going to do something like this, you should probably do it in private. Because it is only you who knows why you are doing this. It is only you who knows that the relationship you now have with the dead person doesn't rely on objects or things for its reality.

FINDING OTHER WAYS TO RELATE

A son tells this story:

I keep my dad with me symbolically through this old truck. One of the things Dad and I had always worked on together was old trucks. That was a big part of our lives. He'd cruise the countryside and find trucks sitting in people's backyards—old clunkers, it didn't matter—and he'd make them an offer: "Hey, I'll give you fifty dollars to haul that old thing off." And they'd say, "Sure, get rid of it." He'd bring the old thing home; and he and I would tinker with it, get it running, and then sell it. Once in a while, we painted them. We painted one bright orange with green bumpers and called it the Pumpkin.

I always wanted one of those trucks, but we were never in the position for me to keep one. Now, when this truck came along Dad and I agreed that it was the best truck we had ever run into. Dad bought it from a rancher up around Sacramento. I don't know why the man sold it. Everything on it was original. So we kept it. When I got ready to leave home, I said to Dad, "If you ever get in a position where you need to sell this truck, you tell me, because I'll find the money somewhere to buy it so we can keep it." It never got to that point, though; and when he died the truck was about the only thing he had left, and I got it. It's a family heirloom, and I feel an obligation to keep it as long as it exists.

So now, when I go to teach my classes at the university, I drive this truck every day. When the transmission jumps out of gear, which it invariably does at about forty miles per hour, I laugh and think, "Oh, that's Daddy saying, 'You're going too fast for this old truck—slow down.'" This old truck keeps me in touch with him. I get in here and talk to him. I don't "talk" to him, really, but I feel close to him when I'm in the truck. It's the kind of connection that I can take with me into the future.

EXPLORING FOR A BELIEF SYSTEM THAT WORKS

A woman said:

I don't know what I believe in anymore. Everything I thought was true in the past now seems suspect. But the other day I did have an insight. I was asking a friend of mine what she thought was in the hereafter, and she said she didn't know, that she had her ideas and these ideas gave her life meaning but that certainly didn't mean they were accurate. She said, "Whatever the hereafter is like, it's going to be completely different from this world. So I relish every day I live on the planet because I want to know as much as possible about life here. I want to do everything there is to do here, and learn everything there is to learn." As soon as she said this, I felt an intense desire to do the same. I realized that this life I have now—as up and down as it may be—is something to be explored, to be known. My attitude really changed as a result of that conversation. I had been moping around, halfway sick, for months, but I decided I didn't want to be sick even one day now! I don't want to miss anything.

RECOGNIZING WHAT IS GOOD FOR YOU

A woman tells this story:

In getting myself pointed toward a new life, I've had to get rid of some old friends. I know this may sound negative, or maybe even tacky, but there are some people who are happy only when things are bad. They enjoy the drama of hard times. I have a few friends who fall into this category. If I'm feeling low and terrible, they want to be right there; but if I'm feeling up and happy, they keep saying things like "I know you really miss David" or "I'm sure glad to see you having a good day—I know it's rough for you," etc., etc.

Well, by now I want to move on, and I think that subconsciously they don't want me to. The other day I ran into a friend at the grocery store, and she said, "Oh, I never see you anymore—you never call." I just stopped my cart right there and said to her, "You know, Karen, you're really a sweet person. I'm fond of you. I'd like always to be your friend. But I haven't called you because all you want to do is talk about the past." Then she interrupted me. "Oh," she said. "I know it's just too painful." And I interrupted her and said, "No, Karen, it's not that it's painful. It's just boring."

RECOGNIZING THAT PROFESSIONAL HELP IS NEEDED TO MOVE FORWARD

A young widow with two children reports:

One morning I realized that I wasn't able to love my children. I was just getting through the day with them the same way I was just getting through the day at work—fifteen minutes at a time. On this particular morning, I realized that I had been coping by shutting off all feelings, including my feelings for my children.

So I made the choice to take my life insurance money—which I was guarding—and get professional help. This was one of the scariest things I had ever done. First of all, people I know just don't go to psychiatrists. It was like an admission that you're crazy. You just don't do it. And, second, it seemed like so much money!

But I was determined to do whatever it took to get back in touch with my love for my children. I said, "I'll go Monday, Tuesday, Wednesday, Thursday, and Friday if it's necessary. I'll tell that psychiatrist everything that's happened since kindergarten if she wants to know!" That's how willing I was to do anything to return to the land of the living.

What I've discovered by getting this help is that I already had many of these problems and they just came to light now. I'm working on these problems now, and already I can see a difference. I've made the choice to change and not live the way I did in the past. Going and asking for help was the first step to my new life.

DECIDING TO DO SOMETHING THAT IMPLIES RESPONSIBILITY FOR THE FUTURE

A widower recalls:

One day I decided, "Hey, I'm sick and tired of eating in restaurants. I'm not willing to keep on running away from myself and from learning how to do things on my own. Tonight I'm going to fix round steak and cream gravy!"

So I stopped by Kroger's and picked up a beautiful piece of round steak—a little expensive and far too much for one person. But I'd just eat the leftovers, I decided. "I'll have parsley boiled potatoes that you can put gravy over, a fresh loaf of bread, and a little salad—lettuce, tomato, some mayonnaise on it," I said to myself.

I started preparing all of this as soon as I got home. I was really anxious. I cooked the steak, cut up the salad, got the potatoes to boiling. Then I thought, "Oh, my God, I don't know how to make gravy." I'd tried when Laura was alive, and it always came out in one lump instead of liquid. "Well," I thought, "it's time for you to learn. If you're going to have gravy, that's what you got to do. What you gonna do, otherwise—invite Mama down from Oklahoma to cook it for you?"

I began. "Settle down and think about it. If you do this first and this second, it's probably going to turn out all right. Do it carefully, do it slowly, take your turn, learn how to do it." I ended up making the most beautiful pot of cream gravy you've ever seen. The only thing was that I made too much, but I saved it and put it on my toast the next morning.

You know, I found myself to some extent—I found this independence, this ability to live on my own—through cooking that cream gravy. After I made the gravy, I took on an even bigger project—doing my own washing. I had always divided everything into man's work and woman's work. Now it was all my work. Riding the crest of the wave of gravy success, I said, "I'm going to do some hot-water washing with some bleach. I'm going to get my things really white."

So I read the instructions on the washing machine and the instructions on the bleach bottle. I put all that information together, and I did a wash and then I did a dry. I remember that when I took those things out of the dryer it was dark. I reached in and bundled them all up and took them to the living room, where I had been listening to music, and put them on the sofa to fold them.

This was another mark of success—success at taking responsibility for putting yourself together again. You know, all the king's horses and all the king's men couldn't do it, so how can you? You don't think that finding out how to put yourself together again consists of things like washing clothes and making cream gravy.

CRITICAL CONSIDERATIONS WHEN WE ARE TURNING INTO THE WIND

Turning Into the Wind seems like such an obvious—and life-affirming—development that we wonder, "Why do people find it so hard? Why do some people actually choose not to do it?" The answers to these questions lie in the complexities of finding a way to honor and hold the past and, at the same time, to commit to stepping boldly toward a new—and unknown—future.

FINDING AN APPROPRIATE FORM FOR THE RELATIONSHIP

I remember wondering after Greg died, "How do I love a dead person?" My feelings for this man were as strong and deep as they had ever been, and the fact that he wasn't present to receive my affection only intensified my attachment.

In his book *Loss and Change,* Peter Marris talks about this dilemma. If the very purpose and meaning of our lives are integrally connected with this lost person, how can we let him or her go? Would that not denigrate the central role that person played in our lives? And if we were able to let that person go, wouldn't such an act devalue what he or she meant to us and, by association, devalue all our relationships? And would we not be callous people if relationships could be changed so easily?

Of course, one way to solve the dilemma is to keep the person in our minds—and as, much as possible, in our lives—the way they were in the past. We see this behavior in the extreme in Queen

Victoria's legendary order that her late husband's shaving articles be laid out every morning as if he were still alive. We see it in a less extreme fashion in the lives of those people who, two or three years after a person's death or departure, have made few if any changes that indicate the person is no longer present.

The fact that we can understand the impetus for this kind of behavior doesn't make the behavior any less debilitating. No matter how hard we attempt to keep those we've lost present in our lives—through such means as talking about them as if they were still alive, avoiding disposing of their ashes or getting a headstone, and keeping their possessions around us as if they had just gone down the street to pick up a newspaper—we aren't successful. In reality, they are absent. So we remain stuck, unable to make even those changes we want to make and know would be good for us. We are stretched taut, wanting to remain close to the person who is gone but going about it in a way that can result only in stagnation. Life is made all the more miserable.

As part of the act of the Turn, we find a way to alter our relationship with the lost person so that she or he remains a part of our lives but in ways that are appropriate. Sidney Zisook, M.D., and his colleagues put it this way: "It is as if the survivor ultimately finds a comfortable place for the deceased, a place where memories, thoughts, and images exist but no longer overwhelm or predominate." It is a mistake, they say, to assume that the death of someone means that the relationship is over, for a healthy adaptation "includes the evolution of a new form of this relationship and its integration into the changing life and personality of the bereaved."

At this point, we begin to make a clear distinction between those "patterns of thought, feeling, and behavior that are clearly no longer appropriate . . . which only make sense if the lost person is physically present," and those that allow us to remain linked to the person in a positive way through maintaining values and pursuing goals that we shared with the lost person. We are able, as Dr. Bowlby points out, to "retain a strong sense of the continuing presence of [the lost person] without the turmoil of hope and disappointment, search and frustration, anger and blame, that are present earlier."

I recently saw an example of a mother and father working to establish this kind of altered relationship. Their son, who had been killed in an automobile accident, and his father were alumni of the same university; both had participated in the same military program, a program that for more than a hundred years had created strong bonds among its members. To perpetuate a record of this shared history, the university had established a collection of class rings worn by the cadets in this program, a collection that went back to the 1800s. The parents of the young man who had been killed decided to give their son's senior class ring to this collection and did so in a lovely ceremony, carried out with strength and dignity.

Through this ceremony, the parents were acting on the reality that their son was no longer present to wear his ring. Every time a future cadet and her or his parents come into the room to look at these rings, the values and ideals of the deceased son's life will be evident. Although finding ways to establish a "new form" for their relationship with their son will, of course, be an ongoing process, these parents have made a positive beginning.

REPLACING MALADAPTIVE THOUGHTS WITH EMPOWERING THOUGHTS

It may be that some people recognize that it's time to make a new plan for their lives, yet they can find no energy to move forward. This often happens when old—and often unrecognized—patterns of thinking bind individuals to discouragement, doubt, and fear.

This often leads to a continued focus on one's own suffering and to living a daily existence that is "morbidly introspective." Such people often also become hypochondriacs.

It is possible, however, for people in situations like this to change. They can, as Aaron Beck, M.D., says "learn to use a new language":

> When an adult . . . attempts to learn a new language, then he has to concentrate on the formation of words and sentences. Similarly, when he has a problem in interpreting certain aspects of reality, it may be useful for him to focus on the rules he applies in making judgments. In examining a problem area, he finds that the rule is incorrect or that he has been applying it incorrectly. Since making the incorrect judgments has probably become a deeply ingrained habit, which he may not be conscious of, several steps are required to correct it. First, he has to become aware of what he is thinking. Second, he needs to recognize what thoughts are awry. Then he has to substitute accurate for inaccurate judgments. Finally, he needs feedback to inform him whether his changes are correct. The same kind of sequence is necessary for making behavioral changes.

When we recognize that it is time to commit to a new shape for our lives, a valuable exercise is to examine what Dr. Beck calls our "automatic thoughts" to see if they are hindering us from changing. We can follow Dr. Beck's simple steps:

1. Become aware of what we are thinking.
2. Recognize when the thoughts are of a detrimental sort.
3. Substitute accurate for inaccurate judgments.
4. Check out our thinking with someone we respect who will listen but will not impose her or his own way of thinking.

Dr. Beck asserts that "it is possible to perceive a thought, focus on it, and evaluate it," just as it is possible to identify and reflect on a sensation such as a backache or an external stimulus such as a request that we turn down the radio. Then we must challenge and replace the thoughts we have that are "maladaptive" with the kind of thoughts that will empower us to move on to the next appropriate form for our grieving process.

CLARIFYING A SET OF BELIEFS THAT CAN BE SUSTAINING

From where we are looking at this point, the future is wide open, yes, but that future is also unknown and definitely uncertain. What are we to stand on? What foundation can support us firmly when we don't seem to have anywhere to step but out into thin air? Will it be only pluck, blind faith, sheer courage, a feckless action that propels us from where we are now to where we know we need to go?

This time of Turning Into the Wind offers us an opportunity to think about what system of beliefs fits our lives now, what values and truths we can hold on to. Researchers tell us:

The bereaved . . . go through a significant and at times radical alteration of their world view—the set of beliefs by which they operate. Following their loss, the bereaved are frequently floundering for direction, often well into the second year. This loss of direction and meaning is precipitated by the disruption of the plans and hopes they shared with their spouses, or by the shattering of belief systems which governed many of their actions: beliefs in being able to control one's destiny, maintain invincibility, belief in a just and merciful God. . . . All such beliefs [for many individuals] are challenged, fall short, and leave a vacuum that only gradually gets filled again.

The important words here are "a vacuum that only gradually gets filled again." Our belief systems are like the phoenix that burns, only to rise to life again from the ashes. At first, we may question everything. Then, as we grapple with what has happened, we begin to discover those things we can say we believe in, those ideas, convictions, and experiences that we return to again and again as the context for our thinking and our actions.

It is valuable to think deliberately about what we can and do believe in that sustains us. For many it is the reconfirming of a traditional faith. For those of us for whom this is true, we have come to see that "faith does not shield us from the facts of life," as Dr. Glen Davidson points out. "God," he says, "does not disappear in the presence of imperfection—death, loss, or suffering . . . the human sufferer can live the seeming contradiction of growing through losing." Dr. Sidney Zisook says that religious faith in the lives of many grievers can help provide meaning, offer help and support through God, and combat loneliness.

For others, "a vacuum that only gradually gets filled again" comes to hold not reconfirmed beliefs, according to researchers, but a "modified" reassertion of these old beliefs and even, at times, "totally new ones, reflecting the finiteness and fragility of life and the limits of control." I know that in my own case the quite dogmatic belief system I had before Greg died—a system that had *me* and *my actions* and *my goals* and *my hard work* at the center—was being replaced, as I reached the place of the Turn, by a much greater sense of reverence, awe, and mystery. It wasn't that what I had believed and acted on before was wrong. It had been useful to have a set of beliefs that focused on what I could do to take care of my own life. Hadn't such a belief system gotten me out of the hills of East Tennessee? Propelled me to college and through graduate school? Supported me in working hard to build a successful career? Given me the determination to be a partner in a good marriage?

No, it wasn't that my old belief system was wrong. It was just incomplete. Until Greg's death, I had never been slapped in the face with something about which I could do absolutely nothing. I had never paid attention to an "Otherness" that I now could not deny: the coincidence of the butterfly outside that high window in a New York office building; the "knowing" that came that day while I was standing in the aisle of the airplane landing in Chattanooga; the unexplainable calm, peace, and courage that now appeared often after I had sat quietly in prayer.

I was also realizing now that in the matter of my belief system I had thrown the proverbial baby out with the bathwater. While I knew that I did not want to live by the doctrinal tenets of the church in which I was raised, I did not have the facility at that time to distinguish between a doctrine and the interpretations of a particular religious group, and fundamental truths, faith, and religious commitments. I was still unable to accept the thinking that I had grown up with. But something else was changing profoundly. I found that I was increasingly able to distinguish between an unexplained way of interpreting, understanding, and using particular beliefs and a conscious belief system and religious commitment that centered on God, with whom I could—and did—have meaningful communication. I now had a spiritual and religious life to which I attended and that I found more and more sustaining.

Dr. Zisook and Stephen Shuchter point out that our reconfirmed, modified, or new belief systems play a very important part in our lives, showing up in our being "more appreciative of daily living, more patient and accepting, and more giving." Our clarified belief system can provide support, these researchers say, for "developing new careers or changing careers, for enjoying ourselves with more gusto, or with finding new outlets for creativity."

Since this time of Turning Into the Wind calls for every bit of support possible, any moments we spend clarifying what we can now say we do believe in will be sustaining.

THE CHOICE

What is the choice of value when we are Turning Into the Wind?

We can choose to replan and change our lives to include
but not be identified by the loss.

This choice to replan our lives to include the loss we have had is an assertion, a declaration, something we just affirm without knowing what the exact outcome is going to be. We are now "stating or putting forward an assertion positively, even if in the face of difficulties." We are proclaiming that we will go forward; we will incorporate this loss into our lives in a way that does not keep us stuck in the past but provides us with a way forward into the future.

A study of widows carried out at Harvard University uncovered an important finding: Those women whose grieving was moving toward a healthy (and even creative) outcome had "at a particular moment . . . asserted themselves in some way and had therefore found themselves on a path to recovery." The authors of the study write: "Often this is a painful task. . . . But when it is completed it became a statement that one era of a widow's life had ended and another was beginning." Each of the women—regardless of the exact form of her assertion—had demonstrated that she was willing to replan and change her life to include the loss but not be identified by it and, thereby, not stay stuck in her grieving.

Dr. Bowlby warns us: If we choose not to begin to "replan our lives the representational models we have of ourselves and of the world about us remain unchanged," and we subsequently find that "our life is either planned on a false basis or else falls into unplanned disarray."

The choice to replan our lives is first and foremost an internal commitment, a private decision: *I will contribute to my own rehabilitation. I will make necessary changes. I will build something new for the future.* The internal commitment comes first; then some kind of external action will naturally and appropriately follow.

What makes this choice difficult?

It takes courage to say, "I am responsible for myself. I must make appropriate changes." It is disconcerting not to know what to do in certain situations. It is a risk to think of doing something that you have no assurance will be successful. It is an act of faith to step out into what seems like "nothing." From this point on, our grief process will center on the longer-term adjustments related to our new role and identity, to new relationships and situations that are not always referenced by the past, and to the resolution of past/present conflicts, as well as resolution of new problems that would not have occurred if we had not asserted that we would move forward.

I don't think it's too dramatic to say that this choice is a life-or-death issue. We will either make an assertion that we are committed to shaping a new life that includes the past but is also expanding, shaping a new life that is appropriate for who we are now, in our current circumstances—or we will live, in the words of an old French saying, as a person whose clock has stopped. (Researchers at the Institute of Medicine put it this way: "Not only is there no movement, but there also is a sense that the person will not permit any movement.")

People who don't make the choice to replan their lives at the appropriate time after a loss have sad fates: some become chronic mourners; some continue destructive behavior; some lose themselves in work and frantic activity; some continue delinquent behavior; some continue to be ill; some sink into chronic depression; and some die. There are also the "hidden" aftermaths of not making the choice to replan and change one's life to include but not be dominated by the change—outcomes that probably do relate to uncompleted grieving but may not be seen as being directly connected. Some people who choose not to commit to the longer-term changes may "feel deeply dissatisfied with their lives; may become super self-sufficient; many feel depersonalized with a sense of unreality." They exist as what Dr. Donald Winnicott calls a "false self." Many are angry and bitter. They become brittle and hard, having "little understanding either of others or of themselves, difficult to live and work with."

WHAT WE NEED FROM FAMILY AND FRIENDS WHEN WE ARE TURNING INTO THE WIND

I remember a friend saying to me one day, "What you need now is tough love and ruthless compassion." And that was how he interacted with me, a fact for which today I am very grateful. He—and others—acted as if they *expected* me to establish my own autonomy, gave support as I started the work of establishing a new identity, even helped initiate certain turning points, such as planning the first vacation I would take alone, and applauded me because I had exhibited a change in attitude and begun to take important steps toward a new future.

One of the things we may have to do at this point is winnow out those companions and acquaintances who always see the glass as being half empty, who want to dwell only on the past, who continue to make sympathetic gestures of rallying around us and relieving us of our roles and obligations, who perhaps are themselves incomplete with their own grieving.

We may also have to ask for the kind of support we need now. Friends and family may be in the habit of responding to us in certain ways out of respect for the difficulties they know we have been experiencing. "You have to retrain your environment" is the way one widow put it. "At this point, the most important thing you can do," she added, "is to let people around you know that you are committed to starting a new life appropriate to the situation you now find yourself in and that you would appreciate their help and their support as you make these uncharted changes."

Once when I was in Santa Fe, I bought a book about D. H. Lawrence's experiences in New Mexico. In one of these essays Lawrence writes about the thoughts and practices of Native Americans, particularly the Aztec tribe, whose stories he had heard and whose ceremonies he had witnessed. Aztecs, he states, so long as they are pure, have "only two great negative commandments:

Thou shalt not lie.
Thou shalt not be a coward.

Positively, their one commandment is:

Thou shalt acknowledge the wonder."

When I was writing this commentary on Turning Into the Wind, I thought of those commandments. For this phase of the grieving process, I don't think we could find any better guidance.

THE TERRAIN OF OUR ACTIVE GRIEVING

Life As It Was   *Life and Loss Integrated*
The Event of Loss   *Freedom from Domination of Grief*

IMPACT: Experiencing the unthinkable
CHOICE: To experience and express grief fully

SECOND CRISIS: Stumbling in the dark
CHOICE: To endure with patience

OBSERVATION: Linking past to present
CHOICE: To look honestly

THE TURN: Turning into the wind
CHOICE: To replan and change our lives to include but not be dominated by the loss

RECONSTRUCTION: Picking up the pieces
CHOICE: To take specific actions

WORKING THROUGH: Finding solid ground
CHOICE: To engage in the conflicts

INTEGRATION: Daylight
CHOICE: To make and remake choices

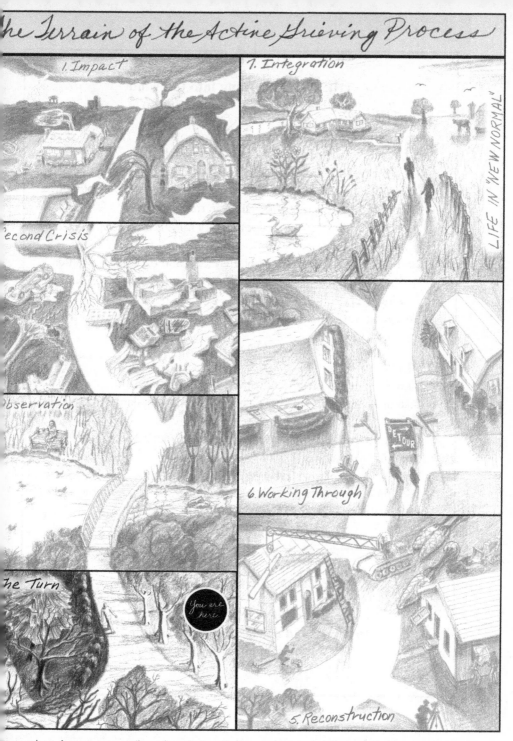

The Terrain of the Active Grieving Process

1. Impact

7. Integration

LIFE IN "NEW NORMAL"

Second Crisis

Observation

6. Working Through

DETOUR

The Turn

You are here.

5. Reconstruction

Remember: A map never tells us how to travel. A map does not determine that everyone travels same route, moves at the same speed, shares a set itinerary. A map does not dictate, prescribe, even describe an individual's movement. A map does, however, name. A map can help us find re we are when we think we are lost. A map shows possibilities and provides ideas for where there is for us to go. At all times, however, every individual is the person holding the map.

THE TURN: Turning into the wind

What Is Normal?

Gaining an awareness that certain responses to the loss, if not changed, will hold us back from enjoying life

Recognizing that only we can begin the longer-term adjustive tasks that must be engaged in if we are to make a new life for ourselves

Becoming willing to stop focusing on the past

Becoming willing to take responsibility for our own happiness and well-being

Starting to reconstitute our belief system and explore our values

Finding ways to express our love for the lost person that are appropriate to how life is now

Assessing our critical role in the kind of life we will have in the future

What Can I Do?

Write in order to explore new possibilities for your life.

Take proactive steps to show a commitment to making a new shape for your life.

Make positive and appropriate changes in your environment.

Organize your affairs.

Assert to yourself and to others that you will be responsible for creating a life that is appropriate to the person you are now and to the situation in which you find yourself now.

THE TURN: Turning into the wind

My active choice?

**To replan and change my life to include but
not be dominated by the loss**

5

RECONSTRUCTION:

PICKING UP THE PIECES

If you're doing nothing, you're doing wrong.
Lord Mountbatten

The surf was so strong that I had to turn up the volume on the cassette player under my lounge chair. Taking advantage of the lull between the summer and fall semesters at the university, I had invited my parents to join me at this isolated spot on the coast of North Carolina. It was early in the week, but the three of us had already settled into a comfortable routine. After breakfast my father fished, my mother crocheted, and I came out to the sand dune in front of our rental cottage to read, write, and listen to music.

The first task of the morning was to set up my "work area"—make sure the rickety side table was close enough to the lounge chair so that I could reach my coffee, stack up the cassette boxes on the sand in a certain order, put out my books, pen, and writing tablet. As I got organized, I kept thinking of a line from *Moby Dick*—something like "When it's November in my soul, I get myself down to the sea." Today, perhaps more than ever, I could understand Ishmael's motivation and appreciate his wisdom. For even though we had been here for only two days, already the rhythm of life by the ocean had begun to enlarge my spirit and wear away my sharp edges.

Haydn's One Hundredth Symphony was playing, and I was reading Anne Morrow Lindbergh's *Gift from the Sea*. This was not a book I had brought with me but one I had found in the bookcase of the cottage. Greg had been reading *Gift from the Sea* on the afternoon he died; the book was lying on his worktable, one passage marked to include in the manuscript on which he was working. It had made me happy to find the book here at the beach, because Greg, never far from my thoughts in the entire fifteen months since his death, had been on my mind a lot since we had arrived here.

I recognized the passage he had planned to use when I came to it: "But I want first of all . . . to be at peace with myself . . . an inner harmony, essentially spiritual, which can be translated into outer harmony." This passage struck me again, as it had when I first read it, as the perfect epitaph. "If Greg had known he was going to die," I thought to myself, "he couldn't have picked a more appropriate final testimony."

But today there was something else about these words . . . I couldn't put my finger on why, but reading the paragraph today bothered—even provoked—me.

I put the book down in my lap and looked out at the ocean. A fleet of shrimp boats was passing in the far distance. The scene was mesmerizing: the flat plan of the ocean, the center poles of the boats rising against the horizon, the high booms turning first left and then right as the nets were moved into the water. As I watched, I realized . . . what was it? Ah, the clue was in the geometry. In looking at these lines and angles, not only was I seeing ocean and boats, booms and center poles, but I was seeing *harmony*.

Harmony that in my own life was not present.

I looked back at the paragraph. *I want a central core to my life . . . purity of intention . . . singleness of eye . . . I want to be at peace with myself . . . inner . . . outer harmony . . . at one.* Those words stung me. I realized that even though I had turned toward the future, even though I had found a new job that brought me into contact with different people and gave me some diversion, those things were not the same as the "purity of intention" that Anne Morrow

Lindbergh was writing about. In spite of these changes, my daily life still had no central core, no true purpose. Where everything meaningful had been when Greg was alive, there was still only a vacuum.

"Great," I said, slapping the book down on the table. "I'll put in my schedule: Get meaning in daily life at ten o'clock next Thursday." I was sick and tired of always having to work on something related to Greg's death. When would life feel just like normal living? When would I be through with all this adjusting? I reached down to change the music, putting a Bob Seger tape into the Sony. As I began to gather up my things to go inside, "Against the Wind" was the song that was playing.

The sun was just starting to go down as I headed out to the beach for my daily run. Off and on all day, thoughts about the passage in *Gift from the Sea* had aggravated me; but as I jogged along, seeing the reflection of the strong afternoon light on the wet sand, I began to feel less irritable. A line from Proust came to mind—"If I were dying," he had said, "and the sun made a patch of light on the floor, my spirit would rise in happiness." It made me happy to remember that quotation.

I thought about the fascination light had had for me since earliest childhood. I could remember sitting alone many days before I started to school, perfectly content to do nothing but watch the light move across the wide boards of our front porch all morning. As an adult, I had finally understood this affinity I felt for light when I read the observation the poet Auden made that in all of our lives there are two or three important images in whose presence our hearts were first opened. I knew that light was one of my images.

As I jogged along, I thought, too, of the day Greg and I first met. It had always been the light of that afternoon that stood out in memory. But I realized, almost with a start, that since Greg died light had not been very important to me. In fact, light was now something I very seldom noticed.

It was then that the idea occurred to me. One way I could start building harmony in my daily life would be to change my home environment. I could move furniture, paint the walls another color . . . why, I could even put in a skylight! The thought made me feel almost giddy. Even as I jogged, I could see the light streaming into the den, making moving patterns on the ceramic tile floor. By the time I got back to the beach cottage, the skylight was already installed and I was sitting under it.

The next day, I woke up excited. The idea of rearranging my house and installing a skylight had released a whole realm of other possibilities. About midmorning I got to my workplace on the beach and took up my pen and tablet. "Decide how you want your life," I tutored myself, "and then start working to make those things happen."

The first thing I did was write at the top of the page: "A Credo for My Life." Then I listed these points.

1. Be good to myself.
2. Have fun.
3. Love others.
4. Make a contribution.

I began to make a list of things I wanted: to create a new beautiful and nourishing home environment . . . to have a wonderful man to share my life with . . . to spend and invest money wisely . . . to eat well and continue to exercise . . . to learn to dance and swim . . . to enlarge my circle of friends . . . to feel safe and secure alone in all circumstances . . . to focus on giving as well as receiving love and care. Making the list, I felt almost euphoric. What friends had told me, I was beginning to realize for myself: I *did* have my whole life ahead of me. I *could* rebuild the central core of my life. I *was* strong and able.

But the euphoria didn't last.

When I got back home I discovered that it is no small task to turn goals set on a beach in North Carolina into reality back in Texas. Putting in the skylight was just one example. When the carpenter came to give me an estimate, he found there was only enough space to put a very small skylight in the den roof. But, he pointed out, if we removed one wall of Greg's office and incorporated that space into the den, we could put in a much bigger skylight. This was much more of an undertaking than I had counted on, of course, but to have a minuscule skylight would defeat the whole purpose. I decided to do the remodeling.

One of my first tasks was to clear out Greg's office. I wrote an advertisement for the typewriter, desk and desk chair, bookcases, and also decided at the last minute to include his motorcycle, which was doing nobody any good stored out in the utility room. When the ad came out on Saturday, several people came to see the items. It pleased me to lower the price of the typewriter so that a young mother who was a new graduate student could buy it. The woman who bought the desk and chair was getting them as a surprise for her husband's birthday, and that made me happy. When I saw that Greg's helmet would fit the teenager whose parents were buying him his first motorcycle, I threw that in for good measure.

But after the last buyer left all my composure disappeared. I felt I had sold every piece of furniture I owned and that the whole house was empty. I walked back and forth, crying, doing my best to avoid looking at Greg's vacant office. I finally went to bed, hoping that when I woke up I'd feel better.

But I wasn't so lucky. The next day was Sunday. When the clock radio came on, Kris Kristofferson was singing. It couldn't have been a worse selection: "There's something on a Sunday makes a body feel alone . . ." The pain in my lower back was severe. "Those are tears in my back," I thought. "The tissues and muscles are knotted up with all my sadness."

I fixed a cup of coffee and turned on the radio in the kitchen. Again, luck was against me. The song playing was "For the Good Times." "The disk jockey," I thought sarcastically, "has picked these just for me."

I couldn't remember ever being so lonely. I called Felicia in Tennessee, but she wasn't home. I wrote her a letter:

It's chilly this morning here in Texas. Right now I'm listening to Emmy-lou Harris and thinking of cold, rainy winter days when Greg and I were so content and satisfied and dwelled in the sky called love.

As I wrote, tears splotched the paper in front of me.

I am so tired of being brave and getting on with it and learning from my experience and beginning a new life—all those positive things that you're supposed to do after losing. Instead, I'd like to roll in a rug called "the world is good."

Over the next weeks, the tension continued. However, I knew I could not run from it. I had to resolve this painful conflict. "Otherwise," I asked myself, "what is your alternative?" I knew the answer: regression and stagnation. Living life in a coma, as a colleague put it.

But nothing pulled me. I was bored, listless. Then Felicia wrote back from Tennessee. Her last line read, "Remember, you are a project under reconstruction."

A project under reconstruction. Now, here was a statement that could give me some perspective. How things were now wasn't how they were always going to be. Everything wasn't final. My life was in process, and this uncomfortable feeling of betwixt and between, this phase of moving forward but only into a new place of unsettledness was just where I was at the present time.

Although Felicia had no way of knowing it when she wrote, I had cut a poem out of the *New York Times* during the past summer that spoke much the same message. After I got Felicia's letter, I retrieved the poem from my journal and taped it up on the bathroom mirror:

Sea Sculpture

I've whittled
A peninsula
out of myself
with bays
and inlets
to anchor in
during storms.
I've carved
with care.
I've harbors
to cruise to
on vacation.
With consideration,
I've chiseled seabreezes
to cool my coastlines
during heatwaves.
I've fashioned my dunes
so they won't wash away.
The ocean keeps me guessing.
The final structure is
still under construction.

Roland Pease

When I answered Felicia's letter, I sent her a copy of a Jack Kerouac quip I had found and also taped this sentence on my bathroom mirror: "Look, walking on water wasn't built in a day." I wanted Felicia to know I had gotten her message.

As much as I knew it was a fantasy dream, I wanted to find someone with whom I could have a relationship like the one I had with Greg. I wanted someone to drink hot buttered rum with when we finished decorating the tree on Christmas Eve, someone to help me dye the eggs that went on the circle of cinnamon buns I made every Easter, someone to curl around when it was time to go to sleep.

I had thought early on that I had found the right person. "How could I be so lucky," I marveled, "that the first man I go out with after Greg's death would be just perfect?" Even now I still remembered his genuineness, his tenderness, how strong and light I felt when he left after that first date. In fact, that was the day I had taken the towel down from the uncurtained kitchen window; somehow the outside had not seemed so threatening.

For a few weeks I had thought our relationship was heaven. I loved to go to the house with big windows he had built himself in the middle of the woods. I loved the meals he cooked—biscuits, chicken-fried quail, gravy. I loved his curiosity. "How would you like to see the underside of a house?" he asked one day when we were stalled behind an old structure being transported down the highway on a trailer. He pulled over to the side of the road; we got out and crawled under the house to see its construction. I loved his teaching me how to shoot skeet. I loved finding philosophy books on his night table.

But I tried too hard to be wanted. I was too needy. I made everything too serious. Things became strained between us. When I pressed for more togetherness than he was willing to give, he left. I know now that it was the potential for a friendship, and not romantic love, that he had offered. And this experience had stood me in good stead when I later met Tommy and started going to the ranch with him, but at the time it had been a very hard lesson.

All I could picture now was a dismal future. When I saw an older woman who looked as if life had not been good to her, I would think, almost in a panic: "I'll look like that soon; then for sure nobody will ever want me."

Then the miracle happened. On the plane flying home from a meeting I had attended in Boston, I met the man I wanted as my future husband. Taller than Greg but with features very much like his, Chandler was everything a woman could dream of—attractive, successful (he owned a software company in Dallas), and kind. We were the same age, and both of our spouses had died within months of each other.

As time passed, I couldn't believe my good fortune. I took Chandler to university football games, where we sat in the president's box with all the other couples. I met his family, and he took me to dinner with the neighbors with whom he and his wife had been a foursome. We shared books, wrote letters. He gave me a beautiful antique copper kettle for Thanksgiving, and I placed an early order with L. L. Bean for a chamois shirt for him for Christmas. Life was again wonderful. I knew we were always going to be happy.

"I have to be in New York this Friday," Chandler called to say, "so why don't you go with me? We can fly up on Thursday, stay at the Plaza, and have the weekend free after I finish my meetings." I loved New York City, and I loved the Plaza. So, of course, I would go. But then I remembered I had to give a talk at Western Illinois University on Friday. I decided to fly from Illinois to New York and be at the Plaza by the time Chandler finished his meetings.

I was sitting in the Houston airport, gate No. 31, when it dawned on me that I was going through St. Louis on the way to Western Illinois University. I knew St. Louis airport almost as well as my own living room; it would be hard to count the times I had flown in and out of there when Greg and I were dating. This would be the first time I had been in the airport since Greg moved from St. Louis to New York when we got married.

I decided to call Greg's best friend in St. Louis before I left Houston to see if he could come to the airport for a short visit. As soon as I dialed the area code—314—it seemed I remembered every call I had ever made to Greg when he lived there. Waves of memories rushed over me. I almost missed the plane, I was so caught up in my reveries.

I suppose I will never know what really happened that weekend in New York. Was it me, or was it Chandler? Or was it both of us? Here I was with a man with whom I had felt a fit from the beginning. But now I was uncomfortable, upset, edgy. Questions haunted: Wasn't I dishonoring Greg by being at the Plaza with another man? How could I replace Greg so easily? The weekend passed in a haze. Even now, I can remember only scattered events . . . didn't Chandler get several telephone messages, perhaps from one of his office colleagues (the woman he later married) . . . didn't I rush back to the hotel one afternoon because I feared I had left my diamond earrings out on the dresser, the earrings Greg had bought me on his fortieth birthday?

No, I really can't say what happened. I just know that I didn't tell Chandler that weekend about the birthday party friends were planning for me in December. And I know that, after the weekend in New York, Chandler didn't call me.

In one way the birthday party was wonderful. I loved what I was wearing: a high-necked Victorian-looking blouse trimmed in lace, jeans, boots, and a new cinnamon-colored cowboy hat. The old barn my friends had rented was perfect for making chili, which we did right on the premises, and for country-and-western dancing. Three friends, who, like me, had Christmas birthdays were also honorees at the party, so there were many wonderful people who came to shower all of us with well wishes.

On the other hand, the party was terrible. The next morning all I could think about was an attractive bachelor's remark. "You scare me," he had said while we were dancing, and then I didn't see him for the rest of the evening. I remembered something similar an acquaintance had said to me some months before. "You act so strong and independent," he'd said, "that I don't know why you ever got married." Thinking back over the party, I wrote in my journal: "I'm so afraid of the next years of my life, of becoming unattractive, aging. No one will want me. I'm discouraged and scared. Feel the emptiness of it all after the party last night. The facade. The faking that hides the loneliness."

I knew I had to go forward, but what do you do when you can't get free of whatever it is that keeps pulling you back? I knew I wanted to stop being a widow and just plain be a human being. But what do you do when, in spite of the commitments you've made and the actions you've taken, it's just not happening?

One afternoon I saw a Lawrence Durrell novel I hadn't read on the shelf in the library. When I opened it later that night at home, it seemed as if the book had been written to me as a personal message. Lines like these were so applicable that they startled me: "Such a lack of theme . . . Everyone who dies takes a whole epoch with them . . . It's always now or never—since we are human and enjoy the fatality of choice. Indeed the moment of choice is always now." I thought, "Darn it, I can't even check out a library book without being forced to see evidence of my predicament."

As coincidence would have it, I saw the graffiti and got the letter inviting me to apply for the job on the same day a few weeks later. I walked into the bathroom in one of the buildings where I taught a class and saw, written above the sink:

"What do I want?"
This is the world's most disturbing question.

Seeing the graffiti made me mad. "Hoodlum," I exclaimed, "defacing public property."

"Come on," another voice said, "people have been writing on walls since cave days. Something else is making you angry."

The second voice was right. It was the message that I found so confronting. What did I want? I had no idea, and that was my whole problem. It was as if all the world were out there and I could make my life up now, within reason, in any new configuration I wanted, but what was that going to be?

The state of mind I was in when I got back to the office made the letter in my mail tray all the more enticing. "The University of South Florida in Tampa will be hiring a new Dean of Liberal Arts this semester. The search committee has been given your name as a possible candidate, and we invite you to apply for this position." I was excited; this could be the answer. I liked Tampa, and the university had a good reputation. I would have new work, make new friends, perhaps meet someone with whom things would go better than they had with Chandler. Yes, it would be a good move. I decided to send in my application.

Every two or three weeks, I got another notification. My application was under consideration . . . the screening committee had made the first cut and my application was still being considered . . .

a group of finalists were being asked to send in additional information, and I was one of them.

Then came the really good news: The committee had winnowed the applicants, and my name was on the final short list. Would I come to the campus for an interview? I bought a new lilac-colored linen suit and an off-white silk blouse for the occasion, and a bunch of dark purple silk violets to pin on my lapel just because they looked jaunty. My spirits were high. This could be the new beginning that I needed so desperately.

The interview schedule was grueling. Dinner with the president and his wife, breakfast with the search committee, meetings with the Council of Deans, with students, with this department chair and that one, each one seeming to be housed as far as possible from the other. By the end of the day, I was physically and mentally exhausted. But I liked what I'd seen—a thriving university, energetic administrators with expansive ideas for the future, a liberal arts college poised for change and growth, a mix of interesting students.

On the plane home, I assessed the situation. I knew they had selected five individuals for the final round of interviewing, so the selection process was almost over. Surely I'd hear something in a week or two.

Liberal arts dean—I liked the sound of the title. I began to imagine a high-rise apartment looking out over Tampa Bay, dinner of pompano baked in parchment, maybe even a little place on the beach that could be a getaway cottage. Already, I could see myself swinging my briefcase as I walked along under the palm trees, going to my office at the university.

"You have a telegram," the secretary said almost before I had time to step through the door when I got back to work on Monday. It was clear that the arrival of the telegram had caused a stir in the office. The president, with whom I had developed a close working relationship, had gotten up and come to his doorway when I arrived, and he stood there drinking a cup of coffee.

"A telegram?" I said in surprise, as the secretary handed me the windowed envelope. I had no idea what this could mean or who it could be from, and my heart was pounding. I always associated telegrams with bad news; even at this moment I was remembering the day, when I was a preschooler, that Mother got a telegraph saying her brother had been shot down in action in France and his status was undetermined.

I opened the envelope where I was standing. No, they couldn't have decided already. I had been there only on Friday. But here it was in black and white: "The search committee is happy to inform you that you have been selected for the position of Dean of Liberal Arts at the University of South Florida. Letter to follow." I looked over at the president, who, it turns out, had already received a courtesy call informing him of my selection, and he was smiling. The secretary came around the desk to hug me. I was stunned by the news; but, oh, I was so happy.

In the letter that arrived a few days later, the committee asked me to indicate in writing within a week my acceptance of the position. I surprised myself when I didn't sit down that very night and type out my affirmative response; but then it had been a long day, and I knew I could do it tomorrow. But the next day and then the next came and went, and I still hadn't written the acceptance letter. "Why," I chastised myself. "Why haven't you sent the letter saying you will be thrilled to take this position? It is everything you could ask for." But for some reason the closer the deadline came the more some other part of me was reneging.

I couldn't understand my behavior. "The best I can describe it," I said to a friend, "is that I've realized this is not just a move to another university. This is a major career change, because I will be moving from a life as a professor to a life as a full-time university administrator." Now, although I worked part-time in the president's office, I was still a tenured professor, teaching in the College of Liberal Arts. And when I left the president's office sometime in the future, I would return to the schedule and lifestyle of a professor, with time for research and writing. By contrast, this new job in Florida would be year-round administration and no teaching.

"You do want to make some kind of change, though," my friend said. "If you don't want to be a full-time university administrator, what would you like the change to be?"

"I don't know," I answered. That was the problem. Perhaps this wasn't the right move, but what move was I going to make? This opportunity was real and present. Anything else was only a blank spot in the future. It was hard to send the letter declining the position.

A few weeks after I made the decision, I came across a quotation that gave me some insight. The words went like this:

Anything is one of a million paths. Therefore you must always
keep in mind that a path is only a path; if you feel you should
not follow it, you must not stay with it under any circumstances. . . .
Look at every path closely and deliberately. Try it as many times as you
think necessary. . . . [Then ask one question.] I will tell you what it is:
Does this path have a heart?
If it does, the path is good; if it doesn't, it is of no use.

[A path with a heart] makes for a joyful journey . . . the other will
make you curse your life. One makes you strong; the other
weakens you. . . . A path without a heart is never enjoyable. You
have to work hard even to take it. . . . For me there is only the
traveling on the paths that have a heart.

I knew I was in the process of making a new life for myself. I also knew that the job I had just turned down would have been, for me, not a path with a heart. So, now, even when it looked as if my life weren't going anywhere, I knew I was in action.

This is what it is like when we are Picking Up the Pieces. When our lives are under Reconstruction. The emphasis of our grief work shifts from internal to external. We start to take action that allows us to check out what is and what isn't going to work for us as we design a new shape for our lives. We are now grappling with the necessity of making long-term changes. We are beginning to do the work that is necessary to resolve the conflict between the pull of the past and our desire to be happy.

This is a difficult time. We feel like an immigrant who must carve out a new life in an unfamiliar land, like a mountain climber who can find no sure footing. The past looks like our only place of safety, our only place of refuge. All the while, when we are trying to move forward, we must accommodate the memory of the past and at the same time reckon with our desire for a new future.

Peter Marris, the British social scientist, helps us understand this dilemma. We need our past, he tells us. In fact, the only way we can understand the present is by referencing it to the past. It is from previous experiences that we discern the principles by which we operate our world. Although these principles may be different from those of our neighbor, they nevertheless provide a framework that tells us the meaning of events—whether they will be "good, bad, or indifferent." Each discovery we made in the past, for instance—if I touch a hot stove, that stove will burn me; if I have a companion with me to watch the sunset, I am happier—leads to the next until finally we have, in Professor Marris's words, "a series of interpretations which gradually consolidate, with more or less assurance and consistency, into an understanding of life." We cannot, therefore, just decide to jettison our past, no matter how much we want to get on to the future. Our past is the basis of everything we have learned about what does and does not make us happy.

Furthermore, it is extremely difficult to separate what we learned in the past from the person(s) with whom we learned it. (This is why it is often as difficult for individuals who disliked or even hated the lost person to reconstruct their lives as it is for those who loved the one who is missing: So much of the structure and shape of the past is tied up with the person who is no longer present that it requires a herculean effort to separate principles for living from the people with whom we have lived.)

What we are trying to do in Reconstruction is to find the activities, the people, the kind of work, the experiences, that will give us a sense of continuity with our past and yet allow us to move beyond it. And this is enormously difficult. We feel a lot of pain as we work to find a way to extract the purpose and meaning from the past and experience it in some new, appropriate form in the present, for so much of that purpose and meaning were associated with the person who is no longer present.

Yet I've seen that, regardless of the difficulty, people step out and begin the tasks of long-term change that are now required. This means having the courage to muddle around, to take action when there is no promise of a positive outcome. The writer Sheldon Kopp said once that he had finally accepted that all of his important decisions had to be made on the basis of insufficient data. We all must grapple with a scary, open future even while we are still figuring out our relationship to the past. The conflict can be excruciating, which is why every serious researcher writing about loss asserts that learning how to make these longer-term adjustments is as much a part of the active grieving process as the earlier, more easily recognized forms of acute grieving. But brave individuals take on the tasks for the same reasons that immigrants work so hard to make a life for themselves in a new country: It is these experiences that allow us, finally, to create a life that both honors the past and has new shape and meaning. People who begin to reconstruct their lives tell stories like the ones below.

LEARNING NEW SKILLS

A woman talks:

I had been married to George for almost fifty years. We had that kind of old-fashioned, traditional marriage where he handled all the finances and outside things, and I handled the family and ran the house. With him gone, I realized I had to learn all kinds of things—like how to reconcile a bank statement and balance a checkbook. And establish a whole new network. You know, like find someone you can trust to tell you what's really wrong with your car and not charge you an arm and a leg for fixing it. Who you can get to fix the lawn mower when it breaks. Who puts up part of a fence when it blows down in a storm and who comes right out when you have a plumbing emergency. Where the safety lane sticker place is when you need to get your car inspected. I saw that I was just going to have to move out and do it. I know some women who carry on about this forever. But the way I see it, you can complain or you can do it. And your life is a heck of a lot happier if you decide just to do it.

MAKING CHANGES

A widow says:

I've made a list of all the things I've been doing out of habit but that I really don't like to do. I've been in a study group for over five years, and it dawned on me the other day that I don't enjoy being there. I've also been in a tennis league for a long time. I realized lately that I was in that activity because some of my friends were participating but that I didn't enjoy tennis. So I've canceled both of those activities and signed up to take a genealogy class at the community college. That's something I've been wanting to do for a long time. I think I've hesitated to make changes like this, thinking that a widow needs to keep doing things with her friends as much as possible. But I realized the other day that a widow can also decide what she likes to do on her own account and do that. I've felt better ever since.

ESTABLISHING A NEW IDENTITY

A senior citizen recalls:

There's the shock of being regarded as a widow. It's . . . the word has a very unhappy connotation. And it's brought home to you on all the forms you have to fill out. Married, divorced, widowed. You have trouble getting used to this thing you are now.

You just don't know who you are anymore. Most women my age have had forty or fifty—I had almost fifty—years of discussing everything with one person. Everything was a joint decision. Now that he is gone, I don't have the same identity anymore.

You know, they invited Marge and David. And suddenly, now, I walk into a room as an alone person. You keep asking yourself, "Do people like me? Do they accept me because I was David's wife or because I'm me? And if it's because I'm me, what do I have to offer?"

I caught myself the other night relying on my relationship with David to insert my own opinion into a conversation. At dinner we were talking about something David always had strong opinions about. So I said, "Well, since David isn't here to say this, I'll say it for him. This is the way he felt, and I agree with his opinion." I saw, immediately, that I was pulling back from establishing my own identity. A friend of mine, also widowed, has found an answer for herself. She moved to another environment, away from all her couple friends. And she is loving her life in this new location. She's made new friends who never knew her husband. I don't quite know how to handle all this yet, but I'm, I guess you'd say, practicing.

REALIZING SOME DIFFICULTIES WERE NOT CAUSED BY THE LOSS

A woman tells this story:

It has been a shock for me to realize that I have other problems besides the death of a husband. I actually am faced with an issue of self-development. And I can tell you, that's a lot more confronting even than the death. I've now got to pick up where I left off as a person when I married Clayton and develop myself from there.

Up till Clayton's death, my life had been my husband, my children, and then my grandchildren. I married when I was sixteen, and Clayton was a dominant person. He received the education; I supported him in the background. I never myself became a whole person. All of who I am did not get developed.

I need now to go back and learn a lot of things. I was a good mother; I was a good wife. But I—this is hard for a lot of people to believe—can't swim. I can't dance. I can't type.

I have realized since Clayton died that my life has been full of excuses—and I had such good ones. I couldn't drive, so I couldn't get out in life and do things on my own. Now I have to learn to drive. Until I do that, I'm still so limited. I must call on someone to get me places.

Someone asked the other day, "Well, do you think you'll do any of these things you're talking about?" At first I said, "I hope I will." And then I said, "I must." I can't keep on like I am. I could, but what would it be? Since my children still live in the same town as I do, I would just become a little old lady, baby-sitting her grandchildren. I enjoy doing that, but that's not a very full life. So I just must develop myself. That is the answer.

I asked myself the other day, "Are you going to get out there and do it?" I keep wanting someone else to make it happen, and I know they can't. It has to be me. It digs at me, something I read in *A Road Less Traveled*—that laziness is evil. I believe that! I know I'm not lazy in things like mowing an acre lot or going over and cleaning my daughter's house. But there's a particular kind of lazy—not doing the kinds of things that I have said I must do, like learning to drive or swim or take classes. That kind of laziness is my own fault. So the big question is "Well, when will you get started?"

EXPERIENCING CONTINUED LONELINESS

A person confides:

It's the loneliness that discourages me as I try to make a new life. I can get through the days very well without brooding. I've joined a few other people in the building in starting a Friendly Hour. First we have refreshments and then a program. We've had a wonderful performance of Dorothy Parker's *So Here We Are*, done by three retired drama teachers. A professor from our local university came and talked about the pleasures of reading. A third program was by a nutrition expert. We have five retired doctors living in the building, so the next program is going to be a symposium in which each doctor talks about her or his most interesting or unusual case. And I've started a personal project—putting together a cookbook.

But because of my eyesight I can't drive at night. That's when it hits me, the loneliness. When there's nobody to nudge. When something comes on TV that's either funny or particularly perceptive or a drama that's well done, and there's nobody you can talk it over with. I don't yet know what to do with this continued loneliness.

LOOKING AT THE FUTURE

A widower says:

I work as a historian at a research center where we write many grant proposals. When one proposal isn't funded, we sit down and write another one. I've started thinking about my life as a widower as something I have to write a new proposal for. But, in a case like this, I don't know yet what kind of proposal to write. I have to do a lot of searching, and I've begun to do some of that. I wish I knew. It's a most uncomfortable place to be in, not knowing what direction your life is going to go in. But from all I can see, being uncomfortable while you think about the future just comes with the territory.

RECOGNIZING THAT EMOTIONS ARE SEDUCTIVE

Listen to a mother whose son died:

It's very difficult when you're involved emotionally to be able to pull yourself out of it. That's one reason I've been very careful not to let myself fall into that emotional trap. It would be easy to do. But I know that there's almost a delight in wallowing in my emotions, if I allow myself to continue to do it. There's a certain pleasure in feeling melancholy—"Oh, poor me." A certain pleasure in telling people, "Oh, I've gone through so much."

I've learned that if you get in the emotional trap, there is nothing that is automatically going to trigger your getting out of it. One of the things I use to move myself out of an emotional trap is to repeat some lines I learned a long time ago. I think Rossetti wrote them: "Go, you may call it madness, folly. I would not, if I could be, be glad. I love this melancholy." By repeating those lines, I remind myself that there is an alternative. I've even gotten to the place now where I can laugh at myself when I succumb to the emotional trap. I think that is very important.

IDENTIFYING CERTAIN PRIORITIES

A man says:

One of my main aspirations is to have a wife. That's what I miss. To come home and spend the evening by myself is a difficult thing. The kids did something thoughtful—they got me one of those timers that turn the lights on. At least then I didn't have to walk into a dark house when I got home from work.

There's a book called *Creation Is a Patient Search*. It's about architecture, but I've borrowed the author's ideas and applied them to my own situation. Searching for a wife is a creative search and requires patience. I've got the whole world to search through. So, I'll just conduct a creative search, with patience, and I'll find a new wife. I'm sure of it.

TAKING ON NEW PROJECTS

A woman recalls:

I felt new energy the minute I decided to take on a new project. I finally had something to focus my time and attention on. I joined with a team of people who were putting together a special for public television about business leaders, educators, and professionals who were offering new solutions to age-old problems. While I was working on this project, I wasn't home crying. It was real simple. I couldn't be in two places at the same time, and I couldn't think two thoughts at the same time. As long as I was working on this project and working with other people, I wasn't dwelling on my miserable little existence.

I've discovered that every new thing I do is like a little grain of sand. I add one grain of sand to another. It's beginning to feel as if at some point they will form a block of granite that I can stand on.

EXPERIENCING CONFUSION

Listen to this story:

It's a shame to have to say at age thirty-three, "What am I going to be when I grow up?" But the truth is, I don't know what to do with the rest of my life. I've sold the business that Jack had. It wasn't something I wanted to run. But I do want to do something. I majored in Russian in college, so maybe I'll go back to graduate school. But I've got to think of the three girls I have to raise. Can you imagine, a few years from now, having three girls in college at one time. So financial study would also be valuable. How do I choose? What if I make a mistake? You can't make many mistakes at my age and in my circumstances and have it not seriously affect your future and the future of lots of other people. It just seems to be important to make the right decision, but what is that right thing to do? At least I'm thinking about this, but there is still a lot of confusion.

CRITICAL CONSIDERATIONS WHEN WE ARE PICKING UP THE PIECES

We have all had times when the task at hand and our ability to meet that task were a marvelous fit: We were able to accomplish what had to be done with velocity and ease and a sense of deep satisfaction. Not so during the experiences of Reconstruction, when we are Picking Up the Pieces. As the stories above show, this is a time of groping and stumbling, of not knowing yet taking a step forward anyway, of making changes without any certainty of achieving a good outcome. It is a time when we are beginning to think about goals and dreams for the future but often have little clarity about how those goals and dreams can be accomplished. This is a time when we have to "try out" new roles and new activities, with all the awkwardness and chance that such speculative efforts entail.

I think it was the writer Thomas Szasz who said that you have to be humble to learn. During these experiences we have little choice but to be humble, because we are finding out, often painfully, that although the past pulls powerfully, everything about how to create a new life for ourselves is yet to be learned. This requires us to examine our ways of thinking and behaving in order to determine what can be useful and what will be destructive and detrimental.

NEW IDENTITY/NEW ROLES

Naturally, the mutual roles we shared with the person who is no longer present still assert themselves, if only as habits. This behavior is familiar and often automatic. Even this far into our grieving process, we still find ourselves often thinking and acting as if the past were still present (or certainly wishing this were so), only to have to acknowledge once again, in still another abrupt "test of reality" that the person is not here and will not be here, and that our old thoughts and behavior are inappropriate.

Now we are required to begin to relinquish these old roles and identities and reinvent ourselves in ways that are appropriate to our present circumstances. This would be painful enough by itself (we all remember facing such tasks during adolescence), but, added to the grief we feel for the loss, the situation seems overwhelming. That is why we go down many blind alleys, often look and act so indecisively, and walk around in such a quandary. We don't know who we are yet in this new situation, and it seems that we are always practicing. Ernest Morgan describes it this way: "One aspect of bereavement that I had not anticipated was the loss of identity. With Elizabeth gone, I was no longer me! After forty years of sharing on such a broad spectrum of life, I did not have a separate identity. This was . . . very strange, and several years were required to get over it."

There is no way around this confusion and trial and error. It is no small task we are undertaking—forging a new identity, finding new ways of relating and new sources of satisfaction—so we should not disparage ourselves when we don't always go in a straight line toward a new destination. "Such disorganization," Dr. John Bowlby writes encouragingly, "though painful and perhaps bewildering, is nonetheless potentially adaptive."

We often also find ourselves in a delayed developmental crisis. We see that we do not have certain skills and behaviors that we must have if we are going to be able to move forward successfully. I think about the person who has to learn financial management, starting with how to reconcile the checking account monthly. This was as challenging to this particular person as traveling abroad alone would be for another person. These experiences require us to change in fundamental ways, to take on things we have never done and don't know how to do, to decide what we are going to do and start doing it, to catch ourselves in certain negative behaviors and alter those behaviors. And, Dr. Beverley Raphael reminds us, while "this may be an immensely painful and difficult process for some, when it is satisfactorily worked through, the new identity may be more stable and secure and linked to the core aspects of the self." This is, of course, the result we want to achieve: a more stable and secure identity, linked to the core aspects of ourselves. When we are at work making these fundamental changes, we are living a transforming process.

SELF-PERPETUATING EMOTIONS

This is a time, again, of strong emotions. We may even feel the way we felt when we were first responding to the loss. If this emotion runs its course, all is well. We honor and empty out our sadness, our regret, our longing. We are released and can move forward. But this may not happen. Our emotions are capable of acting as an autonomous system. This means that the emotion can trigger itself again and again with no new stimulus. We then become the puppet of the emotion. One of the greatest challenges we face at this point in our grief process is understanding how our emotions operate so that we can distinguish between the healthy expression of emotion and the unhealthy feeding upon themselves of which our emotions are also capable.

David Burns, M.D., suggests an activity that he calls "Hot Thoughts/Cool Thoughts" as a way of working with destructive emotions. First you write down the thoughts associated with the emotion: *I will never be happy again; I miss those Sunday nights so much—when we put supper on TV trays and watched 60 Minutes; I do not want to go to this party alone* . . . These are the "hot thoughts," the thoughts that keep the emotional system turning on itself. Then write down a "cool thought" for each "hot thought" you've written—an answer or an observation: *I may not ever be happy again, but it's too soon to know; I will invite Stan and Marty over to watch 60 Minutes next Sunday; I will weigh the advantages and disadvantages of going to the party alone.*

Dr. Burns also suggests making a chart that he calls "Daily Record of Dysfunctional Thoughts," which can help the person who is caught in a self-defeating emotional cycle. The chart has five columns: first the "provocative situation" is described; then the emotion that has been triggered is named; then "hot thoughts" are recorded in the third column and "cool thoughts" in the fourth column; the outcome of the situation is written in the final column. Even though this and the "Hot Thoughts/Cool Thoughts" approach are simple, the research done by Dr. Burns and others has shown them to be highly effective in giving individuals control over their emotions.

Other researchers have reported on the value of writing. One suggestion is to write about a particularly painful episode or traumatic experience for twenty minutes on three different days. Some experiments have found that writing even for such a short period of time makes a measurable difference in the functioning of the immune system. And many of us have had the experience of writing our thoughts down and finding that during the process we got clarity or a new idea or some kind of opening for the future.

How can we make the distinction between the times we need to release our emotions and the times we need to discipline our emotions? People tell me that they soon learn to tell the difference because of how they feel afterward. When individuals "bump" into a pocket of emotion that needs to be expressed and choose to vent their feelings, they report that they feel cleansed, washed out, released, free when the experience is over. On the other hand, when the emotion is part of a seductive, repetitive cycle, individuals say they feel worse when the experience is over. (If it is ever over. Some people remain stuck in these defeating cycles.) They say that no matter how long the thoughts and feelings persist, they never feel "finished" with the experience and find instead that feelings of resentment, anger, fear, and even depression increase as a result of the persistence of the negative emotion. To learn to recognize the difference between authentic emotional release and self-destructive emotional cycles is one of the tasks we must undertake when we are Picking Up the Pieces.

RECOGNIZING DIFFERENT KINDS OF LONELINESS

Of course, from the very beginning loneliness has been part of our response to the loss we have sustained. We often feel, when we start Picking Up the Pieces, even more isolated, separate, without companionship, not nurtured. We are now required to be "out in the world" more as we begin to build a new life for ourselves—having "active interchange with the world" is how one researcher puts it—and this seems to accentuate our aloneness. We are making decisions by ourselves; this often increases our sense of being by ourselves and of being vulnerable. As we begin to make plans, it becomes all the more clear that the person who is gone will not be a part of this new life.

In his study of relationships, Robert Weiss of Harvard points out two kinds of loneliness: the *loneliness of emotional isolation* and the *loneliness of social isolation*. The *loneliness of emotional isolation* is experienced when we lose a person whose presence provided us with a sense of place, of belonging, of meaning, attachment, and security. The *loneliness of social isolation* is experienced when we do not have relationships that provide us with the opportunity to discuss mutual interests, exchange ideas and information, engage in social events, and feel a sense of companionship.

During this phase of our grief process, we often feel both types of loneliness. We feel the *loneliness of social isolation* as we work to establish a new identity; perhaps we are not invited to places where we used to go as a couple, do not feel comfortable with groups where we are known as part of a couple, have less interest in things we used to do. This kind of loneliness can be at least partially assuaged by a decision to participate in new activities, make new friends, take the initiative to invite people over, and volunteer in civic, church, and community activities.

But the *loneliness of emotional isolation* is another matter. This is the loneliness we feel because we have no mutually committed relationship, no one with whom we are "affiliated" in a one-to-one relationship. In most cases, even the valued connection with our family, friends, and children do not diminish this kind of emotional loneliness. Part of the emotional loneliness may be the need and desire for sexual intimacy, and it almost certainly includes a longing for closeness.

For some, the *loneliness of emotional isolation* is alleviated by a new intimate, long-term relationship with a life partner. For others, however, the emotional isolation comes to be lessened by another form of relationship, one that is different from a relationship with a life partner but is close and intimate nevertheless. This may be with a friend, a sister, or a mother. It might, for a man, be achieved through a relationship with "buddies." Others find emotional loneliness lessened by their relationship with God, with themselves, with nature, or with pets.

Often, however, at this point we are only "in process" in dealing with our loneliness—of both the social and the emotional variety—making some connections here, others there, committing time to this relationship and that. Nothing is firm. Nothing feels totally familiar. This can make the activities of Reconstruction all the more difficult. I found it valuable, when I was at this place in my grief process, to try to distinguish between the challenge of the new tasks of planning and creating a new shape for my life, and the sadness of the social and emotional loneliness that were still such a part of my daily experience.

I suppose it is because I fell into more than one trap related, particularly, to trying to establish a new primary relationship that the following information seemed very important when I read it. Dr. Beverley Raphael warns about the negative relationships we might be tempted to make because we are lonely:

A fantasy relationship with the lost idealized partner. In this trap, the partner is "ever-loving, perfect, unable to desert or die," and the bereaved finds fault with all other relationships and becomes hostile and negative.

A *replacement relationship*. The bereaved becomes attached to "someone who is seen symbolically, unconsciously, or actively as a replacement for the lost person." Perhaps another spouse or partner who "is valued only in terms of his [or her] similarity to the dead spouse" and, hence, with whom the relationship is usually doomed. Perhaps a child is expected to take over the role of the person who is gone, causing psychological damage to the young person that can last a lifetime. Perhaps a person working in the field of bereavement—a member of the clergy, a counselor—is latched on to "fill the gap."

A *self-destructive relationship*. The bereaved attempts to punish herself or himself by establishing a relationship that will bring pain and feelings of low self-worth.

An *avoidance relationship*. The bereaved, deciding never again to risk becoming close to another person, chooses someone who is incapable of giving and receiving intimacy.

A *compulsive caregiving relationship*. The bereaved finds someone who will always be weak, helpless, bothered, or needy to do and care for, counting on the fact that this person will require so much support, and for so long, that separation will be impossible.

While all of us may, at some point in our movement through grief, establish one of these negative relationships, it is crucial that we come to recognize the damage being done and choose not to stay in such situations. Otherwise, we are living on a relationship dead-end street.

It is certainly true that the loneliness we experience until we are again part of a satisfying social structure, or until we have "reaffiliated" and achieved a new emotional intimacy, makes the work of planning and creating a new shape for our lives more difficult. (This "reaffiliation" can take many shapes: a faith-filled relationship with the Divine, perhaps another primary relationship, a new closeness with a family member or friend, or the presence of a loving pet.) One thought that I hung on to while I wobbled through this period was that loneliness was, at least, open-ended, existing in a space of possibility. There was always the possibility that at some unexpected point in the future the loneliness might end.

There is still one other aspect of loneliness that I think we have to be honest about: There are some situations in which nothing will ever assuage or eradicate our loneliness. There is the loneliness that can never be filled when someone loses a child. To pretend that it is otherwise is to trivialize the loss. Such a profound ripping of bonds of connection and love can only be integrated into the whole of the picture of one's life. It can never be compensated for or amended in any way.

There is, too, the loneliness an adult feels after the loss of a parent. Some who have not experienced the loss of a parent might pooh-pooh the impact of such a loss—after all, the parent had lived a long life; the sick person is finally out of her or his misery; the surviving adult children have their own lives to return to. These justifications and explanations are logical and reasonable, but they are also often irrelevant. For there is no relationship more long-lasting than that between parent and child. And for many, no relationship is more special. For some, too, there may be no relationship more fraught with misunderstandings and resentments.

After my own parents died, I said to a friend one day, "You know, now I understand why there is a character who is an orphan in so many folktales and fairy tales. It is a lonely, painful, and demanding experience to be an orphan." A friend whose mother died last year told me about her thoughts when she found out she had been nominated for an award of national recognition: "The first thing that popped into my head was to call my mother. I knew there was no one in the world who would have been more proud of my accomplishment than my mother." The only kind of "reaffiliating" we can do, in the words of another friend of mine who had lost both parents, is to "become our own father, become our own mother." Perhaps this is what many adult children mean when they say that they grow up in some special way after the loss of a parent. "I've realized since my father died," one young woman told me, "how much I still depended on him. Since he is gone, I have had to become much more responsible for myself. I'm beginning to feel much more capable."

THE CHOICE

What is the positive choice we can make when we are Picking Up the Pieces?

We can choose to take specific actions.

Dr. John Bowlby says it this way: We now have a choice to begin "active interchange between ourselves and our external world." When we are involved in this active interchange, he reminds us, we are in the process of organizing our lives toward some new goal or object. This activity will probably result, as the stories in this chapter have shown us, in a mix of subjective experiences—"hope, fear, anger, satisfaction, frustration, or any combination of these." But no matter how much we go back and forth, up and down, during the interim we are still moving forward. By taking action—which inevitably involves risking changes, some of which work out and some of which don't—we are finding out what it will take for our lives to be satisfying. We are "trying out" alternatives to see what will be the appropriate shape for our new future.

What makes the choice to take specific actions more difficult is that in some cases we can so easily be swept back to the past. As Dr. George Pollock puts it, "Little episodes that are suddenly recalled may serve as poignant reminders of the past. They may rekindle the dying fire of grief and tears for a short time." Yet, Dr. Pollock points out, at the same time as we are experiencing this painful pull of the past, we are finding in our daily lives "various manifestations of adaptive mechanisms attempting to integrate the experience of the loss with reality so that life activities can go on." We have begun the work of "more lasting adaptation" even if it is not finished yet.

Lily Pincus discusses the seemingly contradictory experiences we have: "People who believe strongly in self-discipline and control may be puzzled by regressive behavior in themselves and others," she says. "There are no distinct boundaries or timetables." In fact, the regressive experiences are often a "filling up, a replenishment of the self, in order to become a stronger, better integrated, more separate person."

Melanie Klein, psychotherapist and author, gives further insight into why the choice to take specific actions is difficult:

The pain experienced in the slow process of testing reality in the work of mourning seems to be partly due to the necessity, not only to renew the links to the external world and thus continuously to re-experience the loss, but at the same time and by means of this to rebuild with anguish the inner world, which is felt to be in danger of deteriorating and collapsing.

The choice to take specific actions will result in "contradictory drives toward maturity and regression." This is unavoidable, because we are in a new situation. "All the usual responses are completely out of tune and inadequate to meet it." Therefore our behavior "becomes unpredictable." As Lily Pincus says pointedly, "It is not just losing a state in which one had found one's balance, but rather as if one has lost one's balanced self. In attempting to re-gain it, one may try out some new ways of coping, giving up certain wishes, defining a new task."

That is what happens during Reconstruction. We begin the work to make the replanning of our lives not just an idea but a reality. We begin the work necessary to design and create a new shape for our lives. To gain a new balanced self, we "try out" new ways of liv-ing. We initiate an "active interchange" with the external world.

WHAT WE NEED FROM FAMILY AND FRIENDS WHEN WE ARE PICKING UP THE PIECES

We must remember that although we have made much movement in our process, we are still grieving. This time of longer-term ad-justments is still "a period of ongoing mourning." The problem is that many of our family members and friends (and certainly our em-ployers) will not recognize this set of experiences as part of the grieving process and will assume that, because we are now "out and about in the world," everything is back in balance. And we may hesitate to tell them what we are experiencing—the ambivalence, the sadness, the fears, the loneliness—because we too think that, by this time, we should no longer be grieving. We often think we are being weak, slipping back into the past, when we thought we were moving forward into the future.

It is important, therefore, that we let those close to us know where we are and what we are experiencing. We can't afford to wear a facade that attempts to hide the situation or to act as if the changes we are making are easy when, in truth, they are hard. If we do let people know what we need, many (though, I'm afraid, not all) will give their support and help.

This is a time when participating in some kind of life-skill group can be very useful. This might mean continued participation in a grief program that deals with the entire mourning process, not just the acute first phases. This might mean a group-counseling experience. It might be a testing-and-practice job-skills program. It might be one-to-one life coaching with a professional who knows how to negotiate the rocky terrain of life changes. If we seek out the kinds of groups or situations that focus on making successful life changes, we will meet some people who can be role models. We can seek advice from these individuals, talk over specific problems, include them in our support network. Both these new acquaintances and our old friends and family can help us in practical matters we must now engage in—learning how to manage our finances, how to write a good résumé, how to cook a wholesome meal for one or locate excellent child-care facilities. It is important to us, and to our friends and family, that we ask for this kind of help when we need it.

Edna St. Vincent Millay once wrote about human beings' ability to do amazing things even while we are in the very midst of terrible pain: write music, play tennis, laugh, even plan. I put Millay's lines in a small picture frame and placed the frame on my bedside table. I played these lines in my head like an anthem, an anthem celebrating resilience and courage. *In the very midst of terrible pain, I can plan.* It is a theme song for the time of Reconstruction, a time of Picking Up the Pieces. A time when, in spite of everything, we start to plan and build a new life for ourselves. We begin to take specific actions.

THE TERRAIN OF OUR ACTIVE GRIEVING

Life As It Was *Life and Loss Integrated*
The Event of Loss *Freedom from Domination of Grief*

IMPACT: Experiencing the unthinkable
CHOICE: To experience and express grief fully

SECOND CRISIS: Stumbling in the dark
CHOICE: To endure with patience

OBSERVATION: Linking past to present
CHOICE: To look honestly

THE TURN: Turning into the wind
CHOICE: To replan and change our lives to include but not be dominated by the loss

RECONSTRUCTION: Picking up the pieces
CHOICE: To take specific actions

WORKING THROUGH: Finding solid ground
CHOICE: To engage in the conflicts

INTEGRATION: Daylight
CHOICE: To make and remake choices

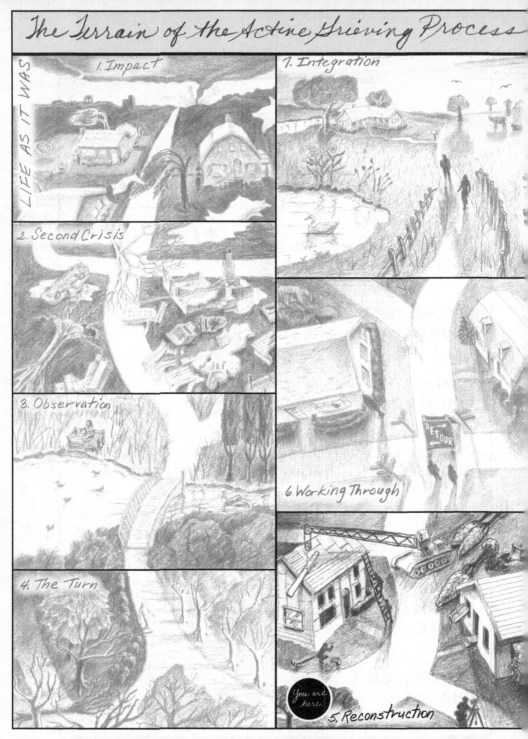

To remember: A map never tells us how to travel. A map does not determine that everyone travels the same route, moves at the same speed, shares a set itinerary. A map does not dictate, prescribe or even describe an individual's movement. A map does, however, name. A map can help us find where we are when we think we are lost. A map shows possibilities and provides ideas for where else there is for us to go. At all times, however, every individual is the person holding the map.

RECONSTRUCTION: Picking up the pieces

What Is Normal?

Beginning to make changes that are hard but beneficial

Working to establish a new identity that is appropriate to present circumstances

Recognizing that other issues not directly related to our loss must also be dealt with

Distinguishing between the loneliness we can do something about—the loneliness of social isolation—and the loneliness that exists until we can make a "reaffiliation" that brings deep emotional connection

Making commitments to new projects

Developing new skills

Setting new priorities

Acknowledging that in our grieving we are now engaging in long-term tasks of adjustment and change that are difficult and take time

What Can I Do?

Take specific steps to learn new skills that you recognize you now need.

Work with a career counselor, a life coach, or a group of individuals who are committed to making life-enhancing changes.

Stop doing things that only remind you of the past.

Make new friends.

Talk to someone about any emotional pain, sadness, fear, or sense of helplessness that might recur as you begin to construct a new future.

RECONSTRUCTION: Picking up the pieces

My active choice?

To take specific actions

6

WORKING THROUGH:

FINDING SOLID GROUND

For a long time it had seemed to me that life was about to begin—real life. But there was always some obstacle in the way, something to be got through first, some unfinished business, time still to be served, a debt to be paid. Then life would begin. At last it dawned on me that these obstacles were my life.

Alfred D'Souza

Sometimes the way a solution shows up is just amazing. For months I had continued to stew about the future. What kind of work would I do? Continue teaching? Choose some other type of employment altogether? Perhaps work in the area of communications for a large corporation? I debated, too, about moving. Didn't I need a new location? Wouldn't I be happier in a new environment? At least twenty times a day, if not two hundred, these questions nagged me.

Then one morning, in that hazy time between sleep and waking, I knew the answer.

"Mother, can I go to the library after we eat? Judy Blake said she'd go with me."

I was eight years old, and it was the middle of summer. My mother and I were in the kitchen of the house that stood at the foot of Lookout Mountain. She was slicing potatoes to fry for lunch.

"You can't walk to that library in this hot, broiling sun. You'll get heat-stroke."

"But, Mother, I've got to go. All my books are due today. I'll walk in the shade . . . let me go . . . please let me."

"Well . . . if you promise to wear something on your head . . . and you'd better not take those shoes off! If you come back from that library barefooted with tar all over your toes, I'll give you a spanking. Last time, I think you just tried to find melted tar to step in."

I loved to go to the library in the summer. You could talk to Mrs. Miller then without having to elbow a hundred kids who were standing around her desk waiting to check out books or to ask her something.

"How many books this week?" Mrs. Miller asked. She was reaching into the little tray where she kept the stars for our reading records, which were displayed on bulletin boards all around the library.

"Ten," I answered proudly.

"Ten!" Mrs. Miller responded, with just the right amount of appreciation. "It's a good thing we keep getting new books. At this rate, you will have read all the books in the library!"

Then came the blessed moment. Mrs. Miller reached into that wonderful, magical second drawer on the left that almost always held some books she had been saving. "How about this Caddie Woodlawn?" she asked me. "Or these two biographies, one about Jane Addams and the other about George Washington Carver?

"You know, Elizabeth," Mrs. Miller said as she handed me the latest treasures, "anybody who loves books the way you do is bound to become a writer. Why, you know what? I bet someday we'll have books you've written in this very library!"

For several seconds in this between-sleep-and-waking state, I could not figure out what was happening. How could I be a girl of eight and also an adult woman? Then I realized that I had been dreaming. No, not dreaming, for everything I had seen had really happened. What I had been doing was recalling something I hadn't thought of in decades. I had been remembering.

And when I got up the memory would not leave me. All during breakfast, I thought about Mrs. Miller and her prediction. Had I been moving toward becoming a writer ever since that day and just hadn't known it? Was that why I majored in the eighteenth-century novel in graduate school? Was that why I became a teacher of literature and writing? Had the scholarly books I had done and the college textbook Greg and I were working on when he died been just links in the chain of events that would finally lead to my becoming a full-time writer?

As I sat there at the breakfast table, I began to formulate the answers to the questions that for months had been hounding me. What I really wanted to do with my life was write. And I wanted to write something besides the academic articles, monographs, and textbooks I had been doing. I wanted to write about life, not just about teaching and writing. I wanted to write all kinds of books on all kinds of subjects—books that, Mrs. Miller, if she were still librarian, would want in the Rossville library.

But how could I do that? How could I make a living? Everyone knew the precariousness of book publishing, how writers never know if a book will be accepted and, even if it is accepted, whether it will be bought and read by the public. I had no one to support me, no cash in reserve to fund such an excursion. How could I even think of giving up my secure job for such unpredictability?

It must have been my day for remembering, for at that point my mind again went back to my childhood. Grandma Harper and I were sitting in the rocking chair on her front porch, on the farm in middle Georgia. I could hear myself asking, "Tell me the Civil War story again, Grandma. Please, please . . . will you tell me?"

All the men were fighting in the army. Your great-great-grandpa got captured and died in a Union prison in Rockford, Illinois. They said he died of typhoid fever, but we always thought he starved to death. Then when the troops got pinned down in Franklin, Tennessee, that's when your great-grandpa knew he had to join the fight.

That left only the womenfolk on the farm. Grandma Anna and her daughter Susan took the silver and china they prized so highly, and they buried it before the Yankees came through, below the house in the little swamphead. During Sherman's march, soldiers came through our section and stole all the horses that were left, except for one broken-down, sway-backed mare.

One day a stray soldier came into the yard. In a few minutes he came around the side of the house with three or four chickens tied together in his hand. Then he went into the kitchen and cut down the only piece of meat the womenfolk had, the remains of a cured ham. When the soldier came out, he said, "Thank you, ma'am. I'll just take these chickens and this ham."

Grandma Anna said, "That's the last piece of meat we have in the house. Those are our last chickens. Over my dead body you'll take them."

In the meantime, the soldier had crawled up on the sway-backed mare. Not only was he taking the food the woman had but he was also stealing the only animal they had left to farm with.

From under her long apron, Grandma Anna pulled an old double-barreled, muzzle-loading shotgun. The gun was loaded only with dried peas and sand, but the soldier didn't know that. He didn't know the women had no ammunition.

"You won't use that gun," the soldier said.

"You believe that?" she replied. "Sometimes it pays the difference to have the difference," she said as she pulled back both hammers on the gun. And with that she pelted him right on the backside.

When she did, he fell off the other side of the horse, turned the chick-

ens loose, and dropped the ham. But Grandma Anna got more than she
bargained for. That soldier was so cut up from the sand and dried peas
that she had to take care of his wounds before he could go on to search for
his regiment.

Grandma and I always laughed hard at the end of the story, thinking of the predicament our ancestor's bravery got her into. Then we'd sit there awhile longer, rocking. I always knew there would be more if I kept still and waited.

"After Appomattox," Grandma would continue, "one of their men came back—but he was never to be well again—and the other one didn't. The women salvaged what they could, moved to a smaller piece of land, and started over."

And then Grandma would look at me and say, "Now, that's what it means to be a Harper woman." That, I knew, was the point of the whole story.

"Well," I thought as I sat at the breakfast table, "perhaps it is time for me to carry on the tradition. Surely some of the blood of those brave women runs in my veins. Surely I have inherited at least some of their grit and determination. When, then, am I going to start acting like a Harper woman?"

I don't know the exact moment that I made the final decision. I just know the day I took action. When I got the next semester's schedule in the mail, I sat down and wrote the department head a letter: "The program that Greg and I started together in the department and that I have been continuing has been gratifying. But it is time now for me to make a change. I am resigning as a commitment to becoming a full-time writer."

I had worked out a plan for supporting myself, for a while at least. I had a long-term consulting assignment with a nonprofit organization publishing a book on world hunger. I also had leads on one or two coaching jobs, working with executives who wanted to learn to do their own writing. Probably the most important thing I was counting on was the royalties from the textbook Greg and I had been writing. This book was now finished and about to be published. I made out a budget that pared my living expenses down to the bone, so I thought I could make it. But I was to find out almost before I got started how precarious these plans were and how quickly a source of income could disappear. I was to discover how unpredictable the life of a self-employed person could be and how much I would have to be on-the-spot resourceful.

The editor of the textbook had called from New York. "By having the book shipped directly from the printers, we're going to be able to introduce it in San Francisco at the convention for the Modern Language Association," he told me. "We've made reservations for you and hope you'll be there."

Of course I would be there. I was counting on this book to be a major source of income, but it was also important to me for many other reasons. The book was the culmination of more than a decade of research and teaching; it presented an approach to writing that Greg and I had developed and believed in. It was the last project he and I had worked on together. And there had been the uncertainty after Greg's death—should I go ahead and finish the book? How much longer would the project now take than had been planned? How would the market respond?

It was past midnight when I arrived in San Francisco. I was very tired when I finally reached the hotel and planned to fall into bed immediately. These plans changed, however, when I walked into my room. For the first thing I saw, lying on the desk, was the new book!

It was beautiful. There was a Kandinsky painting on the cover, and on the first few pages were four-color photographs of a young couple building a cabin. I had used the metaphor of building a house to talk about writing, and that section of the book, I thought, was especially eye-catching. I was proud of it.

I continued to leaf through the book. It was so exciting to see what had once been scribbled on yellow legal paper now appearing as printed words on the page. I felt like a kid at Christmas. The fatigue had left me.

Then a piece of folded paper fell out of the book. "Call me no matter what time you get in," the note read. "All I can say is 'I'm sorry.'" It was signed by my editor.

I was dumbfounded. Why was he sorry? Had something happened that he thought I knew about but didn't? I stared at the words on the note as I called the room number he had listed.

"Have you seen the book?" was Robert's first question.

"Yes," I answered. "I love it. It's so beautiful."

There was a long pause. "Well, have you noticed the second color?"

"The second color?" I echoed. "No, I didn't pay any attention to the second color. Is something wrong with it?" I was turning as fast as I could to find a page with a second color.

"Yes, something is wrong," Robert answered. "The second color isn't the warm brown we specced. It's purple!"

Now I saw. All the headings in the book, all the explanations under the drawings, everywhere color had been used for emphasis . . . all of these were *bright* purple.

"Well," I said quickly, trying to toss the mistake off lightly. "I bet English teachers will love purple for a change. The color will get the book a lot of attention."

There was a long pause, and then Robert said. "Elizabeth, this is really serious. Our marketing department spent several thousand dollars doing research to determine the best second color for this book . . . you know that many of the ideas in the book are innovative, so it was critical that the design and color be traditional. This bright purple trivializes the book, makes it look trendy. We'll never be able to sell it in the conservative English market."

I did see the gravity of the situation. And I was getting angry. "Well, what happened?" I asked, realizing that my voice was several decibels louder. "How, after all that research and planning, did we end up with a book with purple as the second color?"

"It was a clerical error," Robert answered. "Someone confused two orders as the book was going to press."

I just stood there, holding the phone for a few seconds, trying to think of something to say. But there was nothing. Robert's voice was low as he closed the conversation. "I really am sorry, Elizabeth," he said. "Everyone in the company is sick about the mistake. But the book is dead. All we can do now is try to cut our losses." I knew what that meant. No special sales thrust. No special advertising. Everybody trying to forget the book instead of trying to sell it.

I hung up the phone and fell across the bed, crying. So many years' work . . . for nothing. An approach to writing that was fresh and effective . . . to be discounted. All thoughts of the sale of the book being a source of income . . . a pipe-dream fantasy. I was sick. Discouraged. Devastated.

When I finally got up and went to the bathroom to wash my face, I could see that it was almost daylight. The sky was beginning to show pale pink and yellow on the horizon. Since it was useless to think of sleeping, I pulled a chair out onto the small balcony and just sat, looking.

At some point while I was sitting there, something snapped in me. "I will not have it be this way," I said defiantly. "I will not have it. Too much work and effort have gone into this project for such a miserable ending. I just will not have it." Was it my grandma's voice I was hearing in the background? . . . *Then after Appomattox the women salvaged what they could, moved to a smaller piece of land, and started over.* Was finding a way to salvage this book what it meant now to be a Harper woman?

I had never been more resolved in my life. The situation had to be remedied. Whatever it would take, I was going to do it. As the sun came up and the city in front of me took on definition, I made plans—plans that I was going to put into effect as soon as the stores opened.

Ten o'clock found me on Union Square, waiting for the doors to be unlocked at I. Magnin's. I headed straight for the men's department. "I want to buy some purple shirts," I said to the salesman. "Solid purple."

If he had said there were no men's shirts in solid purple, I was prepared with an alternative plan. But plan B turned out not to be necessary, for the gentleman said, "Let's go over to the sportswear department. Pierre Cardin has designed some solid-colored shirts this year in bright colors, and one of them is purple."

It was probably the most purple shirt I will ever see. I couldn't imagine anyone in normal circumstances buying it. "It's a little bright," the salesman said tentatively, "but it's the only thing we have in purple."

"I'll take two," I said without hesitation. "One large and one medium. I'd like them gift-wrapped," I added, "and may I now see the ties you have in paisley?"

I asked the gentleman to pull out every paisley tie that contained the color purple. We spread these out on the glass countertop, and I began choosing. "How many do you need?" the salesman asked. It was clear that he was no longer making ordinary assumptions. If this lady bought two Pierre Cardin solid-purple sport shirts, who knows how many purple paisley ties she needed?

"Ten" I answered.

Expanding our definition of purple to allow for lilac, violet, and blue purple, we found ten paisley ties that filled the bill. "Please gift-wrap those, too," I said.

Everyone was at the booth when I walked into the exhibit area. The national sales manager was there, as well as my editor. "I have something for you," I said, handing each of them a box containing the shirt. Then I gave each of the sales reps one of the gift-wrapped ties.

"Do you want us to open these now?" the men all asked me. They seemed a little pleased but mostly awkward.

"Yes," I responded. "Now is the time to open them."

It was one of those situations where the gift is so bad that it's wonderful. These were not men who wore loud purple shirts and purple paisley ties. These were men who wore wing-tipped shoes and conservative button-down collars. That, of course, made these shirts and ties all the more ridiculous.

At first the men didn't know how to react. Were they supposed to like these? Were they supposed to show their appreciation? But then, first one and then the next began to laugh. Soon all of us standing around this serious college textbook publisher's booth were laughing. Bending-over-double laughing. Holding-the-shirts-up-in-front-of-themselves laughing. Matching-paisley-tie-to-pin-striped-suit laughing.

Suddenly the color purple had lost its heaviness, its significance. One could even imagine, standing there, that these men might be able to sell a new college textbook to a conservative market, even if it did have a second color that was purple.

The next few days proved that supposition to be accurate. The reps had good reports. Professors liked the books, and many said they would be ordering. I knew that by the time the news of this success at the national convention reached the entire sales force the book would stand a good chance of being heavily promoted. Naturally, this made me happy. But I was also mentally and physically exhausted. I had no idea that a person had to work this hard to be a Harper woman.

Even though the textbook sales were going well and I had been able to get the consulting jobs that paid the bills while I worked on a new book proposal, I was still a basket case about money. Even if I could see making ends meet for a particular thirty-day period, I was already worrying about the next one.

I wasn't used to generating income by the month or by the project. Since I was twenty-one, when I got my first teaching job, I had received a regular paycheck. Now I always had to keep my eye on how much I needed, how much had already come in, how much was expected. And I was always afraid that the next month nobody would need or want my services and I wouldn't be able to make it. I knew millions of individuals chose to be self-employed and thrived on the challenge, but in my case it just about made me crazy.

On the other hand, I had never been more content with the nature of my work. My schedule was flexible; I could set it any way I needed to in order to have time to write. The consulting jobs were with interesting, creative people who brought to my life a whole new, non-academic perspective. The proposal I was working on was going well. I knew this was what I wanted to do.

The conflict, however, was taking its toll. It was wintertime, the days were gray, and my spirits were grayer. I had now been self-employed long enough to realize that the cycle was never-ending:

see how much money you have to have, find a way to earn it, finish those projects, see how much money you still have to have, find a way to earn it. . . . "I've just swapped one disadvantage for another," I told myself. "A teaching job that paid well but left little if any time to write, for a life with plenty of time to write but nothing sure to count on."

It had gotten so bad that I was having nightmares. One morning at about four-thirty, I spoke to myself very honestly. I had been tossing and turning for much of the night, having awakened with a start, dreaming that I was shriveled and old and dying in poverty. "You have got to do something to break the hold this thing has on you," I told myself. "It's beginning to affect everything, including your enthusiasm for writing."

As I lay there, I realized the root of the difficulty: It wasn't the type of work I had chosen that was the problem but the fact that I had no self-confidence. I claimed that I didn't like always having to think about budgets and income, but the truth was that underneath that complaint was a constant fear that no one would hire me, that my books would not be good, that I wouldn't be capable of getting work when I needed it. What I had to do something about was the level of my self-confidence, not the way I had chosen to work.

I was surprised at how much it helped just to identify the problem. Now I had something I could grab hold of, something I could work on. I was so sick of the way this unspoken, unacknowledged fear had been sucking energy away from things I deeply cared about and spilling its ugly spew over the new life I was building. "What you need to do," I instructed myself, "is to take some action so drastic that in the future you will feel courageous just by remembering that you did this." But what could I do that would be that drastic?

"Give some money away," came the answer from somewhere inside.

"Give money away? Are you crazy?" I felt fear making pleats in my stomach as the internal dialogue continued.

"What was it that Ralph Emerson said—if you are afraid to do something, that is the thing you should do if you want to build character?"

"But I don't have any money to give away; I'm barely making enough as it is."

"Yes, you do. You have your teacher retirement."

"My teacher retirement! But I can't give part of my teacher retirement away; that's absolutely my only security."

"You don't have to give it all away, but you might give five thousand dollars to that organization you consult with that's working to help end world hunger."

"But five thousand dollars is a big chunk of money."

"I know, but you did say you needed to do something drastic to break the back of this fear that is constantly gnawing away at you."

"Yes, but I didn't mean that drastic!"

The more I thought about it, however, the more I could see that making that donation would be making a statement about my belief in myself: that I could take five thousand dollars out of my teacher retirement because I had confidence that I could add that and more to a new retirement fund out of my self-employment; that I saw myself as the kind of person who could make a contribution of that magnitude; that I was a strong enough person to do something that I was scared to death of doing.

So I gave the five thousand dollars. And although it wasn't the last thing I would have to do to build my self-confidence, it made a big difference.

As the months passed, I felt more and more centered in my work; I felt that I had reconnected with what gave me meaning and purpose. I had picked up the thread again—a thread that, in effect, had been present all my life in some form or another. The plays and stories I had written as a child. All those poems I had taken so much care to print in that little brown spiral notebook. The social studies assignments that I would always ask if I could turn into a story—*Miss McKensie, do you care if I write about the everyday life of a set of twins living in colonial America? I'll be sure to get in all the information about the war with the English.* Then the academic study in literature and writing. All those books and articles I had edited or written. Marrying and working with Greg, who was a writer. I felt that what I was doing now had always been there and I had just come to it.

But I couldn't feel that way about other areas, particularly about my personal life. What I had shared with Greg had been like a destination, a place I had dreamed about all my life, the place I most wanted to get to. What was there to reconnect with there? Nothing. So even when my work was going well, I still had to fight off feelings of "What's the use?" Everything was still so empty; I was so lonely.

First came the dream, then the cookbook, and then the student's letter.

The dream was very simple. There was a large green plant that had been thrown aside on the lawn. But when I picked the plant up, I made a wonderful discovery. The plant had roots! I knew in the dream that the plant could be repotted and that it would grow. In the dream I ran across the grass, holding the plant, saying, "It's got roots. It's alive. I can replant it." The discovery in the dream made me deliriously happy.

Then there was the cookbook. I was standing in an organic-food store, about to choose some fruit and vegetables. Lined up for sale around the top of the bins were all kinds of cookbooks: a vegetarian cookbook from the famous Green's Restaurant; a small spiral-bound book with a luscious apple tart on the cover; a volume that contained what looked like a hundred ways to cook pasta. My eye went to one book a bit down the bins from where I was standing. *Cooking for One*, the title read. I almost didn't go look at it. But when I did, I found myself excited about it. I had no idea that you could make crème brûlée for one or prepare an African lamb dish with chutney, nuts, and raisins in a single serving. It felt almost like the days when Greg and I were poring over cookbooks to find something to take to the gourmet cooking-club tasting suppers. I bought the cookbook and ingredients for three or four dishes. I had found another thread—my love for cooking—another thing that had had meaning for me in the past and that I was now bringing forward.

A few days later, I received a long letter from one of Greg's graduate students from whom I hadn't heard since shortly after Greg died. Chuck wrote:

> *Greg was the first person close to me who ever died. He was my mentor, the teacher I wanted to be. And he just passed right out of my life. He went out so quickly, so irretrievable, so irrevocably. I couldn't go to the funeral, so I didn't get a chance to say goodbye. I did say goodbye one night out in the backyard of my house, but things still always seemed unfinished. But something happened recently that allowed me to see the place Greg has, and will always have, in my life. It happened as I was completing a writing seminar prior to taking my doctoral orals.*

Then the student told his story. Dr. Graves, the professor in the writing seminar, had instructed the graduate students: "Read Scott Momaday's tribute to his grandmother—'Now that I can have her only in memory, I see my grandmother . . . standing at the wood stove on a winter morning and turning meat in a great iron skillet;

sitting at the south window, bent over her beadwork. . . .' Then write a model of Momaday's paragraph, using as the subject someone whom you can now have only in memory."

The student told me he had chosen Greg, and that this was what he had written:

Now that I can only have Greg in memory, I recall the sense of continuity that was shattered when he fell off a road in east Tennessee and out of all our lives forever. I think of Greg and I see Kris Kristofferson, grizzled beard, deep voice, sparkling, deep-set eyes. He was my teacher, my colleague, my friend, who showed me how to step across a boundary and leave all the tangled messes behind. It was the crossing that mattered.

Once we were going into a Japanese restaurant. You had to cross a little bridge to get to it. Greg was bothered by something that had happened at the university . . . I didn't know what it was, but something had disturbed him. As we started to go into the restaurant, Greg said, "When I go across this bridge, I'm leaving the problem here and I'm going over there. It's not going to be with me anymore, and we're going to go ahead and have our time together."

We did have a wonderful time, and it was one of my greatest lessons in life, watching Greg do that. What he taught me was to let go of things and move on. I think that's why I had such a hard time letting go of him—because he taught me how to let go and I couldn't imagine letting go of that. Continuity. The smooth movement from here to there, from then to now, and on into tomorrow without getting caught in any one place too long. That's what he taught me, and it's always with me.

The student ended his letter: *I'm convinced the reason we are here is to remember, if we understand memory to be that uniquely human ability to create from the past a sense of meaning in the present and a trembling anticipation of possibility in the future.*

When I finished Chuck's letter, I knew I had gained wisdom: A person who is gone can live on in memory as an *active* agent in one's life, not just as someone you love and miss, not just as a nostalgic sadness. Greg had been remembered by his student; and that remembering had altered the quality of the student's life in the present and informed his life for the future: ... *if we understand memory to be that uniquely human ability to create from the past a sense of meaning in the present and a trembling anticipation of possibility in the future.*

That, I realized, was how someone we love and have lost can remain in our lives forever, in a way that is neither morbid nor regressive. And in a way that honors that person at the same time that it makes room for others. *We make meaning of the memories.* From the memories we extract values, ideals, insight, pleasures, awareness.

This, then, was how Greg would fit into my life. I knew, for instance, that I would always care for my family in a different way because Greg had enabled me to see them in a new light. I would always feel more connected to the out-of-doors because with him I had learned new ways to see the woods, the mountains, the sea. I would always be more awake to the sensuous pleasures of life—colors, smells, sounds, tastes—because I had been able to experience them with him. And I would always know what love was, because he had loved me.

I would always enjoy the opera and the ballet, which I shared with him. I would always read books about the Lewis and Clark expedition, because I had followed the trail with him one summer and caught a glimpse of how that trek symbolizes a journey that is possible for all of us. I would always like red geraniums by the front door and eggs scrambled with brie. I would always want to drive a clean car, and I would always ask if the saltwater taffy had been made on the premises.

It was just a pleasant interlude, but the experience told me that I could really have fun again.

It was New Year's Eve, and Felicia and I were in Mexico City. Felicia's boyfriend, Brad, had recently been transferred here, and she had invited me to join her when she came for this holiday visit. We were now seated in an elegant hotel dining room, regaling the two men who sat across from us with stories about what had happened to us during our sight-seeing activities. Did they want to hear about the woman who had enticed the parrot she was carrying on a stick to bite me on the elbow when she wanted to pass us on the sidewalk? Or perhaps they would rather hear about the taxi driver who couldn't understand our Spanish and delivered us to an open-air market way out in the suburbs instead of to the downtown cathedral that we had set out for. Or perhaps they'd like to see all the tiny glass turtles and frogs and prisms we had bought at the park from the street vendor. . . .

The colleague Brad had brought as my date for the evening was taking all this hilarity in stride, and I liked him for it. The men soon matched us, story for story, with their own tales of adventure that accompanied being transferred from the United States to a foreign city. We were a lighthearted foursome.

It was almost midnight. "Let's have our champagne downstairs in the discotheque," Brad suggested. "Then we can dance till morning if we want to." I was stunned when we entered the room. I had never seen a club as beautiful as this one. Dark blue velvet banquettes curving around tables covered with white linen, silver, and crystal. A domed ceiling of lights that looked so much like stars and planets that, if you had not known better, you would have sworn you were looking up into the heavens. Beautiful people everywhere. Bright dresses, tuxedos. "This certainly doesn't look like your ordinary discotheque, does it?" I whispered to Felicia as we were being seated. "Can you believe this elegant place?"

I realized as we sat down that I couldn't remember when I had last felt so at ease, so natural. "What's the difference?" I wondered. Then I answered my own question. Not once had I looked at the man across the table as anything except someone to enjoy being with on New Year's Eve. I wasn't worried about whether he would like me. I wasn't thinking about an ongoing relationship. I was here. With no agenda. What a free feeling.

At midnight, we ate the customary twelve grapes to mark the turn of the year and then began dancing. I felt exuberant. The beat of the song was strong, and I was moving in rhythm to it. In this moment there was no yesterday, and there was no tomorrow. There was only *now*. I was just dancing.

I tried to explain the wonder of this experience to Felicia on the plane ride back home. But how do you tell someone that you had learned how to live your whole life while dancing? The truth was that I had. Hold nothing back. Engage fully with what you are doing at the moment. Focus only on the thing right in front of you. Live in the present, not in the past or the future. The extent to which I could do this in all areas of my life, I realized, was the extent to which I would experience being free and happy.

These are the experiences of Finding Solid Ground. A time of Working Through, finding new solutions, forming new assumptions, resolving old issues. We begin to define our place in life around us, to reinforce our competence, to assume new roles alongside the old ones that are necessary or appropriate for us to continue. We reassess our talents and capabilities. We find new ways to live our lives.

During this time, we often experience life as a double thread: We must solve problems and deal with issues related to the new life we are building, and we must do the same for problems and issues that continue from the past. At first glance, it may look as if each of these arenas is an additional demand put on top of the one before. But often we are surprised to find them working in tandem. The confidence we gain as a result of solving a new problem, for instance, will often engage us in facing and solving a knotty problem from the past. As we find ourselves able to act in the present, we discover new ways to experience continuity from the past.

But there is a gap. All of this Working Through isn't done in a day. It takes time for the plans and assumptions that were changed for us externally by the loss to change internally as well. There is much trial and error, much scratchy unsettledness as we engage with the conflicts. We "proceed by tentative approximations"; we "grow by delays." But we can take satisfaction from the fact that we are not only solving problems and working out issues during this period but we are also altering ourselves. We are being changed by the experiences: to become more independent, more competent, more knowing; to realize more fully our potential, to become more our true self.

A number of men and women who have lived in this gap time of Finding Solid Ground say this period of their mourning process includes the experiences related below.

EMERGENCE OF NEW ASPIRATIONS

A man reports:

Probably the hardest thing for me to tolerate after Leslie died was the lethargy. I lost all ambition. Up until that time I had been gung-ho about everything; I had a game plan that excited me. I worked out regularly at the gym. My brother and I were turning a small electrical company into a good business. I had high goals in life and total confidence that I would reach them. But with Leslie gone I just didn't care about anything. I tried to fight it, but it's a contradiction in terms, I guess, to think you can fight lethargy.

Lately, though, something has started to change. It's like I'm waking up. The thing that has excited me is the idea of simplifying my life. I'm looking to see how many things I can get rid of around the house that are just clutter. I've got my brother interested in simplifying at the office. I'm getting him turned on to the idea of building a smaller but more quality business. It's a game now for me to find as many ways as possible to make things more simple.

But I also have to admit that sometimes it's upsetting. Many of the changes involve things related to my life with Leslie. We were into buying old—I mean really run-down—houses and fixing them up to rent. We fixed them up together, and then Leslie managed them. Now, every time I sell one of those houses, I feel like another part of Leslie is gone. But the rewards of simplifying are strong. So I just keep moving on with the project.

REACTIVATION OF FEARS

A young woman relates this story:

Only someone who has ever had a firstborn die a crib death can know what it takes to decide to have another baby. Right before Kimberly was born, I dreamed again and again about Tommy's death. That made me afraid something was wrong with the baby I was carrying. We didn't even talk about the possibility of crib death, just whether or not she would have all her fingers and toes— would there be anything wrong with her?

Even though it's highly unlikely that a second baby in a family will die of crib death, we still keep Kimberly hooked up to a monitor. The fear is residue left over from Tommy's death, I know. One day, when Kimberly was about three months old, the monitor's beeper went off. It's customary for babies to breathe irregularly at times; and if the monitor beeps you're supposed to stand there and count to ten to see if the baby corrects herself, which is what is normal. My first thought, of course, was that she was dead; and it was the hardest thing in the world to stand there and count to ten to see if she started breathing again. I knew I had to, though; I had to face that fear. In just a few seconds, everything was back to normal. That experience has given me the courage to take her off the monitor more often.

TAKING THE INITIATIVE

A mother tells this story:

One day the thought came to me: "I'd like to start dating." I hadn't been interested in men for a long time. I had concentrated all my time and attention on Ben and Tracy, doing everything I could to make their adjustment easy. But as time passed I realized I was lonely. I really missed male companionship.

I had never thought of John as a potential date. I saw him often at the boys' school, where he was the principal, and I knew that he had been divorced for many years, but beyond that I knew little about him. Then one night I dreamed about him. The next day I asked another volunteer at the school who had known him for many years what he was like, and she said he never dated. "He reminds me of an ascetic monk," she said. "His life is devoted to the students."

I debated for several weeks, and then I got up the nerve to call him. "I'd like to have an appointment," I said to him, and we set a time when I could come in. "I'll get right down to the purpose of my visit," I said as soon as I sat down in his office. I was nervous; I had no idea what would be the outcome of this venture. Would things now be so awkward between us that it would be impossible for me to continue to volunteer? Would he laugh? Would we both be totally embarrassed? But I went ahead. I told him about the dream I'd had of him. And then I said, "I would like to get to know you better. Is that a possibility?"

Of course, I shocked him to death. The first thing he did was sit back in his chair. He was speechless. When he finally managed to speak, his words were, "I admire your courage." Then he started two or three other sentences and couldn't finish them.

I interrupted. "I've made you uncomfortable, haven't I?"

"Yes," he answered.

And I replied, "I'm sorry."

"No," he said, "you shouldn't be sorry. It's not you. It's me."

So then we talked a little more and he said, "Do you know how long it's been since I dated? I don't even know how to date."

"Well, I don't either," I answered, "but I can ask my sister. She knows all about those kinds of things."

That was where we left it. The next time we saw each other, he waited for me outside the meeting room and said, "Well, how would you like to go out next Friday night?"

"I think it would be great," I answered.

We made the arrangements. Then, as he was leaving, he said, "I'm looking forward to it," and I said, "Me, too."

We dated and went through all the ups and downs of that process—including working out things that concerned the boys—but my hunch all along was that we'd finally get married! Which we are doing this coming May. And the whole school is invited to the wedding.

NECESSITY TO TAKE RISKS

A young widow recalls:

Of all the things Ed had been involved in, the only piece of the business that I could see being able to make a living at was running the two doughnut shops. They were potentially income-producing, and the kids and I had to have an income. I knew it was a big gamble. I had never even run anything before, much less a doughnut shop. And I knew I would be excused if I said, "I just can't do this." Everybody would have understood and said, "Oh, that poor widow."

But I saw the possibility in the doughnut shops. "The risk of making them better," I told myself, "has got to be worth what you're going to lose if it doesn't work out." So I made a choice. I knew this was for the long haul, not just something I could flit in and out of in a few days. I decided I would get into those doughnut shops and work to change things over time and not be stopped by my fear of economic failure. I knew things were going to be changed anyway, and I decided I would be the one in those shops doing the changing. If time for the next property payment came around and I couldn't meet it, I'd just say, "Hey, I can't do this. I don't know how to run a doughnut shop." But if I succeeded, the kids and I would be in much better shape financially.

It's now been two years, and I'm happy to report that I'm making it. Oh, there have been more new problems to solve than you can shake a stick at. Nothing seems to have gone easily or smoothly. But a big equipment loan just came due at the bank, and it made me feel so good to know that every penny of the money used to pay off that loan had been earned since I had been managing. Yes, this was a risk, but it has certainly been worth it.

COMING BACK FROM FAILURE

A mother of three tells this story:

I had to get another job. So I decided to go into business for myself. It was a risk, but it was also the only way I could see being able to make it.

At first I did great. The business grew; I rented larger office space and hired someone to help me. Unfortunately, I hired someone who was also a friend who I thought knew a lot about bookkeeping, but it turned out she didn't know as much as I thought she did. Then several people who had been clients from the first month I opened died or moved away. The economy in our area took a nosedive, too, and I must have written off $10,000 in accounts receivable. Finally, I couldn't keep everything going, so I had to declare bankruptcy.

I filed Chapter 13 because I wasn't willing to run out on the debt, so for the next five years I'll be paying off everything. This is hard on my sense of self-worth, and I'll be honest and say that it's taking a while for me to put it all in perspective. I am embarrassed and feel like a failure. But I've come to the conclusion that because I went bankrupt doesn't mean I'm any worse a bookkeeper. So I'm again letting people know I'm in business, and I'm starting to get some referrals. The irony is that the bankruptcy may end up helping my business. It has made me very knowledgeable about bankruptcy law and has allowed me to help some of my clients avoid similar situations.

ESTABLISHING A NEW IDENTITY

A woman recalls:

It had always been through this other person that I fulfilled myself in life—take care of a man, help him with his work, raise his children, keep his life in order and on track, and make him look good. That was my life's purpose, and had been for twenty-six years. Suddenly, with him gone, all that wasn't there any longer, so I had to reassess all my values, all the things I believed in, and start over. Or just start, I guess. Just start.

I was terribly frightened. My children were grown. I had moved to unfamiliar territory. I had no idea what to do with the rest of my life. It was like, "My God, what am I going to do?" I wasn't at all prepared to live my own life. I had no idea what it was like to be my own person, to be responsible for my own time, my own emotions, my own circle of friends.

Now, however, I'm beginning to get something of a new identity. I looked at some of the things I did most successfully when I worked with my husband and realized that over the years I had developed a lot of skill in strategic planning. So I've zeroed in on that and I'm offering my services to small businesses that need help with their planning.

I've also taken up ballroom dancing, something I had always wanted to do but never did because my husband wasn't interested. It's opening up a whole new world to me. The people are very different from those in the business world. These new friends are very interesting people. New doors are opening in my personal life, my emotions, my self-expression. I've discovered that I'm having to unlearn just about everything I knew about dancing. And the stamina required—it's amazing. There's no end to the challenge. It's exciting and so open-ended. I have won first place already in several competitions, and I'm going to Hawaii to compete again in January.

I still have my ups and downs. It's not easy to become a new person. But one day when I was moaning and groaning to a friend about all the decisions I have to make now, she looked at me and said, "Don't you ever get tired of whittling on your own finger?"

Boy, that was a breakthrough. Now every time I start thinking negative thoughts, I say to myself, "Brenda, you're whittling on your own finger."

NECESSITY TO EXAMINE ASSUMPTIONS

A young man whose father died and who himself just recovered from a life-threatening disease says:

The way I see it, everybody has a kind of contract with the world. According to the terms of that contract, the world acts in a certain way and you act in a certain way and the world responds in a certain way. It's a contract that builds up over time.

And I think one of the most fundamental clauses in that contract is the immortality clause. The immortality clause says the world doesn't go on without you and those you love in it. We wouldn't admit to believing the immortality clause if we were pinned down to it, but we act as if it is true nevertheless. We believe that the world will stay the way it is while our lives unfold as they are supposed to.

Then something comes along to contest that clause. With no warning, with no signs pointing to it, with no pain beforehand. Like my father dying. Like my going in three years after for a regular checkup and finding out at age twenty-nine I had cancer. All of a sudden everything is shattered. It's a horrible thing.

So I have realized that the clause has gotten canceled, and I have to rewrite the contract completely. The whole contract with life has to be renegotiated because none of it makes sense any longer. I'm now in the process of doing that renegotiation.

RECOGNIZING THAT CERTAIN PROBLEMS WERE ALREADY THERE

A widow reports:

At first I blamed my problems on Jim's dying. But I know now that some of these problems already existed. For instance, since his death I've realized that it's very difficult for me to show affection; and I said this was related to being in mourning. But the truth is that I have always had trouble showing affection. When Jim was alive I wasn't the only parent to love and nurture the children, so any deficiency on my part wasn't so apparent, at least to me. Now, I've had to work hard to learn how to show them my affection.

My relationship with my in-laws is another area that I had been able to handle by hiding behind Jim. If I got upset with them, I'd tell Jim and he'd say he'd talk to them or he'd do some kind of mediating. Now if I don't want to go someplace they want to go or if I don't want to do something or don't want the kids to do something, I have to come right out and say it. I now have to deal with them as an adult, on a one-on-one basis. I'd like to go on claiming this problem is all because of Jim's death. But I know it isn't. I know these problems were already there, and now there's just no convenient way to hide them. I'm having to find ways to solve the problems I've avoided for years.

ACHIEVING CLARITY

A mother says:

When our adult son committed suicide, I was so angry at him. "He didn't have to do this," I said again and again. "He had many other alternatives." But now I see that, yes, he did have other alternatives, but he also had the alternative of suicide. That was an alternative. Certainly not the alternative I would have chosen, but it was his choice. He thought that he could be free of whatever trauma he was living in his life, and therefore I have to respect that even if I don't agree with it.

And I don't hold our family or God responsible. For a long time I kept going back over our lives. What did my husband and I do wrong? Perhaps we didn't provide him with what he needed. And how could God allow this? Where was God's love?

I no longer ask these questions. My husband and I did make some mistakes, but that's part of being human. And any mistakes we might have made didn't cause our son to choose to kill himself. Even if we hurt him inadvertently or overlooked some way we could have helped him, we still didn't have the power to determine how he responded to what happened to him. Over that, nobody but the single individual has any control. And God gave all of us free will and, I think, honors us by letting us make our own choices. So it wasn't God's fault either. Somehow, it seems releasing just to say that our son made a decision based on the best thinking he was able to do at the time; and, while we wish with everything in us that that decision had been different, it *was* our son's decision.

WORKING THROUGH ONGOING ISSUES

A grandmother recounts:

I think the loss of a child may be one of the hardest things to get over. When my grandson Jason died, I became very bitter, very angry with God. How could an innocent baby die when there were so many mean, evil people walking around alive in the world? How could a bright child's potential be denied?

I have finally worked through this issue for myself. I read *Why Do Bad Things Happen to Good People* and realized that there are random events in the world. I also came to recognize that loss is part of being human, and that we were never promised a life without pain. That God loving us is not inconsistent with death in the world.

I've also stopped asking why. For so long I was dominated by that question. But I see now that I can never find a satisfactory answer. I now know the question "Why" is not a good question. So I have ceased to ask it. And I'm at peace even though I don't know the answer.

There is one issue, though, that is still ongoing in our family. Some family members want us to stop talking about Jason. But I know I have to be able to speak of him when I'm sad or on special occasions when I especially miss him. Talking was the best therapy I found after his death. I had one friend who encouraged me to talk as much as I wanted to. Fortunately, one friend will do; you don't have to have a whole support system to talk to.

By this time, though, I don't feel a need to talk about the death all the time. But if it's Christmas I'll say something like "I'm sorry Jason isn't here to get and give presents." The rest of my family never respond when I speak about Jason. They won't talk about him or the death at all. At first this bothered me a lot, but now I just remind myself that I've got to do what keeps me healthy, no matter what others do or don't do.

FINDING SOLUTIONS

A father recounts:

Money is tight now. Before, I had taken the money we had for granted. We weren't rich by any means, not even close; but we had some cash flow we could live with. We could go skiing and things like that. All of a sudden, with only my paycheck, I didn't have the money to go skiing or do anything extra. And I have a lot of pride. It was just adding one more insult to injury—to go from being solid middle-class to being a pauper.

So it's taken me a while to stop being a victim of the situation and do something about it. I kept thinking, "Just to go out to eat on a basic date anymore must cost fifty or sixty bucks!" And I was living on fifty bucks a week discretionary money. But lately I've started getting real creative about what to do. I'll go running down the Hike and Bike Trail, and I've met some neat women that way. Women who like to do things out-of-doors and don't demand that a lot of money be spent on them. I've started perusing the paper to see what's going on around town, like free concerts.

Sometimes I think you develop a real good sense of humor to keep from going crazy. The decision is yours: to be miserable or to be happy; to make light of it or let it depress you. And I've decided to choose to make light of it as much as I can.

BRINGING MEANING FROM THE PAST INTO A NEW FORM IN THE PRESENT

A widow tells this story:

Family was always important to my husband and me. His four brothers and their wives would come to see us, all at the same time, and we would have such a good time together. I enjoyed cooking for them—"the old-fashioned way," they called it. I enjoyed every minute—making biscuits for every meal, bowls of cream gravy, fried pork chops.

After my husband died, we didn't have family events like that anymore. We were all still close, but we just didn't visit the way we did before. I really missed that experience of "family." Then I discovered one day that writing about the past put me back in touch with all those good feelings. I wrote a little vignette about my childhood—about the day my papa's drugstore burned down—and although it was simple and might not be great writing, I really enjoyed it. So I began putting together a collection of stories from the past, which I gave to all the family one Christmas.

The funny thing was that to write those stories I ended up visiting every one of the four brothers to get facts and details. It was a new way to enjoy family.

Dealing with Surprises

A widow talks:

It took me about three years—I remained a part of a grief support group in my parish this entire time—to move far enough in the grieving process to decide it was time to sell the family home. My husband and I had lived in the same house for over fifty years. All of our eight children were born and grew up there. So it wasn't easy to part with the house and a lot of the furnishings.

But I loved the condo I bought. It was light and airy, with an atrium tall enough for me to grow trees! Now it was time for the first Thanksgiving since I moved into my new place. All the children and all the grandchildren were coming for dinner, as they did every year.

I bought the turkey and the ham and planned the dishes: baked-squash casserole, sweet potatoes with marshmallows broiled on top, stuffing (both with and without oysters—to please everybody). The day before Thanksgiving, when I started preparing the food, was the first time I realized that in the new condo I didn't have two ovens. I had always had two ovens; it had been a necessity to have two ovens with our large family. Now I had only one oven—and a small one at that—and there was no way I could prepare all this food and have it ready on time with only one oven.

This situation caught me completely off guard. I began to castigate myself for making the move. I felt I had made the biggest mistake in the world. I was distraught. Then I thought, "I love this place. Surely there is some way I can solve this problem." I called the condo manager and asked if the clubhouse kitchen was available. "On Wednesday before Thanksgiving?" he said. "You bet. It's completely open." So my dilemma was solved. I made up all the food and then sent family members down the street to the clubhouse when it was time to bake what I couldn't fit into my own oven. We still laugh about that. It's a whole new set of memories.

FINDING A COMFORTABLE PLACE IN YOUR THOUGHTS FOR THE PERSON WHO IS GONE

A woman tells this story:

The day after my mother died, I drove to the funeral home to take some clothes for her to be buried in, and my thirteen-year-old son was with me. When we got to the parking lot outside the funeral home, I started to cry. I said to William, "You know, all that we have left of Nanny is in the funeral home." And he looked at me like I was crazy.

"Why, Mama," he said, "you know we'll always have Nanny with us. We'll always think about her and what we did and what a nice time we had together. She's not going anywhere—she'll always be with us." I thought, "What an idiot I am. Here's a thirteen-year-old boy who has it all figured out."

As time has gone on, I've realized just how right he was—that we would always have Nanny in memory. And I think you should think about those things—you can't stop yourself from thinking about them anyway; something is always reminding you. So we still talk about her, and now it's not hard to talk. We can even make jokes about things that happened. I think we have a tendency to make saints out of people who have died, and they become perfect in our minds. For a while. And then, all of a sudden, you realize they were just human beings like everyone else. They didn't always do the right thing, and sometimes you even got disgusted with them.

I still talk to my mother, too. She was a wise woman. When she was alive, I would talk things over with her. She would always insist that I make my own decisions, but she always had some very helpful things to say. So now, if I have something I'm trying to figure out, I have a conversation with her. The only difference is that I both ask and answer all the questions. She also had a wonderful sense of humor. The day before she died, the doctor was using some instrument to look into her eyes and she thought he looked so funny twisted around trying to see what he needed to see that she burst out laughing. To this day, the doctor still mentions that when I see him. I find myself now seeing more humor in situations than I used to, and I often think of her when I'm laughing.

CRITICAL CONSIDERATIONS WHEN WE ARE FINDING SOLID GROUND

Needless to say, the tasks that make up these experiences of Working Through—tasks that include problem-solving, grappling with old issues that have resurfaced, working to establish a new identity, and numerous other challenges—tax and strain us. This is clearly a working-things-out period in our lives, and most of the time we feel that there is little, if any, respite from this labor. How do we keep ourselves moving forward under these circumstances? How do we deal with all the thorny issues?

FINDING WHAT SUPPORTS

I remember a poet writing that instead of feeling as if he were just one person, he felt as if he were a whole boardinghouse full of people who would never come to dinner at the same time when he called them. That's often how we feel during these experiences. We know what we need to do, but some renegade pieces of us won't join the confederation.

Each person comes up with her or his own repertoire of support. I think of my neighbor, whose wife died unexpectedly, walking several miles every day at about 4:00 A.M. I think of another friend— a woman who has remarried and is working to merge two households—who schedules into her busy life at least an hour every day to listen to tapes that inspire and instruct her. "I know I've got to work on myself," I've heard her say again and again. "I've got to work on my own thinking. That's the only thing that will make any difference." This woman looks at least ten years younger than her years, and I have to believe the regimen of private study and quiet reflection that she does each day with her tapes contributes to and enhances her beauty.

Current research shows that people who know that their thoughts and behavior affect their lives don't feel helpless in the face of adversity. The *New York Times* reported that it has now been proved that "optimism—at least reasonable optimism—can pay dividends as wide-ranging as health, longevity, job success, and higher scores on achievements tests" (and, I would add, success in doing our active grieving). "Our expectancies," says Dr. Edward Jones of Princeton University, "not only affect how we see reality but also affect the reality itself."

Dr. Michael Scheier of Carnegie Mellon University, reported that people who think from an optimistic viewpoint handle stress better than those who think from a pessimistic viewpoint. Optimists, for instance, respond to being turned down for a job by formulating a plan of action and asking other people for help and advice; pessimists try to "forget the whole thing" and assume "there is nothing they can do to change things."

...artin Seligman of the University of Pennsylvania has ...out that it is the way people explain their failures to them- ...es that determines the degree of their future successes (and also their health; an attitude of helplessness, for instance, is associated with a weakened immune system). Those who look from a pessimistic viewpoint, Dr. Seligman points out, "construe bad events . . . as resulting from a personal deficit that will plague them forever in everything they do." They punish themselves for their setbacks. By contrast, he says, those who think more optimistically see "the same setbacks as being due to mistakes that can be remedied. They feel they can make the necessary changes." Those who take the stance that there is nothing they can do are much more prone to depression.

Dr. Seligman's research shows that people with a disposition toward pessimism can learn what he calls "flexible optimism." In his best-selling book, *Learned Optimism: How to Change Your Mind and Your Life*, he discusses simple steps for intervening in pessimistic thoughts. Something happens that we experience as negative. We have beliefs about that. Those beliefs lead to consequences. Dr. Seligman suggests that writing down what happened, noting what we think when this situation occurs, and then paying attention to what we do afterward are the beginning steps. Then we can do one of two things: we can distract ourselves from these thoughts by deliberately putting our thoughts somewhere else or, better yet, we can dispute the thoughts by (1) checking the evidence, (2) looking for alternatives, (3) asking what are the implications, or (4) asking how useful we find these beliefs and consequences.

Talking to the person who is gone has also proved to be a valuable way of supporting oneself while Finding Solid Ground. I. O. Glick and his colleagues at Harvard point out: "Often the widow's progress toward recovery was facilitated by inner conversations with her husband's presence . . . this continued sense of attachment was not incompatible with an increasing capacity for independent action." Dr. John Bowlby adds, "That for many bereaved people this [talking to the lost person] is the preferred solution to their dilemma has for too long gone unrecognized." With this internalization, he says, it's as if the lost persons "can be summoned to life and made to appear three-dimensional, in the mind as a stage where, like veteran actors, they play once more their classic role."

One specific action that some grief groups suggest is the use of a tool called project management. When an individual decides to make a particular change, accomplish a certain goal, or do a specific activity that is not part of her or his ordinary repertoire of actions or that is especially hard, that person decides whether the goal or proposed activity is important enough to be turned into a project. (Turning something into a project shows a commitment to making the change or to accomplishing the desired end.)

"Turning an idea into a project" means that the idea is put in writing and a structure is created that supports the accomplishment of the project. For instance, questions like these are answered: What is the purpose of this project? What makes this project worth doing? What is likely to go wrong, and what will you do when this happens? What tools, equipment, supplies, information, and so on do you need to do this project? Who can coach you in this project? What is the timeline? When will your next project be?

Men and women have used the tool of project management to do everything from putting a fifty-year collection of photographs into albums to learning to drive at the age of seventy to setting up a budget to manage personal finances to finding a solution for how to discipline their children. People are amazed to discover that a tool as simple as project management can give them such a sense of control and personal power. (But didn't Einstein say that the most elegant things are the simplest?) A tool like project management can provide just the liftoff, order, and purpose needed.

There were three things that made a huge difference to me as I searched for what would support me during the turbulent times when I was Finding Solid Ground. The first was spending some time every day alone in silence. I recently read a quote from a career counselor: "When I tell my clients that the first step toward finding their perfect job, spouse, or living situation is to sit still, they look at me as though I've turned into a snake. Stillness scares them, and rightly so. If we hold still long enough, we begin to feel what we really feel and to know what we really know. . . . If you can do this—get used to sitting still—eventually you will begin to sense a very deep self that defies all labels, a calm soul who has experienced your whole life . . . without ever being dominated or extinguished. This is . . . you."

I add prayer to the time I sit in silence, and I've found that keeping this commitment to spending some time, any amount of time—alone in quiet and in communion with the Divine every day (or not, when I didn't) created the opportunity for me to be sustained, guided, transformed, and supported in ways I could never have imagined or set a goal for.

There's a second thing: walking out-of-doors. You never know what you might see that will go deep inside to your very soul and give you strength that you had not even dreamed of. One day while out walking I happened upon tiny alpine flowers poking their yellow, pink, and blue heads up out of the ice and snow. I was feeling particularly low and sad that day. But as I stood looking at the bright colors of those hearty plants that grew and flourished in what seemed to me very harsh circumstances, I thought, "Surely I have alpine flowers in my heart. Surely I can flower in bright colors in adverse circumstances just as these tiny plants in front of me do."

And a third: art and music. I remember one day, walking alone in a small gallery, I came upon a picture I had seen maybe twenty years before on a Christmas card. It was Henry Raeburn's portrait

The Reverend Robert Walker Skating (c. 1794). The Reverend Walker, a Scot clergyman, is skating alone on a big pond. His face is serene. His motions look fluid, even in paint. The grayish sky, with a swath of pink, reflects with a pale rose glow, even down on the blue-gray-green of the ice. There's a barely visible left bank of the pond in the far distance. Then there's the minister, "exactly the curve of a black feather, blown across the empty lakescape on a wintry wind." There's the black of his hat, jacket, and knee breeches and leggings; the white of his neck cloth; and his red checks. I was stopped in my tracks. I felt one of the deepest wells of joy that I have ever felt. The joy just spouted up like a geyser. I actually laughed out loud at my first sight of the painting. Who can explain the power of a picture to touch the very core of who we are? Who can explain the wellsprings of joy that reside, even alongside the raw of pain? I have never forgotten that moment; and the thought of that portrait and of my joy in coming upon it sustained me many times afterward while I was struggling to keep Finding Solid Ground.

Then there was Beethoven's Ninth Symphony, ending in "Ode to Joy." I remember playing this symphony over and over. There was something so triumphant about the piece of music. I would flash back to the time Greg and I heard the piece by the San Francisco Symphony. That was the night I actually "heard" geometric shapes: circles, rectangles, squares. Perhaps the experience was related to harmonics—that phenomenon in music where one note pressed on the piano will always vibrate with higher and higher overtones. People who are in the know on such things tell us that harmonic overtones will always be arranged in identical order, and that this order is preordained by nature and governed by universal physical law. I didn't know any of this that night, but I do remember thinking of Keats's line "Beauty is truth, truth beauty." When I was so pressed by the necessity to engage in conflicts during my grieving process, I would play the Ninth Symphony and be sustained by the truth and beauty that I felt I could hear in every word and note.

RETRIEVING THREADS OF MEANING AND PURPOSE

One of the most crucial and most difficult of all tasks during the mourning process is to retrieve the threads of purpose and meaning that ran through the life we had before the loss and find a way to bring those threads into our present circumstances, albeit in a different form. There is no quick fix that allows this to happen. I've seen men and women attempt to find immediate purpose and meaning through "practical busyness"—by taking classes, going on trips, joining groups. But such a flurry of activity does not give these people what they want. It is not possible just to tack on activities and expect these to matter deeply to us. It has been over a lifetime that the purposes that give our lives meaning have been learned and brought together. Any new purposes we establish, therefore, "remain meaningless until they can be referred to those which have gone before." And such helter-skelter activities can actually be dangerous; they can result in a fragmentation—a disintegration— of our identity that is "more lastingly damaging" than the loss that led to our needing to retrieve a purpose from the "wreck of dead hopes."

As Peter Marris tells us:

A sense of continuity can, then, only be restored by detaching the familiar meanings of life from the relationship in which they were embodied, and reestablishing them independently of it. . . . Thus grief is mastered, not by ceasing to care for the dead, but by abstracting what was fundamentally important in the relationship and rehabilitating it. A widow has to give up her husband without giving up all that he meant to her. . . .

[This is a] task of extricating the essential meaning of the past and rein-
terpreting it to fit a very different future. . . . This is what happens in the
working through grief.

Professor James Carse, of New York University, has another way of talking about the reestablishing of meaning and purpose. When we do find a way to pick up the threads of the past and connect those threads with something in the present, we discover that, as hostile a force as it is, loss has not taken away all of our freedom. We still have a very important freedom, he says: *the freedom to "re-constitute the continuities" that the loss has destroyed.* When we experience this, we realize that we do have "the power to sustain continuity [even] in the face of death." And this, the professor says, is the highest form of freedom.

ENGAGING WITH QUESTIONS THAT MATTER TO US

Earlier in our grieving, many of us were plagued with questions about the "eternal verities," as some people put it. What is life all about? Why am I here? Why do the things happen that do happen? Does God care? What do I believe? Where does faith fit into a rational life? Who and what can I trust? When it was all we could do to get through a day or deal with our first thrusts out into life again, such questions debilitated. At the time, they truly were, in the words of Armand DiMele, "messy-dot questions." It was impossible for us to see the big picture; all we could see on the canvas was thousands of messy dots.

By this point, however, we have gained distance, perspective, and strength. Engaging with such questions now often seems like movement forward. We find succor in participating in a quiet weekend retreat, in listening to a lovely hymn during a church service, in taking a philosophy course or talking to a wise person.

Perhaps it is a time when we reaffirm what we believed in before the loss, but from the vantage point of who we are becoming rather than who we were then. Perhaps we find a new code of honor, a new creed, a new reason for living. Perhaps making a contribution is now more important to us than it was before. Perhaps we know we want to do work that is more meaningful.

Becoming more and more clear about what sustains us, what matters, what we can and do have faith in, and what we are committed to gives great support when we are Working Through and Finding Solid Ground. Howard Thurman, the great mystic, poet, and theologian, puts it this way:

> As a person, each of us lives a private life; there is a world within where for us the great issues of our lives are determined. It is here that at long last the yea and nay of our living is defined, declared. It is private. . . . The important thing, however, is the fact that beyond the zero point of endurance there are vast possibilities. . . . This simple fact of revitalizing human endurance opens a great vista for living. . . . There is a bottomless resourcefulness in individuals that ultimately enables them to transform "the spear of frustration into a shaft of light." Under such a circumstance even one's deepest distress becomes so sanctified that a vast illumination points the way to the land one seeks.

Albert Einstein talks about the importance of engaging in life with wonder and a passion for comprehension. (*Wonder* in the *American Heritage Dictionary* is associated with awe, surprise, astonishment—and puzzlement and doubt.) He says:

> To know that what is impenetrable to us really exists, manifesting itself as the highest wisdom and the most radiant beauty, which our dull faculties can comprehend only in the most primitive forms—this knowledge, this feeling is at the center of true religiousness. . . . There is, after all, some-

thing eternal that lies beyond reach of the hand of fate and of all human delusions.

By engaging in questions that matter—as Howard Thurman and Albert Einstein remind us—we do find that core of ourselves where the *yea and nay of our living is defined* and where "the spears of frustration" can be transformed into "a shaft of light." We find bedrock in that *something eternal that lies beyond reach of the hand of fate.*

THE CHOICE

If there is any one thing that has become clear during the experiences of Finding Solid Ground, it is that movement is not automatic. Time does not, contrary to the old saying, "heal all wounds." No, it isn't time that determines whether or not we go forward to a creative transformation of our grieving. What does determine this movement is our choices. What is the choice, then, when we are Finding Solid Ground?

We can choose to engage in the conflicts.

Conflict, we are told, "is a very powerful organizing principle of behavior, simplifying and clarifying immediate purposes." As we weigh the pros and cons, look for solutions, grapple with issues, we are, in effect, determining our values, setting our priorities, deciding on what is and is not acceptable to us. We are drawing the contours of our future.

Choosing to engage in the conflicts isn't easy, for it means acknowledging situations we would rather not deal with. It means sticking with problems until we find a satisfactory solution. It means doing those things that are necessary to change ourselves in order to be consistent with our new life environment. This choosing to engage in the conflicts, however, is "the central, most urgent task" because without this engagement we "cannot repair the ability to learn new meaningful ways of coping." When we have engaged, however, and worked through the problems and issues, we "will find vitality and confidence for other purposes."

There are some areas of special difficulty where the choice to engage in the conflicts may seem truly daunting: (1) the challenge of establishing new primary relationships, if that is something we wish to do; (2) the challenges represented to the family unit; and (3) the extra strain and stress for those who have lost a homosexual partner, a family member, or a friend.

One of the problems that people who start to think about establishing new primary relationships must face is that of awkwardness and unfamiliarity. In an essay that would be amusing if it were not so to-the-bone accurate, Noel Perrin, a newly divorced professor, writes about middle-age dating:

> *I'm dialing a phone number, and when I've touched five digits, I suddenly hang up. For two or three minutes I sit on my bed, my lips moving occasionally, as if I were an actor going over a part. Then I pick up the phone, hesitate, start to put it down again. Instead, I quickly touch seven tones. A woman answers. I am a nervous man in his fifties, calling a woman also in her fifties to ask her to dinner. It will be a blind date. It will be my second blind date this month. Dear god, how I dread it.*

When our loss has been a spouse or a partner, we often don't know what to do when we finally venture to go out with others. We feel awkward: What will I do if the person wants to kiss me? Should I offer to pay half of the meal? Do I keep my ring on or take it off? How do I discuss dating with the children?

Many of us haven't had to think about such questions since we were teenagers or young adults. And now we feel like adolescents facing these thorny issues all over again. There are no rules, which makes the circumstances even more uncomfortable. Noel Perrin suggests a way to ease into middle-age dating:

True intimacy is the whole purpose of middle-age dating. Only what took one date to accomplish at twenty-five may now take five or ten. By middle age, people have developed complex personalities, whole networks of obligations, settled habits. It would be naïve to expect any quick meshing.

We probably need to invent a new kind of dating: fewer evenings, more mornings. Breakfast and a shopping excursion, sometimes, instead of dinner and clasped hands in a movie theatre. It's more work, of course. But then, we're deeper people now. With luck, we might wind up with the kind of rich and tolerant relationship we didn't even dream of when we were young.

Another conflict of these experiences of Working Through is the change that comes in the dynamics of family connections. As Dr. Beverley Raphael alerts us, "The family unit as it was before dies, and a new family system must be constituted. The death," she says, "will be a crisis for the family unit as well as for each individual member." What is the nature of this crisis?

Perhaps before the loss the family's well-being was nurtured by a mother who had chosen the career of a homemaker. When she is gone, there is no one for the family to constellate themselves around, so the family unit disintegrates. Or perhaps the adult children of a family maintained a modicum of congeniality and chose to cover up seething resentments to avoid open conflict while their father was alive, only to reveal their real feelings of anger, distrust, and jealousy after his death. These families must reconstitute themselves, and this reconstitution can be painful.

After the loss, family members must also find appropriate new roles for themselves. Who will take over the lost person's duties and responsibilities? How will the other family members react to this replacement? What dynamics will come into play as family members attempt to cohere into a reorganized unit? How will other family members respond to the changes that occur in the life of the primary mourner? These are difficult questions. Often, doing the work of Finding Solid Ground is a commitment that will be made by some family members and not by others.

Another kind of conflict at the family level is the recognition and response to young children's delayed or prolonged grieving. A young mother whose husband died accidentally some years ago told me about her ten-year-old son, who, until recently, she thought was moving through the grieving process in a timely and normal fashion. Then, suddenly, he became frantic—afraid at every turn that there was some part of his homework he hadn't done because he didn't remember the complete assignment; afraid that he wouldn't get to soccer practice on time; afraid that he wouldn't be able to do the tasks required for his next Boy Scout badge. Fortunately, the young mother was cognizant of the phases of the mourning process and recognized that, though it had been some years since the father's death, her son's behavior might be related to aspects of the loss. She realized that, in keeping with her son's maturation and development, perhaps he was only now facing certain loss issues that he had been too young to experience earlier. The child is now seeing a psychologist once a week—"my other teacher," he says—and positive changes are already apparent in his behavior. Paramount among them is a noticeable increase in the child's spontaneous mentioning of his father. There has also been a noticeable decrease in his frantic behavior.

Another group for whom engaging in the conflicts is awkward and often extremely difficult is partners, relatives, or friends of homosexuals. Professionals who have worked with recovery groups in the gay community point out ways in which this segment of grieving individuals differs from others: They live a lifestyle that is often condemned by others, and they are often shunned themselves because people think they may carry the AIDS virus. They are sometimes plagued by low self-esteem and guilt. They may feel abandoned and isolated because the deceased was their only real "family," their own family being perhaps emotionally and geographically absent. There is no tradition for gay mourning and little societal approval. The survivors usually do not get financial benefits and often lose jointly acquired property. They are often not given a role in the making of funeral or memorial plans. Reentry and resocialization are difficult and often complicated by more deaths and new diagnoses of illness. There are few outside resources or sources of support for gays who are grieving. Caregivers often must deal with their own feelings about loss and about homosexuality in order to offer genuine help. There is an extreme need, during the experiences of Finding Solid Ground, for individuals to recognize and respond to the special needs of members of the gay community, who may be grieving not only for "their dead and dying friends but also for a way of life that is gone and may never come back."

But, as hard as it may be, these painful conflicts must be engaged with. Some kind of balance must be established. Issues such as these make the choice to engage in the conflicts even more difficult, but as we have learned at every juncture in the grieving process, the only alternative we have is to make the affirmative choice, no matter how difficult that choice may be.

WHAT WE NEED FROM FAMILY AND FRIENDS WHILE WE ARE FINDING SOLID GROUND

The kind of people we need around us now are those who know that we have conflicts to work through in order to reestablish ourselves in life—all parts of our grieving—and who also know that we are capable of meeting and resolving these conflicts. Dr. Colin Murray Parkes points out how important such individuals can be: "In a situation in which well-established norms are absent, the expectations of those around are potent determinants of behavior." Choosing to be around people who expect us to grow and change, who expect us to face and handle the challenges of this period of our grieving, can be a powerful incentive for resolving the conflicts that are always a part of change. The kind of people we do not need to be around are those whose "caretaking" and "sympathy" would keep us weak, dependent, and afraid.

This is an excellent time, too, to seek professional advice and support on specific issues and situations with which we are beset. A child psychologist can help us understand a youngster's delayed grieving. A counselor or a coach can assist us in understanding our fear of change. In a group, we can practice new roles that are awkward and unfamiliar. A wise friend can point out areas we need to work in that we may not be able to see for ourselves. A weekend retreat can help us begin to reconstitute our faith.

The bottom line is that during this time of problem-solving, we should seek out and ask for the assistance of those individuals around us who are solution-oriented, who understand the necessity for change, who are not intimidated by risk-taking, who understand that our progress will not occur in a smooth, straight line and who acknowledge and support us for having the courage to engage with the conflicts that are unavoidable as we are Finding Solid Ground.

I happened to be going through the Denver airport at one extremely difficult time while I was Finding Solid Ground. While waiting for my flight, I picked up a paperback at the newsstand, a little book called *Markings* by Dag Hammarskjöld, a private journal he had kept for many years. Only after he was killed in an airplane crash in Africa while serving as secretary-general of the United Nations was the journal made available to the public.

There were many entries in *Markings* that spoke to me. But one sentence in particular stood out. "I am committed to a life of no return," Mr. Hammarskjöld had written. That, I decided, was worth remembering and repeating often. I am committed to a life of no return. The life of balance and promise that I so desperately wanted lay nowhere except ahead; and going forward was, I knew, the only way I was going to reach it.

THE TERRAIN OF OUR ACTIVE GRIEVING

Life As It Was   *Life and Loss Integrated*
The Event of Loss   *Freedom from Domination of Grief*

IMPACT: Experiencing the unthinkable
CHOICE: To experience and express grief fully

SECOND CRISIS: Stumbling in the dark
CHOICE: To endure with patience

OBSERVATION: Linking past to present
CHOICE: To look honestly

THE TURN: Turning into the wind
CHOICE: To replan and change our lives to include but not be dominated by the loss

RECONSTRUCTION: Picking up the pieces
CHOICE: To take specific actions

WORKING THROUGH: Finding solid ground
CHOICE: To engage in the conflicts

INTEGRATION: Daylight
CHOICE: To make and remake choices

Remember: A map never tells us how to travel. A map does not determine that everyone travels same route, moves at the same speed, shares a set itinerary. A map does not dictate, prescribe, ven describe an individual's movement. A map does, however, name. A map can help us find re we are when we think we are lost. A map shows possibilities and provides ideas for where there is for us to go. At all times, however, every individual is the person holding the map.

WORKING THROUGH: Finding solid ground

What Is Normal?

    Experiencing new problems related to changes we are making

    Practicing new roles

    Dealing with breakdowns and finding creative solutions

    Risking

    Determining how to respond to disappointments and adversity resulting from new activities and new commitments

    Continuing to develop a new identity consistent with who we are now and what our life circumstances are now

    Reexamining assumptions

    Realizing the need for self-management

    Reconstituting and reaffirming values and beliefs

What Can I Do?

    Seek out people who are proficient at what I am trying to learn.

    Focus on solving problems rather than being upset that the problems are there.

    Distinguish between problems that are related to the loss and those that are just part of living.

    Replenish yourself by sitting still, praying, taking walks, writing poems, looking at art you love, listening to music, cooking new recipes, gardening, fishing, getting messages.

    Be patient.

WORKING THROUGH: Finding solid ground

My active choice?

To engage in the conflicts

7

INTEGRATION:

DAYLIGHT

The tales we care for lastingly are the ones that touch on the redemptive . . . the idea that insists on the freedom to change one's life.
Cynthia Ozick

I am not afraid of storms, for I am learning how to sail my ship.
Louisa May Alcott

Looking out the window, I could see dark clouds ahead. Streaks of lightning were flashing every few seconds. The pilot, the only crew aboard the small commuter plane, announced, "A thunderstorm has moved in faster than expected. Looks like we're going to be going through the worst of it. Be sure your seat belts are fastened."

The wind began to toss the small plane around as if it were made of paper. We rolled from side to side. Sheets of rain hit the windows. The plane bucked again and again as we hit air pockets. The metal began popping and cracking. It was only four o'clock in the afternoon, but there was now nothing but black outside, punctuated by bursts of lightning. I could see the pilot in the cockpit, his hands gripping the wheel in front of him. The muscle at the back of his right jaw was twitching violently.

I began to sob. I knew the plane was breaking up and we were going to crash. I knew death was imminent.

Suddenly the motion of the plane threw me to the right, the seat belt cutting into my abdomen. The gentleman across the narrow aisle reached out to steady me, and I grasped his hand. Immediately, I was strangely affected. A warmth—a feeling of heat—traveled through my entire body. I continued to hold on to the stranger's hand as I wedged myself back into my seat. The plane rocked as uncontrollably as before, but something amazing had happened. All fear had left me; I was completely at peace.

When we finally passed through the storm, I released the gentleman's hand and looked over to thank him. He must have been in his late sixties or early seventies, a tall, thin man with big hands and a wind-whipped face. I could see nothing in his appearance or his demeanor that would explain the warmth and the strange calming effect his touch had had on me.

"I'm Ernest Naudon," the gentleman said. "A well digger from British Columbia, on my way to the Turks and Caicos Islands. I'm just stopping off at Texas A&M to pick up some equipment."

"What will you do in the Turks and Caicos?" I asked him, searching for a clue that would help me understand what I had just experienced.

"Help build some houses for the poor and a place of worship. I'm of the Baha'i faith, and each year I do three months' work at some pioneer mission. This year it's the Turks and Caicos."

I sat for a few seconds trying to think how to broach the subject. I finally asked straight out:

"You weren't afraid at all when we were going through that storm, were you?"

"No," he answered. "I was not afraid."

"But you knew we might crash, didn't you?"

"Yes," he answered. "I knew we were in great danger."

"Do you mean, then," I asked incredulously, "that you knew we were in great danger and you still weren't afraid of dying?"

"No," he said. "I was not afraid of dying." The man looked me straight in the eye when he answered.

"But how can you not be afraid of dying?" I asked him. "Death is so terrible."

Without answering, the gentleman opened the paperback he had been reading, tore a blank end sheet from the back, and printed in large block letters:

> Know, you are where you are
> Not by accident but by the design
> Of your Creator for your own
> Development or for the development
> Of those around you.
>
> Abdul Baha

Below this verse he wrote a second:

> Is there any remover of difficulties, save God? . . .
> All are his servants and all abide by his bidding.
>
> The Bab

"That," he said, "is why I am not afraid of dying. I know there is a design, and I know I participate in that design by God's bidding. What, then, is there to fear—whether one is dead or living?"

I knew Mr. Naudon believed what he spoke; I had seen the evidence a few minutes ago. I envied this man his peace about dying. I envied him his freedom.

When the plane landed, I walked with him to the terminal. As we shook hands and said goodbye, I made an awkward attempt to thank him. "I certainly hope there is someone like you on the next plane I'm flying," I said.

"Oh, there will be," Mr. Naudon answered with a smile that was as enigmatic as his answer.

The aftermath of the scare in the airplane left me with two recurring memories: the frightening sounds of popping and cracking, which I had been sure meant the plane was breaking, and the inexplicable warmth and sense of calm in which I had been enveloped when I grasped the gentleman's hand. I would lie awake at night, playing these two experiences against each other: the one reminding me of how afraid I was of dying; the other reminding me that, for some, there was another alternative.

The truth was that this was the first time I had considered my own dying. And it was very upsetting. A raft of memories flooded my mind every time I let myself think about it. A filmstrip we saw when I was in the eleventh grade—wasn't it one of Chaucer's tales, where the Grim Reaper came, at his pleasure, through the window with his hourglass and his sickle? The experience of stepping across the threshold of a room in a southern plantation I was once touring, feeling the air suddenly and inexplicably change from pleasant to cold and finding out only after the tour guide had entered the room and told the story that this was the room in which the master of the house had died after putting up a terrible struggle. The shock of being touched personally by the force of death, unveiled and unmitigated, when I saw for the first time a dead body not yet in a mortuary—and that dead body was the body of my husband! No, thinking about my own death was not a subject I found pleasant.

But I wasn't able to forget it. I thought of the truths I had long believed in, truths reflected in St. Paul's "O death, where is thy sting? O grave, where is thy victory?"; in the Buddha's "Death is a temporary end of a temporary phenomenon"; in the Sufis' "Death is the tax the soul pays for having had a form and a name." Until I faced my own imminent death, these truths had been sufficient. But now I realized that a gulf existed between what I believed about death and how I responded when I actually thought I would soon be dying. As a result of that experience on the plane, the shield had been removed that until that moment had protected me from seeing into the abyss called my own dying.

But now the shock of the glimpse had registered. "How much does this unacknowledged, unexamined fear of my own death determine the parameters of my life?" I wondered. "Is it possible," I quizzed myself further, "to express in daily life an attitude and a behavior that include death in the whole picture rather than doing everything possible to exclude it?"

As synchronicity would have it, a friend whom I had told about the airplane incident brought me a book a few weeks later. "I found this," he said. "Thought it might be interesting in light of your recent experience." The book was called *Death and the Creative Life: Conversations with Prominent Artists and Scientists* by Lisl Goodman. Who would have thought that it was from the words of a physicist and a scientist that I would get the first glimmer of how to bring my faith and my behavior together, my first insight into how to build a frame for thinking that included death and life as a whole?

Goodman had interviewed the physicist John Wheeler, famous for his study of black holes and his work in gravitational physics, asking him if he thought he had come to terms with death. Professor Wheeler answered by affirming how much he loved life:

> If my airplane tomorrow night had to ditch in the ocean, I would struggle with all my might to survive. Life is just too precious to give up. . . . Each remaining year seems more precious than ever; but even more, the contact with every friend enhances the preciousness of life.

The editor then pressed the physicist: "But suppose you had finished everything you possibly could?"

"In my office," Professor Wheeler answered, "I keep a two-inch white box for every project that I plan to do someday. . . . The number of new projects that I add each year exceeds the number that I accomplish. So now there are about one hundred and fifty such two-inch boxes in my office—misery for my poor secretary. To me, each is a precious tie to the world. So it is hard for me to think of myself ever being tired of the world."

But, then, would he banish death if he could?

The scientist answered, "Taking a responsibility for the trees at my children's summer place makes me aware of how a great old spreading tree kills the future for promising new young trees which are too close to it. Death is essential for renewal. We know that the earth is renewed from underneath."

And furthermore, he said:

Life without death would be a picture without a frame. To have the body go is proof before one's eyes that the survival of mankind, its essence, is of the spirit—the flame handed on from one runner to another. How else are we to realize that life is more important than the ones who do the living?

The paradox was clear to me as I read the interview. Here was a man, on the one hand, with a hundred and fifty projects waiting, a man who loved his friends and family, a man who didn't want to give up a single precious day of living. On the other hand, he was a man who, tending his children's trees, knew that death was a part of the design of life. A man who recognized that it was death that proved that the very essence of life was spirit.

I read further. Dr. Howard Gruber, a scientist noted for his work on creativity, spoke about a paper he had written titled "And the Bush Was Not Consumed." In it, the scientist said, "I don't speak of death, but about the 'unquenchable flame'":

A creative moment is part of a longer creative process, which in its turn is part of a creative life. How are such lives lived? How can I express this particular idea that such an individual must be a self-regenerating system? Not a system that comes to rest when it has done good work, but one that urges itself onward. And yet not a runaway system that accelerates its activity to the point where it burns itself out in one great flash. The system regulates the activity and the creative acts regenerate the system.

Then Dr. Gruber added:

If you ask me how I am planning my life . . . I am planning it around the idea that I am going to die. I know I am going to die and I want certain things to be accomplished, so I'm working within certain probabilities about getting old, losing my resources, my energy.

It came to me as I read: Instead of focusing on the fear of death, I could focus on not dying incomplete. This meant that I would strive at all times to be a "self-regenerating system," to concentrate on living my life to its fullest potential. That way, whenever I died—whether suddenly or in old age—at that moment of going I would feel that I had died alive, active, working to do everything I was drawn to do.

As I put the book away, it seemed ironic that the frightening experience I had on that plane had turned out to be such a gift, enabling me to confront the idea of my own dying. And, while the context I had begun to frame for myself was perhaps not as explicit a statement of faith as those lovely words the gentleman had written that day on the plane, there did seem to be something about the insights I had just gained that was sacred.

It happened in the wilds of the Mojave Desert, in Southern California, on a late afternoon in the fall four years after Greg died. The moment—the symbolic moment—when I knew I had reached a new equilibrium, when I was no longer dominated by the necessity to grieve.

The setting was an Outward Bound wilderness-survival course, which I had first thought of taking three years earlier but until now had not been able to muster the courage to tackle. And I still wasn't sure about the whole thing. In fact, since being here I had questioned my decision to take the course at least ten times a day, if not a hundred. What was a klutz like me doing rappelling five hundred feet down a mountain, climbing fifty-foot boulders, hiking ten hours at a stretch, hoisting a fifty-pound backpack, and learning to assemble a camp stove and read a compass? It was only with great difficulty that I could remember the litany I had repeated to get myself here: *It's a new experience, a physical challenge, something you have never done before, it will keep you young, an opportunity to expand your limits.*

And now I had even graver doubts about the wisdom of such an adventure. We had reached that dreaded point in the schedule: It was time for the experience known as the solo. Each of us was going to be left alone to fend for ourselves in the desert. "Naturally," our course leader said, "you'll learn from the physical challenge of having to survive." We all laughed nervously. The course leader smiled and continued: "But perhaps the greatest benefit you will gain from doing the solo is the time you spend in conversation with yourself. Take this opportunity to ask important questions: What do I want in life? What gives my life meaning? You know, those universal questions that people in all cultures have asked as far back as there is record.

"Consider writing in a journal. Drawing pictures. Making a piece of art from found objects. Building something from the dirt and wood around you. Or just sitting, doing nothing."

I had cleared the site where I had been dropped off, unrolled my sleeping bag on the ground, gotten out my food and water. It was late afternoon—I guessed there were two or three hours of daylight left—when I sat down with my journal. A "commonplace book," I called it, because I put everything in it—not only my own jottings but quotes I found meaningful, poems, clippings from magazines and newspapers, addresses given out on National Public Radio for ordering tapes and transcripts of their programs. The pages, in addition to my own journal-keeping, were a hodgepodge of many things that over the past couple of years had interested or inspired me.

"I wonder what I will find here?" I asked as I adjusted myself next to a Joshua tree. Even though I picked up the book often at home to write or add an entry, I had never sat down and read it from beginning to end. "Will I find out something about myself that I do not know? Will there perhaps be some pattern behind what looks like a bunch of random entries?"

The first entry I turned to was the paragraphs I had copied from Woody Guthrie's posthumous autobiography, word pictures of a family gathering to eat:

Chow is now on! Red bean a green bean a white bean a flitter, corn bread dry bread a wheat bread fritter! Come get it before I throw it to th' hogs in th' pen!

I laughed. Discover myself in these extravagant lines? Find a pattern that said something about the eternal questions of existence? In words like these?

But I also realized as I read this entry that, for a Southern girl, this passage was a celebration of family. It was a celebration of the simple things in life. It was gathering, eating, playing. Life real, life lived at its marrow. The passage was a reminder of my roots, and it was a pointer toward what I wanted now and in the future.

I brought my mind back from its reverie. I noticed the bushy purple cactuses all around me and out of the corner of my eye caught a glimpse of a jackrabbit moving across the desert in the distance. Now, what was our assignment?

"Hold a conversation with yourself. Think about your life. Reconsider the eternal questions," the leader had said. I turned on in my journal.

Why, I had even saved an obituary. For Buckminster Fuller. In the obituary, some of Bucky's own words had been quoted:

> *I live on earth at present, and I don't know what I am*
> *I know that I am not a category. I am not a thing—a noun.*
> *I seem to be a verb, an evolutionary process—an integral function of the*
>   *universe.*

These words by this scientist reminded me of those earlier sentences: *We are a self-regenerating system . . . Life is a bush that will not be consumed . . . Life is more important than those who do the living . . .*

Below the obituary, I had taped another quote by Bucky:

> *My brother collected stones.*
> *I collected papers with my name on them*
> *As written or printed by someone else*
> *Letters, postcards . . . school reports . . .*
> *As a consequence of surprises*
> *Emanating from my collection's*
> *Progressive patterning*
> *In 1917, at the age of 22,*

I made a grand strategy decision.
I determined to make myself the guinea pig
In a lifelong research project. . . .

I leaned back against the Joshua tree and gazed up at the sky. That was an interesting way to think about the evolution of one's life . . . as a lifelong research project. In that context, I wondered, "By the end of a woman's life, what kind of investigation would the death of a husband have turned out to be? How would such a life-changing event fit into the lifelong research project?"

The end of a woman's life . . . My eye alighted next on an excerpt from an interview with Marguerite Yourcenar, the French novelist. When she was in her late eighties, an interviewer had asked Mme. Yourcenar to speak about what she thought was the purpose of living. I had copied:

I believe that perfecting oneself is life's principal purpose. . . . We may not reform the world, but at least we can reform ourselves, and we are, after all, a small part of the world.

Yourcenar went on to quote the eighteenth-century philosopher Saint-Martin, who had said of his friends:

They are the beings through whom God loved me.

This seemed to me, as I sat that afternoon in the desert, a worthy purpose for a person to have for her life: to be someone through whom God loved others.

I had placed a Howard Thurman quote next to Yourcenar's words:

Each of us, in our own way, finds the stairs leading to the Holy Place. We gather in our hands the fragments of our lives, searching eagerly for

*some creative synthesis, some wholeness, some all-encompassing unity
capable of stilling the tempests within us and quieting all the inner turbu-
lence of our fears. We seek to walk in our own path which opens up before us, made clear by the light of [the Divine] Spirit and the radiance
which it casts all around us. . . . The assumption is that the individual is
ever in immediate candidacy to get an "assist" from God—that she is not
alone in her quest. Through prayer, meditation and singleness of mind,
the individual's life may be invaded by strength, insight, and courage sufficient for her needs. Thus she need not seek refuge in excuses but can live
her life with ever-increasing vigor and experience . . . an ever-deepening
sense of fulfillment.*

I knew immediately the reason for this entry in my commonplace book: The quiet time and prayer that had begun with my
meeting Betty Unterberger, the history professor, had by now become the very context of my life. I knew that an awareness of the
possibility and the promise of a well-tended and honored inner life
that focused on partnership with the Holy Other would now always
be my first commitment. I continued, as Howard Thurman said, to
receive that "assist" from God. I was blessed by being "invaded by
strength, insight, and courage sufficient" for my needs.

A few pages over, I saw an entry that made me laugh out loud.
Somewhere I had come across the phonetic transcription by a
French composer of a nightingale's song:

*Tiou, tiou, tiou, tiou—Spe, tiou, squa—tio, tio, tio, tio, tio, tio, tio,
tix—Coutio, coutio, coutio, coutio—Squo, squo, squo, squo—Tzu,
tzu, tzu, tzu, tzu, tzu, tzu, tzu, tzi—Corror, tiou, squa, pipiquiZozozo-
zozozozozozozozozozozo, zirrhading—Tsissisi, tsissisisisisisisis—Dzoree,
dzoree, dzoree, tzatu, dzi—Dlo, dlo, dlo, dlo, dlo, dlo, dlo, dlo, dlo—
Quio, trrrrrrrr—Lu, lu, lu, lu, ly, ly, ly, ly, lie, lie, lie, lie, lie—Quio*

didl li lulylie—Hagurr, gurr, quipio—Coui, coui, coui, couri, qui, qui, qui, gai, gui, gui, gui—Goll, goll, goll, goll guia hadadoi—Conigui, horr, ha diadia dill si—Hezezezezezezezezezezezezezezeze courar ho dze hoi—Quia, quia, quia, quia, quia, quia, quia, quia, ti Ki, ki, ki, io, io, io, ioioioioio ki—Lu ly li le lai la leu lo, didl io, quia—Ki-gaigaigaigaigaigaigai guiagaigaigai couior dzio dzio pi.

I decided I must have put this piece in my journal to help me keep perspective, because right beneath it I had written two other quotes. The first one read:

> *There are three things which are real:*
> *God, human folly, and laughter.*
> *The first two are beyond our comprehension*
> *So we must do what we can with the third.*

And then came what someone had told me were Socrates' last words: *Please the gods, may the laughter keep breaking through.*

It was at this moment that I recognized that the work of grieving for Greg was over. Not, of course, that I believed I would never feel sadness again, or longing or pain. Not that the experience of his death would not be a part of me forever. Not that issues, particularly about myself, that had been revealed, though not caused, by his death were not present for me to continue to grapple with. But what I now realized was that my life was no longer dominated by the presence of loss. I had found balance. Daily life was now a "new kind of normal." I did again take joy in living. I did have enthusiasm and energy. I felt full to the brim with possibility. Most of all, I felt privileged to be able to live this Awesome Mystery, the Gift of Life. Yes, I had done the work that was necessary to be able to say, "I have grieved."

After I prepared my noodles and vegetables, ate my bickie crackers and peanut butter, cleaned the boiler so it would be ready for making coffee the next morning, it was time for bed.

I would be lying if I said I wasn't scared as I climbed into my sleeping bag and zipped it up around me. But I wasn't nearly as afraid as I had thought I would be. Even when I woke in the wee hours of the morning and saw a coyote standing near the end of the bedroll, I yelled only five times to scare him away, instead of ten or twenty. And I think I was even able to go back to sleep, maybe sometime shortly before daybreak.

This is Daylight. The set of experiences that culminates in Integration, in our recognizing that the loss is now a part of who we are. We feel released. No longer do we feel dominated by the loss; we are no longer forced to do combat with debilitating memories every day. Our life is no longer one gaping hole of emptiness and pain. We have changed. We are stronger. We have a renewed interest in living. We enjoy an increased sense of play and freedom. And, once again, when we look up we can see a horizon.

All of this is possible because we have chosen to experience fully and actively the *complete* grieving process. Not just the acute first phases of grief—as important and essential as these are—but the daunting longer-term phases, those sets of experiences that require us to change ourselves in order to be consistent with our new life situation.

Dr. George Pollock calls this process we have just been through a *transformational mourning-liberation process.* He asserts that this process is normal, found in all people and throughout history. He also says that this process—which we have navigated with varying degrees of success on any given day—is *a universal means of adapting to unwanted change.*

And there are gains we have made as a result of our hard work to move forward through the full grief process. Dr. Pollock calls these gains *creative outcomes* and says these creative outcomes include:

- the ability to feel joy, satisfaction, and a sense of accomplishment
- a return to a steady state of balance
- the experience of an increased capacity to appreciate people and things
- a realization that we are more tolerant and wise
- a desire to express ourselves creatively
- the ability to invest in new relationships
- the experience of a sense of play and freedom
- a deepening of our faith

We do not experience these creative outcomes because we have been able to re-create how things were before the loss. No, we have achieved much more than that. What we experience now, because the mourning process is what Dr. Pollock calls an *adaptive-transformational process*, is a "new creation." A new creation that, he says, derives "its energy and perhaps inspiration and direction from the past," to be sure, but is nevertheless a "successor" creation, not a replacement. We have been changed by the grieving process, and as a result we have changed things around us.

The women and men with whom I have talked speak of the satisfaction that comes during the experiences of Daylight. It is as if a parenthesis had closed, a chapter completed. There is a certain degree of clarity, a way of thinking, a kind of recognition that marks the lives of those who have finished their grieving. It is experiences like these that they report during this period when they recognize that the loss is now integrated and they are reaching Daylight.

FINDING DEEPER RESOURCES

A mother says:

Oh, I admit it was awful. I had been living in a real comfort zone. I had everything made. My husband made good money; he was loving and caring. I had two beautiful children I adored; my whole purpose in life was to be a good wife and a good mother. And I was great at both of those things. Then he was gone. I could no longer afford to go out to eat in fancy restaurants. I had to get a cheaper car. I had to do everything myself.

But today I no longer dwell on what I lost but look instead to see that I've made it in the past and I'm making it now. This is not just wishful thinking or sheer determination talking. I have looked around and seen evidence that I've achieved a lot in this long, painful process. I see that I've been forced to take a new path and to see that a world that I thought was perfect and working so well can be interrupted and then destroyed. I've had to call on my resources; I've had to dig deeper. I've had to call on something I had forgotten was there, things I hadn't ever given myself credit for. And, you know, to tell you the truth it's kind of exciting.

REINVENTING ONESELF

A young man recounts:

The whole structure of my life was shattered to smithereens by the death of my mother. I was eight and didn't understand what had happened—that my mother had become addicted to barbiturates three years earlier and was dying from this addiction. Within these three years, then, we went from a very Midwestern, middle-class, very typical early-fifties St. Louis kind of family to a disintegrated, poor, Deep South kind of family. It was just incomprehensible. Very bewildering. Confusion and more confusion. I changed from being very outgoing to never going out—just staying home and reading and having no friends. Our family just withdrew as a group.

So as an adult I've had to reinvent myself—come up with a personality and a person to be. When someone asks how you do that, I say, "You pick what you like. You learn." For a long time I was a very unfocused, undirected person. But life placed me in contact with people who taught me that I could pick and choose from the menu of what I had seen and say, "Well, I like that and I like that, and I don't like that. That's a good way to be, and that's not a good way to be."

I made choices. I just became aware of reality and that I had to make choices, and those choices were my life. Everybody, of course, has to do that, but loss forces you into an absolute realization of that. And I'm still doing it. Making choices isn't something that you do once and then no more. Making choices is for the rest of your life.

RECLAIMING PLEASURE

A friend tells this story:

I used to be an avid deer hunter. Nothing could keep me away from the lease during the fall of the year. After Whitney's death, I was no longer interested in killing deer. For a long time, there was only a void in my life where deer hunting used to be. No hobby or activity seemed to give me any pleasure.

I surprised myself the other day by thinking, "You know, old boy, you've got your pleasure back!" It was like waking up to life again after being so long in the twilight world of grieving our daughter's death. I've found something new to involve myself in—duck hunting. Well, actually it's more like duck observing, I suppose, because what I'm interested in is figuring out the world of ducks, not shooting at them. I'm reading about duck hunting. I've got a great old book, *Travel and Traditions of Water Fowl,* that I'm reading. A classic in the field. So I'm looking into ducks now. And once I figure out ducks, maybe I'll go for wild boar or something. I'm really enjoying it. I heard my wife on the phone the other night talking to her sister. "I thought for so long that Joe would never be excited about anything again," she said. "It's so wonderful to see him engrossed in his books and heading out to the duck blind early in the morning."

MAKING A WISE CHOICE

A woman talks:

It's now been five years, and when I feel what I would generally call pain, I can usually transform that into something else by looking for the explanation: I'm learning something new or doing something that is uncomfortable or letting go of another piece of the past. I'm getting to the place where I can have a sense of humor about it. I know now that everything in life is temporary—everything—and that even what we call pain is just going through an experience we didn't expect.

So often I have to remind myself that there is a choice. I have my life here, and back there is the life I used to have. But by this time I've come up with a mental picture that keeps me from getting caught in the contradiction. I see a railroad track, with me on one of those little one-wheeled scooters railroad workers ride to check on the track. One side of the track is the unfulfilled dreams of my life before the loss. The other side is the joy, fulfillment, and wonderful things in my life now.

On any given day, I can travel on my one-wheeled scooter along either of those tracks. If I want joy, peace, and harmony, I can go down one track. If I want to think about what I lost and will never have again, I can hop over there and be miserable for a while. It's really kind of nice. It's like, "Get over there and be sloppy sad." And then it feels so much better when you do go back to the fun part. It's always a choice. And most of the time now I feel wise enough to choose to be happy.

NAMING POSITIVE OUTCOMES

A *widow writes:*

If I had to say how I have been changed by actively grieving, I would use one word: *quieter.* I'm quieter in my spirit. Wisdom did come, as researchers predict it can, from participating in the full grieving cycle. I'm on the go less. I don't try to do everything that comes along. What is even more amazing is that I don't even set goals anymore. I make commitments and keep them. I get things done that are there to be done. But I have no goals I'm striving for, no gold ring I want to reach. I let life take its course. I follow—as one philosopher puts it—the movement of the showing. I work and work hard. I take action when action is needed. But I don't push for my idea of what ought to be happening.

It's a paradox, isn't it? I'm not drifting. I'm not waiting for things to just happen. I am an active participant in the enterprise. But somewhere along the way I've realized that any goal I set, any direction I lay out precisely, might be too small or too limited or too one-dimensional. This I do not want.

I now have time to do things that I didn't even want to do before the death—like water flowers, cut bouquets, visit antiques stores, hunt for bargains in thrift stores. My home is much more a home and less a place to stay when I wasn't working, volunteering, going, doing, as in the past. I express my creativity more. Not long ago, I took a two-hour course on making collages at an art-supply store nearby—and my new husband had the piece I made framed. "That's art," he said, when I brought it home.

What began in the grieving process as stillness has now evolved into a richly textured spiritual life. Being in relationship with God is now always my first commitment. Learning how to love more and more graciously and totally is my highest intention. All this could, I suppose, sound platitudinous. Pompous. Even pious. Funny, though. It's none of that. It's my life. That is truly how I have changed. I experienced through death another kind of death—death of the view of life that I had before the loss. The view I have now of life allows me to be much more at peace. Much more confident. Much more able to wait. And even more in awe of Mystery.

Engaging with Life Fully

A son recalls:

Before my father was killed, I would say that I was very much with the program of life. I excelled in sports—I had a room full of trophies. I had medals for singing. I made straight A's in school. I was honor society and class president. I did all the achievement-oriented things that regular everyday life is about—winning and succeeding.

Then for a long time—years, really—after my father's death I wasn't interested in succeeding or participating. But now I think differently. I'm going to take what I've learned since my father's death and bring that back with me into the mainstream of life where most people live—which is to be successful and have a nice house and great cars and win awards in your industry and be all you can be. Go for the gusto . . . tonight's Miller time . . . living it up . . . taking a vacation to Hawaii . . . and all that.

And I know all that is absolutely meaningless. It just has no meaning in and of itself. It can't, when you put your face up to the fact that you're going to die and all that is going to be left here. You get real clear, when somebody dies, that none of that stuff means anything.

So when I say that I'm integrating back in with life I mean I'm going to hold the reality that those things have no meaning in and of themselves, *and* I'm still going out there and get them. That's the game to play. That's how life is set up; that's how you grow; that's what there is to do. So if you're going to get with the program you've got to get back out there and participate.

I think what grows when you do that, when you change and master something you hadn't mastered before, is your soul. And the soul is just something you might take with you. If I don't do that, all that learning I've done since my father's death would be of no use if I didn't bring it to bear somewhere. It would have been for naught.

LIVING WITH LOSS AS PART OF LIFE

A mother says:

I don't think you ever get over the loss in your heart. I think you have to acknowledge the fact that, when you love someone and that person is gone, you're going to miss him or her. And that has nothing to do with your spiritual strength or trust or even with whether you've been true to your grieving. It's a perfectly human thing to continue to miss a child who has died. When Christmastime comes, Christmas Eve, and there's no Cliff who's going to walk in the door with a big sack of presents and say, "Hi, Mom!" I have a hard time.

But there's no agonizing over Cliff now. There is peace and a quiet calmness. Dean and I are comfortable with the situation. If something beautiful happens or we're somewhere Cliff would have been with us, we'll say, "Hi, Cliff, wish you could see this . . . how's it going, ol' boy?" Something like that, but it's not heavy.

INTEGRATING A SPIRITUAL APPROACH TO LIFE

A man says:

The important thing to do is put the arbitrary occurrence in a larger context. There isn't anything I can do in terms of how the cards fall. Sometimes I can control them, and sometimes I can't. So I've begun to get the picture that there's something bigger that's running the show, and I have to learn to get along with whatever it is that's running the bigger program. So I guess that's what I mean when I say that I'm beginning to find my place. And it's taken a lot of trial and error. Trust is important. Trust in yourself and trust in the overall process. You just have to do it and see what works. That's how you learn to get along with the bigger program. I think I have to say that when you finally come back and integrate with life, if you're aware of what really happened to you and of what the overall program is in life, then your integration is going to be intertwined with a spiritual approach to life. It's surprising to hear myself say that, but I truly believe that it's so.

FINDING CONTENTMENT

A widow recounts her situation:

We were married for fifty-four years. He lived to be seventy-eight. I'm eighty-three now, and I've have been widowed for four years. Of course, he still lives on for me. I have tapes of his speeches, and I listen to them sometimes. There's one tape he made with the grandchildren when they were small, and he's so natural. He laughs, and I just love to play that tape.

Of course, I don't associate him with my new apartment, but when I turn on programs that we used to look at together, that's when I think of him. And I surprise myself by crying a lot when I'm watching sad movies. I just weep and wail, use up ten handker-chiefs, and cry and cry.

If I die tomorrow, it's all right; but if I live ten more years, I'd like it. But I don't have the least fear of dying. I trust in the goodness of the universe. If I die, I think God knows what's best for me. If there's something to preserve, He will. If not, He won't. The Great Intelligence knows the best.

I'm perfectly content. I stay busy. Keep house, get the groceries, fix my meals, vacuum the rug. And, of course, I do my reading and play my music: Beethoven's C-sharp Minor Quartet, the medita-tion from Massenet's *Thaïs*, the "Song to the Evening Star" from Wagner's *Tannhäuser*, Liszt's *Liebesträume*. I agree with Beethoven that "music is in very truth the mediator between the life of the senses and the life of the spirit."

And I stay out in the yard as much as I can. I couldn't live with-out my swing. My swing is not only a tranquilizer when I swing gently but an energizer when I swing vigorously, as high as I can. I'm instantly in a state of joyful, exultant, childlike wonder that keeps me young at heart. And I walk every day to the park to see the squirrels and get in some exercise.

GAINING PERSPECTIVE

A man says:

You've got to be able to see that this is some sort of learning process and that you don't always know everything that is happen-ing. It's like the old Chinese story of the farmer whose champion stallion ran away and all the neighbors gathered to say, "That's bad." And the old farmer said, "Maybe." The next day the stallion came back with a whole herd of wild horses, and the neighbors all said, "That's good," and the farmer said, "Maybe." Then the farmer's son broke his leg trying to tame one of the wild horses, and the neighbors said, "That's bad," and the old farmer said, "Maybe." Right after the son broke his leg, the army came through and drafted all the young men and took them off to war, but they left the farmer's son because his leg was broken. All the neighbors said, "That's good," to which the old farmer only said, "Maybe." And, of course, the story never ends.

That illustrates to me that whatever is happening now, you don't really know what is going on. And I've seen during these years of grief work that this is true. It's a real irony, isn't it, that I would have ended up coming out of this thing an optimist!

CLARITY ABOUT WHAT ONE BELIEVES IN

Listen to this man:

I'm very clear that loss is just the other side of gain. It's going to happen to you. If you live long enough, you're going to lose it all. And sometimes you lose it all before you live long enough, like our son dying before he even started school. When I was a kid, a young man, I was terribly concerned about getting my philosophy together. But as I've done my grieving I've given up on that and settled on a pretty simple deal: The object of life is to gain wisdom. And that's what I'm trying to do. I've come up with some guiding principles: The world is full of creeps, so try not to be one. Remember that what saves us is style and grace. Have tolerance, reserve judgment, and be easy on people, because we're all weak. Just try to conduct yourself with a little dignity. Be quiet. Don't pop off.

I read a book one time . . . I think it was called *The Master Game*. The author divided the book into Object Games and Metagames. And the greatest player of Metagames was Jesus Christ and other life masters, like the Buddha. The purpose of a Metagame is to endure, to keep on playing, to share enlightenment. In the Object

Game, though, the purpose is the worship of money or prestige or recognition or winning. My aim is to play the Metagame.

I relish life. I get up earlier in the morning now more than ever. I bounce out of bed. I guess it's curiosity. I like to get up and watch the sun come up. I like to feel the sun on my back. I enjoy a pretty day. I enjoy a cold, rainy day. It's life. And it beats the alternative all to hell. And what gives life meaning, I've come to see, is love and affection and knowledge.

EVALUATING THE CHANGE

A widow says:

I know it's a terrible thing to say, but it's the truth: I'm happier now than when my husband was living. He was one of those overbearing men who gave a woman no opportunity to have any self-confidence. He was tough and hard and wanted me to be just the way he thought I should be. I could never cry; he forbade it. He just told me what to do and I was supposed to do it.

Even with all the pain that came with his death, I see by this point that I'm better off now. I have a chance to find out who I am. I'm thinking about going to school. I went on my first vacation this past summer. I bought a blousy top the other day that I knew he would have hated, and I even said when I saw myself in the mirror, "Is this me?" But I knew it was; I just wasn't used to asserting my own self-expression. But I'm learning. And life continues to get better.

COMING TO TERMS WITH DEATH

A brother says:

I spent every possible minute at the hospital with Frederick, and the closer he came to dying the more I stared my own death in the face. This was my kid brother! If he could die in his thirties, I could, too. It really shocked and unnerved me.

One day I carried *Little Big Man*, which has been one of my favorite novels since high school, with me to the hospital. I remembered that great scene at the end of the book when Old Lodge Skins says:

> *There is no permanent winning or losing when things move, as they should, in a circle. For is not life continuous? And though I shall die, shall I not also continue to live in everything that is? The buffalo eats grass, I eat him, and when I die, the earth eats me and sprouts more grass. Therefore nothing is ever lost, and each thing is everything forever, though all things move.*

When I finished reading that, something inside me shifted. Late that afternoon, I climbed up on Frederick's bed with my guitar and I sang one of our favorite beer-drinking ballads, even though he was in a coma. And then I said, "You know, buddy, we'd love to have you stick around; but it looks like you're on your way out. So, if you are, I want you to know that it's okay with me. I love you, but I'll dismiss you." I left the hospital, and Frederick died, they said, in the next thirty minutes.

That whole experience really affected me. I'm different now about my own death and everybody's. I've decided that the timing of death may be sad, but death itself is not sad. I mean, we are here, then we're not here. But we live on in some form or another. I am now not bothered.

INTEGRATION

ANSWERING PERENNIAL QUESTIONS

A woman says:

Since Carl's death I have thought a lot about questions that religion raises. Why are we here? What is the purpose of life? You know, if you're a scientist, as I am, you have to think that there must be something higher than what we can study. How can you explain a cell? All that marvelous organization? I mean, how can you explain that 100 percent on a scientific basis? I'm not sure that you can.

I've decided the purpose of life is to try to live as good a life as you can, and it should be happy. You should try to enjoy yourself. You should try to do something for other people. You should try to make a difference in the world. That's why we're here—to make a difference. It doesn't have to be a huge difference, but everyone should contribute something to change the world and make it just a little bit better. You should not be a liability to society, but you should try to leave something positive behind you. That's how you live your life until it's time to die.

FINDING A PURPOSE FOR BEING

A son comments:

One of the things that happens when the whole structure of your life falls apart—like your mother dying when you're young—is that you start wondering early what you're supposed to be doing here. When it becomes clear to you that the purpose of life isn't for you to be perpetually happy, then you have to ask, "If not that, what?"

I've given a lot of thought to this, and I think our purpose here on earth is to get organized. To organize ourselves to do something. Everything, if you look at everything, if you look at the universe, and especially astronomically, all of the processes that are going on are organizing themselves toward some end, and then that isn't the end. Like a star. It is formed out of moving clouds that swirl into a center, and it becomes a star. Then it explodes and becomes a black hole and then absorbs everything. But then it turns into something else. Things constantly organize themselves toward an end, but it's not the end; it's the start of something. And to whatever end our process is, our purpose on earth is to be a part of that. I think, when we finally get down to it, what we are supposed to be doing is just being here, being who we are.

ESTABLISHING A NEW RELATIONSHIP

A newly dating father says:

They billed themselves the Non-Desperate Singles. I had tried out the singles scene off and on during the first couple of years and felt so silly and uneasy. But a friend at the office told me this group was different, so I decided to go. And it was there that I met Linda. We both grew up in small towns not far from each other in northern Ohio, and I had dated one of her friends in high school. But Linda and I didn't remember each other, even though we're in the same senior prom picture in her high school annual. We left the party and went out to get a bite to eat. Since that night Linda and I have never dated anyone else. It's been two years now, and we're planning to get married at the end of the summer. We've worked through many problems—our relationship comes first, but we've had a lot to consider about the kids. We each have a freshman in college, and Linda still has a child at home. Just the logistics—do you buy a house with enough bedrooms for each child, even though some will soon be leaving? Things like that. We've set some goals now, and we're working toward them. She's quite a lady—a bright, fun lady.

INTEGRATION

SEEING THE GLASS AS HALF FULL

A mother says:

I noticed people thought that since I had lost a young child, who suffered for seven years before she died, I would be very heavy and significant about life. But the truth is, through the pain I learned that you can be miserable anywhere you want to be, and you can be happy anywhere you want to be. It's what you make of yourself.

Once when I lived in Okinawa, it wasn't the best living conditions, and there were wives there who were just miserable. They sat around all day being miserable. Well, hell, anybody can be miserable. It doesn't take much of a person to be sad and miserable. It takes a heck of a person to make the best out of what's the worst. When you go to the commissary and you want butter and they say, "Well, there's no butter; there's not going to be any butter for two weeks," what do you do? You ask, "Well, do you have any whipping cream?" "Yes, we've got whipping cream." So you buy whipping cream and make butter out of whipping cream. Add a little salt and a little yellow food coloring, and you got butter. That's how you should take life. That's what life is. Whipping cream.

ENJOYING BEING OUTRAGEOUS

A widow tells this story:

I find that since I've lived through the traumatic experience of loss I prefer lively people—people who are doing things. It's as if surviving and returning to life brings with it a new kind of lightness and freedom. In fact, I don't mind if people are outrageous. I enjoy being outrageous myself at times now. I like people who are willing to take a risk, and being outrageous is taking a risk, isn't it?

About three years after Tom died, I was in England. The fad in London that summer was spraying your hair all kinds of fanciful colors—green, pink, blue, purple. You could wash the paint out, so if you didn't like blue hair, the next day you could try red or yellow or green.

Well, that fall I had a huge class—225 students in biochemistry—and one day before I went to class I sprayed my hair electric blue with some of that hair paint I had bought in England. I just went into the room—me, this sixty-year-old scientist—and started my lecture. After a few minutes, this serious kid sitting in the front row raised his hand and said, "Dr. Williams, why is your hair blue?" I looked him right in the eye and said, "Because I just felt like being outrageous." He continued to look puzzled all during class, but I went right on with my lecture. On the teaching evaluations at the end of the term, several students commented, "That blue hair was marvelous!" Now, can I prove that my ability to have fun like that and my having experienced Tom's death are related? I can't, of course, but I *know* there is a connection.

EXPERIENCING DEEPER COMPASSION

A young man says:

Loss is the *disease* of human life. It's what happens to you, and you cannot stop it. And the damage to the spirit is the *illness* that you suffer after that loss. You can't stop the disease, but you can address the illness. You can actually work at getting over the illness.

I had to learn how to address the illness of the spirit when, within a three-year period, my mentor died, my father died, and I almost died of cancer. I had to let go of the disease itself (the loss) and concentrate on handling the illness (the damage to my spirit). The way I found to do that was to reach out to the community. To create a lot of horizons in my life. To reduce hierarchies.

I grew in compassion. I was no longer above people. I realized I didn't exercise power over them. I was no longer the toughest guy around. I became a person among people, recognizing that there really is a human family. I gave up isolation and became willing to be a part of the human community.

If you choose to work on the illness of loss—the damage to the spirit—you grow to understand the term *compassion*, which is a fellow feeling. Community actually becomes communion. Communion is the act of love, which is the giving of one's self. Not in a namby-pamby way, which means "I'm going to do all for my fellow man." Communion is just giving up that sense of isolation and becoming willing to share deeply in the human condition.

I've come to see that love and loss are exactly the same four-letter word. The degree to which we can feel loss, I think, is just the degree to which we can feel love. And the degree to which we recover from the illness of loss is just exactly the degree to which we can recover the capacity to love.

CRITICAL CONSIDERATIONS WHEN WE EXPERIENCE DAYLIGHT

It seems to me that one of the saddest things we could ever say after a loss is that, like the speaker in T. S. Eliot's poem, "we had the experience but missed the meaning." When I listen to women and men talk about their experience of really engaging in the grieving process, however, I know that they will never have to speak that lament. For these are courageous individuals on whom nothing has been lost. They have observed themselves, taken note of what helped and what hindered, and changed accordingly. And, because of the choices they have made, they are now able to say at Daylight, "We have done the work of grieving." What ways of thinking and behaving brought them this sense of accomplishment?

SEEING THE EXPERIENCE OF GRIEVING AS A LIFE RITUAL

During rituals—which anthropologists also call rites of passage—an individual passes through three states (1) the state of separation (imagine an ancient initiation rite) would occur when the young man or woman being initiated is isolated from regular societal life and taken perhaps to a forest or to a tepee to begin the tasks of the ritual; (2) the state of transition, or "limen" (the time during which the tasks are faced, either successfully or unsuccessfully); and (3) the state of aggregation, or reincorporation (when the young person is brought back from the place of initiation to take her or his new place in society).

In our experience of moving actively through the full grieving process, we might think of the event of the loss as our point of separation. The mourning process up to this point has been our period of transition, of our limen. Now when we are at Daylight, or Integration, we are entering the final ritual state: reincorporation. We are emerging from the experiences of mourning and returning to a life that again has balance and structure. We are finding that we have integrated the loss into our lives and can now integrate ourselves back into the world.

What has made this possible, of course, is our willingness to engage in the ritual. As the anthropologists Victor and Edith Turner point out, individuals are "inwardly transformed and outwardly changed" when they take on the difficult and challenging tasks of a ritual. A rite of passage, they remind us, is a time of "betwixt and between," a time when our experience is that we are traveling through a "realm or dimension" that has few or none of the qualities of our lives in the past and few or none of the qualities our lives will have in the future—a time they compare "to death, to being in the womb, to invisibility . . . and the wilderness," like falling into the dark and living in floating worlds.

But the Turners also point out that the ritual, which, to be sure, is marked by this terrible ambiguity and confusion, is also marked by enormous potentiality. It is a time of "major reformulation," a time of open-endedness and of possibility, a time of not only what is but also of what may be. According to the Turners, any time that our "previous orderings of thought and behavior are subject to revision"—as they certainly are during mourning—there is a strong chance that we will come up with "hitherto unprecedented modes of ordering relations between ideas and people." We experience a "freedom of thought" that helps us reformulate our lives and come up with "new experimental models" for living.

BEING ABLE TO THINK ABOUT MORTALITY

Dr. Beverley Raphael tells us that the "death of a loved one means not only the loss, but also the nearness of personal death, the threat to self. All the personal and internalized meanings of death will be evoked by the death. . . . All the personal vulnerabilities associated with loss will be aroused by its closeness to the self." Through the loss, we have been put in touch with our own mortality.

And Lily Pincus says bluntly that the bereaved who are not able to face their own death "cannot successfully make [the necessary] adjustment." Being willing, then, to think about, to ponder, our own mortality allows us to integrate loss into the whole of living. We have been touched by loss, and we have to come to terms with that profound experience.

In an article titled "Facing Your Own Mortality," Jane Brody, a personal-health columnist and science writer for the *New York Times*, writes: "If any good came from my mother's death at age 49, it was my recognition, at age 17, of *my* mortality and my decision . . . to live each day as though it might be my last." She goes on to say, "Taken to the extreme, fear of death can rob people of life, keeping them from taking the kinds of risks that can yield rich rewards." My experience in talking with people who have been willing to think about their own death confirms Jane Brody's assertion. The freer one is to consider one's own dying, the freer one is to experience full living.

Yet this is not easy. Ernest Becker, citing the work of Frederick Perls, tells us that we have four layers of tactics that we use to avoid such painful subjects: the first two are our "glib, empty talk, 'cliché,' and role-playing layers." Many people, he says, never go beneath these. The third layer is the "impasse" we use to cover our feelings of "being empty and lost," and that is a tough one to penetrate. Finally, there's the fourth—the "fear-of-death layer"—which is the "terror that we carry around in our secret heart." It is only when we penetrate all the way to that fourth layer, Becker says, that we are able to find our "authentic self." And, I would add, only then are we able to come to terms with our own mortality.

Lily Pincus writes:

Thinking and talking about death need not be morbid; they may be quite the opposite. Ignorance and fear of death overshadow life, while knowing about and accepting death erases this shadow and makes life freer of fears and anxieties. The fuller and richer people's experience of life, the less death seems to matter to them—as if love of life casts out fear of death. A child therapist once said to me, "Children of parents who are not afraid of death are not afraid of life." In that sense, education for death is education for life.

"Education for death is education for life." Do we need more incentive for being willing to think about our own dying?

INTEGRATION

RECOGNIZING HOW WE HAVE BEEN ALTERED

Almost everyone who has grieved, at some time or another, has heard words like these spoken by well-meaning people: "You will come out of this stronger"; "Someday you will be able to see how much this loss has taught you"; "Having gone through this tragedy, you are going to be able to contribute so much more to others." Such bromides, of course, rang hollow to our ears at the time, for we were grieving the loss of someone who was an integral part of the very structure of our life. We were not trying to fulfil the requirements for a curriculum of self-development we never signed up for.

But when we assess at Daylight, we find that we truly *have* changed. And that change *does* have some positive repercussions. Therefore, when we take note of such "pluses," we are not trying to persuade ourselves or others. We are just reporting.

Heinz Kohut, M.D., talks about the kind of "attainments of the ego" and the "attitudes and achievements of the personality" that we recognize as part of the legacy of choosing to move through the full grieving process. He gives these attainments a wonderful name: *victorious outcomes*. Among the victorious outcomes of fully grieving, he lists:

An enlarged capacity for empathy
The ability to think beyond the bounds of the individual
A recognition that there has been an increase in one's wisdom

We say someone is empathetic if she or he is able to look at other people, notice how they are behaving and what they are saying, and then, using this data, accurately imagine what they are experiencing inside even though these inner experiences cannot be directly observed. To express empathy, we have to intentionally curb our usual ways of thinking—analyzing, critiquing, scrutinizing, and so forth—

and recognize instead the humaneness of all individuals: that others hurt just the way we do. Others are as confused or off-center or frightened as we have been. At Daylight, many of us recognize that the experiences of the grieving process have resulted in our being much less judgmental and much more humbly empathetic.

Other transformations I've observed in the lives of people who have reached Daylight include other victorious outcomes mentioned by Dr. Kohut:

A new outlook on life
Ability to put attention on what really matters
A kind of "quiet pride" in knowing and being able to acknowledge that
   human existence is finite
Heightened capacity for humor
Increased ability to hold life's ups and downs in perspective

The work of Susan Nolen-Hoeksema also confirms that "the majority of bereaved people report finding something positive in their loss experiences." Among these gains are a sense of personal growth, a sense of personality change, the realization of personal strengths, a re-prioritizing of life goals, a greater appreciation of relationships, and a diminished fear of death. The people who reported outcomes such as these also identified things that had helped them as they were grieving: engaging in active problem-solving, seeking social support, expressing their emotions to others, and participating in hobbies or exercise. They also did not deny the importance of the loss; nor did they engage in long-term maladaptive behaviors such as excessive consumption of alcohol. Nolen-Hoeksema concludes that "indeed . . . most people are resilient and even grow in the wake of traumas."

*   *   *

It's as if individuals who have mourned have an elevated place from which to view life that enables them to see events as if they were being played out on a stage. When I am talking with individuals whose way of thinking and seeing has been altered in this way, I remember that scene in *Troilus and Cressida* where Troilus, already killed in battle, is now in heaven looking down at the war that is still fiercely being waged. But Troilus can now only laugh as he watches. For he knows that such skirmishes mean nothing in the overall scheme of things. He now has life and death in a new perspective.

People who have fully grieved a significant loss and faced their own mortality in the process are not as easily ruffled by day-to-day problems as those people who have not engaged in a similar set of experiences. They display a kind of detached cosmic humor that allows them to put the vagaries, the caprices, of life in perspective. Dr. Kohut describes this trait not as a "picture of grandiosity and elation, but [as] a quiet inner triumph with an admixture of undenied melancholy."

We have formed new attitudes. People around us take note of our new attitudes and say that we have increased in wisdom. "She has become so wise," one will say. "He is a much deeper person now," another remarks. "It's as if he is in touch with the wisdom of the ages" or "Have you noticed how much her faith has deepened?" This achievement of wisdom occurs when we accept our limitations and discover how to be comfortable with the way life itself operates.

What contributes to our being able to attain this wisdom? Attention to forming, reestablishing, and maintaining a set of cherished values. Individuals have told me again and again that they have finished their grieving with a greater clarity than they have ever had in their lives about what they believe in, what they think matters in life, about their relationship with God, and about what they are willing to give their commitment and time to. A sense of proportion, too, is the mark of this hard-won wisdom and "a touch of irony toward the achievements of individual existence, including even [our] wisdom."

When we talk, then, at Daylight, of how loss has altered us, it is not just an attempt to convince ourselves that some good has come out of our experience. We have been genuinely changed; our characters, our personalities, our thought structures, and our value systems have been affected. It is a hard-won shift, to be sure, but a change through which our very self has been altered.

UNDERSTANDING THE TIME FRAME OF THE FULL GRIEVING PROCESS

"Did it have to take so long?" is one of the questions people frequently ask when they finally reach a "new normal" and a place of balance and equilibrium. "And did it have to be so painful? Did I have to make so many mistakes and see things so slowly?" It's as if we wish the wisdom and insight we have gained could be retroactive. But what we see so clearly now has come only because we allowed ourselves to do the work of the full grieving process, with all the time that such a journey entailed.

Someone talked to me when I was grieving about the difference between two kinds of times. There is *Chronos time*, which describes a continuum of past, present, and future. It is the kind of time measured by clocks and calendars—time measured chronologically. *Kairos time*, on the other hand, refers to "the time within which personal life moves forward." Kairos time is measured by the movement we experience as a result of moments of awakening or realization. Kairos time refers to a deepening process that results from our paying attention to the present moment, a process through which we are "drawn inside the movement of our own story."

As we experience the full grieving process, Chronos time is valuable only in that it gives us a span within which to experience our own kairos time. The passing of days and weeks and months and years does not, as we have seen so clearly, within itself bring resolution to our conflict. We each have our own "entelechy"—to use a word favored by anthropologists—that means our own "immanent force controlling and directing development." Therefore the calendar time it takes to finish the work of our grieving depends completely on our own kairos time (which we move through by making our choices) and on our own entelechy. That's why the grieving process is different for every person. Why there's no right and wrong speed with which people do their grief work. Why a cliché like "Four seasons of the year brings an end to grieving" has no meaning to someone who is engaged in authentic grief work.

Nevertheless, people ask, "How long does it take? What can I expect? Am I progressing in a normal fashion?" The best I can offer is some average statistics, and we all know how mythical are all things "average." So, mindful of the caveat, here is what some research findings say about the time it takes for individuals mourning significant losses to complete the grieving process:

Dr. John Bowlby, remarking on those who successfully follow through the process of mourning, says:

> The majority of those who do [recover a state of health and well-being] are more likely to take two or three years to do so than a mere one.

Dr. Beverley Raphael, in *The Anatomy of Bereavement*, suggests that even though survival may be clear by the end of the first year:

> There is no fixed end point of mourning during the first or even second year. . . . There are many end points.

The Institute of Medicine, in its comprehensive report on bereavement, says:

> Despite the popular belief that the bereavement process is normally completed in a year, data from systematic studies and from clinical reports confirm that the process may be considerably more attenuated for many people and still far well within normal boundaries. . . . Thus a precise endpoint in time cannot be specified.

Glen Davidson of Southern Illinois College of Medicine, citing his study of twelve hundred adult mourners carried out over a two-year period, reports:

> Near the end of the second year the bereaved person begins to feel a sense of release, renewed energy, makes judgments better, [and regains] stable eating and sleeping habits.
>
> The mourning process is complex and the period of mourning lasts far longer than most people expect.

Dr. Sidney Zisook and his colleagues report on a study of three hundred widows and widowers:

> One of the most important findings of this study . . . was that for many widowed persons the time course of grief was much more prolonged than generally expected. In general, we can say that the widows and widowers in our study appear to be relatively well adjusted by the end of four years.

When people lament how long the process takes, I think of a conversation an adult student and I had when I taught college many years ago in the hills of Tennessee (in the first two-year, public college to open in that part of Appalachia). The woman came up to me after class one day and said, "You know, my kids and grandkids are embarrassed at me coming over here to this college. They say, 'Mama, you know how old you're gonna be when you graduate from there in two years? You're gonna be seventy.' And I just look at them and say, 'Well, how old am I going to be in two years if I don't graduate?'"

It is *our life* we are living while we move through the active grieving process. Whatever amount of time it takes for each of us personally, we will be the beneficiaries of all the "creative and victorious outcomes" that await us when we finally reach Daylight.

FACTORS THAT MAKE GRIEVING VARIABLE

There are so many variables that play a part in each griever's movement through the full grieving process. Let's look at a few of these variables:

The griever's personality and style of responding to unpleasant events. Since moving through the mourning process depends on our willingness to make hard choices, individuals who establish "dependent, clinging, ambivalent" relationships and who pull back from making decisions on their own will find their mourning extended, fixated, arrested, or perhaps stopped altogether until they are willing to change their behavior. Also, if an individual's habit is to avoid painful situations and realizations, to draw back from working through difficult problems, then the length of the mourning will depend on how soon (and if) she or he becomes willing to change this habitual behavior and begin to engage in the grieving.

The degree to which the lost person was a part of or involved in what gave the grieving person's life order, structure, and meaning. If the lost person was central to the organization of the grieving person's life or to her or his sense of self, the mourning process is likely to take longer than it would if that individual was part of the grieving person's life but not central to it. This means that it is not possible to make blanket judgments about what one individual's death will mean to another. It is possible, for instance, for the death of a brother whom one seldom saw and did not know well to have less impact than the death of a next-door neighbor who was central in those things that gave life meaning. And a husband who was violent and despicable may have to be mourned as extensively as if he had been loving and generous, simply because he was central to the organization and structure of the life of the family.

The nature of the loss. Sudden deaths or losses, the death of a child or a young person, violent or traumatic deaths, and suicides present special problems in grieving. There is often more shock, a greater sense of injustice, more guilt and blame, and a greater sense of helplessness in such situations, and this greatly complicates mourning.

With some losses, such as graduation or after getting a promotion, several of the phases of the grieving process might telescope into each other, creating a quick mourning period. Other losses—such as a death that is unfair, untimely, or happens before our very eyes—seem to attach themselves at a particular bent in our psychological makeup and we may have some sets of experiences for what seems like an inordinate amount of time.

What about the opportunity to anticipate the loss? What effect does this have on the grieving process? Although knowing in advance does give individuals a chance to prepare, this advance preparation may not, in the long run, shorten the mourning period. Researchers have found, for instance, that at the end of one year there is no difference between widows and widowers who experienced anticipated grieving and those who did not (although those who have a chance to prepare do show less likelihood that their mourning will become pathological). The fact that a loss can be anticipated and planned for may be offset by the emotional drain that occurs as a result of a long illness, the ambivalent feelings of both relief and sadness that occur when the death finally happens, or by the emotional bonding and attachment that developed during the period before death.

The kind of support given by family and friends. If those who are grieving have around them people who understand the mourning process and assist them appropriately in each of its phases, they will move through the grieving with greater velocity. If those who are grieving feel loved, supported, and aided, and if their family and friends act as if they know that they are capable and expect them to take the actions that allow them to move through the mourning process, then the outcome of grief will reflect these favorable conditions. If, on the other hand, family and friends are uncomfortable with mourning, if they act as if the grieving person should already be finished mourning, or—heaven forbid, but it does occur—if they actually encourage the grieving person to remain helpless and dependent, then the grieving time will be extended.

Past losses and the degree to which they have been mourned fully. Imagine that when a woman was a child of seven or eight, her mother died. And imagine that, as a child, the woman had no guidance in how to mourn and, subsequently, buried the loss as best she could, developing a way of life that always managed to skirt that delicate, painful, and complex issue. Then the woman's husband died. His death, reaching deep into her psyche, activates the earlier, ungrieved loss of her mother (and possibly many more losses). In such a circumstance, the length of the grieving process may reflect the fact that multiple losses must be mourned.

The amount of unacknowledged ambivalent feelings a person has toward the lost person. The more not-yet-dealt-with ambivalence the grieving person feels toward the lost person, the longer and more difficult the mourning period is likely to be. Perhaps there is unexpressed or unacknowledged resentment and anger. Perhaps there is guilt over disagreements and arguments that were never worked out. Perhaps there is relief that the person is gone, even while there is sorrow, and the grieving person does not forgive herself or himself for this seeming contradiction. In order to deny negative aspects of life with the lost person, individuals may idealize the past and thereby make their mourning more difficult. Any or all of these feelings of ambivalence—unacknowledged and not dealt with—may trigger negative images of one's own worthlessness, which must then be worked through, thereby often adding additional time and complication to the mourning.

The social, economic, and personal circumstances in which the individuals must do their grieving. People who have financial difficulties concurrent with the loss, who are emotionally upset about other issues, do not have good health from the beginning or become ill during the mourning process, or are constrained as a result of previous sex-role conditioning (e.g., men don't cry; women are helpless in the face of making decisions) will find that these factors complicate their grieving.

Phyllis Silverman, professor at Harvard, points out that there is a "male model" of loss, in which one speaks of "learning to break away from the past." People—and they might be women or men—who follow this model prefer to "get on with life" and quickly involve themselves in work or other activities. A "female model" of grief, however, emphasizes connection rather than disengagement and separation. Those who identify with this model, Silverman says, are more comfortable behaving in ways that indicate "you

don't break your ties with the past, you change your ties." People—
and this, too, can be men and women—who follow the female
model are more inclined to display grief to others, to reach out to
one or more individuals around them, and to talk openly about the
loss. Those who are inclined toward the male model will keep their
grief to themselves, work hard to avoid losing control in front of
others, and refrain from asking for help. In the female model, feeling related or connected is of paramount importance, while in the
male model feeling independent and autonomous is critical to the
mourners' having a positive view of themselves. These varying ori-
entations create different approaches to making the choices that
the full grieving process requires and, thereby, often determine how
long the process takes.

These variables affect not only the length of time of our grieving
process but also the "smoothness" with which we move through it.
I don't think I have ever talked to anyone who reached Daylight
who did not at some point in the conversation say, "I wish I had
done certain things differently when I was going through the
process; I wish I hadn't hurt that person; I wish I hadn't been so destructive to myself; I wish I had made the right decision; I wish I
hadn't spent that money; I wish I had made the necessary choices
sooner; I wish . . . I wish." I always remind the individual that these
kinds of regrets are unavoidable. Given the complexity of what we
must experience during the active grieving process—we are, after
all, doing work at the deepest level of self—we will not proceed in
a straight line. Our route will be convoluted. It will take the time
appropriate for our individual movement from Experiencing the
Unthinkable to Daylight.

One final point about time and progress: There is a strong con-
sensus of opinion among those in the medical and health communities that education can make an enormous difference in the
success with which individuals manage their active grieving. I agree

with this observation. My contact with individuals who are grieving tells me that it is often the lack of information about grief and
loss—not want of courage, heroism, willingness, or desire—that
prolongs the process.

THE CHOICE

Since Daylight represents a time when we recognize that we have
achieved the *creative and victorious outcomes* described by researchers, what choice could there possibly be left to make? It
would seem that none was necessary. In fact, have we not reached
Integration because we have already made the choices? But it is
part of the wisdom and learning that accompany our grieving to acknowledge this inevitable truth:

We can choose to continue to make and remake choices.

I think it was Madame de Stael, the eighteenth-century French
novelist, who said, "The human mind always makes progress, but it
is a progress of spirals." This is the way of life, too. And the way of
loss. The loss we have just mourned represents just one of the innumerable losses we will need to grieve for during our lifetime. (No
one has pointed out this fact of life more persuasively and
poignantly than Judith Viorst in her book *Necessary Losses*.) In fact,
at times, in order to move through the grieving process we have
had to create other losses. When we make changes in order to start
to create a new identity, for instance, we often have to leave behind
certain activities, habitual ways, even people, and each of these
losses starts a mini-process of grieving inside our larger, ongoing
process. Spirals within spirals.

Losses, too, often reactive earlier losses. Lily Pincus says, "The loss . . . of an important person strikes at the deepest roots of human existence, recalls the experience of previous attachments and losses, and reactivates the pain of earlier bereavements, physical as well as psychological in nature." Therefore we have to be willing to continue to make and remake choices that will allow us to experience the *transformational-mourning-liberation* process for all of our resurrected and our future losses.

Recognizing that life does present us with both a repetition and a succession of losses is part of the wisdom we gain as a result of engaging in the full grieving process. We also have a larger context for holding our losses that, while giving them their due, makes them only part of the mosaic of our lives and not the total picture.

One way of thinking of this larger context is to see our lives as an ongoing adventure. It's telling, I think, that the dictionary definition of *adventure* is "an undertaking involving danger and unknown risks," and that the word's root means "that which arrives." Paul Tournier, in a book called *The Adventures of Living*, written while he was a practicing physician in Geneva, Switzerland, says that the adventure each of us lives is a manifestation of ourselves, a form of self-expression. "Each individual," he writes, "plays the cards he holds, and that is his adventure." And we want to play this adventure, Dr. Tournier asserts, because the instinct of adventure is closely linked with what prompts us to make some personal mark that will survive us—some creative work, some contribution to our family and others, some commitment to new paths, some original invention.

Given that adventure always includes the possibility of risk, the adventure that life is goes from "resurgence to resurgence, because of obstacles it meets and the problems to which it gives rise." And that is where loss comes in. Obstacles and problems include losses, and the grieving process is our way of responding. Even this response, Dr. Tournier would say, is a sort of adventure, for he asserts,

"The greatest of adventures is not action; it is our own development."

The renowned British educator James Britton tells us that it is language that we use as a way of "working upon our representation of events." It is with language that we regulate our lives. We set our direction through the words we use. Because we have the use of language, we have "a power of coordinating, stabilizing, and facilitating other forms of behavior." This includes mourning. Which brings us back full circle to making choices. We make choices only through language—spoken language, internal language, body language. These choices are what allow us to direct our grieving.

To be willing to continue to make and remake choices allows us to participate, as Ernest Becker says, in the "mysterious way in which life is given to us in evolution on this planet. . . . Who knows," he says, "what form the forward momentum of life will take in the time ahead or what use it will make of our anguished searching. The most that any one of us can seem to do is to fashion something—an object or ourselves—and drop it into the confusion, make an offering of it, so to speak, to the life force." This is reason enough to commit to doing the work that is necessary to move through our losses.

WHAT WE NEED FROM
FAMILY AND FRIENDS AT DAYLIGHT

Now, at this point in our grieving process it is not so much a matter of what we need from our family and friends as what we can do to contribute to them and others. One of the things we recognize after we have experienced and worked through a loss is how pervasive grief and sadness are in the world. We are more aware of the pain and confusion around us; we can often intuit or recognize what a grieving person needs simply because we have had a similar experience. We have become—without ever desiring it—one of the "wise ones," as Armand DiMele used to say to me. And on this wisdom we can now draw, not only for an understanding of our own future losses but also for helping others to understand theirs.

I remember a grandmother whose grandchild had died saying, "I would get so desperate for someone to talk to that I would go shopping just so I could tell the salespeople that my grandson had died." Now this grandmother makes it a point to spend time with people who have experienced a loss, allowing them to talk about the event as much as they want to. "I realize now," she said, "that so many people are uncomfortable hearing grieving persons talk about the loss. I make a special effort, therefore, to give them an opportunity to talk." This is just one example of the kind of contribution we are able to make after we have made the choices involved in the grieving process.

Even though we have now been released from the suffocating weight of our own grieving and find our lives in balance, the love and companionship we have with our friends and family continue, of course, to be important. It will be important not only for those times in the future when we experience a recurrence of our sadness and grief or suffer a new loss, and for the times when our family and friends will, in turn, need our support in a loss, but also for the times of quiet togetherness, of joy, of celebration and play. For we recognize now, probably to a much greater degree than we did in the past, how integral friends and family are to our well-being and how nurturing are the bonds of love in our life.

When I was mourning, William Stafford sent me a poem he had written called "Rescue," which goes like this:

A fire was burning. In another room
someone was talking. Sunlight slanted
across the foot of my bed, and a glass of water
gleamed where it waited on a chair near my hand.
I was alive and the pain in my head
was gone. Carefully I tried thinking
of those I had known. I let them walk
and then run, and then open their mouths the way
it used to cause the throbbing. It didn't hurt
anymore. Clearer and clearer I stared
far into the glass. I was cured.

From now on in my life there would be a place
like a scene in a paperweight. One figure in the storm
would be reaching out with my hand for those
who had died. It would always be still in that scene,
no matter what happened. I could come back to it,
carefully, any time, to be saved, and go on.

It seems so long ago now, that July afternoon when, driving along the road to find my husband, I instead found myself a widow. And today I think I can say that I understand the poem that Bill sent me.

For there is something redemptive—"*come back to it, carefully, any time, to be saved, and go on*"—about the mourning process, something that resides in the power and opportunity we have to make choices. These choices, of course, allow us to make for ourselves a new life in the external. For instance, I no longer teach school but, instead, write books, consult, speak, and lead retreats. Several years after Greg died, I married a wonderful man with whom I deeply enjoy the adventure of living.

But the real impact, I think, of the choices we make when we are grieving resides in their power to alter our very way of being. As Emily Dickinson once wrote:

> *Heavenly Hurt, it gives us—*
> *We can find no scar,*
> *But internal differences,*
> *Where the Meanings, are.*

And, as awkward as our progress may have seemed as we mapped our own movement through loss and grief, we created these *internal differences*, these *Meanings*, by our personal choices. In so doing, we have given shape to our here-and-now most precious life.

THE TERRAIN OF OUR ACTIVE GRIEVING

Life As It Was   *Life and Loss Integrated*
The Event of Loss   *Freedom from Domination of Grief*

IMPACT: Experiencing the unthinkable
CHOICE: To experience and express grief fully

SECOND CRISIS: Stumbling in the dark
CHOICE: To endure with patience

OBSERVATION: Linking past to present
CHOICE: To look honestly

THE TURN: Turning into the wind
CHOICE: To replan and change our lives to include but not be dominated by the loss

RECONSTRUCTION: Picking up the pieces
CHOICE: To take specific actions

WORKING THROUGH: Finding solid ground
CHOICE: To engage in the conflicts

INTEGRATION: Daylight
CHOICE: To make and remake choices

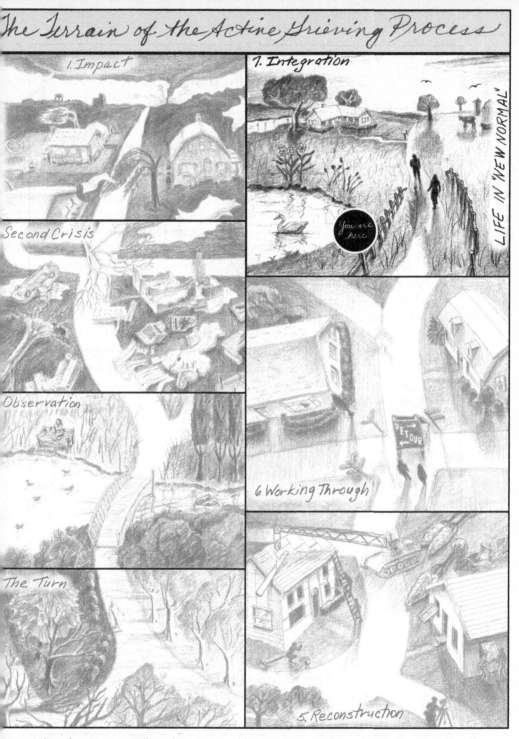

remember: A map never tells us how to travel. A map does not determine that everyone travels e same route, moves at the same speed, shares a set itinerary. A map does not dictate, prescribe, even describe an individual's movement. A map does, however, name. A map can help us find ere we are when we think we are lost. A map shows possibilities and provides ideas for where e there is for us to go. At all times, however, every individual is the person holding the map.

INTEGRATION: Daylight

What Is Normal?

Feeling released

Being able to identify in our lives many of Dr. Kohut's *victorious outcomes*: an enlarged capacity for empathy; the ability to think beyond the bounds of the individual; a recognition that there has been an increase in one's wisdom; a new outlook on life; the ability to pay attention to what really matters; a kind of "quiet pride" in knowing and being able to acknowledge that human existence is finite; a heightened capacity for humor; an increased ability to hold life's ups and downs in perspective.

Being able to identify in our lives many of Dr. Pollock's *creative outcomes*: the ability to feel joy, satisfaction, and a sense of accomplishment; a return to a steady state of balance; the experience of an increased capacity to appreciate people and things; a realization that we are more tolerant and wise; a desire to express ourselves creatively; the ability to invest in new relationships; the experience of a sense of play and freedom; a deepening of our faith.

Having a clearer sense of what we believe in and what truths we choose to live by

Looking up and being able to see a horizon

What Can I Do?

Acknowledge and celebrate the hard work you have accomplished.

Share your wisdom with others.

Honor your sense of humor.

Keep exploring; be adventurous.

Stay in touch with what gives your life meaning.

Keep some time for stillness and quiet.

Remind yourself of what you have learned when you face another loss.

INTEGRATION: Daylight

My active choice?

To be willing to make and remake choices

Addendum

Helping Children and Teenagers Deal with Loss

HELPING CHILDREN AND TEENAGERS
DEAL WITH LOSS

It is extremely difficult to grieve fully oneself and, at the same time, to facilitate a child's or a teenager's grieving. Yet this is what parents, grandparents, aunts, uncles, siblings, and friends are required to do. Professionals offer these suggestions to help us at this difficult time in this often heartbreaking task.

A GRIEVING PROCESS

The first step—researchers, doctors, and counselors tell us—is to recognize that children experience a mourning process also, although in different ways, at different ages and to different degrees, and in different proportions from adults.

Grace Christ has written a thorough book, *Healing Children's Grief*, based on the large-scale study of families coping with the illness and death of a parent from cancer that she and a colleague conducted at Memorial Sloan-Kettering Cancer Center. On the subject of children's resilience, Christ writes: "But we have found that while children do go through pain, they can also learn, grow and recover with the help of supportive adults. What is apparent from the research in this study is that the way a child responds to loss is the result of a complex interweaving of circumstances. . . ." These circumstances include, according to Dr. Christ's research, the emotional responses and parenting abilities of the surviving parent (when the death is a parent), the presence or absence of financial difficulties, and the child's own natural strengths and weaknesses.

One of the most useful findings of Grace Christ's study was the fact that children of different ages cope with death in different ways. The lists that follow represent Elizabeth Neeld's distillation of Professor Christ's research:

Children Three to Five Years Old

Characteristics of their grieving:

Expressing anger and sadness for many days or months

Regressing in areas such as eating and toilet training

Displaying sleeping difficulties

Showing anxiousness when separated from caregivers

Complaining of stomachaches, headaches, bumps, and bruises

Recalling the dead person, but often in a distant or casual way

Indicating a desire for a replacement for the dead person

Recommendations for caregivers:

Use concrete details to describe death: The heart has stopped beating, etc. Tell the child that the dead person will never come back. Use other examples of death, such as the death of a pet or of someone else who has died, if this is applicable.

Let the child know what she or he might be feeling—anger, sadness, fear, etc.—and let the child draw pictures or show in play what she or he understands about the death.

Allow children to attend rituals, and make arrangements for someone to take care of them if the event lasts too long.

Reassure the child that she or he will continue to be taken care of.

Provide the child with objects that are associated with the dead person, such as a photograph or a toy they both played with.

Think about how to respond to the separation anxiety, sleeping problems, clinging behavior, etc., that are likely to be present.

Create opportunities for the child to talk about the dead person. Help the child remember pleasurable activities she or he participated in with the dead person.

Be sure the child understands why adults around her or him are experiencing intense emotions.

When anniversaries and holidays come, emphasize with the child the good times related to the lost person.

Allow the child to participate in a play group that includes other children who have had a similar loss.

Remember that the pace of the child's grieving is very different from that of an adult. The child may express intense feelings related to the death off and on for years.

Seek professional help for a child who continues over time to cling, be fearful, have nightmares, who becomes preoccupied with dying, displays acute sadness, has trouble functioning at school, or shows continuing signs of developmental regression in toilet training, eating, etc.

(Also seek professional help for any caregiver whose problems related to the loss have a negative impact.)

Children Six to Eight Years Old

Characteristics of their grieving:

Displaying sad and angry feelings, but also talking about the dead person in a happy way

Enjoying "talking to" the dead person and imagining that the dead person is watching over them

Enjoying looking at pictures and videotapes that include the dead person

Taking gifts and decorations to the cemetery, though often not spending a long time at the grave

Trying to help adults feel better in their grief

Desiring some possession or object associated with the dead person

Crying during the night, having nightmares and dreams, and talking about missing the dead person

Being angry with God for the death and having thoughts of discouragement and bitterness

Being worried about who will take care of them and whether they will continue to have normal activities like vacations

Recommendations for caregivers:

Encourage the child to be a part of (and to participate in, if the child so desires) rituals and ceremonies honoring the dead person.

Expect the child to ask blunt questions about the death.

Be prepared for the child's wanting to return quickly to normal activities.

Talk with the child about all the different changes that are now taking place in her or his life.

Be sure school personnel, day-care workers, and other adults are aware that the child has suffered a loss.

Keep the daily structure of the child's life as count-on-able as is feasible and possible.

If it is a parent who has died, try to avoid a separation of more than a day or so by the other parent during the first six months of grieving.

Expect intense feelings of grief to be displayed only fleetingly, and that emphasis for the child is likely to be remembering the dead person pleasantly.

Consider a children's bereavement group and bereavement counseling.

If anxiety, depression, guilt, poor self-esteem, or thoughts of suicide persist for more than several months after the death, consider therapy for the child (and the caregiver if problems related to the loss have a negative impact).

Children Nine to Eleven Years Old

Characteristics of their grieving:

Wanting to hide sad feelings and be brave

Fearing other losses

Showing concern about what seems like the injustice of the loss

Worrying about getting a disease

Identifying with the dead person

Displaying muted emotional responses

Complaining of headaches and stomachaches

Expressing anger by being messy, fighting, provoking teachers and parents, testing limits

Wanting to help others in their grief

Recommendations for caregivers:

Encourage participation in rituals and ceremonies honoring the dead person.

Make objects that belonged to the dead person available to the child.

Talk about any necessary changes in routine that the child will be experiencing.

Look at photographs, remember good times, talk about what happened, who did what.

Teach the child that sad feelings are normal and help the child understand that a grieving process is also normal.

Reestablish as many routines as possible as quickly as possible.

Think about the roles the dead person played in the child's life and plan how these roles might be filled now.

Lessen any separation anxiety the child displays as much as possible.

Do not be surprised by rebellion, sulks, messiness, or similar behavior displayed at home.

Seek individual or group grief counseling for the child and the adults in her or his life.

Provide therapy for the child if a return to previous levels of compe-

tence in school, for example, is delayed or if the child's sadness persists without large blocks of pleasure or joy.

Adolescents Twelve to Fourteen Years Old

Characteristics of their grieving:

Bringing home school reports that show drops in grades

Experiencing problems sleeping

Displaying anger, sadness, mild depression, anxiety, fear, acting out, emotional withdrawal, weight gain, stubbornness, or oppositional, argumentative, and demanding behavior

Crying alone

Showing a reluctance to talk about the thoughts and feelings they have for the dead person

Displaying episodic mourning, often triggered by specific events such as birthdays

Talking to adults other than a parent about the loss

Becoming angry about other difficulties such as pressures at school or relationships with peers; needing limits to be set

Identifying with the deceased

Talking with the dead person, dreaming about the person, and sensing the person's presence

Resisting letting expressions of mourning interfere with school and peer activities

Missing the dead person as a caretaker or a role model

Experiencing displaced emotion, such as crying at a movie rather than crying directly about the dead person

Desiring not to show emotion

Recommendations for caregivers:

Encourage as much participation in funeral and burial rites as the adolescent desires.

Understand the adolescent's need to return quickly to normal activities.

Make momentos that belonged to the dead person available to the adolescent.

Create opportunities for the expression of grief and expect expressions of grief to be episodic and of a duration that fits the adolescent's own timetable.

Let the adolescent know that dreaming of the dead person and sensing the dead person's presence are normal.

Emphasize positive experiences, especially around the adolescent's achievements.

Provide the structure, nurturing, and support that had been given by the dead person.

Realize the adolescent's need for limits to be set that prevent destructive behavior at the same time that support is given for her or him to act with independence.

Consider family therapy to deal with conflicts within the family.

Encourage the adolescent to participate in school, athletic, and social activities.

Emphasize positive growth that comes from going through a mourning process; teach the adolescent that there is a normal mourning process that she can go through at her own pace and in her own way.

Seek professional counseling or therapy if uncommon or severe symptoms continue.

Adults, too, should seek counseling if they are experiencing prolonged or severe problems in handling family conflicts or in managing their own grief.

Young Adults Fifteen to Seventeen Years Old

Characteristics of the grieving of this age group:

Displaying a complex grieving process much more like that of adults

Feeling fear about the future—for example, whether there will be enough money

Being selective about whom to share grief with

Experiencing sustained and profound sadness, crying, anger, bitterness, depressed mood with sleep disturbances, a sense of helplessness and of being overwhelmed

Worrying about school performance and often experiencing a decline in school, sports, and other activities

Displaying transient bouts of drinking or taking drugs, having arguments with parents, spending more time away from home with friends

Refusing on some occasions to do chores

Wanting to be alone to grieve, such as at the cemetery

Finding feelings about death reawakened by other transitions, such as going to college

Showing a need to renegotiate relationships with others

Missing the role the person played for the young adult and often idealizing the dead person

Recommendations for caregivers:

Encourage the young adult to participate in the funeral and burial as actively as she or he wishes to.

Do not be surprised when young adults idealize the dead person.

Be sure school personnel know about the loss.

Encourage the expression of feelings and explain the nature of the grief process.

Allow the young adult to select momentos that belonged to the dead person.

Use peer, informal, and formal counseling; offer bereavement counseling and educational services so that the young adult can learn about the process she or he is experiencing.

Bring up the subject of the young adult's plans for the future.

Anticipate the young adult's anger and withdrawal, refusal to help with household chores, etc.

Recognize the young adult's need to be independent and separate.

Identify the positive aspects of the dead person's legacy to the young adult.

Refer young adults with severe symptoms for counseling and therapy; adults who are encountering unusual conflicts with their young people or having difficulty dealing with their own grieving should also seek therapy.

Professionals Give General Advice

Perhaps the most essential advice for adults helping children deal with loss is to communicate with them straightforwardly. To help a child understand, death can be described as "what happens when the body stops working"; or the dead person can be described as someone who "no longer eats or talks or breathes," who has been buried "in a special place and cannot return," and who "feels no pain." Religious beliefs that are central to the family's life can also be discussed and explained.

Almost everyone agrees that children should be included in the mourning rituals. Experts vary on the age at which children should attend funerals. The opinions range from age three to five to seven, but all agree that the choice of whether to attend should be the child's. For many children, being a part of the funeral and burial activities helps them express their sorrow. It is important to be direct when explaining the funeral. What will take place? Who will be there? How long will it last? What does it mean? Answering these questions as completely and as honestly as possible will allow the child to prepare mentally for an event that will very likely be etched in her or his memory forever.

Remember, too, that children experience many of the same fears as do adults: that they caused the death or separation; that they are in danger themselves; that they have been personally abandoned and rejected. They may also be angry. These fears and emotions may be present in the case of both death and divorce, but they may be even more severe when the loss is the result of divorce. Adults therefore should discuss these issues candidly, helping children acknowledge their fears and put these fears in perspective.

The Child Bereavement Trust in Great Britain recommends that adults should (1) always use the words "dead" and "died," and not soften the blow with euphemisms; (2) think twice about sending children to stay with friends or relatives to protect them during family bereavements, because removing children from their usual environment can make matters worse; (3) avoid exposing children to distressing television images, which could further traumatize them; (4) ask children if they want to see the body of the person who has died; and (5) give honest information when children ask questions.

One writer talks about a five-year-old's response to his father's death. The child initially asked lots of questions about the accident in which his father died, and his mother even arranged for him to speak to the policeman who had been there. Then, as the months went on, the boy became increasingly withdrawn and quiet. His mother took him to a service for bereaved children run by a local hospice. There she found books on grief for them to read together. The child began to ask how we knew that his daddy was really dead, so a doctor at the hospice showed him how to test for the pulse, information that brought a big relief to the child. Much of the work of adults in the child's grieving involved giving him the language with which to talk about his father's death. When the boy became angry when he heard other boys talking about their fathers at school, his mother suggested to him that he might be feeling angry because he missed his daddy. She told him that it was all right to feel angry but that it wasn't all right to hit people, and she reminded him that he had had a super dad.

As the young boy progressed through his grieving, he began to speak proudly of his father. In reference to a small memory jar of colored salt that he made in the bereavement program he attended, the child said, "I used colors that Daddy liked so I could have good memories of him. I used purple and white for the sports team he liked, and green because he used to be in the army. The orange and yellow remind me of when we went to the beach and Daddy floated me in the water, because they are the colors of the sun and sand and

Daddy's swimming trunks. I was very upset when my daddy died. I went to play and forgot about it, but I wanted him there a lot."

Things to Do

It is critical that children be encouraged to express their feelings. Simple things like these seem to make such a difference with a child who is grieving:

Deliberately setting aside time and creating an opportunity for the child to talk about the lost person

Preparing a scrapbook together that commemorates life with the person who is gone

Putting pictures in a photograph album

Making sure the child has a picture of the lost person available close by

Carrying out a project with the child that is related to one of the interests of the absent person

Listening

Often, the best thing an adult can do is listen, instead of telling a child what to say or how to act. Professionals say that rather than talking too much to children or teenagers ourselves, we should encourage them to talk. Ask questions that allow the child or teenager to think and remember:

- Can you tell me a funny story about your dad?
- Did you have a favorite time with your brother?
- Where do you think your mother has gone?
- What do you remember the most?

It is important to remember that not every child will respond in the same manner. Adults have varying needs and ways of communicating, and the same is true of children and teenagers. Some may choose to express their loss with pictures, while others will opt for words. If you find that a child or teenager isn't responsive, try sharing your own feelings and the things you've done to help ease the pain. This will allow the young person to see that she is not alone in her suffering.

Teenagers

Special attention should also be paid to the age differences of children experiencing grief and loss. Some adults have told me that dealing with their teenager's grief was more difficult than dealing with their own. Remember that teenagers are particularly vulnerable, even without a loss. They like to be in control. They are coming to terms with their own sexuality, their own choices and individualism, as well as with social and academic pressures. A sudden loss or deviation from their regular lives can throw a teenager off course completely. Try to act as a companion rather than as a director. Encourage adult conversations that treat the teenager with respect.

Allowing teens to express themselves shows our respect for their words and thoughts. Remind teenagers that everyone is free to grieve as she or he wishes. Some respond to death with laughter. One teenager began to sing and dance and was unable to cry when her mother died. It's important to let teens, as well as young children, know that grief can be expressed in many different ways and for varying lengths of time. There is no limit to grief. Wounds heal differently with different people, and the same holds true for the grieving process. It is important never to tell a young person to "move on."

More Specific Suggestions

These suggestions can help ease the stress of both teenagers and children in their grieving:

Find some alone time daily with the child or young person. Be sure she or he knows this is a special time with you, to share feelings and emotions, or simply to sit quietly with your full, undivided attention.

Try not to "fix" situations but to listen instead.

Open up and share your own stories and memories of a loved one or of good times together.

Encourage creative activities, such as art or exercise, that will allow the release of energy and stress.

Remember that children and young people can be extremely intuitive. Don't underestimate what your child will pick up from your own anxieties. Be honest about what you are experiencing, and share what you are doing in your own grief work.

Be patient. It may take some time before a child or a teenager opens up during a difficult time.

Note from Elizabeth Neeld: The following contribution comes from Ione Jenson, educator, author, lecturer, and psycho-spiritual therapist with degrees in education, counseling, and psychology. In 1981 she co-founded a holistic retreat and healing center near Coeur d'Alene, Idaho, where she lives and works. For the past three years, she has been deeply involved in Camp Indigo, a six-week summer program for grades K–5, where children are given a richly textured program in experiential learning, and where conflict resolution and peacemaking strategies are an integral part of the program (www.campindigo.org).

SUPPORTING CHILDREN IN GRIEF
Ione Jenson

Children suffer many kinds of losses, too, and, like adults, they will each suffer and cope in their own unique way. However, it's important to remember that children are inexperienced, and that even though teenagers may seem more sophisticated, they too often lack the experience they will need to see them through some of the more difficult times. This may well be why teenage suicide rates and the incidence of depression among teens have risen as they face a rapidly changing world, often without the inner skills or the adult support needed to aid them in the learning and coping process.

Because very young children have not yet developed the verbal skills they need to express their emotions, they will usually respond to stress and grief by acting out or by reacting. This acting out of feelings may manifest in the form of loneliness, withdrawal, fear, jealousy, moodiness, guilt, anger, or the whole gamut of human emotions. Often, through their drawings, dreams, dramatic play with the use of puppets, or by utilizing the sand tray techniques, these youngsters are able to release some of the intensity of their experience. These expressions provide clues to what is happening inside the individual child and often give the adult crucial information for aiding and supporting the child through the process. Of course, older children, and even some adults who are not practiced or who do not feel comfortable verbalizing emotions, will also often express their feelings in outer actions and reactions in much the same manner. This is where love and tolerance, coupled with time and patience, are needed on the part of others who make up their world.

So what are the concrete ways in which we can support our children through the losses they will inevitably experience throughout their lives?

- Keeping the lines of communication open and practicing compassionate listening, with both the mind and the heart, is the single most important thing we can ever do for children under all circumstances, and it is even more important when children are facing challenges they don't understand and that can seem over-whelming at times. Children may ask the same questions over and over in their attempts to integrate the information and make it real, so offer ample opportunity for open communication. If parents are too grief-stricken to handle this, they should make sure that someone who is open and willing to talk with the child becomes involved as soon as possible.

- Including children in as much of the process as is age appropri-ate is vitally important. Even babies are very conscious of the "vibes" of emotionally charged situations, and certainly that holds true for toddlers and young children. Even if children are removed from the situation and sent away to stay with friends or relatives, they know that something important has happened and may feel anxious. If simple explanations aren't given—and even preverbal youngsters understand much more than they are able to voice—their imaginations will create fantasy explanations that may conjure up fears greater or worse than the reality of the situation. Provide ample opportunity for children to express themselves in some form, and follow their lead in determining what works best for them.
- Remember that children are literal and may well misinterpret certain remarks, such as, "Grandma went to sleep, and God took her to live in heaven." To small children, this may stir up a fear of going to bed and going to sleep lest God should take them away from their home and parents. An even greater fear may be that God will take their parents away, too. So, as well intentioned as our explanations to save our children from experiencing grief may be, allowing them to share a little of our grief and to experi-ence their own may be the wiser choice.
- Talking about death in natural ways before it happens to some-one close allows children to articulate questions and fears more easily. Talk about life cycles and the death of plants or casual ac-quaintances or people who are known to the child but may not be closely involved in the child's life. Allow children to grieve the death of pets, and encourage them to plan and participate in a ritual of thanksgiving for the life and joy the pet brought to the family.
- Sometimes children's fear of death centers around what might

become of them in the event that a parent should die. My son expressed this concern one day when he was about five or six years old, and although I assured him that it wasn't likely that anything would happen to either his father or me, I told him that his dad and I had drawn up legal documents that gave his aunt, who loved and adored him and whom he dearly loved in return, legal custody. When he asked to see the papers and wanted to know where we kept them, we complied with his request.

- If death strikes a close family member, remember that play is fundamental to the way children work through their feelings. Support this activity without interfering with it, and just be an observer and available. If children initiate a conversation, or if the play naturally leads into talking, allow it to unfold, but without pressure. Sometimes supportive silence is a huge gift.

- Children may cry and need to grieve and express sadness through tears. If that occurs, grieve with them and don't feel the necessity of hiding your own tears. Shared grief can be very comforting.

- Children may need to withdraw from the intensity of grieving—either their own or that of others—so make room for that if it happens. When I was sixteen, my father died from a sudden heart attack. I was alone with him at his business and held him in my arms while awaiting the ambulance I had called. (CPR wasn't known then.) When my mother finally arrived, she went in the ambulance with my father, so I had the responsibility of closing up the business and calling my two older sisters, who were sixty miles away, and asking them to come immediately. By midnight, I finally said I was going to bed. My sisters thought I was "taking it" better than anyone else because I could go to bed and go to sleep, while in truth I just needed to withdraw from the intensity in the only manner I knew how. It was my temporary escape mechanism.

- A child may feel guilty. In the case of the illness or death of a close family member, the child has probably been angry with the person at one time or another, and wonders if she caused the death because of her words, thoughts, or actions toward the dead person. Children need to be reassured that everyone has those thoughts and feelings, and that they do not cause either the illness or death of another. In the case of death, perhaps the child would like to speak to a picture of the deceased and express her or his feelings. Under those circumstances, it may be helpful to explain to the child that the person was so loving he or she would know the child meant no harm and would certainly understand and forgive.

- Allow children to participate in simple decisions about the service and in simple rituals that are age appropriate. Teenagers, and even small children, may run errands, honor the deceased by lighting a candle, by helping to arrange flowers, or by putting a favorite toy or poem in a place of honor. Invite them to be a part of any rituals that are observed in your own spiritual belief system. At a funeral that I recently attended, five teenage grandchildren got up, one at a time, and spoke of a happy experience they had shared with their grandmother. One spoke only a couple of sentences, another read something he had written, and in doing so each not only recognized the passing of a dearly beloved woman but also celebrated her life with happy memories. It's important to speak of life as well as death.

- Assemble a picture album or a memory journal in which each member of the family writes a word, a thought, or about a gift received that remains close in heart because it was shared by the departed. The sharing could also be tape-recorded and then written up on the computer, where copies could be made for each person who contributed. This can become a lifetime keepsake; for while sadness and emotions may ebb and lose their sharp edge with the passing of time, remembering, loving, and tenderly missing is never erased and will continue throughout our lives.

- Above all, follow your heart and let your child lead you into knowing just what she or he needs. One poignant story follows September 11, 2001. The father of a four-year-old boy was killed in the World Trade Center collapse. The child's therapist told him she had a four-year-old client whose father was also killed when the Twin Towers collapsed and she wondered if this boy might give her four-year-old client some advice. Out of the child's mouth came the most incredible wisdom, as he advised this "four-year-old client" on what he might do that would help him to best handle his loss. Of course, he was advising himself and giving both his therapist and his mother the exact steps they needed to take to help him integrate and work through this life-altering event he was experiencing. "Out of the mouths of babes . . ."

In the end, be present for your children and be present to your own needs. Give yourselves and your children adequate time and sufficient space, and then have patience in allowing the process to take as long as it takes. Don't attempt to extend it, and don't attempt to shorten or by-pass it; it's all an important part of the journey, for, above all else, loss and grief are an integral part of the very fabric and cycles of our existence.

Note from Elizabeth Neeld: The following contribution comes from Colleen O'Grady, a marriage and family therapist who is a supervisor for the American Association of Marriage and Family Therapists, as well as a supervisor, consultant, and trainer of family therapy in child and adolescent psychiatry at the University of Texas Mental Science Institute in Houston. She also supervises family therapy in the Learning Support Center at Texas Children's Hospital in Houston. In addition, O'Grady has a private practice and has worked with teenagers for twenty-five years.

DEALING WITH ADOLESCENT GRIEF
Colleen O'Grady

Living with adolescents can be challenging and very rewarding for parents at the best of times. It can become extremely challenging for the parents of an adolescent who is grieving. All parents want the best for their children, and it is heartbreaking to see a child suffer. The important question for the parent to ask is what is helpful and what "helpful" things may not be so helpful. Hopefully, the following principles will be useful to you.

1. Are they making mountains out of molehills?

Sometimes parents are bewildered at their adolescent's deep distress over something that seems minor, like the betrayal of a friend or rejection from a romantic crush. It is very easy for a parent to minimize adolescents' feelings by either placating them ("You're just being dramatic"; "Don't worry about it, you'll get over it") or getting frustrated with them and cutting them off. If a parent minimizes the grief, there is a strong probability that the adolescent will escalate his distress until he gets the parent's attention. It is important for parents to remember that adolescents are not adults and this may be the first time they have ever had this life experience, which may have shaken their understanding of the world. Parents may say, "I wish that was the only thing I had to worry about," but adolescents aren't able to carry (emotionally) what adults are expected to carry. It may be helpful for a parent to remember some of her first life experiences, which might facilitate a caring, empathic atmosphere.

2. Can parents really understand?

Adolescents desperately want to be listened to by adults. It is very easy for a parent to respond by saying, "I understand. I went through the same things when I was a teenager." Too often, however, a parent shuts down the conversation by understanding too quickly, or by focusing the conversation on herself. Teenagers want their experience to be unique, and they don't want to be just like their parents. What is helpful is for parents to work at understanding their adolescent. This is accomplished by the parents becoming a student of the teenager's culture and experience, which means that when they don't "get it," the parents will allow themselves to be taught. A teenager is very receptive to an adult who is sincerely asking questions and working hard to "get" the adolescent's experience.

3. My teenager won't talk to me!

It can be very frustrating for parents when adolescents won't talk, especially in a season of grief. Often, parents try to talk to their adolescents at reasonable times, such as after school, or at dinnertime. This is both good news and bad news. The bad news is that adolescents don't like to talk at reasonable times, and the good news is that they *will* talk. Many parents have told me that they had significant and healing conversations with their teenagers when they were on their way to bed. Be open to the opportunities that are initiated by your teenager, even if the time is unreasonable.

4. Mary, Mary quite contrary! (How do you give advice to adolescents?)

Parents, have you ever noticed that your teenager can take the opposite side of anything you suggest, and that she can be argumentative? There is an adolescent "logic" that no parent can beat because the "logic" is that the teenager should have his way. So how can parents give advice to their adolescents, especially at a time of loss? There are times when parents must take action in order to protect their teenagers despite the protest. However, at other times it is important for parents to be sowers of seeds and not to push the seeds. Throwing out seeds of advice like "Just think about it" gives the adolescent time to think about it and be receptive. Because the parents aren't pushing, there is less likelihood of arguments. Parents can stay warm and supportive and continue to sow the seeds of advice until their teenagers become responsive.

5. My parents are hiding things from me.

Adolescents are very perceptive, and they will know that something is wrong in the home even if it is not talked about. They know if someone is being "fake." An adolescent who doesn't have clear information even though he senses something isn't right may become increasingly anxious, agitated, and stressful. Teenagers need this information and can share in the responsibility of helping in the home. Parents can make it clear that they are in charge and that they accept responsibility for carrying the major responsibilities. Parents can be role models to their adolescents by being authentic about their thoughts and feelings.

6. Are your adolescents acting out internally or externally?

It is normal for adolescents who are grieving to be extremely sad or angry. It is normal for them to have erratic mood swings, to be happy one minute and to burst into tears the next. However, adolescents are vulnerable to being at risk after losing someone they love and may respond by acting out. When adolescents act out internally, they take their anger and sadness and go inward. If this persists over time without any treatment, it can develop into major depression, anxiety disorders, or eating disorders. Parents can watch for significant changes in eating, sleeping, peer socialization, and school functioning.

Adolescents may also act out externally. Parents need to be alert to whether their adolescent has changed friends to a more "party" crowd. He could be at risk for using alcohol or drugs to numb the pain by "partying" all the time. Parents should also be alert to any changes in grades or in attendance at school. If the anger persists over time and your teenager is getting into frequent fights at home or at school, she could benefit from professional treatment. If you have any concerns about the long-term changes in your adolescent, don't hesitate to call a school counselor, psychotherapist, family doctor, or psychiatrist.

7. Adolescents who are grieving need . . .

• to be in a community of adolescents. Not only are teenagers comforted by their families but they need ongoing comfort from their peers. They may find this in a youth group from church, a small group at school, or at home. There is a depth of relationship that is uniquely forged at times of grief. Part of this depth is the love and caring that transcends ordinary friendships. Adolescents relish this time of realness, where the walls that have separated come tumbling down. Also, spirituality can bring depth to a relationship and offer new meaning in life as teenagers come together and support each other in prayer and song.

• to feel normal. Even though life as they know it will never be the same, teenagers want to find some normalcy. It is important for them to continue to engage in the normal activities of school and home. Adolescents are resilient. They can laugh with their friends, go to movies, and continue to be involved at school while grieving. It is good for parents to continue the normalcy of family routines, rituals, and traditions as much as possible. Parents can reassure adolescents that it is important for them to continue to be normal, but adolescents also need to have their parents' permission to grieve and not participate when they are not feeling up to it.

- to develop new meaning for their life. This meaning can be created from conversations with friends and family. An adolescent may realize that her family is "really behind me and loves me." Some adolescents may get a new sense of belonging with their peers. They may become less self-centered and more grateful, and develop compassion and caring for others. They may decide to move forward, and set goals for the future and give back to others. Many will begin their own authentic spiritual journey, which often continues through their lifetime. For an adolescent, the experience of loss can be the greatest gift for developing a sense of identity and meaning.

WEB SITES

Fortunately, there are more and more good resources for adults to help children and teenagers deal with loss, particularly on the Internet. Check the Internet for sites such as these:

The Dougy Center
www.grievingchild.org
3909 SE 52nd Avenue
Portland, OR 97206
(503) 775-5683

The Dougy Center is a nonprofit organization that provides peer support for grieving children. Through its National Center for Grieving Children and Families, the center also provides support and training locally, nationally, and internationally to individuals and organizations seeking to assist children in grief. The well-organized and colorful site is an additional tool that offers information, resources, and a drop-down state-by-state list of counseling centers in your area. Highly recommended.

Rainbows
www.rainbows.org
2100 Golf Road #370
Rolling Meadows, IL 60008-4231
(847) 952-1770

Rainbows is a not-for-profit, international organization that offers training and curricula for establishing peer-support groups in churches, synagogues, schools, and social agencies. These curricula are available to children and adults of all ages and religious denominations who are mourning a death, a divorce, or any other painful transition in their family.

KIDSAID (Part of Griefnet.org)
http://kidsaid.com

KIDSAID offers a safe place for children to share and to help one another deal with grief related to any type of loss. Run by GriefNet.org, the site allows children to show artwork and stories, talk about pets, family, and peers. Games and contests will soon be added to the site's program.

Fernside
www.fernside.org
2303 Indian Mound Avenue
Cincinnati, OH 45212
(513) 841-1012

Fernside appeals to children who have experienced a loss. It offers kids letters, message boards, and other resources, including a summer camp, to help ease their suffering. Pages include activities, art (posted by kids), questions asked by other kids, recommended books, and feedback for kids to give to the sponsoring organization.

BOOKS

Death and Younger Children (Under Ten)

Appelt, Kathi. *I See the Moon*. Wm. B. Eerdmans, 1998.
Bahr, Mary. *If Nathan Were Here*. Wm. B. Eerdmans, 2001.
Barron, T. A. *Where Is Grandpa?* Philomel, 2000.
Carson, Jo. *You Hold Me, and I'll Hold You*. Orchard, 1992.
Clifton, Lucille. *Everett Anderson's Goodbye*. Henry Holt, 1988.
Coerr, Eleanor. *Sadako*. Scott Foresman, 1997.
Harris, Robie. *Goodbye Mousie*. Margaret McElderry Books, 2001.
Hopkinson, Deborah. *Bluebird Summer*. HarperCollins, 2001.
Johnston, Tony. *That Summer*. Harcourt Brace, 2002.

Joslin, Mary. *The Goodbye Boat*. Wm. B. Eerdmans, 1999.

Joosse, Barbara M. *Ghost Wings*. Chronicle Books, 2001.

Krasny Brown, Laurie and Marc Tolon Brown. *When Dinosaurs Die: A Guide to Understanding Death*. Little, Brown, 1998.

Mills, Joyce C. *Gentle Willow: A Story for Children About Dying*. Magination, 1993.

Mundy, Michaelene. *Sad Isn't Bad: A Good-Grief Guidebook for Kids Dealing with Loss*. Abbey Press, 1998.

Polacco, Patricia. *The Butterfly*. Philomel, 2000.

Romain, Trevor, and Elizabeth Verdick. *What on Earth Do You Do When Someone Dies?* Free Spirit, 1999.

Rylant, Cynthia. *Dog Heaven*. Scholastic, 1995.

———. *Cat Heaven*. Scholastic, 1997.

Santucci, Barbara. *Loon Summer*. Wm. B. Eerdmans, 2000.

Schweibert, Pat, et al. *Tear Soup*. Perinatal Loss, 2001.

Silverman, Janis. *Help Me Say Goodbye: Activities for Helping Kids Cope When a Special Person Dies*. Fairview Press, 1999.

Simon, Norma. *The Saddest Time*. Albert Whitman, 1992.

Sims, Alicia M. *Am I Still a Sister?* Big A & Company, 1988.

Singleton, Joan, and Virginia Kylberg. *Someone Special Died (Kids Have Feelings Too Series)*. McGraw Hill, 2002.

Stafford, William. *The Animal Who Drank Up Sound*. Harcourt, 1992.

Varley, Susan. *Badger's Parting Gifts*. Mulberry Books, 1992.

Viorst, Judith. *The Tenth Good Thing About Barney*. Aladdin Books, 1976.

White, E. B. *Charlotte's Web*. HarperTrophy, 1999.

Wilhelm, Hans. *I'll Always Love You*. Crown Books, 1989.

Death and Older Children (10+) and Teenagers

Appelt, Kathi. *Kissing Tennessee*. Harcourt, 2000.

———. *Just People, Poems for Young Readers*. Absey & Co., 1997.

Bode, Janet. *Death Is Hard to Live With*. Dell Books for Young Readers, 1993.

Creech, Sharon. *Walk Two Moons*. HarperTrophy, 1996.

Curtis, Christopher Paul. *The Watsons Go to Birmingham*. Bantam, 1998.

Fitzgerald, Helen. *The Grieving Teen: A Guide for Teenagers and Their Friends*. Simon & Schuster, 2000.

Gliko-Braden, Majel. *Grief Comes to Class*. Centering Corporation, 1992.

Gootman, Marilyn E. *When a Friend Dies: A Book for Teens About Grieving & Healing*. Free Spirit, 1994.

Grollman, Earl. *Straight Talk About Death for Teenagers*. Beacon, 1993.

————. *Living When a Young Friend Commits Suicide: Or Even Talks About It*. Beacon, 1999.

Howe, James, ed. *The Color of Absence: 12 Stories About Loss and Hope*. Atheneum, 2001.

Krementz, Jill. *How It Feels When a Parent Dies*. Knopf, 1988.

Paterson, Katherine. *Bridge to Terabithia*. HarperCollins, 1978.

Rylant, Cynthia. *Missing May*. Yearling, 1993.

Scrivani, Mark. *When Death Walks In*. Centering Corporation, 1991.

Smith, Cynthia Leitich. *Rain Is Not My Indian Name*. HarperCollins, 2001.

Spinelli, Jerry. *Maniac Magee*. Little, Brown, 1990.

Stafford, William. *The Animal Who Drank Up Sound*. Harcourt, 1990.

Traisman, Enid Samuel. *Fire in My Heart, Ice in My Veins: A Journal for Teenagers Experiencing a Loss*. Centering Corporation, 1992.

Wolff, Virginia Euwer. *Make Lemonade*. Point, 1994.

Note from Elizabeth Neeld: The following is a list of books on death and tragedy and books on hope posted on the Web site www.looseleaf.org.

Books on Death and Tragedy (Sited on Web Site www.looseleaf.org)

Bridge to Terabithia
Katherine Paterson (HarperTrophy)

All summer, Jess pushed himself to be the fastest boy in the fifth grade. But his victory was stolen by a newcomer—a girl, one who didn't even know enough to stay on the girls' side of the playground. Jess finds himself sticking up for Leslie, for the girl who breaks rules and wins races. The friendship between the two grows as Jess guides the city girl through the pitfalls of life in their small, rural town, and Leslie draws him into the world of imagination, magic, and ceremony called Terabithia. Here, Leslie and Jess rule supreme among the oaks and evergreens—until an unforeseen tragedy forces Jess to reign in Terabithia alone, and both worlds are forever changed. Ages 9–12.

The Dead Bird
Margaret Wise Brown (HarperTrophy)

There is a little bird lying on its side. Its eyes are closed and there's no heartbeat. The children are very sorry, so they decide to say goodbye. In the forest, they dig a hole for the bird and cover it with warm ferns and flowers. Finally, their sweet song sends the little bird on its way. Ages 4–8.

Stopping for Death: Poems of Love and Loss
Edited by Carol Ann Duffy (Henry Holt)

A collection of poems about death, loss, and mourning written by poets from all over the world, including Janet Frame, Alice Walker, and Seamus Heaney. Young adult.

If You Come Softly
Jacqueline Woodson (Puffin)

Jeremiah feels good inside his own skin. That is, when he's in his own Brooklyn neighborhood. But now he's going to be attending a fancy prep school in Manhattan, and black teenage boys don't exactly fit in there. So it's a surprise when he meets Ellie the first week of school. In one frozen moment their eyes lock, and after that they know they fit together—even though she's Jewish and he's black. Their worlds are so different, but to them that's not what matters. Too bad the rest of the world has to get in their way. Ages 9–12.

Books on Hope (Sited on Web Site www.looseleaf.org)

Earth-Shattering Poems
Edited by Liz Rosenberg (Henry Holt)

A collection of the world's most intense poetry, carefully selected to inspire and nourish fervent feelings. From the tragedy of Federico Garcia Lorca's "Lament for the Death of Ignacio Sanchez Mejias" to the beauty of Margaret Menges's "A Love Poem," here is an international collection of language distilled to its emotional essence. Young adult.

Light-Gathering Poems
Edited by Liz Rosenberg (Henry Holt)

Some of the best-known poems by famous poets are here—favorites by Byron, Dickinson, Frost, Ginsberg, Hughes, Keats, Oliver, Stafford, Yeats, and lots more.

There are also several fine accessible poems in translation (including exquisite selections by Issa, Rilke, and Rumi), as well as a few by new American voices. In her lyrical introduction, Rosenberg writes simply about the music of poetry, about rhyme, simile, and metaphor as promising the hope of connection and possibility. Young adult.

Seedfolks
Paul Fleischman (HarperCollins)

This is the story of a blighted neighborhood that is transformed when a young girl plants a few lima beans in an abandoned lot. Slowly, one by one, neighbors are touched and stirred to action as they see tendrils poke through the dirt. Hispanics, Haitians, Koreans, young, and old begin to turn the littered lot into a garden for the entire community. A gift for hearts of all ages, this gentle, timeless story will delight anyone in need of a sprig of inspiration. Ages 9–12.

Cello of Mr. O
Jane Cutler (Dutton)

When a concert cellist plays in the square for his neighbors in a war-besieged city, his priceless instrument is destroyed by a mortar shell, but he finds the courage to return the next day to perform with a harmonica. Ages 4–8.

Miss Rumphius
Barbara Cooney (Viking)

This powerful recounting of the life of a woman who lives on her own terms and still remembers her responsibility to make the world more beautiful is a must for every library. Ages 4–8.

Goin' Someplace Special
Patricia C. McKissack (Atheneum)

It's 1950 in the Southern town where Tricia Ann lives, and she faces painful prejudice when she goes off for a special day away from home. Carried by the wise words of her grandmother and by a touch of tenacity, she finds a place where all are welcome, regardless of their skin color. Ages 4–8.

Baseball Saved Us
Ken Mochizuki (Lee & Low)

Shorty's family had to leave their home and move to a Japanese internment camp during World War II. It was a difficult time; but when his dad built a base-ball field, Shorty began to regain his confidence. Ages 4–8.

Ali, Child of the Desert
Jonathan London (Lothrop)

Ali and his father were in the desert headed for the Moroccan town of Rissani when suddenly a windstorm overtook them and Ali found himself alone. Courage and friendship help Ali to survive. Ages 4–8.

River Friendly, River Wild
Jane Kurtz (Simon & Schuster)

Jane Kurtz uses poetry to explore what it's like to struggle through a flood and pull your life together afterward. Inspired by her own flood experience, this tale is realistic and unforgettable. Ages 4–8.

Goodbye Mousie
Robie Harris (Margaret McElderry Books)

This is the story of a little boy who wakes up to discover that his pet mouse has died. After expressing anger and disbelief, the boy learns that sadness and mem-ories are part of saying goodbye. Ages 4–8.

The Tenth Good Thing about Barney
Judith Viorst (Atheneum)

A young boy copes with the death of his cat, Barney. "An unusually good book that handles a difficult subject straightforwardly." —The Horn Book. Ages 4–8.

The Color of Absence: 12 Stories about Loss and Hope
Edited by James Howe (Atheneum)

The contributors to this collection of short stories for teens include Avi, C. B. Christiansen, James Howe, Angela Johnson, Annette Curtis Klause, Chris Lynch, Norma Fox Mazer, Walter Dean Myers, Naomi Shihab Nye, Michael J. Rosen, Roderick Townley, Virginia Euwer Wolff, and Jacqueline Woodson. Young adult.

BOOKS FOR ADULTS ABOUT GRIEF OF CHILDREN AND TEENAGERS

Christ, Grace H. *Healing Children's Grief: Surviving a Parent's Death from Cancer.* Oxford University Press, 2000.

Dodds, Bill. *Your Grieving Child: Answers on Death and Dying.* Our Sunday Visitor, 2001.

The Dougy Center, ed. *35 Ways to Help a Grieving Child.* The Dougy Center, 1999.

Emswiler, Mary Ann, and James P. Emswiler. *Guiding Your Child Through Grief.* Bantam, 2000.

Fitzgerald, Helen. *The Grieving Child: A Parent's Guide.* Simon & Schuster, 1992.

Grollman, Earl A. *Bereaved Children and Teens: A Support Guide for Parents and Professionals.* Beacon, 1996.

———. *Straight Talk About Death for Teenagers: How to Cope with Losing Someone You Love.* Beacon, 1993.

———. *Talking About Divorce and Separation: A Dialogue Between Parent and Child.* Beacon, 1989.

Hospice of Lancaster County. *A Teacher's Guide to the Grieving Student.* Hospice of Lancaster County, 1995.

Huntley, Theresa. *When Your Child Loses a Loved One.* Augsbury Fortress, 2001.

James, John W., and Russell Friedman (with Leslie London Matthews). *When Children Grieve: For Adults to Help Children Deal with Death, Divorce, Pet Loss, Moving, and Other Losses.* HarperCollins, 2001.

Johnson, Joy, and Marvin Johnson. *Children Grieve, Too: Helping Children Cope with Grief.* Centering Corporation, 1998.

Jones, Eileen. *Bibliotherapy for Bereaved Children: Healing Reading.* Jessica Kingsley, 2001.

Kubler-Ross, Elisabeth. *On Children and Death: How Children and Their Parents Can and Do Cope with Death.* Scribner, 1997.

Poust, Mary DeTurris. *Parenting a Grieving Child: Helping Children Find Faith, Hope, and Healing After the Loss of a Loved One.* Loyola Press, 2002.

Scherago, Marcia. *Sibling Grief: How Parents Can Help the Child Whose Brother or Sister Has Died.* Medic Publishing, 1987.

Traisman, Enid Samuel. *Fire in My Heart, Ice in My Veins: A Journal for Teenagers Experiencing a Loss.* Centering Corporation, 1992.

MUSIC FOR CHILDREN AND TEENAGERS WHO ARE GRIEVING

Ann Rachlin makes these recommendations for music for grieving children. Her full suggestions for music for all grievers can be found in the Directory of Resources that follows.

This is a simple list of pieces that may help soothe a grieving young person. They are all loved by my pupils. No age groups are significant.

Bach	Air on the G String
Canteloube:	Songs of the Aurvergne (*"Cradle Song"*)
Delius	On Hearing the First Cuckoo in Spring
Ravel:	Ma Mère L'Oye (*Mother Goose Suite*) *for Orchestra*
	Pavane for a Dead Infanta (*Orchestral*)
	"Sleeping Beauty"
	"Enchanted Garden"
Schubert	*Impromptu No. 3 in G-Flat Major*
Schumann:	Kinderscene
	"By the Fireside"
	"Dreaming"

See Directory of Resources—e.g., pets, gardening, and nature/outdoor activities—for other ways to assist children and teenagers who are grieving.

DIRECTORY OF
RESOURCES INDEX

DIRECTORY OF RESOURCES

Every grief, of course, is different. What provides succor to one of us when we are mourning does not necessarily aid another. While one individual finds solace in solitary gardening or walks along a creek bank, another may be helped most by meeting with a self-help group or talking often with friends. And both the solitary individual and the more gregarious person often choose to seek the support of a professional therapist, counselor, or social worker, a pastoral professional, or a designated grief counselor.

I have, therefore, attempted to provide an eclectic collection of resources that will offer something appropriate for everyone. The value of what follows, then, will not be found in the specificity of the information but in the stimulus these suggestions provide for each individual to make her or his own listings.

ONGOING COMMUNICATION WITH ELIZABETH HARPER NEELD

www.elizabethharperneeld.com is a Web site where readers can find new information, suggestions, discussion, a schedule of author appearances, and opportunities for communicating provided by *Seven Choice's* author Elizabeth Harper Neeld. Individuals who wish to explore the possibility of scheduling Elizabeth Neeld to speak or lead a retreat will find contact information on this Web site.

The Web site is also available for readers to suggest via e-mail any additional recommendations and suggestions for this Directory of Resources.

ORGANIZATIONS, SELF-HELP GROUPS, AND ONLINE COMMUNITIES

Below are organizations, clearinghouses, and service groups that exist to provide information and guidance to bereaved individuals. Many of these organizations also offer online communities that provide an abundance of information, chat rooms, and a virtual place of comfort for those in need.

AARP Grief and Loss Program
American Association of Retired Persons
601 E Street NW
Washington, DC 20049
(202) 434-2277; toll free: (800) 424-3410
www.griefandloss.org and www.aarp.org/griefandloss

An individual does not have to be of retirement age or a member of AARP to benefit from the extremely valuable services offered by this program. More than two hundred local self-help programs throughout the United States are sponsored by the Grief and Loss Program and directed by volunteer widowed individuals who have been trained to assist the bereaved. Bibliographies, pamphlets, and many other resources are available.

There is an extensive Web site that offers bereavement outreach programs, publications, news and research, statistics, assistance with practical matters, online communities, and links to local centers.

Accord
1941 Bishop's Lane, Suite 202
Louisville, KY 40218
(800) 346-3087

Call the 800 number for information on how to locate the source for these materials in your local area. *Grief Magazine*, a quarterly publication offering assistance to the bereaved in practical as well as emotional matters, is available for $25 a year.

AIDS Project Los Angeles
3550 Wiltshire Boulevard, Suite 300
Los Angeles, CA 90010
(213) 201-1600
www.apla.org

Publications and information on AIDS can be obtained from this organization.

Association for Death Education & Counseling
342 North Main Street
West Hartford, CT 06117-2507
(860) 586-7503
www.adec.org

A professional organization of educators, counselors, medical doctors, nurses, therapists, mental health professionals, clergy, and others specializing in bereavement education and counseling that holds conferences, sponsors research, and offers standards for certification.

Bereavement and Loss Center of New York
Anne Rosberger, Executive Director
170 East 83rd Street, Suite 4P
New York, NY 10028
(212) 879-5655

A private, nonsectarian organization, this center offers professional counseling services for individuals who have suffered loss of various kinds: widows, widowers, parents who have lost children, children who have lost parents, individuals who have lost significant others, and individuals and couples who have experienced prenatal death.

***Bereavement* Magazine**
4765 N. Carefree Circle
Colorado Springs, CO 80917-2118
(888) 604-4673
www.bereavementmag.com

The magazine, which offers support and other resources, is published six times a year.

Centering Corporation
7230 Maple Street
Omaha, NE 68134
(402) 553-1200
www.centering.org

This nonprofit organization is a leader in providing supportive literature for grieving families. Its excellent, economical publications run a wide gamut: grief related to the death of children, miscarriage, stillborn deaths, the death of siblings, death by suicide, the death of grandparents, and much more. Its publications are durable and beautifully designed. Filmstrips, a newsletter, and workshops are also part of the corporation's offerings. Catalog of publications available.

Compassionate Friends
PO Box 3696
Oak Brook, IL 60522-3696
(630) 990-0010
www.compassionatefriends.org

One of the largest self-help organizations in the world for bereaved parents, siblings, and grandparents. It provides more than 650 local chapters in the United States and Canada, with national and regional conferences. Its mission is to assist families toward the positive resolution of grief following the death of a child of any age and to provide information to help others be supportive. The Compassionate Friends is a national nonprofit, self-help support organization with no religious affiliation or fees, and it offers a thorough Web site with easy-to-navigate pages. To locate a chapter in your area, call the number listed above or log on to the Web site.

Mental Health Association of Colorado
6795 East Tennessee Avenue, Suite 425
Denver, CO 80224
(303) 377-3040; toll-free: (800) 456-3249
www.mha.org

Offers support, information, and referral services for the public and for professionals; a ten-week support program; and a facilitator's program. The institute's *Bereavement Support Group Leadership Manual* is also available.

National Self-Help Clearinghouse
Graduate School and University Center of the
City University of New York
365 Fifth Avenue, Suite 3300
New York, NY 10016
(212) 817-1822
www.selfhelpweb.org

This clearinghouse provides information about self-help groups in all areas of interest. Upon receipt of a self-addressed, stamped envelope, the staff of the clearinghouse will send information about its services and publications.

National Sudden Infant Death Syndrome (SIDS) Foundation
1314 Bedford Avenue
Baltimore, MD 21208
(410) 415-6628 (in Maryland)
(800) 221-SIDS (outside Maryland)
www.sids-id-psc.org

An organization of more than sixty chapters and numerous parent contacts and support groups offering services to families in which a child has died of SIDS. Information about publications, local chapters, and parent contacts are available by telephone.

Parents of Murdered Children
100 East Eighth Street, Room B41
Cincinnati, OH 45202
(513) 721-5683
www.pomc.org

A national self-help organization with local chapters across the United States, Parents of Murdered Children provides resources and support for families that have lost a child as a result of murder.

Parents Without Partners
1650 South Dixie Highway, Suite 510
Boca Raton, FL 33432
(800) 637-7974
www.parentswithoutpartners.org

This organization of mutual support groups (more than eight hundred throughout the United States and Canada) offers educational, social, and family services to single parents and their children. Publications are available for widowed, divorced, and unmarried parents.

GriefNet
PO Box 3272
Ann Arbor, MI 48106-3272
www.griefnet.org

GriefNet.org is an Internet community of individuals dealing with grief, death, and major loss. The organization offers more than thirty-five e-mail support groups, links, and a special KIDSAID section for children. It provides assistance to people working through loss and grief issues of all kinds. GriefNet is supervised by Cendra Lynn, Ph.D., a clinical grief psychologist, death educator, and traumatologist based in Michigan. The site is very well organized.

Counseling for Loss & Life Changes
Kent Counseling & Wellness Center
420 West Main Street
Kent, OH 44240
(330) 678-6504
www.counselingforloss.com

Sponsored by the Kent Counseling and Wellness Center in Ohio, Counseling for Loss has compiled information to help people who are grieving the loss of loved ones, security, hope, and peace. The soothing Web design and the easy-to-navigate pages offer comprehensive links, research, and answers to commonly asked questions about loss. Although the list of local support groups is for the Ohio area only, the site is worthy of national recognition.

Willowgreen
10351 Dawson's Creek Boulevard, Suite B
Fort Wayne, IN 46802
(219) 490-2222
www.willowgreen.com

Created by writer, grief counselor, and clergyman James E. Miller, Willowgreen provides information and inspiration in the areas of illness and dying, loss and grief, healthy caregiving, life transition, and spirituality. It features poems and calming book excerpts as well as e-cards to send to those in need.

Webhealing
149 Little Quarry Mews
Gaithersburg, MD 20878
(301) 670-1027
www.webhealing.com

This Web site is offered as a place where people can talk to each other in chat rooms or simply browse to understand the many different paths to healing, strong emotions. There is a special section where you can read and post essays, personal stories, and tributes to loved ones. The site is run by Tom Golden, LCSW, an author, speaker, and psychotherapist based in Washington, D.C.

The Shiva Foundation
www.goodgrief.org
All contact via Web site

This site lists answers to commonly asked questions and alternative ways of dealing with grief. Shiva Foundation offers educational programs, family assistance, lectures, and even exercise programs for families who are looking for meaning after a loss. It also offers an extensive list of books and audiotapes on the subject. The site is run by Deborah Morris Coryell, who has worked in the health field for more than twenty-five years and conceived and directed the Wellness/Education Program at Canyon Ranch in Tucson, Arizona.

William Wendt Center for Loss and Healing
730 Eleventh Street NW, Third Floor
Washington, DC 20001

(202) 624-0010
www.lossandhealing.org

This center provides useful, practical, and accessible information for those interested in learning more about the process of healing around life-changing illness, loss, and grief. The contents of this Web site have been compiled from more than twenty years of experience in supporting the ill and bereaved. It includes information and comments from individuals and professionals who wish to share their experiences. Information on grief and bereavement resources has been provided in an attempt to assist those in locating other useful services and information online.

GROWW

931 N. State Road 434, Suite 1201-358
Altamonte Springs, FL 32714
www.groww.org

GROWW is an acronym for Grief Recovery Online (founded by) Widows & Widowers. The Web site is a support community for all bereaved (not just widows and widowers), broken down by types of grief, with a variety of chat rooms and message boards. The Web site also provides gateways to organizations and agencies that may provide assistance to the bereaved, such as the Social Security Administration or local medical or hospice associations. There is an extensive list of chats and discussions on topics ranging from the loss of adult children to suicide survivors, as well as guidance for kids under eighteen.

Rainbows

2100 Golf Road #370
Rolling Meadows, IL 60008-4231
(847) 952-1770
www.rainbows.org

Rainbows is a not-for-profit, international organization that offers training and curricula for establishing peer support groups in churches, synagogues, schools, and social agencies. These curricula are available for children and adults of all ages and religious denominations who are grieving a death, a divorce, or any other painful transition in their family.

Healing Hearts

19627 SE 284th SE
Kent, WA 98042-8545
www.healingheart.net

Healing Hearts for Bereaved Parents is a self-help nonprofit organization of bereaved parents dedicated to "supporting and serving other bereaved parents and their families." The site is well organized, with articles, poetry, links, and basic resources. It also links people up with pen pals who want to correspond with others who have lost a loved one.

Tragedy Assistance Program for Survivors
2001 S Street NW, Suite 300
Washington, DC 20009
(800) 959-TAPS
www.taps.org

TAPS provides services for those who have lost a loved one in the line of military duty. Licensed counselors are on call twenty-four hours a day and offer assistance and referrals to help families and loved ones in need.

Night Sky
http://antwrp.gsfc.nasa.gov/apod/image/0011/earthlights_dmsp_big.jpg

An uplifting, in-time view of the night sky in many parts of the world.

Chat Rooms

In addition to many of the Web sites listed above, service providers like AOL, Compuserve, and others also offer well-organized chat rooms and message groups on grief and loss.

ABOUT.COM Search Engine

While this is a search engine, if you type in "Grief and Loss" About breaks it down into various areas of grief and loss (loss of a parent, loss of a sibling, loss of a spouse, etc). The site can be very comprehensive and specific depending on your needs.

MUSIC

Many of the individuals with whom I have talked mentioned particular pieces of music that they turned to again and again during their grieving process. For a young man mourning the loss of his best friend, it was Keith Jarrett's *Koln Concert* and *Arhour Zena*. For an eighty-three-year-old widow whose husband of fifty-four years had recently died, it was Beethoven's C-Sharp Minor Quartet, the meditation from Massenet's *Thaïs*, the "Song to the Evening Star" from Wagner's *Tannhäuser*, Liszt's *Liebesträume*, Braga's *Angel's Serenade*, and Beethoven's *Moonlight Sonata*. Others have mentioned the piano music of George Winston and

David Lanz, the tapes and albums of Steven Halpern, and the sound track of *Chariots of Fire*. The music that I found particularly helpful when I was grieving included Jean Michel Jarre's "Oxygene," Kitaro's "Silk Road," Haydn's symphonies (particularly the 93rd, 94th, and 100th), Mozart's Piano Concerto No. 21 in C, Grofé's *Grand Canyon Suite*, Vivaldi's *The Four Seasons*, Smetana's *The Moldau*, Beethoven's *Symphony No. 9*, R. Carlos Nakai's *Native American Flute Music*, Puccini's *Madama Butterfly*, Janáček's *Jenufa*, and Neil Diamond's *Hot August Night* album. More recently, I have learned that these pieces of music have been helpful to those working through the grieving process: the slow movement of the Marcello Oboe Concerto; the slow movement from Rodrigo's *Concierto de Aranjuez*; J. S. Bach's Prelude in E-Flat Minor, as arranged for orchestra; Grieg's Holberg Suite, particularly the movement called "Air"; and other Grieg pieces. The works of Mozart and Gregorian chants have been associated with the healing of the body and spirit in some scientific studies. See also *The Mozart Effect* and accompanying CDs by Don Campbell.

Much is now known about the ability of music to affect an individual's sense of well-being; in fact, music therapy has become a mainstream academic study (New York University, for instance, offers graduate courses in music therapy leading to a master's degree or a doctorate). A. Watson and N. Drury have written a book called *Healing Music* (Prism Press, 1987), which can be a guide to those who wish to use music to aid them in moving through their grieving.

To learn about music therapy workshops, contact the Bonny Foundation, An Institute for Music-Centered Therapy, at PO Box 39355, Baltimore, MD 21212, (866) 345-5465, or log on to www.bonnyfoundation.org.

Discover Dr. Andrew Weil's Sound body, Sound mind: Music for Healing at www.drweil.com; www.andrewweil.com (in the U.S., 888-337-9345).

MUSIC SPECIFICALLY FOR *SEVEN CHOICES*

Note from Elizabeth Neeld: One of the readers of *Seven Choices*, Ann Rachlin, graciously accepted my request to prepare a list of musical selections that are appropriate for people who are grieving. Not only did Ann accept my request but she went beyond anything I might have imagined she would have time to provide. Knowing *Seven Choices* as well as she does, having used it repeatedly in her own grieving and having given it to many others over the past decade, Ann provided music for each set of experiences talked about in the book. With deep gratitude, I offer you Ann's suggestions. But, first, a word about Ann Rachlin herself:

Ann Rachlin is one of the early pioneers of music appreciation for children in the United Kingdom, and the first performer to introduce "fun" to classical music. A gifted storyteller, Ann began teaching music appreciation at St. Anthony's Preparatory School in Hampstead and then branched out on her own, and Fun with Music was born.

In 1968 Ann met the American conductor/pianist Ezra Rachlin, and one year later they were married and had moved to Texas, where Ezra had three orchestras in Austin, Fort Worth, and Houston. In 1970, under his expert guidance, Ann gave her first concert with full symphony orchestra in front of three thousand children. When Ezra added the Queensland Symphony Orchestra in Australia to his schedule, Ann traveled into the outback, where she performed Fun with Music stories for children who had never seen or heard an orchestra before.

Returning to London in 1973, Ann soon found that she had a three-year waiting list for her sessions, a phenomenon that still exists today. Over the years, she has given seventy-four performances of "The Life of Handel and the Water Music on a Barge on the Thames," now available on CD as "Once Upon the Thames." In 1986 she performed a year of family "Funtasia" concerts at the Barbican with the London Symphony Orchestra, with her husband, Ezra Rachlin, conducting. Her music festival appearances include Bath, Leeds, Chester, Brighton, Harrogate, Perth, and Stratford-upon-Avon.

In 1985 Ann became a recording artist for EMI and now produces her own CDs on the Fun with Music Limited label under license from EMI. These include stories of the Russian ballets, *Lives of the Great Composers*, and *Musical Adventures* and are available at leading record shops, by mail order, and online at www.funwithmusic.com. Ann is also a successful writer. Her ten "Famous Children" books are best-sellers in the United States and have been translated into seventeen languages, including Indonesian, Finnish, Czech, and Chinese.

In the summer of 1987 Prince William joined Ann's program for Juniors and was followed a year later by Prince Harry, who entered the Toddlers. They remained with Ann for four years until they went to boarding school. Prince and Princess Michael of Kent, King Constantine and Queen Anne-Marie of Greece, Dame Judi Dench, Jane Asher, Edward Fox and Joanna David, Barry Humphries, Bob Hoskins, Sir Clement Freud, Spike Milligan, and Peter O'Toole also number among other celebrities who have sent their children to Fun with Music. In her classes today, Ann enjoys having many "grandchildren pupils"—children of former pupils—in some cases where both mother and father came to Fun with Music.

When Ezra died in 1995, Ann was determined to continue her work. She has done so with the invaluable help of Iain Kerr, who has worked with her since 1978. She was the subject of *This Is Your Life* in 1996, when Lord Menuhin, Sir Georg Solti, and Lord Runcie, as well as many of her former pupils, greeted her and paid tribute to her life's work with children and music. As founder of the Beethoven Fund for Deaf Children, Ann Rachlin was awarded the Member of the Order of the British Empire by Queen Elizabeth in 1986 for her services to deaf children.

For more information, contact Fun with Music, PO Box 16975, London NW8 6ZL, U.K.; e-mail: info@funwithmusic.com; Web site: www.funwithmusic.com.

MUSIC FOR SEVEN CHOICES
By Ann Rachlin

Note from Ann Rachlin: I lost my father, my mother, and my husband within four years. This is some of the music that helped me through my bereavement.

1. Impact: Experiencing the Unthinkable

Music to soothe, comfort, and allow tears

Rachmaninoff (1873–1943), Russia
    Vocalise (Piano or Orchestral Version)
    Symphony No. 2, Third Movement

When Sergei Rachmaninoff wrote his first symphony, he was so nervous that he sat on the steps outside the concert hall during the first performance. The audience was not enthusiastic, and the review in the newspaper the next day was so vicious that Rachmaninoff was devastated. He completely lost his confidence and did not compose for three years. "I felt like a man who had suffered a stroke and had lost the use of his head and hands," he wrote later. His ability to play and compose was restored by a hypnotist, Dr. Nicolai Dahl, to whom he dedicated the second piano concerto. Soon after the 1917 Revolution, Rachmaninoff was forced to leave Russia for good. In the United States, he established a phenomenal career as a composer, conductor, and pianist.

Massenet (1842–1912), France
    Meditation from *Thaïs*

Jules Massenet kept a diary from childhood and even wrote his "Thoughts After Death":

I have departed from this planet and I have left behind my poor earthly ones with their occupations which are as many as they are useless; at last I am living in the scintillating splendor of the stars, each of which used to seem to me as large as millions of suns. Of old I was never able to get such lighting for my scenery on the great stage at the Opéra, where the back-drops were too often in darkness. Henceforth there will be no letters to answer; I have bade farewell to first performances and the literary and other discussions which come from them. Here there are no newspapers, no dinners, no sleepless nights. Ah! If I could but counsel my friends to join me here, I would not hesitate to call them to me. But would they come?

Chopin (1810–1848), Poland
   Prelude No. 4 in E Minor, op. 28

2. Second Crisis: Stumbling in the Dark

Music to relieve sadness, combat depression, relieve insomnia, and boost self-esteem

Mozart (1756–1791), Austria
   Piano Concerto K. 491, Second Movement

An unsympathetic employer forced Wolfgang Amadeus Mozart's father to stay home and send his young son to Paris, accompanied by his mother. The poor woman suffered greatly on the uncomfortable jour-ney and became ill and died. After her funeral, the thoughtful young Wolfgang showed his great sensitivity by writing two letters to his fa-ther and his sister in Austria. The first told them that Mama was ill and getting weaker. This prepared them for the second letter, informing them of her death.

Barber (1910–1981), United States
   Adagio for Strings

Samuel Barber's most popular works were played after the deaths of Presidents Roosevelt and Kennedy and were also featured in the movies *Platoon, The Elephant Man, El Norte,* and *Lorenzo's Oil.*

Brahms (1833–1897), Germany
   Intermezzo in Eb, Op. 117 No. 1

Schubert (1797–1828), Austria
    Impromptu No. 3 in G-flat Major (Andante)

3. Observation: Linking Past to Present

Music to accompany the necessary time to be alone, to think, and to make connections

Canteloube, Marie-Joseph de Calaret (1879–1957), France
    Songs of the Auvergne, First Series No. 2, "Baïlèro"

My husband and I played this song when we lost our much-loved dog, Maestro. Thereafter, it became our "good morning" music when we were in our country cottage. My partner and I carry on the tradition. However anxious or troubled I am, it never fails to calm me and give me space to think.

Brahms (1833–1897), Germany
    Violin Concerto in D Major, Second Movement (Adagio-Intermezzo)

Rodrigo (1901–1999), Spain
    Concierto de Aranjuez for Guitar and Orchestra, Second Movement

Joaquin Rodrigo went blind at the age of three. His loss of sight heightened his sense of hearing, and he composed songs and concerti that reflect the vibrant colors of his native Spain.

Dvořák (1841–1904), Czechoslovakia
    Serenade for Strings
    Symphony No. 9 in E Minor (*From the New World*), Second Movement

Dvořák collected train numbers. When he had to move to the United States, where he composed his famous *New World* Symphony, he missed his wife and family desperately. To make matters worse, his apartment was nowhere near a train station. He adjusted his life by making a switch to collecting ships' names, memorizing the timetables of all the liners that sailed by his window.

4. The Turn: Turning Into the Wind

Music to give strength to make new commitments

Beethoven (1770–1827), Germany
  Symphony No. 6 in F, Op. 68 (*Pastoral*)

Ludwig van Beethoven began to lose his hearing when he was twenty-eight. At first he was almost suicidal, but it was his music that saved his life. In June 1801, he wrote: "For the past two years I avoid almost all social activities because it is impossible for me to say to people 'I am DEAF.' If I practiced any other profession, it would be easier, but in my profession this is a terrible condition. To give you an idea of this remarkable deafness, I can tell you that at the theatre I must sit very close to the orchestra in order to understand the actors. . . . Sometimes if someone speaks in a low voice I can barely understand; I hear the sounds not the words. If anyone shouts it is unbearable. What is to become of me, heaven only knows!" Yet in the country near Heiligenstad he composed his Symphony No. 6, known as the *Pastoral*. Although he was profoundly deaf, Beethoven accurately describes the song of the birds (the quail, cuckoo, and nightingale), the murmuring of a pleasant brook, and a most perfect musical thunderstorm. After my husband died, I found that listening to the *Pastoral* restored my own equilibrium. No matter how many times I hear it, it is always as fresh as the first time.

Tchaikovsky (1840–1893), Russia
  String Quartet No. 1 in D, Op. 11, Second Movement

Tchaikovsky was devoted to his mother. When she sent him away to school, he was heartbroken. On the first day, she accompanied him by coach and handed him over to the headmaster. Tchaikovsky pleaded with his mother to take him with her, but she bade him be strong and left. As the carriage moved away, he broke loose from his teacher and ran, sobbing after her. He was hit by the wheel of the carriage and flung into the street. His face streaming with tears, he watched as his mother's carriage disappeared from sight. "The worst day of my life," he described it later. His mother died of cholera when he was fourteen. He never ceased to mourn her. It is said that Tchaikovsky obtained the folk-song that is the first theme of the Andante cantabile in his first String Quartet from a carpenter.

5. Reconstruction: Picking Up the Pieces

Music to encourage change

Borodin (1833–1887), Russia
 String Quartet No. 2 in D Major, Third Movement

The beautiful melody became the lovely song "And This Is My Beloved" in the show *Kismet* with added lyrics by R. Wright and G. Forrest. It is said that Borodin composed this beautiful nocturne in 1881 shortly after the death of his composer friend Mussorgsky.

DeliFus (1862–1934), England
 Song of Summer

Frederick Delius was blind and disabled. Unable to walk or use his hands, he had to rely on the devotion of his amanuensis, Eric Fenby, who painstakingly took down his music, note by note. As he began dictating the *Song of Summer,* he spoke of being on a cliff, overlooking the sea in his native Yorkshire. The roll of the waves below and a soaring seagull were all "visible" to the blind composer, and you can see the scene as you listen to this remarkably beautiful music, which was created in spite of the most crippling disabilities. Without the devotion of the young Eric Fenby, Delius would have died totally frustrated, many wonderful musical creations remaining trapped in his frail body.

6. Working Through: Finding Solid Ground

Music to support a change of direction and a new life; to encourage when there are new problems to solve

Schubert (1797–1828), Austria
 String Quartet No. 13 in A Minor (*Rosamunde*), Second Movement

This incidental music to the play *Rosamande* reflects a total change of direction in Rosamunde's life. The heroine, the princess of Cyprus, will shortly return to the scenes of her childhood, renounce her throne, and live a fulfilled simple life among the cattle and country people, far from the troubles and discord of state.

Handel (1685–1759), Germany
Concerto for Two Horns in B-flat (The *Lento* is particularly calming.)
Concerto for Organ No. 13 (*The Cuckoo and the Nightingale*)

When Handel arrived in London he had to forge a new life for himself against all odds. He had to learn a new language and, eventually, overcome by blindness, still continue to compose. He was determined to succeed. He made England his home and is buried, with other great English writers, composers, and painters, in London's Westminster Abbey.

Bruch (1838–1920), Germany
Violin Concerto No. 1 in G Minor, Op. 26

7. Integration: Daylight

Music for living in a new world, enriched with memories and the experience of having grieved and knowing you are alive; music to celebrate victorious and creative outcomes gained by actively and fully grieving

Mascagni (1863–1945), Italy
Intermezzo from *Cavalleria Rusticana*

Rimsky-Korsakov (1844–1908) Russia
Symphonic Suite (*Sheherazade*), Op. 35, Third Movement
Composer's title "The Young Prince and The Young Princess"

Rachmaninoff (1873–1943), Russia
Piano Concerto No. 2

Khatchaturian (1903–1978), Russia
Adagio of Spartacus and Phrygia from *Spartacus*

BOOKS

For those who want to read about loss, the following is a sampling of the many books available on the subject.

Antinori, Deborah. *Pet Loss Audio*. Two-cassete program with twenty-eight-page booklet. See www.petlossaudio.com.

Attig, Thomas. *The Heart of Grief: Death and the Search for Lasting Love*. Oxford University Press, 2000.

Auz, Martin and Maureen Andrews. *Handbook for Those Who Grieve: What You Should Know and What You Can Do During Times of Loss*. Loyola Press, 2002.

Bernstein, Judith. *When the Bough Breaks: Forever After the Death of a Son or Daughter*. Andrews McMeel Publishing, 1998.

Borg, Susan, and Judith Lasker. *When Pregnancy Fails: Families Coping with Miscarriage, Stillbirth, and Infant Death*. Bantam Books, 1988.

Buscaglia, Leo. *The Fall of Freddie the Leaf*. Holt, Rinehart, 1982.

Caine, Lynn. *Being a Widow*. Penguin USA, 1990.

Carpenter, Liz. *Getting Better All the Time*. Pocket Books, 1987.

Chodron, Pema. *When Things Fall Apart: Heart Advice for Difficult Times*. Shambhala, 2000.

Cousins, Norman. *Anatomy of an Illness as Perceived by the Patient: Reflections on Healing and Regeneration*. W. W. Norton, 2001.

Davidson, Glen W. *Understanding Mourning: A Guide for Those Who Grieve*. Augsburg Publishing, 1984.

DiGlulio, Robert C. *Beyond Widowhood: From Bereavement to Emergence to Hope*. Free Press, 1989.

Doerr, Maribeth Wilder. *For Better or Worse: For Couples Whose Child Has Died*. Centering Corporation, 1992.

Donnelly, Katherine F. *Recovering from the Loss of a Parent*. Dodd, Mead, 1987.

———. *Recovering from the Loss of a Sibling*. Dodd, Mead, 1988.

The Dougy Center, ed. *35 Ways to Help a Grieving Child*. The Dougy Center, 1999.

Edelman, Hope. *Motherless Daughters: The Legacy of Loss*. Delta, 1995.

Edelstein, Linda. *Maternal Bereavement: Coping with the Unexpected Death of a Child*. Praeger Publishers, 1984.

Emswiler, Mary Ann, and James P. Emswiler. *Guiding Your Child Through Grief*. Bantam, 2000.

Faber, Rebecca. *A Mother's Grief: A Personal Account of How God Brought Hope and Healing Following the Devastating Loss of a Son*. Tyndale House, 1997.

Feinberg, Linda Sones. *I'm Grieving as Fast as I can: How Young Widows and Widowers Can Cope and Heal*. New Horizon Press, 1994.

Fitzgerald, Helen. *The Mourning Handbook: A Complete Guide for the Bereaved*. Simon & Schuster, 1994.

———. *The Grieving Teen: A Guide for Teenagers and Their Friends*. Simon & Schuster, 2000.

Goodman, Sandy. *Love Never Dies: A Mother's Journey from Loss to Love*. Jodere Group, 2002.

Graf, Ulrike, and Elissa Al-Chokhachy. *The Angel with the Golden Glow: A Family's Journey Through Loss and Healing*. Penny Bear Publishing, 2001.

Grollman, Earl A. *Living When a Loved One Has Died*. Beacon Press, 1995.

———. *Living with Loss, Healing and with Hope: A Jewish Perspective*. Beacon, 2000.

Hall, Donald. *Without*. Houghton Mifflin, 1998.

Huntley, Theresa. *Helping Children Grieve: When Someone You Love Dies*. Augsburg Fortress Publishers, 1991.

Isolina, Ricci. *Mom's House, Dad's House*. Fireside, 1997.

James, John W., and Russell Friedman (with Leslie London Matthews). *When Children Grieve: For Adults to Help Children Deal with Death, Divorce, Pet Loss, Moving, and Other Losses*. HarperCollins, 2001.

Johnson, Joy, and Marvin Johnson, et al. *Miscarriage: A Book for Parents Experiencing Fetal Death*. Centering Corporation, 1980.

Kast, Verena. *A Time to Mourn: Growing Through the Grief Process*. Daimon Verlag, 1988.

Koppelman, Kent. *The Fall of a Sparrow: Of Death and Dreams and Healing*. Scribner, 1999.

Krauss, Pesach, and Morrie Goldfischer. *Why Me: Coping with Grief, Loss, and Change*. Bantam Books, 1990.

Kubler-Ross, Elisabeth. *On Children and Death: How Children and Their Parents Can and Do Cope with Death*. Scribner, 1997.

Kubler-Ross, Elisabeth, and David Kessler. *Life Lessons: Two Experts on Death and Dying Teach Us About the Mysteries of Life and Living*. Scribner, 2001.

Kushner, Harold S. *When Bad Things Happen to Good People*. Avon Books, 1997.

Lafser, Christine O'Keefe, and Phyllis Tickle. *An Empty Cradle, a Full Heart: Reflections for Mothers and Fathers After Miscarriage, Stillbirth, or Infant Death*. Loyola Press, 1998.

LeShan, Eda. *Learning to Say Good-Bye When a Parent Dies*. Avon Books, 1988.

Levy, Naomi. *To Begin Again: The Journey Toward Comfort, Strength, and Faith in Difficult Times*. Knopf, 1999.

Levang, Elizabeth, and Sherokee Ilse. *Remembering with Love: Messages of Hope for the First Year of Grieving and Beyond*. Fairview Press, 1995.

Lewis, C. S. *A Grief Observed*. Harper, 1991.

Margolis, Otto, et al., eds. *Grief and the Loss of an Adult Child*. Greenwood Publishing Group, 1988.

Mitsch, Ray. *Grieving the Loss of Someone You Love: Daily Meditations to Help You Through the Grieving Process*. Vine Books, 1993.

Moffat, Mary Jane. *In the Midst of Winter: Selections from the Literature of Mourning*. Vintage Books, 1992.

Moffatt, Betty Clare. *When Someone You Love Has AIDS: A Book of Hope for Families and Friends*. New American Library, 1987.

Myers, Edward. *When Parents Die: A Guide for Adults*. Penguin Books, 1997.

Neeld, Elizabeth Harper. *Seven Choices: Finding Daylight After Loss Shatters Your World*. Warner Books, 2003.

———. *A Sacred Primer: The Essential Guide to Quiet Time and Prayer*. Renaissance Books, 1999.

Neuman, Gary M. (with Patricia Romanowski). *Helping Your Kids Cope with Divorce the Sandcastles Way*. Random House, 1999.

Rando, Therese A. *Grieving: How to Go on Living When Someone You Love Dies*. D. C. Heath, 1991.

Robertson, Christina. *A Woman's Guide to Divorce and Decision Making: A Supportive Workbook for Women Facing the Process of Divorce*. Simon & Schuster, 1989.

Rollin, Betty. *Last Wish*. Public Affairs, 1998.

Ross, E. Betsy. *Life After Suicide: A Ray of Hope for Those Left Behind*. Perseus Press, 1997.

Schaefer, Dan, and Christine Lyons. *How Do We Tell the Children? Helping Children Understand and Cope When Someone Dies*. Newmarket Press, 2002.

Scherago, Marcia. *Sibling Grief: How Parents Can Help the Child Whose Brother or Sister Has Died*. Medic Publishing, 1987.

Schiff, Harriet Sarnoff. *Living Through Mourning: Finding Comfort and Hope When a Loved One Has Died*. Viking, 1987.

———. *The Bereaved Parent*. Viking, 1978.

Schneider, John. *Finding My Way: Healing and Transformation Through Loss and Grief*. Seasons Press, 1994.

————. *Grief's Wisdom: Quotes for Understanding the Transformative Process*. Seasons Press, 2000.

————. *The Overdiagnosis of Depression: Recognizing Grief and Its Transformative Potential*. Seasons Press, 1994.

Shute, Jenefer. *Free Fall*. Secker & Warburg, United Kingdom, 2002 (can be ordered from amazon.co.uk).

Sontag, Susan. *Illness as Metaphor* and *AIDS and Its Metaphors*. Picador, USA, 2001.

Sprague, Billy, and John MacMurray. *Letter to a Grieving Heart: Comfort and Hope for Those Who Hurt*. Harvest House, 2001.

Stearns, Ann Kaiser. *Coming Back: Rebuilding Lives After Crisis and Loss*. Random House, 1988.

————. *Living Through Personal Crisis*. Ballantine, 1985.

Tatelbaum, Judy. *The Courage to Grieve: Creative Living, Recovery, and Growth Through Grief*. Lippincott & Crowell, 1984.

————. *You Don't Have to Suffer: A Handbook for Moving Beyond Life's Crisis*. Harper & Row, 1989.

Truman, Jill. *Letter to My Husband: Notes About Mourning and Recovery*. Viking Penguin, 1987.

Veninga, Robert. *A Gift of Hope: How We Survive Our Tragedies*. Ballantine, 1985.

Viorst, Judith. *Necessary Losses*. Fireside, 1998.

Wesburg, Granger E. *Good Grief: A Constructive Approach*. Dell Books, 1987.

Wheat, Rick. *Miscarriage: A Man's Book*. Centering Corporation, 1995.

Wieseltier, Leon. *Kaddish*. Vintage, 2000.

Wrobleski, Adina. *Suicide: Survivors—A Guide for Those Left Behind*. Afterwords, 2002.

Zonnebelt-Smeenge, Susan. *Getting to the Other Side of Grief—Overcoming the Loss of a Spouse*. Baker, 1999.

A good source for books on grieving is Compassion Books, 477 Hannah Branch Road, Burnsville, NC 28714.

Some of the books that are most important to me when I am grieving do not deal with the subject of loss directly but with other subjects such as the resilience of the human spirit, the creativity inherent in every individual, and the challenges individuals faced and met as they made real their dreams and visions. Books like these remind us of what we are capable of and, therefore, can often lift us above our sadness and our despair. I urge you to build your own list of books that lift the spirit.

Alexander, Christopher. *The Timeless Way of Building*. Oxford University Press, 1979.

Austin, James H. *Chase, Chance, and Creativity: The Lucky Art of Novelty*. Columbia University Press, 1978.

Bakeless, John, ed. *Journals of Lewis and Clark: A New Selection*. Signet Classic, 2002.

Barry, Sebastian. *Annie Dunne: A Novel*. Faber & Faber (U.K.), 2002 (can be ordered from amazon.co.uk).

Breathnach, Sarah Ban. *Simple Abundance: A Daybook of Comfort and Joy*. Warner Books, 1995.

Beevor, Anthony. *Berlin: The Downfall 1945*. Viking, 2002.

Bentov, Itzhak. *Stalking the Wild Pendulum: On the Mechanics of Consciousness*. Inner Traditions International, 1988.

Bernstein, Leonard. *The Unanswered Question: Six Talks at Harvard*. Harvard University Press, 1976.

Bird, Isabella. *A Lady's Life in the Rocky Mountains*. Konemann, 2000.

Cather, Willa. *Death Comes to the Archbishop*. Vintage Books, 1990.

Choi, Susan. *The Foreign Student*. Harper Perennial, 1999.

Edwards, Betty. *The New Drawing on the Right Side of the Brain: A Course in Enhancing Creativity and Artistic Confidence*. Jeremy P. Tarcher, 1999.

Fiennes, William. *The Snow Geese*. Picador, 2002.

Fitzgerald, Sally, ed. *The Habit of Being: Letters of Flannery O'Connor*. Noonday Press, 1988.

Gao, Anhua. *To the Edge of the Sky*. Penguin Books, 2000.

Guthrie, Woody. *Seeds of Man*. E. P. Dutton, 1976.

Lewis, C. S. *The Chronicles of Narnia*. HarperCollins, 2000.

Lindbergh, Anne Morrow. *Gift from the Sea*. Pantheon Books, 1991.

Lopez, Barry. *Arctic Dreams*. Vintage Books, 2001.

Marai, Sandor. *Embers*. Viking, 2002.

Myers, Robert. *Children of Pride: Selected Letters of the Family of the Rev. Dr. Charles Colkock Jones from the Years 1860–1868*. Yale University Press, 1987.

Nouwen, Henri J. M. *The Genesee Diary: Report from a Trappist Monastery*. Image Books, 1981.

———. *The Return of the Prodigal Son*. Image Books, 1994.

O'Brien, Edna. *In the Forest*. Weidenfeld & Nicolson, 2002.

O'Keefe, Georgia. *Georgia O'Keefe*. Random House, 1994.

Perkins, David. *The Mind's Best Work*. Harvard University Press, 1981.

Patchett, Ann. *Bel Canto*. Harper Perennial, 2002.

———. *Taft*. Ballantine Books, 1994.

Ruth and *Esther*, Books of the Bible.

Sarton, May. *The House by the Sea: A Journal*. W. W. Norton, 1996.

Sendak, Maurice. *Where the Wild Things Are*. HarperCollins Juvenile, 1988.

Shreve, Anita. *The Pilot's Wife: A Novel*. Back Bay Books, 1999.

Shute, Jenefer. *Free Fall*. Secker & Warburg, United Kingdom, 2002 (can be ordered from amazon.co.uk).

White, E. B. *Charlotte's Web*. HarperTrophy, 1999.

Williams, Niall. *As It Is In Heaven*. Warner Books, 2000.

MOVIES AND VIDEOS

Note from Elizabeth Neeld: The following shortlist of films that touch on the theme of grief and loss was provided by Professor John Bradley, Cleveland State Community College, Cleveland, Tennessee.

Ordinary People is one of the best, I think, because of the character of the mother and her way of dealing with the loss of her son.

Two recent films deal with the loss of a son: *The Matthew Shepard Story* was made for television and may not be available on VHS or DVD, but it is told from the points of view of the parents. Stockard Channing and Sam Waterston are excellent. *In the Bedroom*, with Spacek and Wilkinson, also deals with a son's murder. Comparing it with *Matt Shepard* might be interesting.

Brian's Song and *Bang the Drum Slowly* are on the theme of sports and dying.

There is a '60s film *All the Way Home*, adapted from Agee's *A Death in the Family*.

Longtime Companion was one of the first films to deal with the loss of friends and lovers from AIDS.

Old favorites: *Ghost*, *Terms of Endearment*, *Steel Magnolias*, *Our Town*.

For children (and adults), there's *Bambi*, *The Lion King*, *All Dogs Go to Heaven*, *Sounder* and *Old Yeller*.

Prince of Tides, *A Map of the World*, *Deep End of the Ocean*, *Places in the Heart*, *Shadowlands*, *What Dreams May Come*, and *Sophie's Choice* also come to mind.

There is also *Testament*, the story of Jane Alexander and her family surviving but dying after a nuclear war.

Woody Allen's *Crimes and Misdemeanors* deals with a man's guilt after having his mistress murdered. I am very fond of this film and what it says about personal responsibility.

There is *The Pawnbroker*, with Rod Steiger as a Holocaust survivor who hardens himself to all the street violence in New York until he finally makes himself "feel" something by driving a nail through his hand. Powerful performance. Gritty and violent, though.

A search for grief, loss, and death on www.teachwithmovies.org yielded:

Cry, the Beloved Country, Twelfth Night, Hamlet, Prince of Denmark, The White Rose, Twelve O'Clock High, Lorenzo's Oil, On the Waterfront, Billy Elliot, Ganhdi, Gettysburg, A Man for All Seasons, All My Sons, All Quiet on the Western Front, Amistad, Apollo 13, The Black Stallion, Brian's Song, The Buddy Holly Story, Casablanca, The Crucible, Field of Dreams, For Whom the Bell Tolls, Gallipoli, Gone with the Wind, Glory, Great Expectations, The King and I, Liszt's Rhapsody, Knute Rockne All American, Michael Collins, The Miracle Worker, The Mission, Native Son, The Red Shoes, The Adventures of Robin Hood, Romeo and Juliet, Roots, Schindler's List, The Swiss Family Robinson, A Tale of Two Cities, To Live, A Tree Grows in Brooklyn, White Nights

VIDEO

A PSB one-hour documentary video *The Challenge of Grief*, anchored by Elizabeth Harper Neeld and based on *Seven Choices*, is reviewed on www.elizabeth harperneeld.com.

ART

Often during my grieving, when I was in New York meeting with my publisher, I would go to the Museum of Modern Art to see Monet's water lily paintings. There I would sit, sometimes an hour or more, looking at these paintings, which are so large that they fill entire walls. The colors—pinks and purples and blues— the serenity of the water and the flowers, the scale of the paintings, all combined to create in me a feeling of quietness that brought peace to my agitated spirit. Even today, when I'm back in the city, I return to pay homage to these beautiful paintings, remembering what they meant to me then.

There was also a painting at the Metropolitan Museum that I went to see again and again, Jules Bastien-Lepage's *Joan of Arc*. I would stand in front of the canvas, seeing the young woman dressed in her peasant garments, standing among the cabbages in the yard of her parents' cottage. Here was a painting of a flesh-and-blood human being who, regardless of the disadvantages under which she lived and acted, nevertheless found within herself the capacity to make enormous commitments and show much courage. It wasn't that I thought all of this while I was standing there looking at the painting, but I must have known it at some level deeper than words. I was drawn back again and again to look at the painting.

Others who have found solace in art mention other works: Georgia O'Keefe's beautiful flower, shell, and sky paintings; the Dreaming-track paintings of the Australian aborigines; sand paintings of the Navajo; the totem poles of the Northwest Indians at New York's Museum of Natural History. The work of one artist in particular has spoken to thousands about the relationship of grief and loss to forgiveness: the awesome Holocaust paintings of Houston artist Alice Cahana. Whatever one's tastes and preferences in art, there will be some pieces that reach past the pain of loss to touch the depths of one's spirit. To seek out such works for oneself is a worthy activity during bereavement.

Many people who are grieving have also found that painting or drawing themselves, working with clay and other media, making collages, and sculpting have been enormously beneficial as they moved through the grieving process. Check the course offerings of community education programs, as well as the colleges and universities in your area, to locate activities you would like to engage in. Also, you might choose to work with a trained art therapist who will assist you in using art as an expression of your grieving. For information about how to locate an art therapist in your area, contact the American Art Therapy Association, 1202 Allanson Road, Mundelein, IL, 60060; (847) 949-6064 or log on to www.arttherapy.org.

A study of postsurgery patients in Sweden who regularly saw a painting of calm water and trees exhibited less anxiety and required fewer strong pain drugs than patients who saw no art. Dr. Andrew Weil, citing this study, offers these suggestions:

Take time to admire works of art you find beautiful and inspiring, whether paintings, buildings, or statues.

Make your living and working spaces visually attractive.

Doodle.

Keep a visual journal, using imagery to express your feelings.

Learn more from The Art Therapy Sourcebook *by Cathy Malchiodi (Lowell House, 1998).*

PHOTOGRAPHY

There are many photographers' Web sites that display images that uplift the spirit and bring beauty to the eye. I especially enjoy the work of the photographer Joey Bieber, found on her Web site www.bierberco.co.uk. Speaking of Bieber's photographs of Burma, Lord Hindlip, the chairman of Christie's, writes: "Some of the photographs illustrate the poverty and deprivation of the country and the suffering of its citizens, but most demonstrate the extraordinary beauty and serenity of these peace-loving people. Joey Bieber shows us the rivers and temples, the monks, impoverished mothers and their still smiling children, their animals, their whole way of life. She is a wonderful photographer who uses her art for the good of others, in this case the beautiful people of Burma."

A different response to bereavement can be found in Pedro Myer's work called "I Photograph to Remember." (Log on to www.zonezero.com, click on Gallery, and search for the name Pedro Meyer.) Pedro photographed his parents during the final months of their lives. Myer says this about "I Photograph to Remember": "I took all those photographs for myself as a way of dealing with death itself. . . . After all, memory is precisely that, a way of making a moment permanent. I knew full well that my emotions at the time would not allow me to recall, further on, the specifics of any given moment. The photographs have indeed allowed me to return many times to those captured slices of my experience, and flawed as those pictures inevitably are, due to the limitations inherent to the photographic medium, I do get a sense of the way it all happened."

WRITING

Keeping a journal is a lifeline for many people as they experience their mourning. The Progoff Journal method, developed by Dr. Ira Progoff, offers a structure that a number of individuals have told me was useful to them as they "wrote through their grieving." You can learn about the Progoff Journal method by reading *At a Journal Workshop* and *The Practice of Process Meditation*, written by Ira Progoff and published by Dialogue House Library in New York. But, better yet, attend a Progoff Journal Writing Workshop. To learn dates and locations of these workshops (and to receive information about how to purchase the books above, or other books and tapes related to the Progoff Journal method), write to Dialogue House, 80 East Eleventh Street, New York, NY 10003; (212) 673-5880 and 800-221-5844, or log on to www.intensivejournal.org.

James Pennebaker, Ph.D., has shown that people who write about stressful experiences visit doctors less often and have stronger immune responses. In one study, people who wrote for twenty minutes on three consecutive days about a past trauma experienced measurable positive physical and emotional changes after completing the writing. At the Andrew Weil Integrative Medicine Clinic, patients are urged to write in a journal about their feelings, both positive and negative, for fifteen to twenty minutes a day.

And a study in the *Journal of the American Medical Association* (April 14, 1999) found that patients with asthma or rheumatoid arthritis who wrote about a past trauma had a significant reduction in symptoms.

Kathleen Adam's *Journal to the Self: 22 Paths to Personal Growth* (Warner, 1990) is an excellent resource, as is the Center for Journal Therapy (in the U.S., 888-421-2298 or www.journaltherapy.com).

For those who want to write but not necessarily in a journal format, these books and tapes are excellent:

Baldwin, Christina. *Life's Companion: Journal Writing as a Spiritual Quest*. New York: Bantam Books, 1990.

Brande, Dorothea. *Becoming a Writer*. Los Angeles: Jeremy P. Tarcher, 1934.

Cameron, Julia. *The Artist's Way: A Spiritual Path to Higher Creativity*. New York: Jeremy P. Tarcher/Perigee Books, 1992.

———. *The Vein of Gold*. New York: Jeremy P. Tarcher/Perigee Books, 1996.

Metzger, Deena. *Writing for Your Life: A Guide and Companion to the Inner Worlds*. San Francisco: HarperSanFrancisco, 1992.

Neeld, Elizabeth Harper. *Yes! You Can Write*. 1986 (set of six audiocassettes). Available from Nightingale-Conant Corporation, 7300 N. Lehigh Avenue, Chicago, IL 60648; (800) 323-5552.

Stafford, William. *Writing the Australian Crawl: Views on the Writer's Vocation*. Ann Arbor: University of Michigan Press, 1978.

Ueland, Brenda. *If You Want to Write: A Book About Art, Independence and Spirit*. St. Paul: Graywolf Press, 1987.

A most unusual book for writers but an excellent resource is *List Your Self: List-making as the Way to Self-Discovery* by Ilene Segalove and Paul Bob Velick, Andrews and McMeel, 1996.

DANCE AND OTHER BODY-MOVEMENT ACTIVITIES

Many bereaved individuals have told me that bodywork and body-movement activities have been some of the most important components of their successful grieving. For some, it was therapeutic massage, Trager bodywork, or perhaps body movement using the Feldenkrais method. For others, it was dance or low-impact aerobics or yoga. And for many it was a combination of several of these.

For information about a Trager practitioner in your vicinity, contact Trager International, 3800 Park East Drive, Suite 100, Room 1, Beachwood, OH 44122; (216) 896-9383 or log on to www.trager.com. (You may also want to get a copy of *Trager Mentastics: Movement as a Way to Agelessness* by Milton Trager, M.D., published by Station Hill Press, Barrytown, NY, 12507.)

To learn the names of Feldenkrais teachers in your vicinity, contact the Feldenkrais Guild, 3611 SW Hood Avenue, Suite 100, Portland, OR 97201; (503) 221-6612, toll-free (800) 755-2118, or log on to www.feldenkrais.com.

Lillas Folan has done excellent video and audiotapes for learning and practicing yoga, as well as audiotapes for relaxation. These can be ordered online or from your local bookstore.

To learn more about dance-movement therapy or to obtain the names of registered dance-movement therapists in your community, contact the American Dance Therapy Association, 2000 Century Plaza, Columbia, MD, 21044; (410) 997-4040 or log on to www.adta.org.

Also see *Dance as a Healing Art: Returning to Health Through Movement & Imagery* by Anna Halprin (LifeRhythm, 2000).

NATURE AND OUTDOOR ACTIVITIES

A beautiful book, *Listening to Nature: How to Deepen Your Awareness of Nature* (written by Joseph Cornell and published by Dawn Publications, P.O. Box 2010, Nevada City, CA 95959; [800] 545-7475, order online at www.dawnpub.com), has been very therapeutic for many people who were engaged in putting their losses into a broader perspective. So have materials published by such organizations as the Sierra Club, 85 Second Street, Second Floor, San Francisco, CA 94105, (415) 977-5500, www.sierraclub.org; the National Audubon Society, 700 Broadway, New York, NY 10003, (212) 979-3000, www.audubon.org; and books that discuss the Gaia principle, such as James Lovelock's *Gaia: A New Look at Life on Earth* (Oxford University Press, 1987).

Visiting aquariums, walking in redwood forests, hiking in the desert or the mountains, camping, and backpacking are ways in which many individuals have lifted their spirits when they were in the depths of mourning. Gardening has also been a source of effective therapy (even looking at seed catalogs and gardening books, many say, helped).

The outdoor programs offered by Outward Bound, 0110 SW Bancroft Street, Portland, OR 97201, (503) 243-1993, www.outwardbound.org; the travel expeditions sponsored by such organizations as the American Museum of Natural History, 79th Street at Central Park West, New York, NY 10024, (212) 769-5100, www.discoverytours.org; and the biking tours offered by many different companies are just some examples of the kinds of activities many people have found to be valuable as they moved through the grieving process.

GARDENING

Barbara Ann Myrick, Master Gardener, writes: "When you come home . . . stop, take a few minutes, go outside, work for a short time in your yard. You will be surprised at how much better you feel. If you are angry, impatient, nervous, unhappy, or sad, gardening is the answer. Take your emotions out on the weeds, prune the shrubs, 'deadhead' the flowers, cut down that plant you don't like or want, or just dig in the soil. Mother Nature is a great healer. . . . You learn patience by waiting for the results of your labor. You overcome failure through knowledge and trial and error. You relieve stress and depression by working and achieving a beautiful, restful haven. Gardening can ease your pain, calm your spirit, and soothe your soul!" (www.aggie-horticulture.tamu.edu/country/tips/misc/gardentherapy.html)

Researchers suggest at least three reasons for our response to plants: (1) plants serve as a stimulus for a direct, specific, positive response for which the human perceptual system is specifically developed; (2) plants are a part of the aesthetically pleasing and perceptually stimulating aspects of the environment to which humans respond; and (3) by observing plant growth and change, humans learn about life and acquire an understanding that can be applied to other aspects of life (Diane Relf, Professor of Horticulture).

Larry Caplan, Extension Educator in Horticulture at Purdue University, suggests gardening for the senses: making a garden you can taste (golden zucchini squash, red leaf lettuce, purple podded beans); a garden you can smell (honeysuckle, jasmine, wisteria, lavender, rosemary, lemon verbena, oregano, sage, thyme, chamomile, creeping thyme, scented geraniums); a garden you can feel (soft, fuzzy lamb's ear, woolly thyme, pussy willow; fluffy hare's tail grass; silky hibiscus, gardenia, and most lilies; papery feel of statice, globe amaranth, seed pods of honesty or the money plant); and a garden you can hear (the whisper of willows and birch; the rustling of ornamental grasses and bamboo).

Resources abound for those who are interested in gardening. A quick search on a search engine such as www.google.com for gardening therapy turns up pages of valuable sources. Web sites such as www.gardenforever.com; www.gofor green.co/gardening; www.EnglishGardeningSchool.co.uk; www.plants-for-people.org; and www.gardening.about.com are just a beginning.

Excellent books include *The Enabling Garden: A Guide to Lifelong Gardening* by Eugene Rothert; *Dump Your Stress in the Compost Pile* by Douglas Schar; *Buffalo Bird Woman's Garden: Agriculture of the Hidatsa Indians* by Gilbert Wilson; *Butterfly Gardening: Creating Summer Magic in Your Garden* (Xerces Society); and *Gardening with a Wild Heart* by Judith Larner Lowry.

PRAYER

Below are resources that provide inspiration for those who wish to use prayer and quiet time as a resource during their grieving.

BOOKS

Appleton, George. *The Oxford Book of Prayer*. Oxford University Press, 1985.

Ashcroft, Mary Ellen. *The Magdalene Gospel*. Doubleday, 1995.

Brother Lawrence. *The Practice of the Presence of God*. Whitaker House, 1982.

Castelli, Jim. *How I Pray*. Ballantine Books, 1994.

De Caussade, Jean-Pierre. *The Sacrament of the Present Moment*. HarperSanFrancisco, 1989.

Dorsey, Larry. *Healing Words*. HarperSanFrancisco, 1993.

Doyle, Brendan. *Meditations with Julian of Norwich*. Bear & Company, 1983.

Dunman, Maxie. *The Workbook of Living Prayer*. Upper Room, 1974.

Foster, Richard J. *Prayer: Finding the Heart's True Home*. HarperSanFrancisco, 1992.

Judson, Sylvia Shaw. *The Quiet Eye*. Regnery Gateway, 1982.

Knight, George A. F. *The Daily Study Bible Series, Psalms, Volumes 1 and 2*. Westminster Press, 1982.

Mother Teresa and Brother Roger. *Seeking the Heart of God, Reflections on Prayer*. HarperSanFrancisco, 1991.

Neeld, Elizabeth. *A Sacred Primer: The Essential Guide to Quiet Time and Prayer*. Renaissance Books, 1999.

Thurman, Howard. *The Creative Encounter*. Friends United Press, 1972.

————. *Inward Journey*. Friends United Press, 1971.

Tutu, Desmond. *An African Prayer Book*. Doubleday, 1995.

Uhlein, Gabriele. *Meditations with Hildegard of Bingen*. Bear & Company, 1983.

Nilgiri Press carries books—e.g., *Meditation, The Compassionate Universe, Take Your Time, God Makes the Rivers to Flow*—that many have found valuable in their quiet time. Nilgiri Press, PO Box 477, Petaluma, CA 94953, (707) 878-2309.

MUSIC FOR PRAYER TIME

Andrea Bocelli's *Sacred Arias*

Prayers, by Sumi Jo

Mahalia Jackson's spirituals

Chant, by the Benedictine Monks of Santo Domingo De Silos

Agnus Dei: Music of Inner Harmony, by the choir of New College, Oxford

Anne Murray's *What a Wonderful World*

Musical Book of Hours, by Pomerium

Richard Paul Fink's *I Love to Tell the Story*

Domine Deus Taize chants with English verses

The monks of Glenstal Abbey Gregorian chants

Barbra Streisand's *Higher Ground*

A Web site that provides many resources is www.beliefnet.com.

POETRY

Dr. Andrew Weil says: "During difficult times, poetry can let you know that others have been through and made sense of a similar experience. By writing poetry, you can give voice to your own unique experience. When poetry is read aloud, the musical qualities of the language itself can be pleasing."

Discover collections such as *A Book of Luminous Things: An International Anthology of Poetry*, edited by Czeslaw Milosz (Harcourt Brace, 1996); Mary Jane Moffat's *Literature of Mourning* (Vintage Books, 1992); Robert Pinsky's *Americans' Favorite Poems* (W. W. Norton, 2000); and any of the books of poetry by William Stafford.

Poetry readings listed in the local newspapers can be valuable, as can listening to poetry on audiocassette.

Those who are interested in writing poetry should check out *Poetic Medicine: The Healing Art of Poem-Making* by John Fox (J. P. Tarcher, 1997), as well as www.poeticmedicine.com and National Association for Poetry Therapy (in U.S., [202] 966-2536).

Excellent Web sites for poetry include www.poetrysociety.org.uk; www.poetrylibrary.org.uk.; www.poets.org; www.kotapress.com (contains "Loss News" links for the bereaved); and www.library.utoronto.co/utel/rp/indexauthors.html.

PETS

Research has shown that owning a pet can reduce stress; petting a dog, for instance, has been shown to lower blood pressure. According to a study conducted at City Hospital in New York, heart patients who owned pets were significantly more likely to be alive a year after they were discharged from the hospital than those who didn't own pets. The presence of a pet was found to give a higher boost to the survival rate than having a spouse or friends. A study conducted at UCLA found that dog owners required much less medical care for stress-induced aches and pains than did non-dog owners. Pet ownership may affect people physiologically through the soothing and relaxing effect of touch. And speechless communication with a pet, or simply watching a cat or fish, may produce a relaxation response that makes little demand on the viewer. Pets such as dogs and cats provide unconditional, nonjudgmental love and affection. And pets enlarge our focus beyond ourselves and connect us to a larger world. They also make us laugh more. (See www.holistic-online.com/stress/stress_pet-therapy.htm; www.dogplay.com; www.medsupport.org/pettherapy.htm.)

Children see animals as peers, and older children's empathy with animals can carry over into their experiences of people.

The Sussex County LPN Program (www.dog-play.com/dogpill.html) provides this information in a "pharmacology worksheet format": Pets can stimulate spontaneous performance of active ROM exercises, especially of the hand; relax pre-existing contractures due to arthritis; increase motivation to get out of bed in the morning; decrease blood pressure; contribute to survival rate post-MI; decrease risk of the "helplessness/hopelessness" syndrome associated with illness and vulnerability to sudden-death accidents; increase awareness in the cognitively impaired; and stimulate social interaction.

HEALTH AND ALTERNATIVE MEDICINE

Below are examples of the kind of information one can find in the areas of health and alternative medicine to help in dealing with grief. If they are interested in these areas, individuals who are grieving should look for the kinds of health and alternative-medicine suggestions that appeal to them. The following serve only as examples of what is available to the general public:

(1) In a health article in the *Times* (London) May 2002 newspaper, a feature titled "The Art of Self-Healing" contains this information:

According to those who view illness and emotional problems as a challenge that can lead to self-development, many activities can contribute to health, harmonize emotions, and provide a sense of well-being; art, music, sound and movement therapies, rhythmic massage, crafts, cooking, and other such activities. "It's about getting people to make changes that will empower them," says Dr. David McGavin.

The article goes on to describe a successful program at the National Health Services in the United Kingdom that has a nineteen-year history, the Blackthorn Trust and Medical Centre, started by Dr. McGavin (www.blackthorn.org.uk). This is a program in which people with physical and emotional stresses can "have appointments for art or music therapy, massage or counseling . . . they can join the craft group or help in the café, bakery or plant nursery, while job coaches find work placements [for those wishing to go into the public workplace]." This program won the Prince's Foundation for Integrated Medicine award in 2001 for good practice. (See the *Times*, May 14, 2002, p. 11.)

(2) Stephen Levine recommends simple exercises that help when one is grieving.
   1. Just taking a deep breath, as if directly into your heart and feeling the sigh of letting go in the exhalation. Love is breathed in; sorrow is breathed out.
   2. When we suffer a loss, we can locate the very tender spot at the center of the chest. Tapping this grief point can balance energy in this area. Some people tap as they walk.
   3. Soft-belly practice. Sit quietly. Let attention rest on the abdomen and ride the rising and falling of the breath. Inhalation: belly rising with the tide; exhalation, the tide goes out. Soften the belly to allow awareness to settle in.
   Do this several times a day. (See "You Shall Be Released," O, *The Oprah Magazine*, April 2002, p. 239.)

---

(3) Other alternative health suggestions made by health practitioners and medical doctors:

Fresh flowers in living space

Green plants, especially *Spathiphyllum* (peace lily); *Howea forsterana* (kentia palm); *Fiscus benjamina* (fine-leafed fig); *Dracaena* "Janet Craig"; and *Epipremnum aureum* (devil's ivy); check www.plants-for-people.org

Wind chimes

Music, especially Mozart and Gregorian chant

Essential-oil essences (avoid synthetics), particularly lavender, jasmine, ylang-ylang, patchouli, tangerine, orange, and lemon

Bath oils and salts, particularly tangerine and lavender

Candles (Note from Elizabeth Neeld: Aroma Naturals makes wonderful candles using real essential-oil essences, no synthetics. 800-46-AROMA [phone]; 800-955-9481 [fax]; www.aromanaturals.com.)

Breathing exercises

Tonics

Dr. Bach's Rescue Remedy for the treatment of grief

Hawthorne berries

Lemon balm

Rose oil

Colored lights, particularly rose and violet

Perelandra Microbial Balancing Program: Immune, Respiratory, Lymphatic, Nervous, Endocrine, and Digestive Systems Balancing Solutions

Homeopathic Ignatia 30CD, a dried seed from the St. Ignatius bean, for sadness, crying, and loss of appetite accompanying grief

Valerian root (150–300 mg of standardized extract, 0.8 percent valeric acid content in capsule form) for sleeplessness

Homeopathic Kali bromatum 30C (potassium bromate) for remorse or helplessness

5-htp (hydroxytryptophan) for depression

Phenylalanine or tyrosine for fatigue

Ignatia from the Ignatia amara plant for emotional distress

Colostrum capsules 3,000 mg7 to boost immune function

Yoga, meditation, a strong network of friends and family, work with a grief counselor, a grief-support group for nurturing oneself

RELIGIOUS-SPONSORED PROGRAMS

Beginning Experience is a weekend program designed to help widowed, separated, divorced, and otherwise bereft individuals make a new beginning in life. Participants should have gone past the initial acute grieving experience and have reached the point of desiring a new beginning. An interfaith endeavor sponsored by the Catholic Church and the Episcopal Church, the weekend program, which begins on Friday evening and concludes on Sunday afternoon, is quiet, reflective, and spiritual. For information about Beginning Experience, log on to www. beginningexperience.org. In addition, many other churches, synagogues, and houses of worship, hospitals, family-service agencies, hospice groups, and federal governmental agencies offer programs and services for the bereaved as well as sponsor bereavement and divorce recovery programs on a local level. Ask your doctor, a member of the clergy, or health department personnel for information about such offerings in your area.

PROFESSIONAL THERAPY AND COUNSELING

More and more bereaved individuals are realizing the value of working with someone who understands the grieving process and who can, therefore, serve as a guide through the experience. No longer believing that one has to be "sick" or "weak" to engage in the valuable self-care work of therapy or counseling, many who are mourning are asking their doctors, associates, priests, rabbis, ministers, family, and friends to recommend a therapist, analyst, or counselor with whom they can work. The best person to ask for a recommendation, of course, is a bereaved individual who has found the work of a particular professional to be helpful and beneficial.

Bereaved people with whom I have talked consistently offer one piece of advice about how to evaluate your experience with a counselor, analyst, or therapist. They say this in different words, but the message is the same: Ask yourself if you feel you are "winning" in your commitment to move through the grieving process. If you are "winning," continue the therapy or counseling. If you are not, find another counselor, analyst, or therapist.

NOTES

INTRODUCTION: A PROLOGUE

Page xv

Mapping of the terrain: The editors of the Institute of Medicine's *Bereavement: Reactions, Consequences, and Care* state, "Despite the nonlinearity of the grieving process, most observers of it speak of clusters of reactions or 'phases' of bereavement that change over time. Although observers divide the process into various numbers of phases and use different terminology to label them, there is general agreement about the nature of reactions over time. Clinicians also agree that there is substantial individual variation in terms of specific manifestations of grief and in the speed with which people move through the process" (p. 48).

Active grieving process does exist: Terms used in talking about the grieving process vary. The Institute of Medicine, in its study *Bereavement: Reactions, Consequences, and Care,* edited by Marian Osterweis, Fredric Solomon, and Morris Green, uses these definitions: *Bereavement:* the fact of loss through death. *Bereavement reactions:* any psychological, physiologic, or behavioral response to bereavement. *Reaction* is not meant to suggest automatic, reflex responses or to imply that any particular reaction is universal. *Bereavement process:* an umbrella term that refers to the emergence of bereavement reactions over time. *Grief:* the feeling (affect) and certain associated behaviors, such as crying. *Grieving process:* the changing affective state over time. *Mourning:* in the social science sense, the social expressions of grief, including mourning rituals and associated behaviors. This definition of *mourning* is a departure from Freud's usage, where the term refers to an internal psychological state and process (pp. 9–10).

Beverley Raphael, a professor of psychiatry at the University of Newcastle in New South Wales, Australia, in *The Anatomy of Bereavement* uses these terms: "*Bereavement* is the reaction to the loss of a close relationship. Sometimes *grief* is also used to describe this reaction, but in this work *grief* will be used to refer to the emotional response to loss: the complex amalgam of painful affects, including sadness, anger, helplessness, guilt, and despair. *Mourning* will be used here to refer to the psychological mourning processes that occur in bereavement: the processes whereby the bereaved gradually undoes the psychological bonds that bound him [her] to the deceased" (p. 33).

George Pollock, M.D., whose work based on his research as professor, Department of Psychiatry, Northwestern University Medical School, director of the Chicago Institute for Psychoanalysis, and president of the Center for Psychosocial Studies in Chicago, has for more than twenty-five years provided a definitive perspective on loss and grieving, uses the term *mourning process* to cover both acute grieving and chronic grieving. *Chronic grieving* includes the adaptive mechanisms that allow an individual to integrate the experience of the loss with reality. In his seminal article "Mourning and Adaptation," published in the *International Journal of Psycho-analysis*, vol. 42, parts 4–5, Dr. Pollock says, "The *acute stage* of the mourning process refers to the immediate phases following the loss of the object. These phases consist of the shock, grief, pain, reaction to separation, and the beginning internal object decathexis with the recognition of the loss. . . . As the acute stage of the mourning process progresses, the chronic stage gradually takes over. Here we find various manifestations of adaptive mechanisms attempting to integrate the experience of the loss with reality so that life activities can go on" (p. 352). Dr. Pollock considers *bereavement* (loss of a meaningful person by death) to be a subclass of *mourning* and refers to bereavement, as well as to other kinds of losses, in his discussion of the mourning process. (See Pollock, "Process and Affect: Mourning and Grief," *International Journal of Psycho-analysis,* vol. 59, parts 2–3, p. 273.)

For purposes of simplicity and familiarity, in this book I use the terms *grief, mourning, active grieving process*, and *mourning process* interchangeably to refer to the full range of experiences that allow individuals to find their way from the first impact of the loss through the longer-term adjustment and adaptation phases through to integration and a new equilibrium and balance in life. These experiences include the emotional and psychological responses to loss as well as the longer-term adjustments and adaptations that help people develop new identities, establish new purposes, and build new assumptive worlds. I use *acute grieving* to refer to the initial intense emotional responses that occur following a loss.

I am deeply indebted to the writings of the individuals cited above, and to others whose works are cited in later notes, for my theoretical understanding of the complete active grieving process, as well as for the illumination I have gained about my own mourning process.

Structure of this book:

Impact: Experiencing the Unthinkable: These reactions are universal, and they are automatic. The responses are elemental, ancient, connected to human beings' need for balance and order in our lives and to our desire to remain bonded to those around us. For millennia, such bonds have been synonymous with survival. Many of the responses we make during Impact are instinctual; we share them with other animals—such as greylag geese and the primates—that search for their lost partners and are sad when they cannot find them. Elephants mourn their dead. They will stop at a carcass of one of their own, become quiet and tense, and then slowly and cautiously begin to touch the bones as if they are trying to recognize the animal. See Colin Murray Parkes, M.D., *Bereavement: Studies of Grief in Adult Life*, p. 40, as well as Pollock, "Mourning and Adaptation," *International Journal of Psycho-analysis*, vol. 42, parts 4–5, pp. 359–360. Also see Cynthia Moss's *Elephant Memories: Thirteen Years in the Life of an Elephant Family*. Chapter 3 of this book, called "Migration," contains a moving account of an elephant family's response to the death of one of its members from a gunshot wound (pp. 72–75). Chapter 10, "Life Cycle and Death," details additional information about elephants' reactions to death (pp. 270–271).

Second Crisis: Stumbling in the Dark: These reactions occur in full effect weeks, months, and, for some, even years after the loss. Hence these clusters or sets of experiences may, when encountered, not be associated with the loss. They may, for this reason, go unattended, be misdiagnosed or, worse yet, be belittled as weakness or an unwillingness to "get on with life" after the loss. It is easy to call the first experiences of acute grieving in *Impact* a *crisis*. However, the fact that the phase of delayed responses, gradual recognition of the full implications of the loss, and of dealing with painful thoughts of guilt, blame, anger, and despair is a most serious crisis—in effect, a *second crisis*—is often overlooked. But a *crisis* it is. Death, illness, and accident rates increase enormously during this time—which can be anywhere from one to six years after the loss occurs. (For statistics, see "Second Crisis: Stumbling in the Dark" commentary in this book.) Suicides increase during this phase of the grieving process. Destructive behavior, misuse of relationships, and the beginnings of what can be a lifetime of pathological mourning often begin at this point. During these experiences, too, people often find themselves in such a deep slough of despair, hopelessness, and depression that they have difficulty even imagining life being any different.

Observation: Linking Past to Present: Anne Morrow Lindbergh once said that if suffering alone made one wise, all the world would be wise. "To suffering," she says, "must be added mourning, understanding, patience, love, openness, and the willingness to remain vulnerable." One of the differences between those who suffer and become wise and those who suffer and do not become wise is the experiences of Linking Past to Present. Sifting through memories, reminiscing, acknowledging ambiguity in relationships, observing—these experiences result in reflection, discernment, and assimilation, and they can lead to wisdom.

Observation is not synonymous with acceptance. In fact, acceptance can be the booby prize in the grieving process, because most people, when asked their definition of *acceptance* in this context, will indicate that the word means something like *resignation*. Observation, instead, is a time of "living in the question," of forgiving oneself, others, and life; of noticing how the loss has changed or is changing us, altered our environment, scattered our past. It is a time of reminiscing, of acknowledging ambivalence, and of sifting through memories. It is a period of keeping open the mourning process in order to have time to think, to experience. It is a time of ambiguity as well as clarity; a time of not knowing and a time of wonderment.

The Turn: Turning Into the Wind: John Bowlby, in *Loss*, speaks of the critical importance of these experiences in the active grieving process: "If all goes well . . . [the griever] starts to examine the new situation in which he finds himself and to consider ways of meeting it. This entails a redefinition of himself as well as of his situation. . . . Until redefinition is achieved no plans for the future can be made. . . . Once this corner is turned a bereaved person recognizes that an attempt must be made to fill unaccustomed roles and to acquire new skills (p. 94). Bowlby also says that if we choose not to begin to "replan our lives," the representational models we have of ourselves and of the world about us remain unchanged and, subsequently, we find that "our life is either planned on a false basis or else falls into unplanned disarray" (*Loss*, p. 138).

Reconstruction: Picking Up the Pieces: Raphael, in speaking of these longer-term adjustments and adaptations, asserts in *The Anatomy of Bereavement*: "The time for the longer-term adaptations will vary enormously. . . . The period of readjustment may be seen as a period of ongoing mourning" (p. 57). George Pollock also states, "This mourning reaction is an ego-adaptive process which includes the reaction to the loss of the object, as well as the readjustment to an external environment wherein this object no longer exists in reality" ("Mourning and Adaptation," *International Journal of Psycho-analysis*, vol. 42, parts 4–5, p. 343).

In *Bereavement: Reactions, Consequences, and Care*, the editors cite the Widow-to-Widow Program conducted by Phyllis Silverman from 1964 to 1974 at Harvard University. The goals of that program did not center around "recovery"; instead, the work with the widows centered around change. Recognizing that it is never possible to return "to all prebereavement baselines," the program taught that reaching a constructive outcome to the mourning process depended on the mourners' "ability to adapt and alter their images and roles to fit their new status." Commenting on this program and its emphasis, the editors observed, "Although emotional support from a person who has also been through the experience was considered important, the women's most fundamental need was to learn how to change" (pp. 242–244).

In *Loss,* John Bowlby says that a mourner will do one of two things: he will either "progress toward a recognition of his changed circumstances, a revision of his representational models, and a redefinition of his goals in life, or else [he will stay] in a state of suspended growth in which he is held prisoner by a dilemma he can't solve" (p. 139).

Working Through: Finding Solid Ground: Pollock points out that "the need to give up a house, a social group, or the like as a result of the separation may serve to institute new mourning processes and increase the integrative task of the ego, but these also are gradually worked through." He also says, "New mourning experiences can serve to revive past mourning reactions that may still have bits of unresolved work present ("Mourning and Adaptation," *International Journal of Psycho-analysis,* vol. 42, parts 4–5, p. 354).

Peter Marris, the British social scientist who has studied the complexities of change in a variety of settings—bereavement, slum clearings, entrepreneurial enterprises in Africa, and others—writes in *Loss and Change*: "A sense of continuity can, then, only be restored by detaching the familiar meanings of life from the relationship in which they were embodied, and re-establishing them independently of it. This is what happens during the working through of grief" (p. 34). Marris also states: "The working out of a severe bereavement represents, as a personal crisis, a general principle of adaptation to change. Life becomes unmanageable, because it has become meaningless. The context of purposes and attachments, to which events are referred for their interpretation, has been so badly disrupted by the loss that it at first seems irreparable" (p. 38). He adds, "The meaning of life must be retrieved and reformulated, so that it can continuously survive the relationship which may no longer contain it" (p. 40).

Integration: Daylight: Pollock asserts that mourning is a "normal transformational adaptive process [that has] an outcome of gain and freedom once the process has been completed." It is a "change-creative-gain sequence," he says. The active grieving process, available to all of humankind as "one of the more universal forms of adaptation and growth," Pollock continues, is what allows us to deal with the trauma of our loss; and through this process we find a way to achieve "continuity, integration, cohesiveness, preservation, survival, and further additional development." Because we choose to experience the full grieving process, we achieve what Pollock calls a "creative outcome" when we finish our grieving, defined by him as the ability to feel joy, satisfaction, and a sense of accomplishment; a return to a steady state of balance; the experience of an increased capacity to appreciate people and things; a realization that one has become more tolerant and wise; a desire to express oneself creatively; the ability to invest in new relationships; the experience of a sense of freedom and revitalization. See Pollock, "Process and Affect: Mourning and Grief," *International Journal of Psycho-analysis*, vol. 59, parts 2–3, pp. 267–273; "Mourning and Grief," *International Journal of Psycho-analysis*, vol. 42, parts 4–5, pp. 345, 354–355; and "The Mourning Process and Creative Organizational Change," *Journal of the American Psychoanalytic Association*, vol. 25, no. 1, pp. 11–28. Pollock also says, "It is my belief that the mourning process, a universal adaptive process to change and loss with an outcome of gain and freedom once the process has been completed is a means of re-establishing balance intrapsychically, interpersonally, socially, and culturally" (ibid., p. 18).

Of this active grieving process, Pollock says, "The mourning process can have four outcomes: *normal resolution* which results in creative activity, creative reinvested living, creative products. Memory traces become the end product intrapsychically of the resolved and complete mourning process; *arrestation* of the mourning process at various stages; *fixations* at various earlier stages which become reactivated when a mourning process is initiated; and, finally, *pathological* or *deviated mourning process* that are variously diagnosed as depression, depressive states, apathy. These may result in anniversary suicides, anniversary homicides, serious delinquent behavior, psychotic decompensations, etc." ("Process and Affect: Mourning and Grief," *International Journal of Psycho-analysis*, vol. 59, parts 2–3, p. 273). Citing John Bowlby, Pollock defines *pathological mourning* as "(1) anxiety and depression where a persistent and unconscious yearning to recover and reunite with the lost object is present; (2) intense anger and reproach, frequently unconscious, directed toward various objects, including the self; (3) absorption in caring for others who have been bereaved; and (4) denial that the object is permanently lost" (ibid., p. 266).

Caveats about any mapping of the terrain of an active grieving process:

(1) The clusters of experience are not a series of tightly defined steps moved through in a linear, lockstep arrangement. (For this reason the word *stage* is too rigid to describe the parts of the process. The Institute of Medicine cautions against using the term *stage* "because it may connote concrete boundaries between what are actually overlapping, fluid phases. The notion of stages might lead people to expect the bereaved to proceed from one clearly identifiable reaction to another in a more orderly fashion than usually occurs. It might also result in inappropriate behavior toward the bereaved, including hasty assessments of where individuals are or ought to be in the grieving process" [*Bereavement*, p. 48]). The process is recursive, characterized by movement that is back and forth and overlapping. Yet the clusters of experience do occur in a sequence. That sequence, although not an uninterrupted chain of happenings occurring one right after the other, does gradually move in a forward direction: toward reorganization, reorientation, and an achievement of equilibrium. Raphael writes:

"... such phases are not clear-cut or fixed, and ... the bereaved may pass backward and forward among them or may indeed become locked in one or another, partially or completely" (*The Anatomy of Grief*, p. 33). Pollock says of the phases that "though somewhat unidirectional, [they] do on occasion oscillate and revert back temporarily ... as part of the back and forth transformational process" ("Process and Affect," p. 262).

(2) No two people experience the complete grieving process at the same pace or in the same manner. Also, the various phases of the process assume different proportions for different kinds of losses. Yet we can speak of grieving as a universal phenomenon experienced through history by all people.

Pollock writes: "The mourning process ... is a universal adaptation, goes on throughout the life cycle of the individual, is found in all cultures, and, when ritualized, can be found throughout man's existence in his religious, social, and cultural practices ("The Mourning Process and Creative Organizational Change," *Journal of the American Psychoanalytic Association*, vol. 25, no. 1, p. 16). He also says, "Mourning is a normal transformational adaptive process, found in all people and throughout history" ("Process and Affect," p. 273).

(3) Some individuals report that they experience no intense distress during their grieving. They are able to find a way to think about their loss, they report, that allows them to bypass many of the phases of the grieving process. Such people, as one psychologist put it, bear their grief "lightly." For more information, see "New Studies Find Many Myths About Mourning," Daniel Goleman, *New York Times*, August 8, 1989, p. C1.

(4) The active grieving process is not to be confused with the process through which people may move when they find out they are dying. The valuable research of Elisabeth Kubler-Ross, in which she identified five stages—denial, anger, bargaining, depression, and acceptance—experienced by individuals prior to the occurrence of their own death, has been mistakenly identified by many as a description of a complete or full grieving process. The two processes, however, are very different. Survivors of loss must, again, make active interchange with life, replan their lives to include but not be dominated by the loss, make adaptations and adjustments in daily living, learn new skills, create new circumstances and situations, work through ongoing problems and challenges, and find a "new normal" and equilibrium and balance. The two processes—grieving one's own death and grieving as a survivor after a loss—are very different; and much confusion and not a little damage have resulted from the misapplying of Kubler-Ross's five stages to survivors of a loss for whom her work was not appropriate.

The mapping I have included here, though based on my own experiences and research, also includes, amplifies, builds on, and adds to phases delineated by other researchers.

Bowlby, whose pioneer work was conducted with the World Health Organization and at the Tavistock Clinic and Tavistock Institute of Human Relations in London, lists in *Loss* these four phases: 1. Phase of numbing that usually lasts from a few hours to a week and may be interrupted by outbursts of extremely intense distress and/or anger. 2. Phase of yearning and searching for the lost figure lasting some months and sometimes for years. 3. Phase of disorganization and despair 4. Phase of greater or less degree of reorganization (p. 85).

Glen Davidson, professor and chairman of the Department of Medical Humanities, Southern Illinois University School of Medicine, lists these phases in *Understanding Mourning*: 1. Shock and numbness: resistance to stimuli, judgment-making difficult, functioning impeded, emotional outbursts, stunned feelings. 2. Searching and yearning: very sensitive to stimuli, anger/guilt, restless/impatient, ambiguous, testing what is real. 3. Disorientation: disorganized, depressed, guilt, weight gain, loss of awareness of reality. 4. Reorganization: sense of release, renewed energy, makes judgments better, stable eating and sleeping habits. (pp. 50, 59, 68, 78).

Sidney Zisook, M.D., University of California, San Diego, UCSD-Gifford Mental Health Center, lists these phases in *Biopsychosocial Aspects of Bereavement*: 1. Shock—denial and disbelief. 2. (A) Acute mourning: intense feeling states—crying spells, guilt, shame, depression, anorexia, insomnia, irritability, emptiness, and fatigue. (B) Social withdrawal: preoccupation with health, inability to sustain usual work, family, and personal relationships. (C) Identification with the deceased: transient adoption of habits, mannerisms, and somatic symptoms of the deceased. 3. Resolution: acceptance of loss, awareness of having grieved, return to well-being, and ability to recall the deceased without subjective pain (p. 25).

Beverley Raphael, M.D., in *The Anatomy of Bereavement* refers to: 1. Shock, numbness, disbelief. 2. Emotional experience of separation pain: intense yearning, pining, and longing . . . restlessness, agitation, and a high level of psychological arousal, preoccupation with the absent person, pain and emptiness, anxiety and helplessness, anger and aggression. 3. Psychological mourning: intense reexperiencing of much of the past development of relationship, undoing the bonds that built the relationship, crying, sadness, regret, resentment, guilt, despair, disorganization. 4. Longer-term adjustments: engaging in adjustive tasks, defining identity, relinquishing old roles, establishing new patterns of interaction and sources of gratification, evolving new and satisfying roles, interactions, and sources of gratification (pp. 34–58).

Serves as a mirror: In *Loss and Change* Peter Marris writes: "Bereavement presents unambiguously one aspect of social changes—the irretrievable loss of the familiar. And since it is a common experience in every society, the reaction to bereavement is perhaps the most general and best described of all examples of how we assimilate disruptive change. If we can understand grief and mourning, we may be able to see more clearly the process of adjustment in other situations of change, where the discontinuity is less clear-cut" (p. 23). He also says, "I have been writing of death. But these suggestions can, I think, be adapted to any severe personal loss" (p. 154). George Pollock writes: "I have studied the loss through death as it is simpler to date the loss and subsequent mourning. I believe the general principles are applicable to other loss situations, e.g., divorce, serious illness with prolonged separation, etc." ("Process and Affect: Mourning and Grief," p. 271).

I. IMPACT: EXPERIENCING THE UNTHINKABLE

Pages 1, 105
   Epigraph: For notice of this Shakespeare reference and the Thomas Paine epigraph introducing Chapter 3, I am indebted to John Schneider's *Stress, Loss, and Grief,* pp. 79, 9.

Page 23
   Brains secrete: Institute of Medicine, *Bereavement: Reactions, Consequences, and Care,* p. 162.
   Virtually closes its boundaries and defenses: Beverley Raphael, *The Anatomy of Bereavement,* p. 34

Page 24
   Restlessly by day and night: Cited by Colin Murray Parkes, *Bereavement,* p. 40
   Elephants mourning: See "Earth Week," *Houston Chronicle,* November 26, 2001, p. 18A.
   Moss: *Elephant Memories,* Chapters 3 and 10.

Page 25
   Long evolutionary history: See Raphael, *The Anatomy of Bereavement,* p. 3, and Parkes, *Bereavement,* pp. 40–42.

Page 34
   Flight-or-fight: See Wayne Barrett et al., *The Brain: Mystery of Matter and Mind,* pp. 98, 99.

Page 35

Medical studies: For comprehensive information about the relationship of grief and health, see the Institute of Medicine's *Bereavement: Reactions, Consequences, and Care,* Chapters 2, 3, and 6.

Page 41

Many theories: For a review of such theories, see Allan L. Combs, "Synchronicity: A Synthesis of Western Theories and Eastern Perspectives," *ReVision,* vol. 5, no. 1, pp. 20–27.

Page 43

Mourning is treated: See Geoffrey Gorer, *Death, Grief, and Mourning,* p. 131.
Lily Pincus: Death and the Family: The Importance of Mourning, pp. 253–254.
Anthony Storr: Solitude: A Return to the Self, p. 3.

Page 44

Be swept by pangs of grief: See John Bowlby, *Loss,* p. 243.
Optimal "level of grieving": Parkes, *Bereavement,* p. 162.

Page 45

Need from families and friends: Beverley Raphael summarizes the chief goals of care in the early phase of grieving: "to facilitate the emotional release; to assist the bereaved in recognizing and expressing their yearning for the lost person; to facilitate reality testing by a review of the death and its meaning; to promote other social support; and to initiate the basis for an ongoing caring relationship" (*Anatomy of Bereavement,* p. 358).

Page 46

Damage done: Bowlby, *Loss,* p. 193.

Page 47

Pluck at the heartstrings: Parkes, *Bereavement,* p. 161.

Page 50

Mapping the terrain:

(1) The clusters of experience are not a series of tightly defined steps moved through in a linear, lockstep arrangement. (For this reason the word *stage* is too rigid to describe the parts of the process. The Institute of Medicine cautions against using the term *stage* because it may "connote concrete boundaries between what are actually overlapping, fluid phases. The notion of stages might lead people to expect the bereaved to proceed from one clearly identifiable reac-

tion to another in a more orderly fashion than usually occurs. It might also result in inappropriate behavior toward the bereaved, including hasty assessments of where individuals are or ought to be in the grieving process" [*Bereavement*, p. 48]. The process is recursive, characterized by movement that is back and forth and overlapping. Yet the clusters of experience do occur in a sequence. That sequence, although not an uninterrupted chain of happenings occurring one right after the other, does gradually move in a forward direction: toward reorganization, reorientation, and an achievement of equilibrium. Raphael writes: ". . . such phases are not clear-cut or fixed, and . . . the bereaved may pass backward and forward among them or may indeed become locked in one or another, partially or completely" (*The Anatomy of Grief*, p. 33). Pollock says of the phases that "though somewhat unidirectional, [they] do on occasion oscillate and revert back temporarily . . . as part of the back and forth transformational process" ("Process and Affect," p. 262).

(2) No two people experience the complete grieving process at the same pace or in the same manner. Also, the various phases of the process assume different proportions for different kinds of losses. Yet we can speak of grieving as a universal phenomenon experienced through history by all people.

Pollock writes: "The mourning process . . . is a universal adaptation, goes on throughout the life cycle of the individual, is found in all cultures, and, when ritualized, can be found throughout man's existence in his religious, social, and cultural practices ("The Mourning Process and Creative Organizational Change," *Journal of the American Psychoanalytic Association*, vol. 25, no. 1, p. 16). He also says, "Mourning is a normal transformational adaptive process, found in all people and throughout history" ("Process and Affect," p. 273).

(3) Some individuals report that they experience no intense distress during their grieving. They are able to find a way to think about their loss, they report, that allows them to bypass many of the phases of the grieving process. Such people, as one psychologist put it, bear their grief "lightly." For more information, see "New Studies Find Many Myths About Mourning," Daniel Goleman, *New York Times*, August 8, 1989, p. C1.

(4) The active grieving process is not to be confused with the process through which people may move when they find out they are dying. The valuable research of Elisabeth Kubler-Ross, in which she identified five stages—denial, anger, bargaining, depression, and acceptance—experienced by individuals prior to the occurrence of their own death, has been mistakenly identified by many as a description of a complete or full grieving process. The two processes, however, are very different. Survivors of loss must, again, make active interchange with life, replan their lives to include but not be dominated by the loss, make adaptations and adjustments in daily living, learn new skills, create new circumstances and situations, work through ongoing problems and challenges, and find a "new

normal" and equilibrium and balance. The two processes—grieving one's own death and grieving as a survivor after a loss—are very different, and much confusion and not a little damage have resulted from the misapplying of Kubler-Ross's five stages to survivors of a loss for whom her work was not appropriate.

2. SECOND CRISIS: STUMBLING IN THE DARK

Page 53

Epigraph: From "Years Vanish Like the Morning Dew," in *In the Midst of Winter: Selections from The Literature of Mourning*, Mary Jane Moffat, ed.

Page 72

Keystone, whole structure of meaning, important anxieties, resentments: Peter Marris, *Loss and Change*, p. 33.

Escape from this distress; purposes are learned; painful retrieval: Ibid., pp. 33–34.

In the course: John Bowlby, *Loss*, p. 91.

Restore the bond: Ibid.

Page 78

Sympathetic illness: Beverley Raphael says in *The Anatomy of Bereavement*, "Many bereaved widows and widowers experience transiently body symptoms reflecting the dead partner's terminal illness" (p. 215).

Page 79

A sudden accident: Lily Pincus, in *Death and the Family*, comments on the occurrence of accidents following loss. Speaking of her own accident after the death of her husband, she writes: "I managed to fracture my ankle within ten days of my arrival in Israel. . . . When I asked the orthopedic surgeon who treated me whether people often fracture bones after bereavement, he said, without even looking up from my injured foot, 'Naturally, people lose their sense of balance,' and perhaps some have to fracture limbs or hurt some other part of themselves before they can acknowledge what has happened to them. Is it possible to enable them to do so in a less self-destructive way, by encouraging and supporting them in their mourning process?" (p. 13).

Page 82

Assumptive world: See Colin Murray Parkes, *Bereavement*, Chapter 7. Also see James Britton's essays, Chapters 8–10, in *Prospect and Retrospect*, ed. Gordon Pradl.

Page 83

A year ago: Albert F. Knight, "The Death of a Son," *New York Times Magazine,* June 22, 1986, p. 34.

Page 84

Don't burn our widows: Parkes, *Bereavement,* p. 9.
The Guardian: "Private Lives," Section G2, p. 12, March 22, 2002.

Page 85

No allowance for grieving: Julie Rose, in "Mourning a Miscarriage," *Newsweek,* August 3, 1987, p. 7, gives a poignant account of society's reaction to the loss of an unborn child.

Page 86

Will attempt to defend ourselves: Bowlby, *Loss,* p. 72.
Protect themselves: Ibid., p. 21.

Page 87

Bereavement may also be fatal: Raphael, *The Anatomy of Bereavement,* p. 62.
Increase of almost 40 percent: Parkes, *Bereavement,* p. 16.
4.8 percent died within the first year: Ibid.
The mortality rate: Institute of Medicine, *Bereavement: Reactions, Consequences, and Care,* pp. 21–22.
Suicide rate: Institute of Medicine, *Bereavement: Reactions, Consequences, and Care,* p. 26.

Page 88

There is some evidence: Ibid., p. 35.
Partial list: For a discussion of illness and grief, see the Institute of Medicine's *Bereavement: Reactions, Consequences, and Care,* Chapters 2–3.
Seven illnesses, chronic depression: Glen W. Davidson, in *Understanding Mourning,* discusses Lindemann's list and his own, pp. 21–22.

Page 89

Second and third years: Institute of Medicine, *Bereavement: Reactions, Consequences, and Care,* p. 35.
Sick role: See Davidson's *Understanding Mourning,* pp. 71, 72.
Derelict role: Ibid., p. 70.
All studies: Institute of Medicine, *Bereavement: Reactions, Consequences, and Care,* p. 40.
Antisocial, delinquent: Raphael, *The Anatomy of Bereavement,* p. 61.

Page 90

Misuse of personal relationships: Ibid., pp. 219–221.

Pathological mourners: Raphael, *The Anatomy of Bereavement,* pp. 59, 60; pp. 205–209; also Bowlby, *Loss,* Chapter 9.

New and special role: Raphael, *The Anatomy of Bereavement,* p. 60.

Page 91

As though nothing: Ibid., p. 205.

Toned down: Ibid., p. 206.

Intense pervasive anger: Ibid., p. 208.

The best that can be determined: Davidson, *Understanding Mourning,* p. 23.

The levels of morbid outcome: Raphael, *The Anatomy of Bereavement,* p. 64.

I suggested: Bowlby, *Loss,* p. 246.

Page 92

It is characteristic: Ibid.

To know, and name, and express: Raphael, *The Anatomy of Bereavement,* p. 358.

Sadness: Raphael, *The Anatomy of Bereavement,* p. 45. Beverley Raphael also points out on page 216: "There is often a semantic confusion: the bereaved widow states her feeling as depression when she really means sadness, for the word sadness has become little used, particularly when speaking of personal feelings which are most frequently labeled depression." See also David Burns's chapter "Sadness Is Not Depression," *Feeling Good,* p. 207.

Do little to improve: Ibid., p. 214.

It is important: Davidson, *Understanding Mourning,* p. 70.

John Schneider: From private correspondence, March 2002. See www.seasons center.com

Page 93

If a mourner is developing an illness: Davidson, *Understanding Mourning,* p. 70.

Page 94

Mental dysfunction: See Morton Hunt's "Sick Thinking," *New York Times Magazine,* January 3, 1988, p. 22.

Acute grief frequently creates: Zisook and Shuchter, "A Multidimensional Model of Spousal Bereavement," in *Biopsychosocial Aspects of Bereavement,* p. 43.

I think a stranger: Peter Marris, *Loss and Change,* p. 153.

Page 95

Grief may give way: Institute of Medicine, *Bereavement: Reactions, Consequences, and Care,* p. 284.

Page 96

Standard of care: Glen Davidson, in *Understanding Mourning,* reports on physicians' tendency to interpret the prescribing of barbiturates or tranquilizers as a "standard of care," citing statistics that showed that 87 percent of physicians in Illinois indicated they held such a position (p. 22).

The majority of the general public: "As many as 89 percent of the general public polled in 1980 understood mourning basically to be an illness, whose characteristics must be suppressed. . . . Most of those polled thought it appropriate for physicians to prescribe drugs as a means of suppressing the symptoms" (Davidson, *Understanding Mourning,* pp. 22, 23).

Unlearning process: Parkes, *Bereavement,* p. 173.

Page 97

Alternatives: Davidson, *Understanding Mourning,* p. 70.

Page 98

All of my work: Maya Angelou, *Phenomenal Woman,* Random House, 2000.

Alexander Shand: John Bowlby in *Loss* says: "Shand, drawing for his data on the works of English poets and French prose-writers, not only delineates most of the main features of grief as we now know them but discusses in a systematic way its relation to fear and anger. As a sensitive and perspicacious study his book ranks high and deserves to be better known" (pp. 24–25).

Despair tends to elicit courage: Alexander Shand, *The Foundations of Character,* p. 492.

3. OBSERVATION: LINKING PAST TO PRESENT

Page 110

Time to stop traveling: Natasha Lynne Vogdes, in Fredric Leer, "Running as an Adjunct to Psychotherapy," *Social Work,* January 1980, pp. 20–25.

Page 117

I want: Gina Cerminara, *Many Mansions,* p. 284.
Realize first: Ibid., p. 286.

Pages 121–122

Mourning requires; at the nub; allows an update: Quoted in Daniel Goleman's "Mourning: New Studies Affirm Its Benefits," *New York Times*, February 5, 1985, p. 23.

Page 122

A very intense: Beverley Raphael, *The Anatomy of Bereavement*, p. 44.
Not growing: Ibid., p. 47.
Piece by piece: Ibid., p. 187.
Many powerful: Ibid., pp. 186, 187.

Page 123

Studying and investigating: Webster's *New Collegiate Dictionary*.
The work of mourning: Anthony Storr, *Solitude*, pp. 31, 32.
To confirm: John Bowlby, *Loss*, p. 232.

Page 136

No gradual transitions: From Liz Carpenter's *Getting Better All the Time*, p. 42.

Page 137

To discover: Storr, *Solitude*, p. 20.
In the presence of someone; actual presence; have an experience; a large number: D. W. Winnicott, "The Capacity to Be Alone," in *The Maturational Processes and the Facilitating Environment*, pp. 34, 35.
The capacity: Storr, *Solitude*, p. 21.
The ability; private behavior; lift the weight: Quoted in Daniel Goleman's "Talking to Oneself Is Good Therapy, Doctors Say," *New York Times*, February 4, 1988, p. B12.

Page 138

One of the principal means; inventory; a thread of continuity; has not vanished; comes close; offers guidance: Pietro Castelnuovo-Tedesco, " 'The Mind as a Stage,' Some Comments on Reminiscence and Internal Objects," *International Journal of Psycho-analysis*, vol. 59, part 1, p. 22.
Occurs silently; simultaneously observer; may even be positively: Ibid., pp. 20, 21.
As buffer; that something; has enough substance: Ibid., p. 23.
Peopled: Ibid., p. 24.

Page 139

Contradictory and interdependent: Lily Pincus, *Death and the Family*, p. 118.
The greatest obstacle: p. 268.

Page 140
Critical to the issue: Raphael, *The Anatomy of Bereavement*, p. 187.
When the bereaved: Ibid., pp. 187, 188.

Page 141
A major bereavement: Colin Murray Parkes, *Bereavement*, p. 85.

Page 142
Wrong doings: Glen W. Davidson, *Understanding Mourning*, pp. 58–59.

Page 145
It often helps; with a column; easier to see: Goleman's "Talking to Oneself Is Good Therapy, Doctors Say," p. B12.

Page 146
Lucia Adams: The Bryan/College Station Eagle, November 19, 1988, p. 2A.

Page 148
Matter of balance: Raphael points out in *The Anatomy of Bereavement* that this time of review is "both private and public" (p. 44).

Page 149
Karma Repair Kit: Richard Brautigan, *The Pill Versus the Springhill Mine Disaster*, p. 8.

4. THE TURN: TURNING INTO THE WIND

Page 159
Physical alteration: This is a common occurrence reported by bereaved individuals. There is a point in their grieving when they experience an actual visceral change. This physical alteration, which is both spontaneous and unexplainable, is followed by a sense of peace, release, ease, and confidence.

Page 160
Relapse nine months after: Beverley Raphael writes in *The Anatomy of Bereavement:* "It is interesting to note that there is sometimes an upsurge of distress, or even a peak of morbidity, about nine months after the death. This may, perhaps, be linked to deep inner fantasies that something left behind, some bit of the dead person, will be reborn again then. And when it is not, and his 'death' continues, then fresh pain is once more experienced. Other peaks of renewed mourning . . .

are often related to a special occasion: festivals without the deceased . . . anniversaries of the relationship or death which reiterate that the dead person is of the past" (page 58).

Page 163

To commemorate your release: John Bowlby in *Loss* references a study that shows a grieving mother's emotions "changed in parallel with the direction of her concern." When she began to think of her son and his fate instead of concentrating all her attention on her own suffering, she began to care for her son tenderly and became calm (p. 144). Bowlby also states, "In healthy mourning a bereaved person is much occupied thinking about the person who has died and perhaps of the pain he may have suffered and the frustration of his hopes" (p. 248).

Page 164

The first anniversary: For a full discussion of behavior associated with the anniversary of the event of loss, see George Pollock's "Anniversary Reactions, Trauma, and Mourning," the *Psychoanalysis Quarterly*, vol. 39, no. 3, pp. 347–371.

Pages 166–167

"A Song": From *Embassy News*, vol. 4, no. 1, p. 20. Unfortunately, despite weeks of research and efforts, I was unable to locate the author of this poem.

Page 167

The cycle of life: Lily Pincus, in *Death and the Family*, speaks of "the ever-recurring theme of 'one life for another.'" She points out that such an experience can "suggest the joyful experience of rebirth, the completion of the life cycle, and the continuation of the dead" (p. 274).

Page 168

The Words of Jean-Paul Sartre; freedom crashed down; let us say: Melvin Maddocks, "The Words of Jean-Paul Sartre," *Christian Science Monitor*, April 21, 1980, p. 22.

Page 171

Because it is necessary; cognitive act: John Bowlby, *Loss*, p. 94.

Page 172

Mourning is: Anthony Storr, *Solitude*, p. 32.

Page 183

Appropriate form for the relationship: Peter Marris points out in *Loss and Change* that "recovery from grief depends on restoring a sense that the lost attachment can still give meaning to the present, not on finding a substitute" (p. 149).

Page 184

It is as if: Sidney Zisook et al., "Adjustment to Widowhood," *Biophychosocial Aspects of Bereavement,* p. 70.

Includes the evolution: Sidney Zisook and Stephen R. Shuchter, "The Therapeutic Tasks of Grief," *Biopsychosocial Aspects of Bereavement,* p. 181.

Patterns of thought; to retain: Bowlby, *Loss,* p. 96.

Page 186

Morbidly introspective: Bowlby, p. 68.

When an adult: Aaron Beck, *Cognitive Therapy and the Emotional Disorders,* p. 217.

Page 187

It is possible: Ibid., p. 235.

The bereaved: Zisook and Shuchter, *Biopsychosocial Aspects of Behavior,* p. 46.

Page 188

Faith: Glen W. Davidson, *Understanding Mourning,* p. 46.

Page 189

More appreciative: Zisook and Shuchter, *Biopsychosocial Aspects of Bereavement,* p. 46.

Page 190

A study of widows: See Glick et al., *The First Year of Bereavement,* p. 153. I am indebted to Bowlby, *Loss,* p. 101, for my first knowledge of this reference.

At a particular moment: Bowlby, *Loss,* p. 101.

Often this is a painful: Glick et al., *The First Year of Bereavement,* p. 153.

Replan our lives: Bowlby, *Loss,* pp. 138, 94.

Page 191

Not only is there: Institute of Medicine, *Bereavement: Results, Consequences, and Care,* p. 54.

Page 192

False self: D. W. Winnicott, "Ego Distortion in Terms of True and False Self," *The Maturational Processes and the Facilitating Environment,* pp. 146, 147. "False self" also cited in Bowlby, *Loss,* p. 225.

Brittle and hard: Bowlby, *Loss,* p. 225.

Page 193

Only two great: D. H. Lawrence, "Indians and Entertainment," in *D. H. Lawrence and New Mexico,* Keith Sagar, ed., p. 36.

5. RECONSTRUCTION: PICKING UP THE PIECES

Page 199

When it's November: The line accurately reads: "Whenever I find myself growing grim about the mouth; whenever it is a damp, drizzly November in my soul; whenever I find myself involuntarily pausing before coffin warehouses, and bringing up the rear of every funeral I meet; and when my hyhpos [depression] gets such an upper hand on me, that it requires a strong moral principle to prevent me from deliberately stepping into the street, and methodically knocking people's hats off—then, I account it high time to get to sea as soon as I can." Herman Melville, *Moby Dick* (New York: W. W. Norton, 1967), p. 12.

Page 200

But I want first of all: Anne Morrow Lindbergh, *Gift from the Sea,* p. 23.

Page 205

Sea Sculpture: Roland Pease, *New York Times,* July 22, 1981, p. C2.

Page 209

Lines like these: Lawrence Durrell, *Nunquam,* pp. 20, 280, postface.

Page 213

Anything is one of a million paths: Carlos Castaneda, *The Teachings of Don Juan: A Yaqui Way of Knowledge,* pp. 106, 107, 160, 185.

Page 214

We need our past: Peter Marris, *Loss and Change,* Chapter 1.

Good, bad, or indifferent: Ibid., p. 10.

A series of interpretations: Ibid., p. 8.

Page 217

Establishing a new identity: For an excellent personal account of the difficulties related to establishing a new identity, see Rhoda Tagliacozzo's "The Legacy of Widowhood" *New York Times Magazine*, July 31, 1988, p. 12.

Page 224

One aspect of bereavement: Ernest Morgan, *Dealing Creativity with Death*, p. 23.
Such disorganization: John Bowlby, *Loss*, p. 246.
This may be: Beverley Raphael, *The Anatomy of Bereavement*, p. 57.

Page 225

Hot Thoughts/Cool Thoughts: David Burns, *Feeling Good*, pp. 151–155.
Daily Record of Dysfunctional Thoughts: Burns, *Feeling Good*, p. 154.

Page 227

Nurturance: Raphael, *The Anatomy of Bereavement*, p. 201.
Two kinds of loneliness: R. S. Weiss, "The Provisions of Social Relationships," *Doing Unto Others*, Zick Rubin, ed., p. 23.

Pages 228–229

Negative types of relationships; ever-loving; someone who is seen; is valued: Raphael, *The Anatomy of Bereavement*, p. 219.

Page 229

Fill the gap: Ibid., p. 220.

Page 231

Active interchange; hope, fear: Bowlby, *Loss*, p. 246.

Page 232

Little episodes: George H. Pollock, "Mourning and Adaptation," *International Journal of Psycho-analysis*, vol. 42, parts 4–5, p. 354.
Various manifestations: Ibid., p. 352.
More lasting adaptation: Ibid.
People who believe: Lily Pincus, *Death and the Family*, p. 122.
The pain experienced: Melanie Klein, "Mourning and Its Relationship to Manic-Depressive States," *International Journal of Psycho-analysis*, vol. 21, p. 136. I am indebted to Pincus, *Death and the Family*, p. 126, for my first exposure to this important research.
Contradicting drives: Pincus, *Death and the Family*, p. 44.
All the usual: Ibid., p. 45.

Page 233
It is not just: Ibid.
Replanning our lives: Bowlby, *Loss,* p. 138.
A period of ongoing mourning: Raphael, *The Anatomy of Bereavement,* p. 57.
Also see Pollock, "Mourning and Adaptation," *International Journal of Psycho-analysis,* vol. 42, parts 4–5, p. 352.

Page 234
Edna St. Vincent Millay: Sonnet clxxi.

6. WORKING THROUGH: FINDING SOLID GROUND

Page 260
Proceed by: Peter Marris, *Loss and Change,* p. 34.
Grow by: Attributed to Pope Gregory.

Page 275
Optimism—at least reasonable optimism; our expectancies: "Research Affirms Power of Positive Thinking," Daniel Goleman, *New York Times,* February 2, 1987, p. 15.

Pages 275–276
Michael Scheier; Martin Seligman: Ibid.

Page 276
Learned Optimism: Martin Seligman, *Learned Optimism: How to Change Your Mind and Your Life,* pp. 228–234.

Page 277
Talking to the lost person: Glick et al., *The First Year of Bereavement,* p. 154. Cited in John Bowlby, *Loss,* p. 98.

Page 278
When I tell my clients: O, *The Oprah Magazine,* June 2001, p. 149.
Henry Raeburn's portrait: Unless it is on loan to another museum, this portrait can be seen at the National Gallery of Scotland in Edinburgh.

Page 280
Practical busyness; remain meaningless: Marris, *Loss and Change,* p. 34.
More lastingly damaging; wreck of dead hopes: Ibid.
A sense of continuity: Marris, *Loss and Change,* p. 34.

Page 281

Reconstitute the continuities; the power to sustain: James Carse, *Death and Existence*, pp. 8, 9. For an excellent discussion of the relation of death to life, see Carse's full introduction, pp. 1–10.

Page 282

Howard Thurman: See *Disciplines of the Spirit*, pp. 18, 22–23; *The Creative Encounter*, p. 68; *For the Inward Journey*, pp. 80–81, 232. For a fuller discussion of this and the Albert Einstein quotes below, see Elizabeth Neeld's *A Sacred Primer*, Renaissance Books, pp. 39–51.

Albert Einstein, wonder: From "Constructing a Theory: Einstein's Model," by Gerald Horton, *The American Scholar*, summer 1979, pp. 309–340.

Albert Einstein, To know that what is impenetrable: from "What I Believe," cited on the Quintessential Quotations Web site (http://user.deltanet.com/lumiere/quotes.htm).

Page 283

Is a very powerful: Marris, *Loss and Change*, p. 98.

Page 284

The central, most urgent task: Ibid., p. 149.

I'm dialing: Noel Perrin, *New York Times Magazine*, July 6, 1986, p. 37.

Page 285

True intimacy: Ibid.

The family unit: Raphael, *The Anatomy of Bereavement*, p. 54.

Page 286

Young children's delayed or prolonged grieving: Jane Brody mentions other signs that could mean a child is experiencing unhealthy grieving: "performing poorly in school . . . physical complaints (stomachache, sore or tight throat, loss of appetite, fatigue), anger toward the deceased, anger toward others, adopting the mannerisms or symptoms of the deceased, idealizing the deceased or latching on to a relative or friend as a replacement for the deceased." *New York Times*, August 12, 1987, p. 18.

Page 287

Gay community: See S. J. Klein and William Fletcher, "Gay Grief: An Examination of Its Uniqueness Brought to Light by the AIDS Crisis," in *Journal of Psychosocial Oncology*, vol. 4, no. 3, pp. 15–26.

Their dead and dying friends: Klein and Fletcher, p. 24.

Page 288

In a situation: Colin Murray Parkes, *Bereavement,* p. 175.

Page 289

I am committed: In one entry in *Markings,* Dag Hammarskjöld writes: "It must have been late in September. Or, perhaps, my memory has invented an appropriate weather for the occasion" (p. 29). My memory, too, invented the sentence "I am committed to a life of no return," although that invention occurred immediately upon completing the initial reading of the book. For it was those words, as I meshed them from two statements Hammarskjöld made, that became a touchstone for me during my own experience of Finding Solid Ground. What Mr. Hammarskjöld actually wrote was this: "Committed to the future—Even if that *means 'se preparer a bien mourir'* " (p. 65) and "There is a point at which everything becomes simple and there is no longer any question of choice, because all you have staked will be lost if you look back. Life's point of no return" (p. 66).

7. INTEGRATION: DAYLIGHT

Page 293

Ozick epigraph: From *Partisan Review* essay "What Literature Means," by Cynthia Ozick.

Alcott epigraph: From Scott Peck's *Abounding Grace* (Andrews McMeel Publishing, 2000).

Pages 299–301

If my airplane; in my office; taking a responsibility; a creative moment; if you ask me: Lisl Marburg Goodman, *Death and the Creative Life: Conversations with Prominent Artists and Scientists,* pp. 79, 80, 81, 110–113.

Page 303

Chow's now on: Woody Guthrie, *Seeds of Man,* p. 61.

Page 304

I live on earth: Quoted in "An Obituary for Bucky," by John Pastier, *Arts & Architecture,* fall 1983.

My brother collected: From "The Archives: Bucky's Own Thoughts on the Archives," *Buckminster Fuller Institute Newsletter,* vol. 2, no. 6, p. 1.

Page 305

I believe: Marguerite Yourcenar, *With Open Eyes*, pp. 201, 205, 259–260.

Each of us: Howard Thurman, *For the Inward Journey*, pp. 84–86. Substitution of pronouns in this excerpt made by Elizabeth Neeld.

Page 306

Tiou, tiou: French composer Lescuyer, writing in *Language et Chant des Oiseaux*, reprinted in George Herrick's *Michelangelo's Snowman: A Commonplace Collection*, p. 14.

Page 308

Transformational-mourning-liberation: George H. Pollock in "Aging or Aged: Development or Pathology," *The Course of Life*, vol. 3, p. 553.

Page 309

Creative outcomes: See George Pollock's "Mourning and Adaptation," *International Journal of Psycho-analysis*, vol. 42, pp. 354–355; "The Mourning Process and Creative Organizational Change," *Journal of the American Psychoanalytic Association*, vol. 25, pp. 13–28; "Process and Affect: Mourning and Grief," *International Journal of Psycho-analysis*, vol. 59, pp. 267–273.

New creation; its energy; successor: George Pollock, "Process and Affect: Mourning and Grief," p. 270.

Page 320

There is no permanent: Thomas Berger, *Little Big Man*, p. 433.

Page 326

Rituals: See Victor Turner and Edith Turner, *Image and Pilgrimage in Christian Culture: Anthropological Perspectives*, p. 2.

Inwardly transformed; betwixt and between: Ibid., p. 249.

Realm or dimension: Ibid., p. 2.

To death, to being in the womb: Ibid., p. 249.

Page 327

Death of a loved one: Beverley Raphael, *The Anatomy of Bereavement*, p. 23.

Bereaved who are not able: Lily Pincus, *Death and the Family*, pp. 124–125.

If any good; taken to the extreme: Jane E. Brody, "Facing Your Own Mortality," *New York Times Magazine*, October 9, 1988, pp. 20, 35.

Page 328
Four layers: Ernest Becker, *The Denial of Death*, p. 57.
Thinking and talking: Pincus, *Death and the Family*, p. 250.

Page 329
Heinz Kohut: See Heinz Kohut, "Forms and Transformations of Narcissism," in *Journal of the American Psychoanalytic Association*, vol. 14, pp. 243–272. All quoted material in this and following five paragraphs is from this source.

Page 330
Susan Nolen-Hoeksema: "Growth and Resilience Among Bereaved People," pp. 122–124.

Page 332
Chronos time; Kairos time; the time within; drawn inside: See Peter A. Campbell and Edwin M. McMahan, *Bio-spirituality*, pp. 84–85.

Page 333
Entelechy: Turner and Turner, *Image and Pilgrimage in Christian Culture*, p. 25.
A majority: John Bowlby, *Loss*, p. 101.
There is no fixed end point: Raphael, *The Anatomy of Bereavement*, p. 47.

Page 334
Despite the popular: The Institute of Medicine, *Bereavement: Reactions, Consequences, and Care*, p. 52.
Near the end of the second year: Glen Davidson, *Understanding Mourning*, pp. 16, 78. For a discussion of the time periods of the phases, see Chapters 5–8.
One of the most important; in general: Sidney Zisook, Stephen R. Shuchter, and Lucy E. Lyons, "Adjusting to Widowhood," *Biopsychosocial Aspects of Bereavement*, pp. 52, 71.

Page 335
So many variables: Raphael, *The Anatomy of Bereavement*, pp. 62–64, 221–227.
Dependent, clinging, ambivalent. Ibid., p. 225.

Page 338
Men don't cry: Diane Cole writes in *Psychology Today*, vol. 22, no. 12, pp. 60–61 of the differences in the ways men and women mourn.
Male model; female model: Ibid., p. 61

Page 339

Education: Speaking of the importance of education, the editors of the Institute of Medicine's *Bereavement: Reactions, Consequences, and Care* write: "Although there are no studies to document the effects of information on the bereavement process, the committee was struck by the widespread view that thorough information of several types can be beneficial and often seems to be lacking . . . people need information" (pp. 289–290).

In Death and the Family, Lily Pincus says, ". . . education for death is education for life, and should be an underlying feature in all education in schools, universities, and through the media" (p. 250).

Page 341

The loss through death: Pincus, *Death and the Family,* p. 171.
Paul Tournier: The Adventure of Living, pp. 87, 49, 91, 240.

Page 342

James Britton: Prospect and Retrospect, Gordon Pradl, ed., pp. 83, 91.
Mysterious way; who knows: Becker, *The Denial of Death,* pp. 284, 285.

Page 344

A fire was burning: "Rescue" by William Stafford, published in *The Small Farm,* spring/fall, 1979. A gift to the author from the poet.

ADDENDUM

Page 351

Grace Christ: Healing Children's Grief: Surviving a Parent's Death from Cancer, Oxford University Press, 2000. In this Addendum, Elizabeth Neeld has interpreted and extrapolated from Grace Christ's research on characteristics and recommendations (children ages 3–17) regarding parent death from cancer as presented in *Healing Children's Grief.* All research in this section is, therefore, credited to Grace Christ; all interpretation is the work of Elizabeth Neeld.

Page 361

The Child's Bereavement Trust: www.childbereavement.org.uk.

Page 362

Five-year-old: "Jane Hughes on Coping with the Death of a Parent," *Self, Times Magazine,* February, 2002, pp. 96–97.

DIRECTORY OF RESOURCES

Page 414
Andrew Weil: "Healing with the Creative Arts," *Dr. Andrew Weil's Self Healing newsletter,* May 2000, pp. 1, 6–7.

BIBLIOGRAPHY

Al-Qusabi, Ghazi. "A Song." *Embassy News*, vol. 4, no. 1 (1980): 20.

Angelou, Maya. *Phenomenal Woman*. New York: Random House, 2000.

Barrett, Wayne, et al. *The Brain: Mystery of Matter and Mind*. New York: Torstar Books, 1984.

Beck, Aaron. *Cognitive Therapy and the Emotional Disorders*. New York: New American Library, 1979.

Becker, Ernest. *The Denial of Death*. New York: Free Press, 1997.

Berger, Thomas. *Little Big Man*. New York: Delacorte Press, 1989.

Bowlby, John. *Loss: Sadness and Depression*. New York: Basic Books, 2000.

Brautigan, Richard. *The Pill Versus the Springhill Mine Disaster*. New York: Mariner Books, 1989.

Brody, Jane E. "Facing Your Own Mortality." *New York Times Magazine* (October 9, 1988): 20.

———. "The Facts of Death for Children." *New York Times* (August 12, 1987): 18.

Burns, David. *Feeling Good*. New York: New American Library, 1980.

Campbell, Peter A., and Edwin M. McMahon. *Bio-Spirituality*. Chicago: Loyola University Press, 1985.

Carpenter, Liz. *Getting Better All the Time*. New York: Pocket Books, 1988.

Carse, James. *Death and Existence: A Conceptual History of Human Mortality*. New York: John Wiley & Sons, 1980.

Castaneda, Carlos. *The Teaching of Don Juan: A Yaqui Way of Knowledge*. New York: Pocket Books, 1985.

Castelnuovo-Tedesco, Pietro. " 'The Mind as a Stage.' Some Comments on Reminiscence and Internal Objects." *International Journal of Psycho-analysis*, vol. 59, part 1 (1978): 20–25.

Cerminara, Gina. *Many Mansions*. New York: New American Library, 1999.

Christ, Grace Hyslop. *Healing Children's Grief: Surviving a Parent's Death from Cancer*. New York: Oxford University Press, 2000.

Combs, Allan L. "Synchronicity: A Synthesis of Western Thoughts and Eastern Perspectives." *ReVision*, vol. 5, no. I (1982): 20–27.

Davidson, Glen W. *Understanding Mourning: A Guide for Those Who Grieve*. Minneapolis: Augsburg Publishing House, 1984.

"Depression," *Newsweek* (May 4, 1987): 48–57.

Dickinson, Emily. *The Complete Poems*. Thomas H. Johnson, ed. Boston: Little, Brown, 1976.

Durrell, Lawrence. *Numquam*. New York: Viking Press, 1979.

Eliot, T. S. *Four Quartets*. Ft. Washington, Pa: Harvest Books, 1974.

Fried, Martha Nemes, and Morton H. Fried. *Transitions: Four Rituals in Eight Cultures*. New York: W. W. Norton, 1980.

Gibbons, Reginald, ed. *The Poet's Worst*. Boston: Houghton Mifflin, 1979.

Gillham, Jane E., ed. *The Science of Optimism: Research Essays in Honor of Martin E. P. Seligman*. Philadelphia: Templeton Foundation Press, 2000.

Glick, Ira. O., Robert S. Weiss, and C. Murray Parkes. *The First Year of Bereavement*. New York: John Wiley & Sons, 1974.

Goleman, Daniel. "Mourning: New Studies Affirm Its Benefits." *New York Times* (February 5, 1985): 19.

———. "New Studies Find Many Myths About Mourning." *New York Times* (August 8, 1989): CI.

———. "Research Affirms Power of Positive Thinking." *New York Times* (February 3, 1987): 15.

———. "Talking to Oneself Is Good Therapy, Doctors Say." *New York Times* (February 4, 1988): B12.

Goodman, Lisl Marburg. *Death and the Creative Life: Conversations with Prominent Artists and Scientists*. New York: Springer Publishing, 1981.

Gorer, Geoffrey. *Death, Grief, and Mourning*. Manchester, N.H.: Ayer Publishing, 1979.

Greenspan, Stanley, and George Pollock, eds. "Aging or Aged: Development or Pathology." *The Course of Life, Volume III: Adulthood and the Aging Process*. Washington, D.C.: U.S. Government Printing Office, 1980.

Guthrie, Woody. *Seeds of Man*. New York: E. P. Dutton, 1979.

Hall, Nor. *The Moon and the Virgin*. New York: Harper & Row, 1980.

Hammarskjöld, Dag. *Markings*. Leif Sjoberg and W. H. Auden, trans. New York: Ballantine, 1993.

Herrick, George. *Michelangelo's Snowman: A Commonplace Collection*. Ipswich, Mass.: Ipswich Publishers, 1985.

Hunt, Morton. "Sick Thinking." *New York Times Magazine* (January 3, 1988): 22.

Institute of Medicine, Osterweis, Marian, Fredric Solomon, and Morris Green, eds. *Bereavement: Reactions, Consequences, and Care*. Washington, D.C.: National Academy Press, 1984.

Klein, Melanie. "Mourning and Its Relationship to Manic-Depressive States." *International Journal of Psycho-analysis*, vol. 21, part 2 (1940): 125–153.

Klein, Sandra Jacoby, and William Fletcher III. "Gay Grief: An Examination of Its Uniqueness Brought to Light by the AIDS Crisis." *Journal of Psychosocial Oncology*, vol. 4, no. 3 (1986): 34.

Kohut, Heinz. "Forms and Transformations of Narcissism." *Journal of the American Psychoanalytic Association*, vol. 14 (1966): 243–272.

Kubler-Ross, Elisabeth. *Death: The Final Stage of Growth*. New York: Simon & Schuster, 1997.

Kutner, Lawrence. "Death Is No Friend, So Take Care When Introducing Him." *New York Times* (March 10, 1988): 19.

Lawrence, D. H. "Indians and Entertainment." *D. H. Lawrence and New Mexico*, Keith Sagar, ed. Salt Lake City: Gibbs M. Smith, 1982.

Leer, Frederic. "Running as an Adjunct Psycho-Therapy." *Social Work* (January 1980): 20–25.

Lindbergh, Anne Morrow. *Gift from the Sea*. New York: Pantheon Books, 1991.

Lindemann, Erich. *Beyond Grief: Studies in Crisis Intervention*. New York: Jason Aronson, 1979.

Lukas, Christopher, and Henry Seiden. *Silent Grief: Living in the Wake of Suicide*. New York: Jason Aronson, 1997.

Maddocks, Melvin. "The Words of Jean-Paul Sartre." *Christian Science Monitor*, vol. 72, no. 103 (1980): 22.

Marris, Peter. *Loss and Change*. New York: Pantheon Books, 1974.

Melville, Herman. *Moby Dick*. New York: Bantam Classics, 1981.

Merton, Thomas. *Raids on the Unspeakable*. New York: W. W. Norton, 1970.

Milosz, Czeslaw, ed. *Postwar Polish Poetry*. Berkeley: University of California Press, 1984.

Millay, Edna St. Vincent, and Norma Millay. *Collected Poems*. New York: Lightyear Press, 1997.

Moffat, Mary Jane, ed. *In the Midst of Winter: Selections from the Literature of Mourning*. New York: Vintage Books, 1992.

Morgan, Ernest. *Dealing Creatively with Death: A Manual of Death Education and Simple Burial*. Jenifer Moran, ed. Hinesburg, Vt: Upper Access Book Publishers, 2001.

Moss, Cynthia. *Elephant Memories: Thirteen Years in the Life of an Elephant Family*. Chicago: University of Chicago Press, 2000.

Nolen-Hoeksema, Susan. "Growth and Resilience Among Bereaved People," pp. 108–127 in Gillham, Jane E. (ed.), *The Science of Optimism: Research Essays in Honor of Martin E. P. Seligman*. Philadelphia: Templeton Foundation Press, 2000.

Parkes, Colin Murray. *Bereavement: Studies of Grief in Adult Life*. New York: Routledge, 2001.

Pease, Roland. "Sea Sculpture." *New York Times* (July 22, 1981): C2.

Perrin, Noel. "Middle-Age Dating." *New York Times Magazine* (July 6, 1986): 37.

Pincus, Lily. *Death and the Family: The Importance of Mourning*. New York: Schocken Books, 1974.

Pollock, George, and Stanley Greenspan, eds. "Aging or Aged: Development or Pathology." *The Course of Life, Volume III: Adulthood and the Aging Process*. Washington, D.C.: U.S. Government Printing Office, 1980.

Pollock, George H. "Mourning and Adaptation." *International Journal of Psychoanalysis*, vol. 42, part 1 (July–October 1961): 1–30.

———. "Anniversary Reactions, Trauma, and Mourning." *Psychoanalytic Quarterly*, vol. 39, no. 3 (1970): 347–371.

———. "The Mourning Process and Creative Organizational Change." *Journal of the American Psychoanalytic Association*, vol. 25, no. 1 (1977): 3–34.

———. "Process and Affect: Mourning and Grief." *International Journal of Psycho-analysis*, vol. 59, parts 2–3 (1978): 255–276.

Pradl, Gordon, ed. *Prospect and Retrospect: Selected Essays by James Britton*. London: Heinemann Educational Books, 1982.

Raphael, Beverley. *The Anatomy of Bereavement*. New York: Jason Aronson, 1995.

Rilke, Rainer Maria. *Duino Elegies*. Gary Miranda, trans. New York: North Point Press, 2000.

Rose, Julie. "Mourning a Miscarriage" *Newsweek* (August 3, 1987): 7.

Schneider, John. *Stress, Loss and Grief*. Baltimore: University Park Press, 1984.

Seligman, Martin E. P. *Learned Optimism: How to Change Your Mind and Your Life*. New York: Pocket Books, 1998.

Shand, Alexander. *The Foundations of Character: Being a Study of the Tendencies of the Emotions and Sentiments*. London: Macmillan, 1920.

Shuchter, Stephen, and Sidney Zisook. "A Multidimensional Model of Spousal Bereavement." *Biopsychosocial Aspects of Bereavement*, Sidney Zisook, ed. Washington, D.C.: American Psychiatric Press, 1987.

Storr, Anthony. *Solitude: A Return to the Self*. New York: Ballantine Books, 1989.

Thurman, Howard. *Creative Encounter*. Richmond, Ind.: Friends United Press, 1997.

———. *For the Inward Journey*. Richmond, Ind.: Friends United Press, 1984.

Tournier, Paul. *The Adventure of Living*. New York: HarperCollins, 1979.

Turner, Victor, and Edith Turner. *Image and Pilgrimage in Christian Culture: Anthropological Perspectives*. New York: Columbia University Press, 1978.

Van Gennep, Arnold. *The Rites of Passage*. Monika B. Bizedom and Gabrielle L. Caffee, trans. Chicago: University of Chicago Press, 1961.

Weiss, R. S. "The Provisions of Social Relationships." *Doing Unto Others*. Zick Ruben, ed. New York: Prentice-Hall, 1975.

Winnicott, D. W. *The Maturational Processes and the Facilitating Environment*. New York: International Universities Press, 1984.

Yourcenar, Marguerite. *With Open Eyes: Conversations with Matthieu Galey*. Arthur Goldhammer, trans. Boston: Beacon Press, 1986.

Zisook, Sidney, Stephen R. Shuchter, and Lucy E. Lyons. "Adjustments to Widowhood." *Biopsychosocial Aspects of Bereavement*. Sidney Zisook, ed. Washington, D.C.: American Psychiatric Press, 1987.

Zisook, Sidney, and Stephen R. Shuchter. "The Therapeutic Tasks of Grief." *Biopsychosocial Aspects of Bereavement*. Sidney Zisook, ed. Washington, D.C.: American Psychiatric Press, 1987.

Zisook, Sidney, ed. *Biopsychosocial Aspects of Bereavement*. Washington, D.C.: American Psychiatric Press, 1987.

INDEX

<small>INDEX</small>

ABOUT THE AUTHOR

For the past two decades, ELIZABETH HARPER NEELD, Ph.D., has researched, written, spoken, and consulted about grief and loss, personal and organizational change, and the possibilities of living a centered, balanced life.

She is an internationally recognized and accomplished author, consultant, and adviser. She has written eighteen books, consulted leaders from *Fortune* 500 and *Fortune* 100 companies, as well as numerous foreign companies, faced with the challenges of responding to rapid, unpredictable change, and has offered wisdom and practical insights borne of personal experience to people rebuilding their lives after change.

Dr. Neeld is committed to work that helps lift the human spirit. An example of this commitment was her involvement in helping to facilitate a gathering of grassroots leaders from Northern Ireland and the Republic of Ireland who were meeting to find ways to ensure the success of the Good Friday peace accord for Northern Ireland. After the September 11, 2001, terrorist attack she also made available copies of *Seven Choices*, which were distributed by the American Red Cross to their national staff and to individuals being served by the Red Cross New York Disaster Relief Center.

Formerly professor of English and assistant to the president at Texas A&M University, Elizabeth Neeld is listed in *Who's Who in America* (53rd edition), *Who's Who in the World* (13th edition), and *Contemporary Authors* (vol. 141). She currently serves on the advisory board of the American Association of Retired Persons (AARP) Loss and Grief Program.

Dr. Neeld lives with her husband, Jerele, in Austin, Texas.

For more information, see Elizabeth Harper Neeld's Web site, www.elizabethharperneeld.com.